URBAN PEOPLE AND PLACES

To Katrina and Silas. (M.I.B.)
For Caroline, Jillian and Ted. (L.C.M.)
For Danny, Erika, Chris, Jeannine, Evelyn, Gabriel and Susan. (D.J.M.)

URBAN PEOPLE AND PLACES

The Sociology of Cities, Suburbs, and Towns

Daniel Joseph Monti
Saint Louis University

Michael Ian Borer
University of Nevada, Las Vegas

Lyn C. Macgregor
University of Wisconsin, Madison

Los Angeles | London | New Delhi
Singapore | Washington DC

Los Angeles | London | New Delhi
Singapore | Washington DC

FOR INFORMATION:

SAGE Publications, Inc.
2455 Teller Road
Thousand Oaks, California 91320
E-mail: order@sagepub.com

SAGE Publications Ltd.
1 Oliver's Yard
55 City Road
London EC1Y 1SP
United Kingdom

SAGE Publications India Pvt. Ltd.
B 1/I 1 Mohan Cooperative Industrial Area
Mathura Road, New Delhi 110 044
India

SAGE Publications Asia-Pacific Pte. Ltd.
3 Church Street
#10-04 Samsung Hub
Singapore 049483

Acquisitions Editor: Jeff Lasser
Editorial Assistant: Lauren Johnson
Production Editor: Brittany Bauhaus
Copy Editor: Dan Gordon
Typesetter: C&M Digitals (P) Ltd.
Proofreader: Jeff Bryant
Cover Designer: Edgar Abarca
Marketing Manager: Andrew Lee

Printed in the United States of America

Library of Congress Cataloging-in-Publication Data
Monti, Daniel J.

Urban places and people : the sociology of cities, suburbs, and towns / Daniel J. Monti, Jr., Saint Louis University, Michael Ian Borer, University of Nevada, Las Vegas, Lyn C. Macgregor, University of Wisconsin, Madison.

pages cm
Includes bibliographical references and index.

ISBN 978-1-4129-8742-4 (pbk. : alk. paper)
ISBN 978-1-4833-0990-3 (web pdf)
ISBN 978-1-4833-1533-1 (epub)

1. Sociology, Urban. I. Title.

HT151.M5596 2014
307.76—dc23   2013031342

This book is printed on acid-free paper.

14 15 16 17 18 10 9 8 7 6 5 4 3 2 1

BRIEF CONTENTS

DETAILED CONTENTS

ACKNOWLEDGMENTS

I t is customary for authors to thank those persons who were instrumental in helping them write their book or assisted them in carrying out the research that went into it. In our case, there are social scientists, historians, reformers, and writers going back at least 200 years upon whose work we relied. There are social philosophers whose writings can be traced back even further in time. But most especially there are the countless millions of men, women, and children from our culture and others who made the stories we tell here and the evidence we assembled here possible to tell and assemble.

To all of them we owe a debt that cannot be repaid other than by having taken their lives and work seriously.

Thank you all.

—Dan Monti

—Michael Ian Borer

—Lyn Macgregor

ABOUT THE AUTHORS

Michael Ian Borer is associate professor of sociology at the University of Nevada, Las Vegas. He holds a BA from Lafayette College, an MA in religious studies from Boston University, and a PhD in sociology, also from Boston University. He is the editor of *The Varieties of Urban Experience: The American City and the Practice of Culture* (University Press of America, 2006) and the author of *Faithful to Fenway: Believing in Boston, Baseball, and America's Most Beloved Ballpark* (NYU Press, 2008). His work has been published in the *Journal of Popular Culture, City & Community, Social Psychology Quarterly*, and *Symbolic Interaction*, among others. He served as the 2011–12 vice president of the Society for the Study of Symbolic Interaction. His research focuses on urbanism, popular culture, the "sacred," and collective memory, and he is currently working on a book about the uses and abuses of imagination and nostalgia in American popular culture and the roles they play in the everyday culture of Las Vegas.

Lyn C. Macgregor earned her BA at Boston University and doctorate in sociology at the University of Wisconsin–Madison. She is the author of *Habits of the Heartland: Small Town Life in Modern America* (Cornell, 2010). After spending several years on the faculty at the University of Montana, she returned to Madison where she is currently the associate director of the Robert F. and Jean E. Holtz Center for Science & Technology Studies.

Daniel Joseph Monti is professor of sociology and public policy at Saint Louis University. A graduate of Oberlin College and the University of North Carolina and former Woodrow Wilson fellow, he is the author of over 50 scholarly articles and seven books on subjects ranging from educational reform and inner-city redevelopment to youth gangs and American urban history. His most recent book, *Engaging Strangers*, deals with civic life in contemporary Boston and the role of business in creating a thriving and orderly culture in that city. He currently is working on a pair of edited books dealing, respectively, with the culture of entrepreneurship and civility in urban life and a book detailing the redevelopment of St. Louis. The latter will constitute the longest study of inner-city redevelopment ever undertaken and focus on the role that major institutions and corporations play in fostering the city's economic and civic revival.

INTRODUCTION

Telling the Story of Cities, Suburbs, and Towns

This book, as its title indicates, is about urban people and places: how they develop, how they are organized, the problems we associate with them, and the various ways we deal with those problems. It is also a book about the way we talk about these places and people, how we make sense of them, and, ultimately, what the places we build and inhabit tell us about ourselves and the way we live together. We pay some attention to urban places and people in Asia, Africa, Central and South America. In fact, our treatment of cities and urban people on those continents is actually quite detailed for a book not dedicated to comparative urbanization. But our discussion of those cities, whatever its strengths and limitations, is intended mostly to help us better understand and appreciate the kinds of cities we know best: those of Western societies and more economically developed countries.

Though pre-urban settlements have been around for at least 10,000 years and have a rich history in most parts of the world, a serious study of cities and urban life didn't begin until the mid-19th century. That's when urban places of the sort we would recognize as cities emerged full-blown and spread rapidly across the globe, especially in Western societies that were going through a period of intense industrialization. As you will see, *the connection between industrialization and city building has been crucial to the way that social scientists and historians think about cities and urban life.*

Nonetheless, cities have thrived as a kind of human settlement long before industrialization, despite taking root in very different cultural settings and on very uneven economic playing fields. The largest cities today have populations numbering in the tens of millions. This doesn't mean everyone living or working there is happy, has a decent place to sleep at night, a full stomach, is clothed well, feels safe, and gets along with everyone around them. Depending on where in the world you happen to be, cities are not organized well enough, and maybe can't be organized well enough, under prevailing conditions to enable many of their residents to meet these basic needs. Cities in most parts of the world continue to grow, however, despite these kinds of problems. *The fact that cities are growing most quickly in parts of the world where it is a daily challenge just to meet people's basic needs tells us something important about the appeal and staying power of this kind of human settlement.*

Clearly, cities perform important functions and serve people in ways they don't believe can be served in other kinds of settlements. Our task right now is to present some of the reasons why cities have become such important sites of human settlement and to lay out the broad outline of how they've changed over time. We introduce two words here that you will see a great deal of throughout the book: *urbanization* and *urbanism*. *Urbanization* is the term we use to describe the story of how cities, suburbs, and urban regions develop over long periods of time in different cultural settings. *Urbanism* refers to the way of life or culture that urban people have made.

Let's begin with some simple but big facts about *urbanization* as a worldwide phenomenon. As Table 1.1 indicates, urban settlements are on track to become the most prevalent kind of settlement in the world by the year 2050. The *percentage* of people living in urban settings in less developed parts of the world—most of Africa and Asia and much of Latin America and the Caribbean—has been catching up with the urban population in more developed parts of the world—mostly North America and Europe—only in the last half century. The *number* of people in less developed countries that live in urban settlements already exceeds the number in more developed countries who live in

these kinds of places; and that gap is likely to become greater in the future.

Two other features of this worldwide phenomenon deserve special attention. First, the overall population in less developed regions of the world will continue to grow rapidly. Second, the percentage of the population in these regions still living in rural areas will be substantially greater than that in more developed parts of the world. Both of these factors will have a profound impact on the way cities and urban areas develop and how well they will be able to accommodate all the people who want to live and work there.

The overall population of less developed regions in 1950 was already twice as large as that of more developed regions. If the population projections of the United Nations prove accurate, there will be more than three times as many people living in less developed regions of the world by 2050 than there will be in more developed regions. Urbanization will not have been accompanied by smaller overall population growth as it has in North America and Europe. Both the urban and rural populations in less developed regions will far outstrip those in more developed regions.

The implications of this rather startling disjuncture in the way urban settlements have developed in more and less developed parts of

Table 1.1 Percentage of Urban and Rural Population in More and Less Developed Regions of the World, 1950–2050

Area	1950	2000	2050
More Developed Regions			
Total population in thousands	813,561	1,194,199	1,245,247
Percentage urban	52.5	73.1	86
Percentage rural	47.5	26.9	14
Less Developed Regions			
Total population in thousands	1,721,532	4,929,924	7,946,040
Percentage urban	18	40.2	67
Percentage rural	82	59.8	33

Source: Data derived from "World Population Prospects: The 2006 Revision and World Urbanization Prospects: The 2007 Revision." Population Division of Economic and Social Affairs of the United Nations Secretariat. http://esa.un.org/unup

the world are important. Dramatic as the growth of cities and urban areas has been in North America and Europe, these figures suggest that *urbanization in less developed parts of the world has unfolded far more quickly and differently than it did in Western societies.* The social, political, and economic impact of urbanization in less developed regions will likewise be substantially different. To the extent that solutions to problems urban dwellers faced in the West are at all applicable, they will have to be applied faster and more broadly in the cities of newly developing countries.

Integrating the economies of newly developing countries more fully with those in the West surely is part of the answer. But it's only one part of a long and complicated answer. Lessons learned in the West about everything from providing the infrastructure to house, feed, employ, transport, and care for so many people living in such close quarters to dealing with the environmental, social, and political consequences of growth will have to be adapted to fit very different kinds of urban settings. Understanding that many of these lessons are still only taken half-heartedly in the West should give us pause. It shows how difficult it will be for people in less developed regions to put into practice what people in Western societies have learned about making cities and having these places work well with their regional neighbors.

All the people in countries with less developed economies who have been moving into cities have another important task on which to work. They will have to learn how to behave in ways that enable them to work effectively at their jobs and with each other in an environment—the city—with which they may have only passing familiarity. This means, among other things, that people must adapt to beliefs, values, customs, codes, ceremonies, groups, and institutions already being practiced in cities *and* learn to supplement these with cultural inventions of their own creation. Absent such learning and exchanges, newcomers will find it next to impossible to thrive in a big urban settlement and get along with the different kinds of persons they see

around them. The good news, as we will see, is that better-established urban residents and new-comers to cities in these countries appear to be making some progress at becoming more effective urban dwellers.

Urbanism, as we've already noted, is the term we use to describe all the stories of how people live in different kinds of urban settlements all over the world. It entails a description of how people, sometimes working collaboratively in groups and at times seemingly quite alone or in conflict with each other, do what it takes to build and keep a city and metropolitan area running even passably well.

The story of *urbanization* overlaps with the story of *urbanism*. How cities and urban regions develop can tell us something about how people live and work there. At the same time, the way of life practiced in urban settlements affects how these places are laid out and operate, whether they can grow, and how the spaces and buildings constructed there are actually used.

We are mindful of how people in non-Western countries and less developed parts of the world make cities and live in their urban settlements. These would include the parts of urban settlements that colonial overseers appended to native cities to make an outpost from which they expected to administer this part of their empire. This book, however, is primarily about urban phenomena in the United States. We will refer to what goes on in cities in less developed regions of the world, but we'll do it mostly to point out how different the process of urbanization has been in the West.

We also will describe some of the ways that urban dwellers live in less developed countries. Again, we will do this primarily to point to some of the parallels in how people in Western societies make cities work for them. Our goal is to better appreciate the cultural innovations people in the West made so they could better adapt to life in cities and leave their unique mark on the place.

Before we begin talking about the development of cities and how people live and work there, we have a few more pieces of intellectual housekeeping that need to be addressed. First, when it comes to telling the story of *urbanization*, the focus of scholars has been on cities and urban settlements as distinctive and important places. They are *central places* where organizations and institutions that coordinate what happens in a large region are found. Cities also are part of a larger *global network* that is thought to have an increasingly large impact on what goes on in these regional centers (Hohenberg & Lees, 1995, p. 2–17).

At crucial points in that network today are so-called "global cities" whose importance has grown well beyond the countries where they are found. They house corporations that coordinate the actions of far-flung manufacturing and investing empires in much the same way as 18th and 19th century colonial powers expanded their domain beyond their national borders. They both ignore the sovereignty of other countries and at times abuse the territorial integrity of other nations and peoples in order to enrich their "investors" (Sassen, 2010). How much influence these global cities have over smaller, less globally connected cities in their country or part of the world is open to speculation and investigation. So far at least, these cities and the people who live and work there haven't become so alike that their cultural differences have been erased or rendered inconsequential.

When social scientists and historians describe the process of *urbanization*, they usually focus on the economic and demographic features of cities and metropolitan areas in different parts of the world. Their objective is to tell how a population occupies a particular locale and how it relates to the larger environment, usually a metropolitan area or region, of which it is part. They focus on how a population sustains itself economically, how it organizes itself in order to best exploit the environment around it, and how its people use all the resources at their disposal.

There are four main questions that people who are interested in the process of urbanization typically ask. We list them below so that they can be referred to more easily as we make our way through the book.

1. How different are cities in different parts of the world and how much have cities changed over the past two or three thousand years?

2. What is the relationship between cities and the areas surrounding them or the larger society of which they are part?

3. How are cities laid out physically and what do different spatial arrangements tell us about the kinds of economic, social, and political relations that people have with each other?

4. What are the best ways to understand and ultimately cure "urban ills" such as congestion, pollution, poverty, and crime that seem to be more common in cities than in smaller, more rural communities?

Researchers interested in the process of urbanization often touch on two or more of these questions in an article or book they write. But it is unlikely that they will address much less answer all four. Scholars usually focus on one or two cities or relations between cities and rural areas in a particular country and period of history. It is only after piecing together the stories of cities and their hinterlands in different historical periods and cultural settings that we begin to assemble something like a theory of how cities are organized and relate to larger geographic entities over a long period of time.

The second way that researchers like to tell the story of cities and metropolitan areas is to talk about the way people actually live there. In this book, we will give the urban way of life or culture that people practice equal weight with the story of how cities and metropolitan regions have developed. Most scholars have treated urban life and culture as something of secondary importance to the bigger economic and demographic realities of urban settlements. The culture and everyday life of urban people have been treated as an effect or result of big economic and demographic changes that happen in urban areas rather than a cause of the big things that take place in cities and metropolitan regions.

One important and unfortunate consequence of looking at the urban world this way is that bigger and compelling economic and demographic changes in urban areas are often portrayed as overwhelming people. People are seen *reacting* to changes over which they seem to have little control. Studies of these reactions—deviant behavior in its many forms, family dissolution, poverty, prejudice, and civil unrest—usually portray city dwellers and the way they get along with each other in a less than favorable light. We don't expect to correct this view of city life in the current book. What we will offer, however, is a more balanced picture of the urban life than the one typically presented in textbooks and academic discussions.

Researchers who talk about urban culture and the ways that people live in different kinds of communities organize their studies around four questions. Again, we list these questions below so that the reader may refer to them more easily as we move through the book.

1. Is there a way of life that it is distinctly *urban*? What elements of this urban way of life are shared by people in different cultures and have they changed over time?

2. Does this supposed new urban way of life encourage the formation of new social collectivities and identities?

3. How does the city encourage or discourage the development of social bonds between citizens of different cultural backgrounds, residences, and occupations?

4. How does urban life affect traditional notions of social deference as they relate to persons' social class position, gender, caste, or race?

As in the study of urbanization, no researcher can possibly answer all four questions in a given piece of writing. Scholars tend to focus on the way community life unfolds in bigger and smaller places, in cities or towns in different historical periods or national settings, and even for specific kinds of people like women or immigrants.

There is undoubtedly a great deal of overlap between the story we can tell about *urbanization* and the story we pull together about *urbanism* or the way people actually live in cities, suburbs, and towns. The overlap is especially apparent in

the way people have talked about and tried to fix urban places and people. Repairing parts of the city was supposed to help heal or fix the people who lived and worked there. As we shall see, however, these stories don't correspond exactly and the story of how we build cities and urban areas usually ends better than the one we tell about urban life.

For instance, we have a pretty good sense of what cities look like in the United States, Canada, and Europe and how they came to be that way. There are lots of tall buildings and monuments, impressive ports and transportation systems, and a great many people making their way in and around the place. Virtually all of these people engage in nonagricultural tasks for a living. They may have gardens, but they don't grow plants for a living. The animals they keep are pets.

Suburbs look and feel different. They vary in size. Though we are inclined to think of these places as "towns," some can be quite large and almost city-like. Others are little more than residential preserves. As a rule, the people who live there don't farm, mine, or harvest other natural resources for a living either.

We tend to think of small towns and villages as rural places, and some of them are. But many small places in most Western societies today are connected to bigger cities. They may be connected more in terms of the way people live than the way these places look and how close they are to a city, perhaps, but they are connected nonetheless.

The urban way of life we associate with cities may be shared more widely than we suspect. Indeed, we think we can say with a great deal of confidence that our way of life in the United States today is more "urban" than it is "rural" and probably has been so for a long time. The same also could be said of life in other Western societies. On the other hand, the size, layout, and look of the settlements in which people live may not be city-like at all.

That is why we need to treat the stories of *urbanization* and *urbanism* as analytically distinct, even though they may overlap quite a bit.

Assembling a picture of what an urban way of life or culture looks like is painstaking work. Our theories about urban life should reflect all the information we have acquired. Social scientists and the people who read and rely on our research, however, have hung onto ideas about how people in cities think and act that have been shown to have little empirical support. We will try to offer a more balanced assessment of the evidence that scholars have assembled over the years.

We certainly will not discount existing explanations or theories for what goes on in cities or dismiss out of hand evidence that cities have problems and that people who live in urban places sometimes behave problematically. Our *cultural approach* to understanding how cities work and people live in urban places, however, gives at least as much credence to the positive contributions that cities make to our way of life. To help readers pull out the information we found most useful in making the case for this particular approach, throughout the book we will *italicize* material that relates to the eight questions we highlighted above. They can then make up their own mind as to whether we have over-sold our preferred way of looking at urban places and people.

The book is divided into four parts. The first part of the book has three chapters in which we pay homage to urbanization and urbanism as worldwide phenomena, compare how they work in more and less developed societies, and then focus on urban places and people in the United States. We emphasize again that the way we build cities and urban areas sometimes complements how people live and work there and sometimes seems to get ahead of people's ability to deal with them effectively. In these chapters, we will see how people in different parts of the world have tried to reconcile how they've built cities and urban areas with the way of life they lead there.

The second part of the book focuses on how we make sense of urban places and people. We have chapters on both classical and contemporary ways of looking at the urban world. Classical theorists tended to look at the way in which industrialization coincided (and in a sense conspired with) the process of nation building to

make a new and very different kind of urban place and people: those we know in Western societies and those in non-Western or less economically developed societies. Contemporary theorists are more interested in specifying how the way we make urban places reflects (and enshrines) differences in people's wealth, power, and social prestige. Much has been written about cities as places where the best which a society has to offer is on full display. There is an equally strong impulse (some would say a much stronger impulse) among both classical and contemporary theorists to look skeptically at urban places, the kinds of people who live there, and the way of life they make. The "cultural" approach favored by the authors of this book certainly doesn't ignore much less dismiss the negative features of urban places and the downsides to the way people live there. What it does is give more equal time or equal space to consider the positive accommodations people learn to make to each other as they struggle and succeed in making a better place for themselves in urban areas.

The primary way in which experts speak about the up and down sides of urban living is found in their writing and research on "community" and "strangers." How communities are organized, how well they work for the people who live there, and perhaps most importantly, how successfully they bring people into contact with others very different from themselves are questions that troubled the Greeks 3,000 years ago and still bother us today. We offer two chapters in the third part of the book on everyday community life and politics in urban places. We also talk more about the overall tenor and form that civic life takes there. This is where our "cultural" approach seems to fill out the picture of urban life better than some of its theoretical competitors, if only by showing how much less strange urban dwellers are to each other than we typically suppose or have been led to believe.

We end the book with three chapters that show how professional thinkers, activists, and reformers have tried to smooth out the rougher edges of life in urban places. Physical changes—what we put under and on top of the ground to make urban places more habitable—are more often involved in answering questions we have about the *size and density of the populations* that try to live and work in cities. Social changes—all the programs, policies, and life-altering practices we promote so people will treat each other better or at least more respectfully—are more often involved in answering questions we have about the *heterogeneity of urban populations*. We have a preference for making physical adjustments, thinking that making a place look better will or should make people behave better. But it is the "cultural" changes—all the "social" adjustments we make in the rules we follow, the roles we fill, and the relationships we make or avoid making— that enable us to make compromises and accommodate ourselves to people and conditions we have little experience with and can't avoid.

THOUGHTS AND REFLECTIONS ON WHAT'S *NOT* IN THE BOOK

Most textbooks are boring, if not dreadful, and all of them are overpriced.

No one really sets out to write a dreadful textbook, but we've all read them and paid handsomely for the privilege. The boring part is understandable, up to a point. After all, the summary of any academic subject, the comprehensive but necessarily superficial rendering of what passes as the state of the art on a given field of study that can be rendered in a semester or academic quarter, is going to hit a lot of subjects in less-than-convincing detail than they deserve.

The trick in writing a textbook that isn't boring, much less dreadful, is to have a sound grasp of the material, the ability to write in a manner that won't put readers to sleep or push them into a homicidal rage, and *really* not like textbooks. Well, we *really* don't like textbooks. We also think (or hope) you will conclude that we have a solid understanding of the field. We have been told that our writing is both informed and accessible. We hope you will agree.

The book's senior author, the one whose name appears first on the list, had successfully resisted writing a textbook for nearly 40 years. He would have continued to do so but for the fact that the other two authors, both closer to the start of their careers than the end, had been his students and were smart and knowledgeable in spots that he isn't. That's really important, because part of what makes textbooks awful is that one author tries to tame an entire subject when, in truth, he's only interested in some parts and faking his mastery of all the other parts.

There's no faking going on inside this textbook. What we chose to write about we know well. And when we didn't know enough about one of the subjects written about in the book we went out and found someone who could fill in the blanks. And believe me, when you write a textbook it becomes apparent quickly how much you don't know about a subject you were supposed to know inside out.

What you leave out of a book is just as important as what you put into it, and maybe even more important. So here's some of what we've left out of our book:

Pictures

Pictures run up the price of a book, are readily available today all over the Internet, and aren't all that helpful in a book of this sort. The reason is simple. Unless you've just crawled out of a cave you have probably seen cities firsthand, already live in a suburb, or saw what Walt Disney imagined towns looked like before corporations and speculators bought up large tracts of farmland, local teens left town for a career in the military or Microsoft, and Wal-Mart started stealing all the town's business. We expect that you're familiar enough with online sources at this point to find more and better pictures than the ones we would have come up with anyway.

Maps

See the discussion of "pictures" above, except for the part about Walt Disney.

Lots of Graphs, Charts, and Tables

These are expensive too. More importantly, the only parts you're interested in are the descriptions of the data which appear in the text right under the graph, chart, or table.

Annoying Inserts

We never read those descriptions of the 1906 San Francisco earthquake, the construction of an iconic building or subway line, the life of a _____ (hooker, gang member, immigrant, impoverished person during the Depression, or any one of a number of different minority groups that already have textbooks written about them), what it's like being part of a crowd walking down Broadway in New York City or some kind of street demonstration, and the urban policies of any U.S. president since FDR. We didn't think you would either.

A STATEMENT ABOUT "LEARNING OBJECTIVES" AT THE START OF EVERY CHAPTER

Really? What is this, high school? If you want to figure out what's important in each chapter, read the book. Pay particular attention to the *italicized* material, like we already told you, and then compose essays that address the questions at the end of each chapter. You'll find that we have three primary learning objectives beyond learning something about urban places and people: critical thinking, the ability to marshal evidence to defend a point, and learning how to write clearly. The rest is up to you.

AN INSTRUCTOR'S MANUAL AND A TEST BANK OF MULTIPLE-CHOICE QUESTIONS

OK, this one may be more for your instructor than it is for you, but you might as well know what was going through your instructor's brain when he or she picked this book instead of one that had a ready-made set of questions.

Instructors love multiple-choice tests because they're easy to grade. Students would especially love multiple-choice for this textbook because we've already italicized the most important points in each chapter. Just read the book. In fact, read lots of books. It won't kill you, and you'll quickly figure out whether we know what we're talking about.

Answer the questions at the end of each chapter using complete sentences. Come up with some questions of your own. Find newspaper stories that relate to the material in the text. Yes, newspapers, not Wikipedia, *newspapers*. Try working on page-long answers to the questions below for starters. Work up to decent five-page essays for questions posed in later chapters.

As we just said, it won't kill you. In fact, it will make you a better person and help convince your parents that all the money they're dumping into your college education is accomplishing more than helping to pay off the new student center or subsidize the athletic department's quest to have its teams ranked nationally.

QUESTIONS FOR STUDY AND DISCUSSION (SEE? WE WEREN'T KIDDING.)

1. Think of the place where you grew up or the place where your school is located. Is it a city? How do you know? What key features does it have that make you think it's a city, a suburb, or a town?

2. What are the differences between urbanization and urbanism? What questions do researchers ask about these two phenomena? Find a newspaper article about a city. Is the story about urbanization or urbanism, or both? Does the article answer any of the important questions scholars ask about urbanization and/or urbanism?

3. Are you taking this class because it fulfills a general college requirement or because you're really interested in the subject?

1

URBANIZATION IN WESTERN SOCIETIES

There are two basic ways to tell the story of urban places and people. The first is to compare the several historical stages through which cities in Western (and more developed) societies appear to have moved. This is generally referred to as an *evolutionary* approach. People who talk about the evolution of cities try to identify some key features about these places or the people who live there and trace the way they changed over a long period of time. It is the perspective we will be using in the present chapter. The second way is to compare cities in more economically developed societies to cities in societies with less developed economies, something we do in the next chapter. This is called, unsurprisingly, a *comparative* approach. The idea in comparative studies is to explore the differences between cities and urban cultures in two or more parts of the world.

The portrayal of urban places as *preindustrial*, *proto-industrial*, *industrial*, or *postindustrial* is predicated on the idea that what people at the time did to make a living is the most crucial piece of information you need to make sense of the place and its people. These names, as it happens, also are used to characterize the level of development of the whole society in which the cities are found. The key determinant in this scheme is how

much heavy manufacturing and actual producing of goods the people living there did, either in the city itself or in the society generally. Cities with lots of industry and manufacturing usually, but not always, have more people living in close proximity to each other. By the time cities enter their late-industrial period or *postindustrial* period, they have begun to spread out along with their manufacturing sites. Cities that didn't have as much manufacturing going on inside their borders during the heyday of the Industrial Revolution didn't grow as much or become as wealthy as cities that had lots of goods being produced within their boundaries.

It isn't necessarily the case that every city will go through the same four stages. The "cities" created by the aboriginal peoples of the United States, for instance, were part of a *preindustrial* society. They didn't last long enough to become *proto-industrial* cities much less *industrial* or *postindustrial* cities. The places that would someday become cities along the eastern coast of the United States began as *proto-industrial* sites or were founded by people who lived in *proto-industrial* societies. Some of the places they made became major *industrial* or *postindustrial* cities. Others did not. Not all cities "evolve" or do so in the same way at the same time.

The correspondence between city building and industrialization isn't perfect either. When you compare cities in the West with those found in less economically developed parts of Africa, Asia, and Central and South America, for instance, the cities on these other continents tend to be much larger. There are fewer of them, but they are bigger, much bigger than places like New York or London. We'll see why in the next chapter. Even in the West, however, the "more industry and bigger city" equation doesn't always work out. Los Angeles, Houston, and Phoenix have grown to be quite large "cities" in the United States without ever having an industrialized core like Cleveland, Chicago, or St. Louis once had. They became big cities by annexing ever greater pieces of territory around their central core as these areas expanded and often contained manufacturing or processing centers. These cities today are much more spread out than older cities in the Northeast and Midwest. Many parts of their "central city" look very much like the suburbs of Philadelphia and Pittsburgh: single-story ranch houses, strip malls, and "big box" shopping malls.

What has remained true about the connection between urbanization and industrialization is that the equation works very well at the national level. *Societies with more manufacturing tend to have more cities and a greater percentage of their people living in urban areas. Societies with less manufacturing have fewer cities, but those cities tend to be extraordinarily large. These societies also have a smaller percentage of their people living in urban areas.* The division between big cities and a rural hinterland in those societies tends to be much starker.

The connection between city building and manufacturing was especially crucial at the start of the Industrial Revolution. City building prior to the 19th century had been something of a hit-and-miss proposition. The fortunes of a city rose and fell with those of the empire that built it. A city thrived when its empire had successful military campaigns, conquered new lands, and populated these faraway places with its own people. Cities that lost their political and economic clout had their population shrink, and were sometimes sacked when their empire waged unsuccessful military adventures or couldn't hold onto the lands it once ruled.

The up-and-down character of city building in Europe may have persisted well into the 19th century and perhaps even past it had its colonization of Africa and Asia not been accompanied by industrialization at home. After industrialization became more firmly established in these societies, colonial powers didn't just leave their armies and governors in new lands to strip them of their natural resources and homemade goods. Empires now had something to sell back to colonized people and new ways to prolong the dependence of these peoples and lands on their colonial overseers. Trading brand-new manufactured goods back to colonies helped cities in more successful European countries grow dramatically. It also enabled the leaders of those cities to wield unprecedented influence over other settlements, not just in their own country and in neighboring countries. That is why virtually every person who writes about the evolution of cities treats industrialization as a pivotal moment in the history of city building.

We will continue this custom by offering a brief survey of how city building proceeded before and after industrialization took hold in Europe. The before-and-after parts of the story can be told by referring to four distinct periods of history. The first period covers the development of *preindustrial cities* and ends in the last decades of the 14th century. The second period covers the emergence of *proto-industrial cities* from sometime around the middle of the 14th century to the middle of the 18th century. The third period is comprised of a relatively short time between the middle of the 18th century to the early-20th century when *industrial cities* grew so dramatically. The most recent part of the story deals with *postindustrial cities* and covers the period between the early-20th century and today.

When and how a particular society industrializes still tells us a great deal about the kind of cities it has. Whether we're talking about urbanization in the West or in newly developing countries, however, the basic criteria that must be met for places to be considered "urban" are the same. They must be permanent settlements of some size where most of the inhabitants don't grow food for a living. With the exception of their recent and comparatively brief flirtation with industrialization, cities rarely produced much in the way of tangible goods or made much profit on their own. Such wealth as they acquired came first and foremost from having successfully appropriated and reinvested the wealth and resources of people who lived outside cities or in faraway lands. For the better part of their recorded history, cities have been surplus gobblers rather than surplus producers.

Whatever surpluses were available to early cities would have been difficult to ship far except by sea because short-distance transportation on land was inefficient and hinterlands were not especially well protected. Occasional fairs made it possible for goods and ideas from faraway places to be brought to the castle gate. Otherwise, there was no good trading or much social and economic intercourse with the surrounding lands except by sea.

Until the onset of industrialization, urban people could make a comparatively good living by appropriating what people in other places had in the way of natural resources or produced goods. The great urban centers of Europe never stopped extracting wealth from the foreign lands they'd colonized. They simply added to the booty they had always taken from these outposts all the wealth they could now acquire by selling people in these same faraway places the wondrous things European "manufactories" were producing for their own people. Though large-scale manufacturing wasn't centered in cities for a long time, we will see that the impact of its comparatively brief presence there was dramatic.

PRE-URBAN AND EARLY URBAN SETTLEMENTS (CITY BUILDING UP TO THE MID-14TH CENTURY)

Archaeologists until recently had put the location of pre-urban settlements in Mesopotamia and the

time of their emergence at around 3500 BCE. The location and timing have changed with the discovery of a large and sophisticated temple complex in southern Turkey called Gobekli Tepe. Built some 11,600 years ago, the religious site predates both Stonehenge and the Great Pyramid of Giza. More importantly, it was used by people when they were still nomadic hunters and gatherers (Mann, 2011).

Prior to the discovery of Gobekli Tepe, archaeologists had supposed that pre-urban settlements emerged only with agricultural surpluses and animal domestication. Such sites in Mesopotamia were estimated to have held between 2,000 and 25,000 people and contain somewhere between 4% and 5% of an area's population. Though some of the people residing in these places may have done a little gardening, they did not earn their keep as shepherds and farmers. They were released from that kind of labor. Most of the jobs they held were new and revolved around the acquisition, storage, and sale of produce and beasts. Their markets weren't just local. Some were located a distance from the village where they lived.

Now it looks like nomadic people traveled great distances first to construct and then worship at a monumental piece of architecture thousands of years before they lived in relatively permanent settlements. *The first settlement may have had more to do with a great cultural innovation—institutionalized religion—than with economics.*

Be that as it may, the small number of residents in early Mesopotamian villages also founded more "leisurely" pursuits, with religion foremost among them. The new customs, art forms, and institutions they created that had little to do with food and shelter. Many of the novel ideas, practices, and artifacts these people produced were offered as cultural goods to people who didn't live in the town.

New ideas, ways of behaving, and cultural artifacts were important exports for early town inhabitants. In fact, as members of a small class of "retainers," they laid the foundation for producing everything from new ways to govern and impressive public works projects to massing and paying for armies that would conquer and pillage in the name of the people who'd raised the money to send them off. The riches they acquired would eventually end up in the treasuries of the ruling elites in early cities like Rome.

The earliest urban settlements were more than places where surpluses could be gathered and used by the small number of people who lived there. They also were political or ceremonial centers. Such commerce and manufacturing that was accomplished in these towns was sufficient to sustain only the elites and their handlers. It was not so large that any one urban settlement could export its surpluses much farther than the next urban settlement, which was more likely reached by water than land. There certainly wasn't enough surplus to sustain ongoing trading among a network of urban places. Instead, residents of these earliest cities consumed most of the surpluses produced elsewhere (either as goods or in the form of tax payments) in the name of their local leader and later for their emperor or empire.

Urban populations remained small because agricultural surpluses were small and unpredictable. *The main way that early urban leaders dealt with the problem of having too many people to feed and house was by shipping a part of the excess population off as armies and colonizers.* These persons were supposed to seize the wealth and natural resources of other peoples. The towns these expatriates built were garrisons supported by hinterland taxes and trade with farther-off places that were guaranteed a measure of peace and prosperity in exchange for their surplus.

This left early urban-based empires a "mosaic of city territories" with bigger cities acting as administrative centers. Local elites had to pay for the services they received and subsidized the provision of such "public" services that would have been made available to people in the city generally. As a result, they either expropriated what they could from other local residents or, in a pattern oddly familiar to anyone who's visited a modern up-scale suburb or gated community, they took off for their rural villas and left the city to stagnate and corrode.

As we've already noted, there was no consistent growth in the number and size of cities in this period and nothing yet like the development of urban regions. The rise and decline of cities correlated with the fate of the empire of which they were part. Intermittent outbreaks of diseases also reduced the size of urban populations. This was especially apparent in the impact that the Black Plague had on Europe's urban populations in the late-14th century.

Cities were compact and poorly laid out. There was little segregation in terms of people living some distance from where they worked or in terms of where different activities took place. Each city had a religious and political gathering spot. Markets usually were located on plazas in front of the local church. They remain that way today in some smaller urban settlements in Europe.

Preindustrial cities exhibited a great deal of inequality. Society was highly stratified into categories of persons distinguished by their relative wealth, power, and social prestige (see Weber, 1947). The differences between wealthy people and everyone else were especially apparent in the way that persons lived in towns or early cities and the way people lived in more rural areas. It is the glaring distinction between urban wealth and grinding rural poverty that provokes some of the earliest statements against the excesses of urban life. But stark differences in the life chances of people also were apparent in the way urban elites lived as compared to the lives that were led by the common people and slaves who also dwelled in urban settlements. *Cities have always been places where distinctions based on wealth, power, and prestige are highly visible and important in marking who had to be deferential to whom.* It wouldn't be until the early- to mid-19th century that city leaders expressed much interest in addressing the persistent differences in life chances that more and less well-to-do people in cities experienced.

Changes in patterns of social deference would come too. A number of persons from disaffected parts of society would find ways to get more of what better-off people had in great abundance. The number able to "move up" and improve their lives could be quite large in the case of a particularly wealthy country like the United States. But these changes didn't happen so quickly or strongly so as to fundamentally challenge the way that wealth and power were distributed. That is why William Julius Wilson (1978) has argued that the persistence of inequality among Black Americans today has more to do with barriers based on their social class than the color of their skin, though race still plays a significant role in the ways that people "see" one another in the United States.

Many of the innovations that city people came up with to deal with inequality came about as a result of trading they did with people in rural areas and faraway lands and by adopting customs and rituals used by people from those places. Town guilds often resisted these changes by engaging in monopolistic practices that limited the impact of new ideas and ways of acting that came from outside their community. Indeed, some urban settlements apparently had rules that kept rural peasants and elites from staying in town overnight, much less for extended periods of time.

By the end of the 14th century, cities had become administrative centers and merchant colonies or "bourgs" that were attached to fortresses. That is where the inhabitants called "bourgeois" could bring luxury goods and added revenues to the lord. These places became capitalist-like enclaves in an otherwise feudal society. Though treated with a certain amount of contempt, the merchants living in these places gained a measure of economic clout and independence despite continuing prohibitions on the part of church leaders against profit making.

The introduction of business people to the city begins a process of political incorporation and liberalization that later put them at the center of municipal leadership in industrial cities. *Merchants and other business leaders in the West have played a big role in building and rebuilding cities since the end of the preindustrial period. Many of the freedoms we take for granted today came from the struggles that small business owners and "petty bourgeois" people went through to solidify their claim to membership in cities.* Trade guilds were the most obvious and prevalent institutions not run by wealthy people. These groups linked

employees and employers together and tightly controlled the manufacture of goods. Even as they administered social benefits to members, they did nothing to open markets to new products or make the economy more productive. Their organization actually helped to legitimate the rule of local elites. In the preindustrial city, however, the idea of loyalty to one's presumed superiors was gradually replaced by practices that were more socially complex. *People imagined themselves in voluntary relationships with both co-equals and non-equals,* and they worked to create both big national moments and many more small and personal moments where this idea was played out (Hohenberg and Lees, 1995, p. 41).

In the West, cities became places where human beings created a variety of bigger ceremonial occasions and everyday experiences that enabled people who came from different levels of society to be together and work together. Some of the same social inventions made it possible for people from the same level of society to find and support each other. The ideal and practice of voluntary association became deeply embedded in the fabric of urban life and in the way scholars came to talk about the changes people made in how they connected with their fellow townsfolk.

PROTO-INDUSTRIAL CITIES (CITY BUILDING BETWEEN THE MID-14TH AND MID-18TH CENTURIES)

Urban growth was less prominent in the first half of this 400-year period than the second half. Swings in the population of any one city could be substantial, however, and there were as many impediments to city growth as there were factors pushing it forward. Changes to conditions that limited growth were slow in coming, but they weren't made any faster than changes in the factors that would have favored urban growth.

Between 1150 and 1450, barriers to capitalism imposed by feudalism were undermined by a series of changes in the ways economies were allowed to operate. Of particular note were a gradual increase in agricultural production and the slow incorporation of merchants and craftsmen as full members in the feudal communities that they had been only grudgingly invited to join. *The important point to bear in mind is that advances in agriculture predated changes in manufacturing.* Displaced agricultural workers would eventually be absorbed in cities as part of a growing mass of factory workers. But until that happened, merchants and craftsmen inside cities busied themselves by finishing the production of luxury goods that were sold to the warriors, priests, and prominent city families that ran and protected the city.

Few new cities were founded during this period. Such urban growth that did occur took place mainly in already large cities. It was attributed to a general economic revival but one that was occasioned especially by more effective use of agricultural land and rural population growth. Cities also benefited from the development of a more central form of government and the security it afforded.

Stagnation or outright decline in many urban centers was due to hunger, war, and epidemics such as the plague. Emigration out of cities was common, too. Notwithstanding population losses of up to 50% in some cities, the populations of most European cities eventually began to grow again during this period.

Increases in the size of urban populations were kept in check by social pressure (e.g., limiting condition of membership in guilds, dowries, and sanctions against out-of-wedlock births, among others) in addition to economic downturns, warfare, and outbreaks of disease. *Urban populations were replenished by migrants from more rural areas.* Proto-industrial cities were still caught up in a cycle of growth and decline that wouldn't end until manufacturing became widespread and more than just the city's elites and protectors were able to acquire the items being manufactured.

Early in this period, there were 3,000 places across Europe, each with up to 2,000 residents. Another 220 places had between 6,000 and 10,000 residents. Already emerging in the late medieval period, then, was the outline of a network of smaller and medium-sized cities that were part of a trading system that had at its center major capital cities like Dublin, London, and Paris. Middle-sized cities like Milan, Cordoba, and Ghent would serve as secondary manufacturing sites and population centers during the industrial period. Their integration into a system built around trade was greatly aided by a set of political, military, and ecclesiastical institutions that gave order to economic exchanges and provided tradesmen with the kind of security and reassurance that they'd not had before.

The larger cities by then had probably grown to between 30,000 and 50,000. But even with so many more urban settlements available to populate, the portion of the people living in cities was probably still no more than 3% or 4%. This was no greater than the share held by most preindustrial urban settlements.

As we already noted, *cities lost their autonomy to central governments during this period despite gaining administrative functions, acting as ports and fortresses, or spas and resorts.* Their influence over the countryside also grew as trade increased, but at least early on these ties were fragile because of poor transportation technology and limited food surpluses. The growing but still comparatively modest level of trading between cities and their hinterland left most cities dependent on trade with cities great distances from where they were located.

Cities had always been centers of trade and consumption. Now they were beginning to make advances in handicraft production, manufacturing, and construction as well. People with substantial wealth began to change where they invested their money. While there still were plenty of major landholders during this period, people started to look at cities and the kinds of investments available there as a way to increase their wealth.

The expansion of urban economies created a more congenial environment where migrants could remain and gain a foothold, no matter how poorly treated they may have been. In particular, there was a decline in the power of local medieval guilds, which had restricted the number of people who could work in different trades. Some portion of the working population did well enough to qualify for membership in the city's middle class. Ethnic groups—confederations of people who could claim membership in an extensive but fictive "kin group"—also provided otherwise unrelated people with an effective way to connect with potentially like-minded city residents (Hohenberg and Lees, 1995, p. 145–150). As we shall see, *ethnic groups and a robust middle class would end up taking on many of the tasks of building and maintaining cities that once fell to small numbers of prominent people who sat at the top of the city's social and economic pyramid.*

The creation of a middle class, no matter how small and timid it was initially, was a dramatic innovation. Urban life was still organized around the great discrepancies in wealth that higher- and lower-status residents possessed. Over 80% of the population of Florence during the 15th century, for instance, was estimated to have been composed of poor and destitute people. A nascent middle class—in the case of Florence perhaps no greater than 16% of the city's resident population—promised to open up the stratification system by allowing more people to acquire a measure of wealth and the ability to spend it in ways that mimicked those practiced by wealthier and higher-status people. A middle class also meant that some residents would rise and fall on the basis of their accomplishments rather than be stuck in the social class to which they'd had the good or bad fortune to be born.

Ethnicity was different. The ancient Greeks had actually invented it as a means to unite unrelated persons into a clan-like entity whose members would provide mutual support and protection. The idea was that they'd also transfer some of these family-like feelings of loyalty to the larger political community or *polis* where they lived. *In the context of late-medieval cities, ethnicity became a means to organize economic and social life. Importantly, membership in ethnic groups was no longer restricted to the highest-status males in the community as it had been in the Greek city-states.* People from different levels of society might claim membership in this fictive family (Smith, 1985). It also afforded members an opportunity to develop organizations and

institutions that paralleled or mimicked those made by more established and prestigious people in the city.

Two other social changes taking place in cities of this era deserve special note. Proto-industrial cities became organized so that different activities and persons were separated into distinctive zones or neighborhoods. Basically, *they invented the practice of spatial and social segregation.* Though contemporary connotations are primarily negative, segregation served a number of important purposes in cities from the proto-industrial period onward.

This is also the first time when we see the size of families beginning to shrink and the family's role in society change. While this trend was apparent in both rural areas and urban settlements, the decreases in family size were especially apparent in cities. *The requirements of urban life changed how families were organized and what services they provided for their members. In general, families would become less important as economic units and more important as sources of social support, which in turn shaped the way cities operated.*

After 1500, the share of the total population that lived in urban settlements began to grow more consistently than it had in the past. Urban dwellers became anywhere from 9% to 12% of the society's population, more than doubling what it had been during the preindustrial period. The growth in urban populations was a response to improved agricultural production and more trade (Light, 1983, pp. 50–62). Newcomers accounted for much of the population increase. They constituted between one third and one half of the population in some cities. Many of the new urban residents had migrated from rural areas; but people increasingly also moved between cities. This large and floating mass of workers was needed to do menial work, and their marginal status was assured by frequent moves.

Although much manufacturing was still done in rural areas, a lot of the finer work that went into finishing and assembling luxury items was completed in cities. This kind of regional integration allowed employers to adjust their workforce during periods of economic fluctuation and for the city to remain a center of market activity, credit, and consumption. This change also spoke to the growing diversification that was taking place in the city's occupational and economic base during this period.

Increases in trade and manufacturing produced more wealth and property income. But these increases still benefited only a comparatively small portion of the population. Families that had a great deal of wealth displayed it through ostentatious consumption and by creating large public monuments in their own honor. These projects provided menial jobs for some urban workers and served as a kind of public welfare.

The influx into cities of so many transient and poor people made better-established families more than a little anxious. Their concern then, no less than our own today, was how to integrate so many poor and unrelated people into the city's economy and everyday social routines. Prominent urban families worried that their way of looking at the world and leadership would be called into question. Occasional outbreaks of civil unrest by less prosperous and settled people added to their concerns. *Then, as today, the response by the city's most important people was to create new modes of institutional life that would make the outsiders' presence less threatening and the city work better.*

All of their reform efforts were made in the name of the "people." They were intended to evoke feelings of trust and transfer the loyalty of city residents from a sovereign to a fictive community literally built into and around the city. Popular culture also bound different persons together. Public drinking houses in colonial and early American cities, for instance, provided one of the few places outside of church where people from different levels of society could socialize. Intermittent displays of public exuberance, annoyance, and even violence directed at outsiders or local people deemed to have behaved badly provided people with another way to share popular feelings about what was going on in their community.

INDUSTRIAL CITIES (URBANIZATION FROM THE MID-18TH CENTURY TO THE EARLY 20TH CENTURY)

As we noted earlier, industrialization really did instigate a great many big changes in Western society. These changes were especially apparent in urban areas. Cities became much larger and there were more of them. Indeed, city building during this period became continuous, unidirectional, and a compelling worldwide phenomenon for the first time. Big changes were seen in how cities were built, how spaces inside cities and increasingly outside them as well were laid out and made available to different kinds of people and businesses, and how urban residents actually used the city and related to each other. We also saw the advent of widespread suburbanization during this period.

The principal engine driving all this growth was the marriage of capitalism to industrial technology. *The development and widespread introduction of heavy industry to cities meant that commerce had to vie with manufacturing for choice pieces of city land. It also meant that economics now took a position equal to and in some ways superior to that of politics and religion as the driving force behind the way cities were laid out.* Just as importantly, economics became a principal way in which people, especially newcomers to the city, were integrated into ongoing urban routines.

It is interesting and perhaps ironic that what really made the brokering of this marriage possible were changes in rural and urban areas that had nothing to do with industrialization. How much people were able to produce in the way of agricultural surpluses, the kinds of craft production rural people did, and how difficult it became for them to inherit or work property their family might have owned for generations all had a profound impact on the growth of big industrial centers. Rural land enclosures and commercial agriculture displaced thousands upon thousands of individual farm laborers who eventually moved to cities. In urban areas, non-craft production was already on the rise and manufacturing-for-export was becoming a more established part of routine economic life. *Improvements to the city's infrastructure and buildings also anticipated the need to focus more on fixed capital investments than on trade in the industrial age.*

Cities formerly had directed and financed much of rural manufacturing and provided markets for goods and workers to finish assembling and refining them. Better transportation and cheaper goods now made sustained urbanization possible by bringing more parts of the manufacturing process to the city. Even with increased migration to cities, however, town populations benefited from short-term increases in rural manufacturing. These same towns also became crucial components in the development of a far-reaching system of smaller and medium-sized urban settlements that served as secondary manufacturing sites and markets for all the new products being built in cities. As we'll see later, these kinds of places aren't as numerous or as well developed in many newly developing nations. The result is that *less developed regions of the world do not yet have an effective network of cities that can act as market centers and spillover sites for big-city populations* (Hohenberg & Lees, 1995, pp. 180–186).

City population growth continued to depend more on migration than natural increase, despite improvements in sanitation, medical care, and cleaner water supplies. Families adjusted to having men doing work like spinning fabric that was once done only by women and children. Rural workers learned how to behave like urbanites by becoming more disciplined in their work schedules and dependent on others for things they used to grow or make for themselves. Some organized assistance made it possible for even marginal laborers and their families to stay in cities during economic downturns instead of returning to rural areas and farm or craft work.

The expansion of city building to new lands was prompted by the mercantile policies of colonial powers. Owing to the Puritans' emphasis on commerce as a godly enterprise, for instance, colonial American towns that would eventually become cities in the North began as commercial experiments, transportation nodes, and craft manufacturing centers. In the South, the feudal ideal of cavaliers took hold in the big plantations maintained by many Black serfs or slaves.

The American South had fewer cities and a smaller urban population for this reason. By 1800, the South had only 2.7% of its population in cities, a figure that would have rivaled that for preindustrial societies. The urban population in the North was between 7.5% and 8.5% of the total population, which would have put it in line with figures in proto-industrial societies. By 1900 and at the height of the Industrial Revolution, only 16% of the South's people lived in urban settlements while 59% of the North's population did. The South remained dependent on the North for finished goods, loans, and investment money into the 20th century.

By this time in Europe, no new cities were being built. Indeed, there were no new European cities built in the 100 years prior to World War II. Urban populations certainly grew. But all this growth took place in existing cities. The urban system in Europe was already in place by the time industrialization took hold.

The situation was much different in the United States. There the number of urban places increased dramatically throughout the 19th and 20th centuries, despite going through its own Civil War and two world wars and suffering the effects of the Great Depression. In keeping with the European model, however, the number of small and medium-sized cities grew much faster than did the number of very large cities.

Regions differed in how quickly they became urbanized depending on the timing of when they experienced nation building, industrialization, and rapid advances in their transportation infrastructure (Hohenberg & Lees, 1995, p. 229, 240). But what Europe's metropolises had in common was that they combined political, service, and industrial activities. Improvements to short-distance transportation made for easier migration and trade within regions and meant that cities were more important as "nodal" centers than "central" places. This same idea has been appropriated by scholars who write about "global cities" today.

All urban areas provide a place where many different clients, suppliers, buyers, and services can be found. And smaller businesses still require the presence of other similarly sized units for goods and information sharing (i.e., the so-called "agglomeration effect"). However, the ratio of manufacturing to service jobs was actually lower in larger cities that had more diversified economies. As a practical matter, then, *the seed for today's "information city" and "postindustrial" city that emerged by the middle of the 20th century and was dedicated to services and less mobile industries tied to them was planted in the Industrial Revolution* (Hohenberg & Lees, 1995, p. 299). The city would remain an economic and social incubator that could not be easily replicated in smaller places.

New technologies allowed for an unprecedented piling up and spreading out of all those persons who moved to cities or worked in them during the industrial era. Vertical construction made for more dense development. Better trains and roads let people spread out. All of this growth had a profound impact on the ecology of cities and metropolitan areas, especially in the way people used natural resources and increased pollution. There also were serious social consequences that came with all the building up and spreading out that people dealt with on a daily basis.

The effect in both cases was to provoke public and private leaders into addressing these problems. The results, as we'll see in chapter 9, were seen in all kinds of campaigns to fix urban places and reform the people who lived and worked in them. Most of this activity was promoted by private groups at first and often served the need of middle- and upper-class persons to do *something* to help as much as it did the down-and-out persons who were the object of reform campaigns. City governments became more directly involved in these planning, rebuilding, and reform efforts only later in the 19th century.

A variety of smaller steps were taken in the civil arena to address some of these problems, too. *People looked for ways to create family-like ties with other city residents when their own families weren't around.* Some persons tried to work closer to home. Neighborhoods became important places for all kinds of socially supportive activities. Ethnicity was practiced more broadly and helped a great many newcomers become better integrated in their new hometown. Many clubs and organizations developed a diverse client and membership base, even as other groups cultivated ties to people identical to those who already were participating or being served.

It may be a surprise to learn that many aspects of urban life in industrial-era cities actively reinforced family and neighborhood ties instead of diminishing them. Furthermore, many elite-inspired customs and tastes came to be practiced by people with less power, status, and wealth. The softening of inequality, including the ways public space came to be used by a variety of people, also took hold as the middle class expanded both its upper and lower boundaries and more elements of everyday culture came to be shared across increasingly fuzzy social class lines.

More opportunities were created for men and women of unequal rank to be included in the same big public ceremonies, enjoy similar leisurely pursuits, and to shop and consume similar kinds of goods and services. Over time, the number and variety of occasions when everyday people take to the streets in a disruptive and violent way diminished. *Public life in cities generally became less rowdy.* One need look no further than the way Christmas has changed from a day of public display and misbehavior to a quiet day practiced indoors with one's family opening gifts it may take months to pay for (Nissenbaum, 1996).

POSTINDUSTRIAL CITIES (URBANIZATION FROM THE MID-20TH CENTURY ONWARD)

By the mid-20th century, the populations of industrialized countries had become overwhelmingly urban and, at least in the United States, increasingly suburban as well. To a certain extent this movement also entailed a shift from areas with older central cities into regions whose cities and metropolitan areas were only now experiencing their greatest growth. The process of urbanization in the United States is one that seems to be driven increasingly by what happens in the South and West as compared with what happens in the North and Midwest where America's first cities were founded.

The push toward building ever more suburbs and building them farther away from central cities may have been delivered something close to a knock-out punch with the economic recession of 2008 and collapse of the housing market that effectively precipitated it. Until then and continuing even today, however, a great many persons undertake long commutes from outlying parts of metro areas, some of which are almost rural in character, to their work closer to the city center. Suburbanization is one half of the big change that happened to the process of urbanization in the United States during the 20th century. The other half of the story involved a massive shift in our population from the Northeast and Midwest to the South and West.

Losses in manufacturing that hammered cities in the Northeast and Midwest compounded and even accelerated a shift to usually sunnier, warmer, and drier parts of the country, if you ignore Florida and parts of the Gulf Coast, which can be quite damp, and Oregon and Washington, which are almost always wet and rarely sunny. The upside for cities and metropolitan areas in the Northeast and Midwest, if there was one, was that these twin population shifts occasioned a massive campaign to rebuild and update their central city cores. *The redevelopment of cities allowed them to attract more service industries and more affluent full-time residents.* It wasn't enough to reverse all the losses they had experienced in their populations and economies, but it did give them a much-needed breather and time to consider what they should do next to recapture the energy they'd once radiated.

A key lesson here has been that areas with diverse economies do better, even in difficult economic times. This has proved especially true of those metropolitan areas that already had a healthy number of advanced services and knowledge-based industries. Doing less well are metropolitan areas whose economies depended upon heavy industry, which can't be much of a surprise to anyone at this point.

More of a surprise, perhaps, is that the process of "decentralizing" (a fancier and nicer word than "losing") businesses, particularly retail stores, and residents, more often White and middle class than not, was already well in place by the end of the 19th century. The out-migration of wholesale and manufacturing enterprises waited until the first third of the 20th century. New industrial enterprises tended to start up in areas outside of central cities. Older industries either remained locked in cities or closed down.

The continued spread of jobs out of central cities and into suburban areas eventually left the latter's economies and populations more diverse and increasingly more "urban" in character. The segregation for which suburbs were once famous began to wear away. The shift was gradual and more apparent in suburbs closer to the central city than farther away. But it was real and persistent. Individual suburban towns may still be more homogeneous than central cities. At the same time, there are more minorities and fewer prosperous individuals living in suburban places than at any other time in the past.

The shift toward suburban development began in earnest during the late 19th century, but accelerated rapidly in the 20th century. It was initiated by more prosperous persons who moved short distances outside of central cities after the Civil War. The movement grew to include less prosperous persons only in the past 50 years. The shift has been so great that today a majority of Americans now live in suburban places.

Minority populations tend to be centered inside a comparatively small number of larger cities, though some, as we just noted, more recently have filtered out into the suburbs. There are a lot of minorities in most states today, and their presence is felt especially in the largest metropolitan areas of those states. Blacks are the dominant minority in 12 metropolitan areas nationally. Over 43% live in these areas, particularly in the New York, Philadelphia, Chicago, and Detroit metropolitan areas and their central cities. Hispanic and Asians predominate in the larger metro areas of the Southwest and West.

Certain kinds of persons have shown a willingness to move into central cities. Minorities and immigrants still use them as a port of entry, even though more than half of the Black and Hispanic poor do not live there. Less than 20% of the non-Hispanic and White poor live in cities. There are sizable pockets of White "gentrification" in central cities today, and middle-class minority settlement inside cities has also increased over the past few decades. A much-talked-about return to the city by older, retired, and childless people has helped energize some neighborhoods in and around the central business districts of cities. It's hard to gauge, however, just how many older people will continue to make such a move.

Certain kinds of economic activities also have tended to centralize inside cities in the last half of the 20th century and first part of the 21st century. City economies are increasingly dominated by professional, technical, and service industries as well as cultural and recreational activities. Historians tell us that this is nothing new. We need to recall here that *from ancient times onward, cities primarily have been sites of consumption rather than production. As we already noted, cities that fared best have had the most diverse economies.* The scale of this postindustrial development, however, surely is unprecedented.

Cities have been refitted for postindustrial economies and populations through the active collaboration of public and private leaders at both the local and national levels for the better part of the last half-century. Early emphasis was put on razing whole sections of cities and outfitting them for the expected arrival of "newer" industries, which did take place eventually, and of more prosperous and White full-time residents, which did not happen as much as persons had hoped. Over the past 40 years, the emphasis had changed to rehabilitating neighborhoods and working with at least some of the local business people and

residents. Much of this work continued to be done with the assistance of governments and public subsidies. In some instances, corporations also played a big part in refitting neighborhoods where their headquarters were located.

We will have more to say about all these changes in Chapter 3, which focuses on urbanization in the United States. We highlight some of the most salient features of urbanization in more developed countries below to set the stage for our discussion in Chapter 2 of urbanization in less developed parts of the world.

LESSONS FROM URBANIZATION IN THE WEST

Cities in the West had their greatest period of growth during the century and a half it took for them to become centers of heavy industry. Not all cities in Europe and North America participated equally in the industrial expansion, but the ones that did saw their populations grow to unprecedented levels during the second half of the 19th century. The important points to keep in mind from the standpoint of understanding how urbanization has unfolded in different parts of the West are these:

1. Cities in the West had the luxury of developing over the course of several centuries, a long period of time when compared to urbanization in many non-Western countries. Cities in the West already had networks of smaller and medium-sized towns and cities with which they had well-established trading arrangements by the time they became industrialized.

2. Advances in agriculture had created large and permanent surpluses in food and displaced workers, men and women who would soon be siphoned off into industrial and wage-earning jobs located in the nation's cities.

3. Populations in rural areas stabilized and even shrunk.

4. There was sufficient flexibility in the economy to allow urban residents in one part of the country

to pick up and move to a variety of urban settlements where the prospect of employment was better.

5. Challenging as it was to acquire public money to invest in urban infrastructural improvements, resources were found so that most urban residents eventually were treated to better services.

We haven't featured the way in which people lived in cities as we described the process of *urbanization.* However, the social changes that had to take place in cities and metropolitan areas so that large numbers of people from different social stations and backgrounds could live and work in such close quarters were equally important. As we noted at the outset of the book, changes in the development of cities (i.e., *urbanization*) were related to the way in which people lived in cities (i.e., *urbanism*).

1. Public and private leaders were well aware of the fact that people from different social classes, backgrounds, and tenure had dramatically different life chances. They were working on this problem before even more people showed up during the industrial era, creating new public and private institutions that would soften the effects of inequality.

2. Merchants became the backbone of a newly emerging middle class inside cities. They pushed for rights and obligations for the maintenance of the city that had once belonged exclusively to wealthy and higher-status people. Among these "privileges" was the ability to create a host of voluntary organizations through which they develop a common view of the world and their place in it. They also were able to acquire luxury goods previously available only to the elite and assert themselves politically into the operation of city governments.

3. The size of families began to shrink, and families took on new roles that better fit an urban world.

4. Ethnicity, a premodern invention, became more widely practiced and managed to include persons of unequal social and economic rank within the putative "ethnic family" or group. Voluntary and enforced segregation, which still occur today, especially in cities with large Muslim populations, provided "outsiders" with an opportunity to develop organizations and sets of beliefs and practices that mimicked those of "insiders."

A really important test of this last innovation is taking place today in Europe as people in cities across the continent are working hard to adjust to the presence of many immigrants, a good number of them Muslim. Two recent reports reveal that European leaders have a serious concern about the progress immigrants are making (Open Societies Institute [OSI], 2010; Rath, 2011). They also talk about what they can do to facilitate the integration of foreign people into the communities where they have settled.

What is striking about Muslims in Europe isn't the religious discrimination they say they have experienced. Occasional displays of ethnic violence, their marginal economic status and relatively poor housing, the negative way in which they are portrayed in the media, and the rise of anti-immigrant sentiment by some political parties certainly are unfortunate (OSI, 2010, pp. 22–23; Sayare, 2012; Meyer, 2012). But they aren't much of a surprise either.

What is most interesting about the Muslim newcomers is how much they have already come to think and act like their new European neighbors. Their views and behavior aren't identical to those of Europeans, to be sure. But they are surprisingly close on a number of points that researchers had good reason to think should matter: how comfortable they feel in their neighborhood; how much they trust local and national officials; their educational aspirations for their children; the number and variety of religious and other voluntary organizations to which they belong; or their sense of personal and political efficacy.

The mimicking of European views and behavior is the first and perhaps most crucial step in the long walk toward integration that Muslim newcomers are taking. At times, they also have collaborated with their European neighbors and local business and political leaders on important matters. Once they begin taking on more of the duties typically assigned to longer-term residents and higher-status people their transformation from cultural outsiders into insiders will be all but complete (Monti, 2012). Public ridicule and displays of aggression toward them will greatly diminish. Officials will recognize them as "legitimate participants in community consultation and engagement" (OSI, 2010, p. 28).

An important element in the Muslim's transformation as it is for all foreign outsiders striving to become cultural insiders is the way ethnic people succeed at being like and different from their hosts at the same time. In the case of European Muslims, some people are more engaged in ethnic-only groups and socialize more with their own people while others have a wider and less exclusive set of personal and organizational ties. Some members of the larger immigrant population keep their feet planted almost entirely in the world belonging to their fellow immigrants. Other people from the same population plant one foot in each world, the one belonging to their fellow immigrants and the one dominated by their European-born neighbors.

An especially important way in which immigrants have always tried to fit in and remain distinct at the same time is by becoming business owners. As Rath (2011, pp. 1–3) observed about Europe's current ethnic entrepreneurs, these people "create their own jobs" and make a place for themselves in their new communities. They don't wait for native business owners to offer them jobs or solicit them to run for public office. When ethnic businessmen and businesswomen are successful, they also create jobs for their friends, relatives, and acquaintances, all of whom are members of the same ethnic group as the business owner. Ethnic entrepreneurs do more than hire people like them and spread around a little more wealth. According to Li (1999), they become leaders in their circle of contacts and friends as well as in the larger community. They are able to do this because they have contacts with suppliers and customers that aren't part of their group. Through these contacts, ethnic entrepreneurs help build bridges to the larger nonimmigrant community and improved their chances for upward mobility. They accomplish this even

as they provide native foods and products to their fellow expatriates and revitalize otherwise run-down neighborhoods.

The larger cultural benefits that accrue to having a more diverse population do not stop with ethnic entrepreneurs and all the good economic and social work they do. Rhys Andrews (2009, p. 428) recently observed that in England the involvement of ethnic people in local associations and political activities helps their nonethnic neighbors every bit as much as it does them. As Andrews puts it, this kind of firsthand observing and engagement "enhances perceptions of mutual respect" among all the area's residents.

Interracial and cross-ethnic contacts have not always been framed in such a positive light, of course. The diverse populations of cities were supposed to increase the chances that different groups would think of each other in a negative light and treat each other poorly. And there was much historical evidence to back up that claim as we shall see in subsequent chapters. Something has changed in the culture of cities during the last century and probably only in the last couple of decades to turn diversity from a bad thing into a good thing. Elsewhere in the book, we will explore some of these changes and how quickly they may or may not be spreading.

Important as these changes may be in the West, of course, there is no guarantee that they would be important in less developed societies or carry the same significance there as they have in Europe and North America. However, the story of city building and urban life in less developed countries today shows that people deal with many of the same problems their counterparts have in more developed countries. They also have adapted Western-style solutions to fit their own urban settlements or had the kernels of such solutions already there to be drawn upon.

SOME CONVERGENCE IN WORLDWIDE TRENDS IN URBANIZATION

Urbanization, as we will see in the next chapter, has been both a cause and an effect of all the changes less developed countries have gone through since the mid-20th century. These people didn't have the luxury of centuries to figure out how to build a freer economy, relatively competent and responsive governments, and a system of smaller, medium-sized, and larger cities connected by trade and good transportation. They had to do all this *and* deal with more rural people moving in faster and in larger numbers than cities in developed countries faced. The rapid urbanization that has occurred in less developed countries has been part of a general improvement in their overall wealth, sanitation, communication and transportation, and the gradual liberalization of their economies. It also has been associated with social and political turmoil, ecological degradation, uneven development, and growing inequality.

Experts used to describe less developed countries as being "over urbanized" and called their cities "primate cities." These catch-all terms were supposed to convey the impression that city building in those countries was unbalanced or imbalanced. They had one or perhaps two large and dominant cities that were the primary focus of everything we associate with urban life in the West. These "primate cities" were often bigger than places like New York and London and were the primary focus of economic wealth, political power, and cultural accomplishment in their country. They had no competitors, much less a healthy system of smaller and medium-sized places around them with which they had strong commercial ties.

The biggest point of convergence between cities in more and less developed societies today is that we saw many American cities exhibit signs of "primacy" and of being "over urbanized" in the second half of the 20th century. They had too many full-time residents and too few jobs for people, especially less well-trained residents and more recent newcomers, who wanted to work. Wealthier persons moved to the periphery of the city or out of the city altogether. The central part of many older cities became filled with rundown slums populated by poor people. Rates of economic inequality rose.

Public services and amenities deteriorated in the face of declining tax receipts.

As the United Nations reported in its *State of the World's Cities 2010/2011*, there is a "legacy of deep divides" in American cities, especially in its larger cities. These cities had "high income inequality due to poverty and racial segregation, postindustrial economic restructuring and combinations of inner-city decline and suburban sprawl." Some larger U.S. cities have levels of income and wealth inequality that come close to matching those of cities in Argentina, Chile, and Ecuador. There is not much comfort to be taken from the fact that U.S. levels are lower than those of Colombia, Thailand, and Nigeria. The report adds that "for many people in the United States, moving up from the lowest economic ranks to the middle class, and from the middle class to the top income echelons, is becoming increasingly difficult." The parallels with cities in less developed countries are telling, if only because many American cities appear to have "caught up" or declined to levels seen in less developed countries.

Cities in the West still have many advantages over their counterparts in less developed countries. But the cities in less developed countries have made progress. We will see that they have become wealthier and managed to reduce the number of people who live under the direst of circumstances. Political liberalization, meaning that national governments no longer determine as much of what happens in the economy, has led to wholesale improvements in the economic outlook for the whole society. Manufacturing all kinds of products from clothing to high-end electronics has created more jobs and let people see improvements in their life chances. Income and wealth inequality remain high, but the level of "consumption inequality" has dropped because less well-off persons are now able to buy goods that are like those that more well-off persons can acquire.

The UN report notes that countries like China and India have made "giant strides" in reducing the share of their respective populations that reside in slums. In China, slum dwellers have gained access to "more than 20 million new and affordable housing units." India has managed to lessen poverty and improve its slum conditions using a combination of strategies. Included among them are building the skills of poor people and giving them access to micro-credit so they can start businesses; providing better services to these areas and funds to buy houses and subsidize their rents; and encouraging the poor to become involved in reclamation projects.

The UN notes that far too many people still live in "shanty towns" and suffer from poor health, bad housing, having too few jobs, and too much crime. Indeed their number has actually been increased since 1990 by "displaced persons" or refugees who continue to move into these places. The weight of these burdens, according to the UN, falls especially heavily on the women and children who live there.

Two other points of convergence between urban areas in more and less developed countries deserve our attention. *The first is that urban areas in less developed countries are gradually connecting. The primary driver in this change is the marketplace.* More goods and services are being produced and shared between cities. The UN now speaks of "mega-regions" and "urban corridors" being created along major transportation routes. It notes that few if any smaller towns or cities have sprung up along these corridors as yet. So it would be inaccurate to talk about what's happening to urban areas in these countries in the same way people in the West talk about their cities gradually growing toward each other. But some important steps toward making a network of cities are being taken.

The second and closer parallel to urban development in the West has been the creation of "urban sprawl." One expression of sprawl is not found in Western cities. It consists of large so-called "peri-urban" areas that have grown around or past the boundaries of incorporated cities. These are areas that are informally tied to the city but have no legal standing. As a result, they lack the "infrastructure, public facilities and basic services that incorporated areas have. They also have "inadequate access to roads" and "little or no public transportation." People familiar with cities in more developed countries like the United States would easily recognize the other kind of sprawl. This would consist of "residential zones for high- and middle-income groups and highly-valued commercial and retail complexes." These areas are "well-connected by individual rather than public transport," meaning that people have to use their cars to travel any substantial distance from home.

It is unrealistic to think that cities and urban areas in less developed countries will look exactly like they do in the West any time soon, if they ever do. No one, for example, foresees as many cities in developing countries attracting the number and variety of foreign immigrants that Western cities drew in the past. At the same time, the UN has estimated that in the last few decades some 5.3 million displaced persons and refugees have come to live in cities in developing countries. Most have settled in sub-Saharan Africa and western and southern Asia. How these people adjust to their new surroundings and how their hosts respond to them will tell us even more about how similar and different city life in developing countries will be to that in the West.

What has happened in less developed countries lately as we will see in the next chapter suggests that there are common properties to the way cities and larger urban regions grow. Given the problems that cities in the West continue to wrestle with, that may not seem like much of a compliment or offer much hope to people trying to make cities in less developed countries work better. But it does speak to a convergence in the strategies people from very different places and cultures use to build their cities and make them work.

QUESTIONS FOR STUDY AND DISCUSSION

1. What are the main similarities and differences between an *evolutionary* and *comparative*

approach to describing the process of urbanization and the way that people live in cities?

2. What are some of the most important factors that led to the development of cities? Can you see examples of those factors in cities that you've lived in, read about, or visited?

3. Describe some of the principal economic and demographic changes that take place in cities and urban areas in the West over the past 400 to 500 years. How did the nature of cities prior to that time set the stage for later urban development?

4. Describe some of the ways in which urbanization and urban life in the West anticipated changes we are now seeing in urban areas in developing countries.

5. What roles do production and consumption play in the development of cities throughout history? How have those roles changed over time?

6. Theorists, as you will see, tend to hold a dim view of cities and the way people live there. Based on what you have read, how will city boosters counter these unflattering views?

INTERNET MATERIALS

UN Habitat, 2010. *State of the world's cities 2010/2011* http://www.unhabitat.org/content.asp?cid=8051 &catid=7&typeid=46

2

URBAN PLACES AND PEOPLE IN COMPARATIVE PERSPECTIVE

We used an *evolutionary* approach or framework in the previous chapter to describe urbanization in Western societies. It was popular among 19th century researchers who tried to make sense of the world in which they were living by reminding themselves of the history their ancestors had made. Obviously, we still find it useful today.

The observations and records that are used in evolutionary arguments let scholars make some sweeping generalizations about cities in general. In no way, however, do they capture all the variations among those cities or the fact that some cities did better and some did worse. This approach also allows us to compare cities on the basis of an important variable—in this case, how industrialized a city or society had become—and enables us to make some broad statements about how people lived in cities during different periods of history. Scholars quickly seized on a question that had bedeviled partisans and critics of cities from the time of the ancient Greeks. That is, how could so many different kinds of people possibly find a congenial and effective way to live with one another in such densely compacted places?

An "evolutionary" way of tracing and making sense of history helps to reveal some important features of cities and urban life. But it probably overlooks many others that would have helped us understand better the kinds of problems and opportunities urban people and places have today. This is one of the main reasons why 19th and 20th century scholars studied cities in parts of the world that weren't like the places they knew in Europe. This *comparative* approach to studying cities and urban life is invaluable. It compels observers to confront their own deeply rooted ideas about how the world works. They see other kinds of people looking at the world differently and making the world work for them in ways that are both different and reminiscent of the ones they know best.

The people and places discussed in "comparative" studies are not identical, not to each other and certainly not to our own. They may have more in common than we imagine, of course. But that's no guarantee that their histories will mimic those of countries like Australia, Canada and the United States in North America, and much of Europe, which have the kind of cities and metropolitan areas we would recognize best. The same could be said of their people, too, even if we never had a chance to visit them, speak their language, or learn their history.

Their cities' large buildings, commercial areas, and many public and private institutions are like those we know in U.S. cities. Their residents, like our own, might like to garden, but few of them engage in agriculture or have anything to do with the production of food. They possess strong manufacturing industries that export finished goods but today would be considered "postindustrial" societies. That is because they have a rapidly growing service sector specializing in finance, technology, health, education, and research. These countries are rich as measured by the per capita income of their citizens. And, finally, their populations are rapidly aging and probably would be shrinking if they were not receiving large numbers of immigrants from other parts of the world.

Countries in Central and South America, Africa, and parts of Asia have cities that look different from the ones we know best (Light, 1983, p. 123), or at least they did until recently. They have large populations, to be sure. Indeed, their city populations are often much larger than those of cities in countries like the United States. Until recently, however, they didn't have much in the way of metropolitan areas and suburbs or anything like the expanse of commercial and public institutions that are so common in the cities of more economically developed countries. There were, again until recently, just a few really big cities and many small towns or villages that were poorly connected by way of trade, lacked an extensive system of roads, and before the advent of wireless phone service had few effective ways to communicate and travel between them on a routine basis.

There are good reasons, then, why city building turned out differently in these different kinds of countries. *Until recently, less economically developed countries had little in the way of independent manufacturing that exported finished goods. Most of their people lived in areas that were substantially agricultural. The service sector in these countries was small. These countries tended to be poor. Their urban populations were growing both by natural increases and migration, but the migrants are coming from rural areas in their own country.* They didn't get as many foreign immigrants. They couldn't feed, house, and employ their own populations much less people from other countries.

There have been recent improvements in the living standards of people in less developed societies, especially for city residents in comparison to people from rural areas. But the difference between their situation and that of people in more developed countries is only decreasing slowly, as measured by the percentage of gross world products each country's people consumes (Light, 1983, p. 123). Part of the reason for the continuing disparity, as we just hinted, is that the larger cities in less developed countries can have more than two and three times as many people living in them as cities in the more developed regions. Furthermore, the number of people residing in shantytowns, which are found almost exclusively in less developed regions and already hold approximately one quarter of the world's urban population, at this point is doubling every decade (Palen, 2008, p. 294).

In this chapter, we will delve more deeply into the way that cities in Latin America, Africa, and Asia have changed in the last half-century. We will explore in a very general way how their respective patterns of urbanization are alike and different. We also will compare these patterns to what has happened in cities in more developed parts of the world.

CITIES IN NON-WESTERN AND LESS DEVELOPED COUNTRIES DURING THE ERA OF URBAN "PRIMACY"

The world's population more than doubled between 1800 and 1900 and more than tripled between 1900 and 2000. Its urban population probably tripled between 1800 and 1900 and grew three times faster than the overall population between 1900 and 2000 (Light, 1983, p. 128). *Most of the increase in the world's urban population in the 20th century can be accounted for by the staggering growth of cities in less economically developed countries.* Looking at these statistics in a slightly different way, it appears that the urban growth rate in less developed countries in the 20th century may well have exceeded the urban growth rate in more developed countries during the height of their urban expansion in the 19th century.

Some less developed countries like those in Latin America are predominantly urban. Indeed, Latin America is the most urbanized continent on the planet. Some countries like those in East Asia and North Africa have populations that are fairly evenly split between their urban and rural areas at this point. The rest are predominantly rural despite large increases in their urban populations in the 20th century. Obviously, this pattern of urbanization is entirely different from the one that has been followed in more developed countries.

The reasons for the difference aren't difficult to understand. *Western societies did a better job of employing and housing their populations and exporting people they didn't need at home to become colonists in faraway lands.* Western death rates declined fairly early because people had more access to clean water, better waste removal systems, and better food. Decreases in birthrates followed suit. Better food and manufacturing could feed and employ part but not all of the larger and increasingly superfluous rural population as cites began to grow rapidly between the late 18th and early 20th centuries. Prior to that, countries that would eventually qualify as being more developed had managed their populations by exporting people to colonial settlements, which turned out, unsurprisingly, to be in less developed regions of the world (Hawley, 1971, pp. 281–283).

Death rates in less developed countries have declined, but birthrates haven't. The fact is that many less developed countries have actually increased their agricultural and manufacturing output at rates as high as or higher than those seen in the West in the 19th century. However, the failure to decrease their birthrates has led to a population imbalance and left these countries with too many people to feed and employ. Inasmuch as these countries were the object of colonization but never built their own foreign outposts and empires, they couldn't get rid of their excess population that way. The result has been that the populations of their cities have become extremely large (Light, 1983, pp. 129–130).

Less developed countries are often said to be "overurbanized" because their cities can't adequately house and employ their rapidly growing populations. To make matters worse, urban populations fed by rural migration also tend to be disproportionately young. Nearly a half-century ago, the youthful migrants were more likely to be female in Latin America and male in Africa and Asia (Hawley, 1971, p. 295). In either case, however, there are still more than enough young men and women around to make many children. This problem was compounded by the fact that the largest city in these countries back then was sometimes the *only* large city in these countries and was many times bigger than other urban places. These countries did not yet have anything like a system of smaller and medium-sized cities dispersed across their territories. Thus, there were usually only one or two main cities to which these people could move.

The original "primate" cities were clustered along seacoasts and were the administrative centers for colonial powers and such export-oriented trade that the colonial overseers could muster. The trade in question, not unlike that in the original American colonies, was one-way. It was designed to take natural resources, raw agricultural products like tobacco or precious metals, to the colonial power overseas. It wasn't designed to allow the colonized people to develop their own commercial and manufacturing capacity.

Primate cities contained most of the country's urban population and dominated an interior region that remained sparsely populated and relatively underdeveloped (Light, 1983, p.129). The population of a primate city may have been larger than the combined populations of the next two or three cities in the country or region. A second class of cities in less developed countries was not on the seacoasts. These indigenous urban settlements served as regional administrative centers, market towns, and concentrations of agriculturalists.

Countries with primate cities and less developed economies tended to be smaller in addition to being poorer. The native populations of these societies were decimated by war, disease, and slave taking. Inside these cities, segregation was commonplace, a pattern somewhat more prevalent in the southern than in the northern parts of Africa. The European model of city building in Latin America had a city center with major government buildings and a church, a market area, and housing for higher-status Europeans. A bit farther out were more modest dwellings for clerks, merchants, and artisans. The city's poor occupied areas farther out yet. The local elite were ceded tracts of land on the outskirts of cities.

These cities didn't begin to grow much less prosper until after colonial powers left and local people were able to trade more directly with Europe and take in just enough European immigrants between 1860 and 1930 to facilitate trade with their former colonial overseers. These immigrants ended up controlling much of the commercial life of these cities. Cities of this sort didn't develop an independent manufacturing base or a class of consumers until the latter half of the 20th century when U.S. manufacturers and manufacturers from other developed countries moved their plants into countries with cheaper labor. Even with that, however, automation limited the number of manufacturing jobs available to native peoples.

URBAN AREAS IN DEVELOPING COUNTRIES IN THE POST-PRIMACY ERA

Much about development in parts of Asia, Latin America, and Africa has changed in the last few decades. Let's begin with differences in their respective populations. United Nations estimates have the number of megacities with 10 million or more residents almost doubling to 34 by 2015. Of these, only six will be in more developed countries (Palen, 2008, p. 295). The rate of urban population growth in less developed regions of the world shows no sign of letting up. The effect on urban areas has been quite remarkable, as we will see below.

CITIES IN CONTEMPORARY LATIN AMERICA

Cities in Latin America and the Caribbean are located in the most urbanized part of the developing world. They also are the engines driving the dramatic economic growth in the region's gross domestic product (GDP). As reported by the McKinsey Global Institute in 2011,

> The region's 198 large cities—defined as having populations of 200,000 or more—together contribute over 60 percent of GDP today. The ten largest cities alone generate half of that output. Such a concentration of urban economic activity among the largest cities is comparable with the picture in the United States and Western Europe today but is much more concentrated than in any other emerging region. China's top ten cities, for instance, contribute around 20 percent of the nation's GDP.[1]

What happens in these cities will have a big impact on economic growth throughout the region. Unfortunately, their populations have grown faster than their local and regional economies could absorb all the new workers who moved there. These cities have used more resources than could reasonably be replenished. They have been unable to generate enough tax dollars to pay local governments to make needed infrastructural improvements. And, finally, they have more social problems than either officials or local people can manage effectively much less eradicate.

As the Inter-American Development Bank argued in 2010,

> New city dwellers have tended to have little or no education or capital. Moreover, guerillas and armed conflicts in rural areas in Peru in the 1980s, in Guatemala, El Salvador, and Nicaragua for several decades, and more recently in Colombia have speeded up the migration to the large cities

among the impoverished inhabitants of rural areas. In this way, the migration process has led to the urbanization of poverty.[2]

The *uneven development* evidenced in Latin American cities has been marked by gross disparities in wealth and opportunities available to the vast majority of newer urban settlers. In Latin America, many of these persons built brand-new shantytowns or expanded ones that had already been established on the outer edges of cities. These are places that had virtually no urban amenities and often became centers for organized gangs whose members controlled much of what happened there. Drug gangs were cleared from one such complex outside Rio de Janeiro in anticipation of the 2014 World Cup and 2016 Olympic Games being played in that city. Welcomed as their removal was, no one was certain how long or how well the "pacification program" would work (Domit, & Barrionuevo, 2010).

The police and army may have been able to clear shantytowns of their more dangerous residents. But they didn't count on the remaining residents putting up much resistance when officials declared that some of the shantytowns would have to be cleared for the 2016 Olympics. The people who still lived there didn't want to leave. As reported in the March 5, 2012, edition of *The New York Times* (Romero, 2012), the 4,000 people in one favela marked for demolition refused "to go quietly" and took their fight to the courts and the street.

Crime and personal insecurity remain big problems in virtually all Latin American cities. In fact, Bryan Roberts (2011, p. 421) has recently observed that gangs, drug trafficking, and the kind of crimes associated with them are undermining other sources of social cohesion that otherwise would be making life in these cities better. Quoting again from the McKinsey Global Institute report, "the average cost of insuring a car against robbery is 33 percent higher than it is in New York." Rio de Janeiro has "33 homicides per 100,000 people each year, compared with four in New York City in 2009." Drug violence has grown dramatically in recent years.

"Monterrey's kidnapping rate of 15.5 per 100,000 is also significantly above average," and is another indication of all the "drug-related crime in the region."[3]

These levels of incivility and disorder are quite high, but probably match those witnessed in 19th century American cities, which also were known for their intemperance and violence. For all the problems that Latin American cities have, however, there are some signs that people in the region are rising to the challenges created by their particular brand of overurbanization. Some of the responses have been positive, others less so. For good or ill, however, they mimic what has been going on in the urban areas of many developed countries for some time.

We have already alluded to the fact that mid-size cities are beginning to become more prominent players in the region's economy. It has been fueled by more liberal trade policies like the 1994 North American Free Trade Agreement (NAFTA). In the case of Mexico, this act had the effect of moving economic activity to smaller urban centers closer to the northern border and American markets. One of the results of spreading out or creating more trained workers in other parts of the country has been to increase commercial ties between bigger cities and these smaller cities. This is an important step in the creation of the kind of commercially inspired "system" of larger, medium-sized, and eventually smaller urban places that countries like the United States have long enjoyed.

A related step taken by governments promises to bring more of the region's workforce out of the "informal" economy and into the "formal" economy. It involves reducing much of the "excessive regulation" that "hobbles entrepreneurship in many cities in Latin America." Governments are making it easier for business people to own property, acquire credit and licenses, and operate a business even as they increase sanctions on things like tax evasion.[4] Improved tax collection increases government resources, which in turn will make it possible for public agencies to provide more and better services to their constituents.

What can happen when a government imposes too many regulations on what business people do and how much money they charge for goods and services became apparent in Venezuela. Federal officials in 2012 introduced such severe price controls on products that manufacturers had to sell their goods on the black market (Neuman, 2012). This move into the informal part of the economy led to marked inflation and a reduction of government tax revenues.

When governments loosen their control and collaborate better with the private sector, there are social as well as economic payoffs. As early as the 1960s, for instance, "companies in Medellín took a lead in . . . pooling resources for investment in community services" by investing in local parks, schools, and social centers for their workers."[5] These practices have become more commonplace across Colombia since then.

The very idea of "corporate responsibility" so common in the United States but only now taking root in some Latin American countries deserves further comment. It is part of the colonial legacy that countries were not encouraged or even allowed to develop their own independent class of entrepreneurs and business people. In Western societies, these men and women assumed broader responsibilities in the community than just providing jobs and decent goods and services at a fair price. They were civic leaders and patrons of all sorts of community-minded and political endeavors. International companies in the United States that work in Latin America today are "exporting" the idea and practice of "corporate responsibility" along with goods and services they want local people to buy. Local business people are learning new civic roles along with making more money.

The results of these changes are predictably better early on for people at the middle and upper ends of the economic spectrum than they are for people subsisting at the margins of society. Better-off people see parts of central cities and waterfront areas revitalized with new housing and entertainment districts, can find malls stocked with goods, and even have gated residential areas to live in (Angotti, 2013, pp. 134–135). Changes to civic roles and routines will come more slowly.

Poorer men and women, as we have already stated, often live in haphazardly constructed and badly maintained housing in neighborhoods with few services and legal protections. The only difference between their situation and that of American minorities living in inner-city slums is that these Latin American settlements are on the edges of urban areas rather than in the middle of the city (Auyero, 2011). Yet that situation has changed dramatically.

The informal economy, which used to provide subsistence-level but otherwise legitimate jobs for the urban poor, doesn't work as well as it once did, either. The gradual introduction of more people to the formal economy certainly helped stabilize and modernize the local economy. But it came with a serious cost: the rise of an illicit drug trade. Together they have diminished the importance of "petty commerce" and the "small-craft workshops" that once catered to the low-income populations living in these areas (Roberts, 2011, p. 420). It will take time for people to adjust to these new economic realities.

In the meantime, the basis for social cohesion in these areas or at least the way it is being expressed these days also has changed. Informal neighboring and efforts to protect these areas from government agencies that wanted to knock down their shanties certainly still take place. But local residents today aren't nearly as resistant to efforts by officials to clear out drug gangs. Furthermore, their grassroots activism has blossomed and moved into the formal political arena where they hope to have their areas certified as legal and serviced by public agencies. The poor and marginalized urban people in Latin America today are fighting to be included in the city rather than resisting efforts to push them out.

The point, as we have previously stated, is that there are promising signs that people in the region are taking steps to address the problems that have come with the kind of cities and economic conditions they inherited. Many of their responses bear a striking resemblance to the way in which people in more Western societies have organized and insulated themselves from the challenges they face. People living in Latin American cities aren't acting exactly as their counterparts in North American cities do, but they are working at it.

URBAN AREAS IN AFRICA AND THE MIDDLE EAST

Africa is in the throes of a profound demographic transformation. As late as the 1990s, "two-thirds of all Africans lived in rural areas" (UN Human Settlements Programme [UN], 2008, p. 4). Within 50 years, half or close to half of the continent's 1.2 billion people will be living in cities, many of them really large. No place, not Europe during its industrialization or in the most quickly urbanizing parts of Latin America or Asia today, would have seen this large or rapid a transition in its rural population into an urban population.

Africa for the moment, in any case, is still the least urbanized continent, with less than 40% of its people living in cities. It may still be by the time this transition plays out. In the meantime, African cities are becoming larger faster than cities in other less developed parts of the world. This growth is most apparent in the continent's largest cities along the coast or on major rivers just off the coast, in places like Cairo, Kinshasa, and Lagos. Although they are growing less quickly today, the consequences of their urban "primacy" are readily apparent and not likely to diminish any time soon.

What happened in Cairo after the 2011 overthrow of Hosni Mubarak's regime shows how people have had to improvise, not just with "do-it-yourself infrastructure" on a grand scale but also in their affairs with each other. As Michael Kimmelman (2013) reported in *The New York Times*, Egyptians "are figuring out anew how they relate to one another and to the city they have always occupied without quite owning— figuring out how to create that city for themselves, politically and socially, as well as with bricks and mortar." A kind of gentrification not sponsored by government is taking place in some

parts of the city as people with money occupy brand-new skyscrapers that replace rundown buildings that had housed poorer people. In other parts of Cairo, grassroots groups work to make neighborhoods more habitable for their poorer residents, sometimes with the help of the Muslim Brotherhood and sometimes without it. "Cairo is in a state of becoming," observed one resident. "We just don't know what it's becoming yet."

For many Egyptians and other African city dwellers the answer to this problem isn't going to be found in older cities but away from the coastline and spread among a number of "intermediate" cities with fewer than 500,000 people (UN, 2008). As we already know, a similar change has taken place in Latin America and was an important step in the development of an "urban system" in North America and Europe. In the case of Africa, the reconfiguration of urbanization as a "regional" phenomenon will be the dominant theme in the continent's development for the foreseeable future.

Much of this development is uncoordinated and unsanctioned by any government body. Such is the case in Tripoli City, Libya. There, population growth has spread beyond the traditional city into surrounding agricultural areas so quickly that different national and regional government offices have been unable to coordinate the reallocation of land. As a result, urban sprawl has been driven by property transactions taking place outside of the formal government system much as it has in Egypt.

Though smaller cities in Africa are growing more rapidly today, most major African cities, as we noted, retain the character of primate cities. This is especially the case in sub-Saharan Africa. As in Latin America and the better part of Asia, their dominance extends over most parts of the country's life. They are population and investment centers, the leading trade and manufacturing hubs, and usually are seats of governmental power as well. The contrast between these places and the relatively undeveloped rural areas surrounding them is striking. Recently, however, cities in South Africa have been doing a better job of developing some of these farther out areas as "suburbs" or at least are incorporating them into the larger urban service delivery system better than they did in the past. This is part of the regional pattern of urban growth to which we have referred.

That said, urbanization has proceeded differently in different parts of the continent. North African countries, according to the United Nations, "have made great strides in improving their cities and reducing the population living under slum conditions through a mix of upgrading and resettlement programmes" (UN, 2008, p. 9). Public–private partnerships between government agencies and businesses have been instrumental in effecting some of these changes as they have been in more developed countries for a long time. That is not all.

> Significant efforts have also been made to encourage the participation of civil society and the activities of non-governmental organizations. Community development associations at the neighbourhood level are emerging and becoming significant partners in developing and implementing community-based initiatives, often with the support of national and local NGOs. (UN, 2008, p. 10)

Cities in west, central, and east Africa, like the countries of which they are part, have not fared as well. The "mostly unplanned and haphazard . . . settlements and mega-slums" characteristic of the region "have become centers of urban squalor, aggravated poverty and human misery." According to the United Nations, these "urban agglomerations" are also "becoming social hotbeds and breeding grounds for unrest and political risk." People do not have routine access to clean water and sufficient food. They do not make enough money to live decent and secure lives much less acquire property. Pollution is endemic. Resources to mount effective building and reform initiatives are lacking.

Cities like Cape Town and Johannesburg in the southern part of Africa have made strides in addressing some of the most obvious and troubling problems that come with the legacy of urban primacy and racial inequality. Their national government has begun to adapt, albeit

slowly perhaps. The new urban world is one in which opportunities and responsibility for running the economy and fashioning more inclusive regulations and programs that will eventually fall to all their people, not just the descendants of White colonialists.

Evidence of this is apparent in Cape Town where deindustrialization "has not produced a large class of Black low-wage service-sector workers" as many observers predicted. Instead, it has produced a class of professional and managerial jobs that are largely integrated or "deracialized" alongside a large class of unemployed Black laborers. "The consequence," Owen Crankshaw (2012, p. 836) observes, "is that the city is becoming divided into racially mixed middle-class neighborhoods and Black working-class neighborhoods characterized by high unemployment."

The political upheaval that South Africa went through has produced a more complex and in some ways more "modern" way of organizing its key cities and problems to deal with. The same thing is happening in Sudan as a result of internal struggles between its "African" and "Arab" populations. Nyla, the second largest city in Sudan, has experienced major growth as its role as the "logistical nerve center" for aid operations during the Darfur crisis expanded dramatically. Rental costs escalated for housing deemed more secure in the center of the city and created pockets of "niche gentrification" that hadn't existed before. Here, too, "new kinds of markets and services have developed for the incoming population." This includes tourist restaurants in downtown Nyla that serve foods not typically eaten by Sudanese and land on the outskirts of the city that is now dedicated to growing vegetables consumed "almost exclusively by the aid worker population" (Bartlett, Alix-Garcia, & Saah, 2012, p. 165).

In other African cities, the UN's "Cities Without 'Slums'" campaign to encourage the development of cityscapes more congenial to Western investors led to a much different reaction on the part of local people. Efforts to clear "slums" have been "resisted, stalled, or derailed by various activist-led rights-based initiatives" and even non-resident property owners in the slum clearance area (Bjorkman, 2013, pp. 125–126). Here as in Latin America, people and property owners in "informal settlements" are demanding to have their claims taken seriously by government officials who would rather see them move away.

The shantytowns of Africa are every bit as much a feature in city life as they are in other developing parts of the world. They house up to one third of all urban residents. The sex ratios in these places tend to favor males and younger people. Poverty, understandably, is rampant. *For all their problems, however, the poor and recently migrated often are able to count on ethnic, tribal, and family ties to help them make the transition into city dwellers.* They are buffered, too, by the gradual diffusion of urban ways into more rural areas, which makes their transition easier.

Changes in women's status are among the biggest adaptations these people have to learn to embrace. More educated women are moving into more modern sectors of the economy, while less educated women make some headway in the informal self-employed part of the economy. Otherwise, they may fall into prostitution and even more marginal economic activities. In general, women's social and economic status has expanded as the size of the families and their importance as economic units decreased. Both are important features of urban life in more developed regions of the world.

Middle Eastern cities include the cities of northern coastal Africa and the major cities of interior Saudi Arabia, Iraq, and Iran. The former flourished through trade with Europe and the Far East. The coastal cities reached their height of influence during the Middle Ages but didn't really grow substantially until the 19th century when Europeans saw them as markets for their goods, as sources of raw materials, and for their strategic military importance (Macionis & Parillo, 2010, p. 375). Cities in the interior of predominantly Muslim societies enabled traders to conduct their business over vast stretches of inhospitable terrain. Divided into many quarters,

Islamic enclaves often were hostile to each other because of religious differences between their respective members. The semi-privacy of the narrow streets provided protection from dust storms and unwanted outsiders contrasted with the courtyards into which residential walled enclaves opened and could be used for communal/family gatherings in a relatively more open and "public" nature.

Colonial powers never tried to populate these countries, but they did end up helping to undermine the traditional bazaars in older cities by trading with people outside those central places. They even set up manufacturing sites in more "suburban" or rural areas, thereby undercutting traditional guilds and their prices as well as the communal social supports that had ensured their continuity (Macionis & Parillo, 2010, p. 377). In an interesting twist on this older pattern, large numbers of people working for international nongovernment organizations (INGOs) have moved into a place like Nyala, Darfur, with the idea of helping the local people deal with the myriad problems they face. The effect of their arrival, however, has been to create a kind of "niche gentrification" that has a big impact on property values and relations between established residents and the migrants that have taken up residence on the outskirts of the old city (Bartlett, Alix-Garcia, & Saah, 2012).

URBAN AREAS IN ASIA

Asia, the second least urbanized region of the world with just over 42% of its people living in cities, had more urban dwellers than any other part of the world two centuries ago and still does today. According to the United Nations, however, Asia is not expected to have 50% of its people living in cities until sometime around 2026. In the meantime,

> The number of megacities (those with populations of 10 million or more) is increasing, and half (12 out of 21) are now in the Asia-Pacific region. Moreover, mega urban regions, urban corridors

and city-regions reflect the emerging links between city growth and new patterns of economic activity. (UN, 2010, p. 4)

There are notable exceptions to this pattern, to be sure. Japan, Australia, and New Zealand already are predominantly urban. Their cities and metropolitan areas look very much like those in Western Europe and North America. But until recently they have been the exception in Asia.

The location and growth of Asia's cities depends in part on whether they were indigenous cities or founded as colonial outposts. The indigenous cities of Asia were built away from the coasts and for religious and political purposes rather than for trade. As was the case elsewhere, colonial cities were built largely along the coasts and were established to administer colonial affairs and to monitor the exportation of the society's raw materials. Hong Kong, Singapore, Shanghai, Calcutta, and Mumbai were all developed to be this kind of foreign-dominated port city.

Across much of Asia today, one certainly can find people who emigrated from their homeland to join the native residents of large cities. But most of the growth that Asian cities have seen comes from rural communities in the same country. Urban migrants often move back and forth between their rural points of origin and new city residences. What LeGates and Hudulah (2013, p. 5) have said of China in this regard appears just as valid in other Asian countries such as Indonesia.

[People] alternate between living in urban and rural areas based on their life cycle (migrating in search of work when young, returning to their village of origin only for the month-long Chinese New Year celebration, to marry or start a business, or to retire when they are too old to work), seasons, (home for planting and harvesting; working elsewhere—perhaps in a distant city—the rest of the year), or economic conditions (working in the global economy where jobs are plentiful, returning to village agricultural work when they are not).

China and Vietnam are among the few nations that attempt to impose limitations on the number of persons allowed to migrate and how long they are allowed to stay in cities. As we already observed, however, migration from foreign countries has become easier and more prevalent, "growing from an estimated 28 million in 1960 to more than 53 million in 2005" (UN, 2010, p. 7). The push factors (e.g., natural disasters, war, internal conflicts, and chronic underemployment) and pull factors (e.g., safety and better jobs) are no different here than they are in other parts of the world.

As is the case in Latin America and Africa, "urban agglomerations in Asia are evolving into mega urban regions and corridors." The population in urban areas has spread here, too, with smaller and medium-sized cities growing faster than nearby big cities. Indeed, "today, 60 percent of Asia's urban population lives in urban areas with populations under one million" (UN, 2010, p. 8).

The movement of people has become so pronounced and permanent a feature of Chinese life that a range of new living arrangements has emerged to accommodate it. There are "suburban private master-planned communities . . . gentrified neighborhoods . . . festival marketplaces, mega malls, and other consumption-oriented spaces" where the "new bourgeoisie" can live and meet (Shen & Wu, 2011, p. 257). Even the Chinese government has gotten into the act, so to speak, by cultivating and promoting arts colonies and festivals as a new commercial tool. "Middle class" tenants buy the public housing units in which they had been living (Zhang, 2010). Migrants living in special enclaves make a place for themselves and earn a decent income in the informal economy even as more marginal workers and migrants turn to spaces like basements and defense shelters for housing. It is no surprise that homeowners' associations have begun to pop up in different Chinese cities and are advocating for their members (Wu, 2012). More surprising, perhaps, local Chinese officials are tolerating their activities (Yip and Jiang, 2013).

Singapore may be governed with something akin to an iron fist, but it is a model of contemporary urban development for the better part of Asia. Surabaya, Indonesia, has carved out a

5,000-acre "city within a city," for instance, that attempts to bring some of the same infrastructural advantages and ordered life that is well known and admired in Singapore. Cleanliness and orderliness are two of the most important qualities that Indonesian officials and developers have tried to build into this planned enclave (Onishi, 2010).

Cities in countries like China and Singapore show the influence of strong central government intervention in matters related to the incorporation of newcomers. They are coping, though not as well as they might want outsiders to think, with the challenge of making room for large numbers of migrants. India, with its comparatively weaker central government and history of intervening in municipal affairs, has cities that show the effect of unregulated growth.

The older cities of India provide further evidence of the two-track focus of colonial-era cities that was carried out in Africa. As Macionis and Parrillo (2010, pp. 378–381) have stated, "Where cities already existed, like Delhi, the British simply constructed a second settlement next to it—in this case, New Delhi . . . resulting in a striking contrast between the indigenous part and the Anglicized part. One typical distinction would be a congested urban center in the old section and carefully planned, often spacious sections nearby." On the other hand, "the older area . . . typically has a form much like that of the Islamic cities. . . . Crowded into a central market . . . numerous small retail shops offer a vast range of goods. . . . Surrounding the marketplace is a residential area strictly divided into quarters, dividing Muslims from Hindu and separating Hindus according to their caste position." Brahmins would be closer to the center and lesser castes distributed farther from it. "The British part of the city . . . is very Western in form, with broad streets, often arranged in a grid pattern. At the center is a trading and manufacturing area, with a railroad leading outward."

The dramatic growth of India's urban population may not have obliterated these differences or made them irrelevant. But it certainly has made them less relevant. Contemporary Mumbai,

The New York Times has pointed out (Polgreen, 2010), is "unable to care for its people" who continue "to stream in from the countryside, where life is even worse. Such migration . . . depletes the rural areas of people and creates huge, unworkable cities." Not unlike cities in England and the United States whose economies were dominated by a single large industry, Mumbai is the textile capital of India because it is close to the cotton-growing areas surrounding the city. It employs nearly half of the city's factory workers. "Most others are employed in the production of silk, artificial fibers, chemicals, and glassware or in the dyeing, bleaching, and printing industries."[6]

Illegal districts and "unauthorized colonies" in a city like New Delhi have become so commonplace that nearly one third of the city's 17 million residents have come to live and work in them. They are not all slums. Indeed, there are many middle-class neighborhoods included among their number and "even a few illegally constructed enclaves [for] the rich" (Yardley, 2013a).

Among the many problems that cities in India face today none is quite so pervasive and annoying to its growing middle and upper classes as the absence of an effective publicly sponsored infrastructure. People may have malls filled with shops featuring designer clothes, access to the most modern communication technologies, golf courses, and fancy cars. But they don't have a functioning water and sewage system. Government offices are hopelessly mired in red tape. Corruption among officials apparently is endemic. Businesses have to provide their own diesel generators for electricity, store lots of water, and set up company-run shuttle services so their employees can make it to and from work in a reasonable amount of time (Yardley, 2011b).

Middle-class activism in the form of newly emerging "citizens' groups" has recently taken hold in Mumbai for just these reasons. According to Jonathan Anjaria (2009, p. 391), "civil society organizations" have taken it upon themselves to control the "unruly" street hawkers that try to take over many of the city's streets and sidewalks.

These groups have brought a degree of orderliness to the city that is consistent with their bourgeois sensibilities. But they also have choked off the political voice and claims of the unregulated sidewalk entrepreneurs whose presence and behavior they find offensive.

The absence of effective government services and public infrastructure was a big part of the thinking behind the construction of a brand-new city, Lavasa, approximately 130 miles southeast of Mumbai. It is eventually supposed to house more than 300,000 and serve as the headquarters for a variety of software and biotech firms and film and animation companies. Such knowledge-based industries are crucial to the development of the "new India." Most important, perhaps, the entire enterprise has been built and will be governed by a private corporation whose investors expect to earn a profit from all the buildings it fills and partnerships it makes with other companies that want to do business there (Kahn, 2011). It is one of five new cities that the national government has pledged to build in *the next five years* in order to relieve overcrowding in its other urban centers and to promote additional commercial expansion on the west coast of the country (Chandrashekar, Krishne, Sridhara, & Kumar, 2013).

A very different problem confronts would-be city builders and managers in China. Cities there have benefited from massive expenditures in public money for improvements in their roads, electrical services, water supplies, and sewage. But top-down government regulations have limited the kinds of political expression that people in India are beginning to practice with great zeal and stymied the kinds of entrepreneurship that allows India to grow despite its ineffective government.

Chinese citizens have mounted protests against local officials in rural areas from time to time in the past, mostly over the acquisition of property that was going to be given to developers. Urban unrest was uncommon. That changed in June of 2010 with a wave of riot-like episodes that lasted over three weeks, apparently without coordination, in a number of cities across the country. The issues that prompted unrest varied from city to city but

included corruption by government officials, aggressive property acquisition practices benefiting developers, police abuses, and ethnic tensions (Von Schirach, 2011).

Officials were surprised and took strong steps to tamp down the violence. Had they studied 19th century European and American history, they might not have been so surprised. The arrival of many migrants in a relatively short period of time led to tensions between people from different countries or, in this case, different regions of the same country. Even with its population still over 60% rural, China still has more city dwellers than any country in the world. More importantly, the number of urban residents has grown substantially in recent decades. Expressions of popular discontent are not likely to dissipate any time soon.

China's biggest urban settlements until the 1970s were its manufacturing and industrial centers, all of which had been Western-dominated port cities. Many other towns and urban settlements grew much larger at the end of the 20th century. Their growth occurred after a new policy favoring rapid industrialization and technological modernization led to a massive migration of over 100 million people from rural to urban areas. Much of the migration was directed to the expansion of small towns (i.e., from 2,000 to over 20,000) and increasing the number of cities (i.e., from fewer than 200 to over 600).

In the course of two decades, the share of China's population that lived in cities had grown from 20% to approximately 43% of the country's population (Jankowiak, 2010). Today, Chinese officials are trying to relocate industries to outlying areas in order to limit migration from rural areas to cities. Public policy remains committed to distributing would-be urban residents to smaller and medium-sized cities. Nevertheless, Shanghai and Hong Kong, both of which were founded as colonial outposts and manufacturing centers, will remain China's main commercial hubs for a long time.[7]

The Chinese government has tried to build some order into its own burgeoning cities and limit the number of rural people moving there to find work. They did this first by controlling the number of people who were granted the equivalent of a visa that would allow them to access public services like free schools for their children, if they elected to move to a city (Mackenzie, 2002). Then, when that proved unworkable, at least in Beijing they introduced their own version of a gated community for rural migrants. The Shoubaozhuang area of Beijing is one of 15 that houses people who moved to the capital in order to find work and a better life. It is a walled and guarded complex that affords a measure of security for its largely poor residents even as it keeps them apart from better-off residents in surrounding neighborhoods (Gao, 2010).

The social walls between recent migrants and more established residents are every bit as large and tough to climb over. According to Wu (2012, p. 547), Chinese migrants from rural areas "do not identify themselves with the places where they live and do not actively participate in community activities." This is not a coincidence, Wu argues. It is done by "institutional design" and has the effect of keeping these people "economic sojourners" rather than making them into effective city residents.

However novel these strategies may have been, they clearly didn't reach enough people or make enough difference in the lives of the people they did touch to keep them from acting out. Though no one expected the 2011 riots to topple local governments, Chinese officials were unaccustomed to having their edicts and practices challenged by everyday urban people. As we already have noted, Chinese leaders were experiencing some of the same disquieting effects that rapid urban growth had brought 19th century European and American cities.

Japan, as we observed earlier, has a much different urban story to tell. It had a strong urban tradition and ancient cities. Among other traits distinguishing its development is the fact that the country was never colonized. It had a series of regional capitals that were protected by a class of full-time warriors. These cities developed a relatively wealthy and powerful middle class that eventually supplanted the warrior class in the

latter 1860s. It was big enough and strong enough to resist European and American colonization efforts by that time. Japan also rapidly industrialized and urbanized in the early 20th century (Macionis and Parillo, 2010, p. 384).

Differences in the nature and timing of their urbanization notwithstanding, countries across Asia are relatively well positioned to take advantage of their own growing domestic markets and international trade. Major cities have for decades participated in manufacturing and benefited from export-led trade and foreign financial investment. Their governments have provided money for improvements in transportation and communication technologies.

Not surprisingly perhaps, the economies in these cities are diversifying and pretty well integrated with a vibrant informal economy. As the United Nations has reported (United Nations Human Settlements Programme, 2010, pp. 11–12), "the informal economy includes the full range of 'non-standard' wage employment . . . such as sweatshop production, home-workers, contract workers, temporary or part-time work, and unregistered workers." These people may not be directly tied into better-established businesses, but they "are clearly dependent on the formal sector for the "equipment, work location and sale of the final products they make."

THE IMPACT OF "PRIMACY" AND "OVERURBANIZATION" IN LESS DEVELOPED COUNTRIES

The effects of colonization on the less developed countries of Asia cannot be overemphasized. It left behind underdeveloped economies based largely on the export of raw materials, which served the indigenous elite well enough but did little to promote wealth generation and consumption by the bulk of the population. Nor did these cities develop the interior of their respective countries. By the time they acquired their independence in the 20th century, they were already well behind Western societies in most important indicators of modernization. Exceptions to this pattern included Hong Kong, Singapore, and the cities of Japan.

A crucial factor in the recent and rapid urbanization of less developed countries was the improvement in agricultural production, which didn't start until the 1960s. People were free to migrate to cities in many instances as we noted earlier. But until recently, development had been uneven at best. Their primate cities "distorted" investment in the sense that capital went to serve the needs of global firms rather than those of the indigenous population. Even with added income in cities, the standard of living in primate cities had been lower than it is in rural areas (Gottdiener & Hutchison, 2006, p. 283). Other than the AIDS epidemic, however, there's been little to slow the growth of spiraling populations in the cities of less developed countries. Adding further to their misery, fertility rates have remained high, and the portion of the population that is less than 21 years old is probably greater than 50% and may be increasing (Palen, 2008, p. 300).

Although the manufacturing capacity of these countries has grown in recent decades, it hasn't generated enough jobs or provided sufficient taxes to provide many basic services in water, waste removal, utilities, and police and fire protection. Pollution and privation are the central features of life in most of these urban agglomerations. This is especially true in the zones surrounding the central city, areas that are occupied largely by the poorest and most recent migrants to the urban area, just as they were in many Western cities. The gulf between more and less prosperous residents probably has grown in recent years. Money that might otherwise go to development efforts elsewhere in the country is siphoned off by initiatives to provide minimal levels of public services in their primate cities. John Palen (2008, p. 304) points out that "the cities of Mexico City, Bogota, and Santiago continue to grow faster than their national populations even though the governments of Mexico, Colombia, and Chile all seek a more balanced growth."

At the same time, primate cities aren't entirely or even necessarily bad. Most newly developing countries simply don't have the resources to support the creation of multiple cities. Thirty years ago, it made good economic sense to focus economic development in a few large cities. Given the absence of effective intraregional and interregional transportation, Hawley (1971, p. 299) argued that "large urban agglomerations [were] a necessary means of concentrating labor supply, capital, technical skills, and other resources required for economic transformation and growth."

Countries need not remain underdeveloped. Only in the last quarter century, Korea, Taiwan, Thailand, China, and India have made great strides in becoming more developed. Mexico and Asia have become destinations for manufacturing facilities being moved from more developed countries. There also are signs that their birthrates are stabilizing. The fact that primate cities continue to grow and that most political movements in these countries emerge from these places suggests that the people there are open to change (Palen, 2008, pp. 299–304).

Competing explanations for why less developed countries have stayed that way so far have tradition-bound people resisting modernizing influences often brought from the outside. Representatives of countries in the West were said to maintain their hegemony over the less developed country through political and economic means: first by opposing progress and then limiting the chances for these countries to make any. And yet, the rapid urban development and industrialization of Russia and Japan in the past 125 years suggest that less developed countries can overcome even stiff political and economic limits placed on them by traditional elites and foreign interests (Light, 1983, pp. 153–154).

PHYSICAL AND SOCIAL ORGANIZATION OF CITIES IN LESS DEVELOPED COUNTRIES

These cities have common features that vary little over time or cultural setting. *The early indigenous cities were physically dense and compact.*

Largely pedestrian or walking cities, their residents traded accessibility over roominess, sanitation, and aesthetics.

Socially, the population was "segmented by tribe, caste, lineage, or previous place of residence." *The city appeared "as a mosaic of residential quarters or enclaves" a "cellular" pattern that didn't break down until the end of the 19th century.* Like most medieval European cities, there was "an absence of any marked concentration of specialized functions" like a central business district. Residential quarters were arranged in such a way that people with less status occupied buildings farther away from the ruling household or a religious edifice (Hawley, 1971, pp. 317–318).

The enclave was the urban equivalent of a rural village in some ways but not so much in other ways. Reproduced in it, for instance, were customary institutions, ethnic or tribal ties, a local market allowing for bargaining and price setting, religious edifices, village associations, and festive rites, friendship ties, and mutual aid. At the same time, these ties could be exploitative, especially when it came to the subject of recent migrants trying to find work. Furthermore, distorted age and sex compositions, the absence of elders, of family obligations, and normal mating opportunities also deprived the enclave of much of its village counterpart's social adhesive and moral oversight. In the end, the presence of rivals in nearby quarters helped to counter the reluctance of some people to remain attached to the enclave and its leaders (Hawley, 1971, pp. 319, 321).

Voluntary associations familiar to village dwellers were adapted to meet circumstances that migrants face upon their arrival in a city. Hawley reported that castes in Indian cities had developed "credit facilities, employment services, and educational aids for their members" (Hawley, 1971, pp. 322, 323). The landholding lineage had "adopted many of the fiscal and management procedures employed in a modern agricultural cooperative." In the *barriadas* and *favelas* of Latin America, transplanted village associations had "equipped themselves to deal with the legal problems of squatting on urban land and have found means to gain representation in municipal affairs." There also were signs of newer associations being created, groups that crossed ethnic lines such as political parties and labor unions.

In Central and South America, many voluntary organizations have their origins in church-related activities. So, too, do the charity work, school building, and hospital construction that they often undertake. Their "evolution" into purely secular organizations has come with the gradual improvement of their members' education and professional status. *It is important to note, however, that many of these organizations draw their members from different social classes, which promotes both consensus building and collaborative engagement across the class spectrum.*

Participation in voluntary organizations varies for different countries. In Asian countries, for example, up to a third of the adult population reportedly belongs to one or two associations. Depending on the country, the kind of organization that predominates is likely to be political, religious, and/or consist of "alumni" from particular schools. "Identity" or ethnic associations are popular as are labor and human rights groups. The motivation for joining organizations in Asia probably reflects the same mix of "affective" and "instrumental" reasons that people in Western societies use when deciding to join groups. Some groups are for fun and serve as purely social outlets for their members. Other organizations are intended to accomplish more practical tasks that are important to their members or their community.

Japanese people do not have many voluntary organizations that work on the national level. But most households are deeply embedded in their local neighborhood association (van Houwelingen, 2012). Family members of different ages find complementary ways to be engaged socially with each other through activities sponsored by the neighborhood group. Old people have their clubs as do children, women, and other adults. They raise funds to beautify their neighborhood, play sports together, do crime patrols and safety checks together, and work on behalf of different cultural activities. These groups help to reinforce the kind of "bonding social capital" that occurs among people who are tied to a particular place and have a lot in common, like their gender or age. They do not act as substitute families, but they do supplement some of the good feeling and chances to join with other people that might otherwise be done by their family.

As in the West, the family changed to the extent that it didn't remain a unit of production like it had been in rural areas. In Nigeria, for example, extended families promoted entrepreneurship by "apprenticing a young member to an experienced entrepreneur" and "supplying the capital for a family-run firm." From this, Hawley (1971, pp. 323–324) concluded that "industrialization is founded in part on the family system." When it ceased to be an economic unit, it still persisted as "a viable mutual aid association."

"Central to the survival of the poor," Goode (2010, p. 189) has similarly observed, were the "informal sharing networks for mutual aid that develop between households . . . based on kinship or *fictive* kinship." In this way, he concluded, one family could "help out the struggling households to which it is linked." It could even include "sharing their residence for a time."

Male unemployment and underemployment along with long commutes yielded more flexible "consensual unions" between men and women that were less financially draining than marriage and divorce. Yet, this hadn't eliminated the presence of males in the household. Fathers were available as time allowed, and a woman's male kin could stand in as father surrogates. "Living in poverty encouraged female-headed households" and "women-centered sharing networks made sense." The act of weaving together incomes from "formal work, the underground economy, and public programs" required a lot of management (Goode, 2010, pp. 190-192) and speaks to the organizational skills of the people involved, especially perhaps the women who were involved.

Many lower-class people working in the "regular" economy had service jobs as messengers, domestic workers, restaurant workers, and laborers. That's why people living in shantytowns are often deeply enmeshed in the informal economy and engage in a great deal of self-help activity with other family members and even people not necessarily tied by marriage but close to the family. This kind of "self-provisioning" included food and clothing production and home construction and repairs. Involvement in the informal economy by way of selling drugs, cigarettes, and items you'd find in convenience stores and sex gained people access to the illicit or illegal economy as well. Bartering was another way marginal people made ends meet (Gottdiener and Hutchison, 2006, p. 295).

The opportunity structures of low-income people may be limited, but work in the informal economy shows they have the ability to adapt and plan that belies notions of a perpetual culture of poverty among the poor. Drug dealing, street mechanics, home-based food production, acquiring money through children's work in government-funded jobs programs, the use of informal credit pools or organized "layaway payment" schemes, self-built housing, and the use of second-hand markets for clothing didn't make people rich. But it did help them to survive (Goode, 2010, pp. 188–189).

Life in shantytowns can certainly qualify as "disorganized" and "destructive" in many ways and more poor people live there than not. When we look more closely at shantytowns, however, they also reveal some very powerful and effective self-regulating elements involving family work and support and broader ethnic and kinship ties (Hutter, 2007, p. 456). Shantytowns thus emerge "as vibrant communities with strong forms of social organizations. They provide an important transition destination for many rural migrates into cities, serving as the initial site for assimilation and acculturation. They also provide a source of cheap and accessible labor for urban industries."

Some shantytowns have developed to the point of becoming working-class suburbs of the cities to which they are appended. While most of the residents are not well-to-do, these places have provided a setting with many stable families and more law-abiding people than they had in the past. Their homegrown leaders are making more credible and effective claims for better water delivery and sewage disposal. Over time, governments have become more accommodating to the people in these residential areas as well (Hutter, 2007, p. 457).

A middle-class way of thinking and associating developed in everything from marriage partners, child rearing, and taking meals with the family to working at salaried jobs. In the West the middle class grew from commerce and industry. In less developed countries, on the other hand, it has been "founded on advanced education and government employment." This means that the middle class in less developed countries has remained more "subservient to the elite which controls the government bureaucracy. A middle class so constituted can hardly be as aggressive or as creative as one based on entrepreneurial achievement," Amos Hawley (1981, p. 326) prophetically observed.

City building showed some capacity to erode ethnic differences over time and alter how institutions like the extended family serve their members. In a general way, they lose some of their importance as people acquire a broader "sense of civic responsibility in both private and public life" through their contacts with other people and ideas (Hawley, 1981, pp. 324-325). The impact these changes might have is limited by the continuing and commanding presence of enclaves and extended family economic activities. But a reconciliation of the two approaches could be possible as well. "It does not follow that the juxtaposition of seemingly incompatible elements" always lead to tension and disorder, Hawley (1981, p. 330) reasoned. "Man has the happy facility of being able to live quite comfortably with inconsistencies in his culture." More generally, the pattern emerging in the expansion of urbanization in less developed countries does not necessarily mean an end, much less an abrupt end, to the continuing importance of ethnic ties and nationalistic sentiments among migrants. This is especially so when the people in question move to a new

country and try to establish themselves in it, as people in Western societies know from the immigrants who moved among them.

"Overall, the group-oriented approach in which the migrant relies on kin and community members for help in getting established in the city is most common among tribal and peasant migrants in the cities of developing countries" (Kemper, 2010). Migrants organize "voluntary associations" to satisfy their needs. Such associations are usually comprised of members of the same ethnic groups or sometimes just individuals from the same rural villages. They assume many of the functions that were performed by kinship groups in the migrants' home villages. In some respects, they operate much like the guilds of preindustrial cities, giving migrants a sense of belonging, providing financial aid in times of need, and organizing recreational activities. They provide strong support groups that ease the migrant into the urban world.

In societies where there's a great deal of circular migration back and forth or transnational moves, migrants can "maintain a strong connection with their natal community, even when they are living far away." They are part of an "extended community" (Kemper, 2010, p. 283). Many of these communities in Central and South America, for instance, benefit from assistance provided by family members who have migrated to the United States. Remittance payments sent home certainly help individual families. But "hometown associations" have sprung up in many American cities and these organizations provide charity services, money when there has been a disaster of some kind, and even make investments back in their home villages. This is exactly what earlier immigrant populations in the United States did (Stack, 1979).

One thing that appears clear is that over a period of time, membership in organizations generally inspires people to become more politically self-conscious. They mobilize on behalf of both local and national issues concerning them as in the provision of better housing and public services. They also become more involved in union activities as more people acquired manufacturing jobs

(Gottdiener & Hutchison, 2006, p. 296). In this way, they mimicked the ways that "poor White women, African American women, Latino women, and multiracial alliances have moved beyond the family to participate in a variety of collective social movements: seeking better schools . . . preventing the removal of a local firehouse, strengthening the role of activist community organizations . . . and reinforcing tenant management in public housing" (Goode, 2010, p. 195).

While many new urban residents eventually become involved in human rights initiatives and political campaigns, it is not at all clear that they have much direct impact on the kinds of policies that officials pursue or on the quality of services they clamor for. At least in Africa, they would appear far more effective in inspiring people to participate more directly in politics than in the implementation of particular programs. The number and variety of clubs, cooperatives, unions, voluntary associations, political groups, and non-governmental press outlets in Egypt, for example, no doubt provided many avenues for people to express their "voice" on the replacement of their longtime leader. Figuring out what to do with the newly-reconstituted government was an entirely different matter.

CONCLUDING THOUGHTS ON URBANIZATION IN MORE AND LESS DEVELOPED COUNTRIES

Cities in less developed regions of the world, as we already noted, did not have the luxury of changing over a long period of time. They also have not had readily available networks of smaller and medium-sized towns and cities around them with which they had well-established trading arrangements by the time they began to grow dramatically. *People moved from rural areas to a big city without having the opportunity to live in places of intermediate size and complexity or the chance to find employment should things in the biggest city not work out.*

Advances in agriculture had created large and permanent surpluses in food and displaced workers in more developed parts of the world. Less developed regions have plenty of displaced agricultural workers but unpredictable food surpluses. To make matters worse, countries in less developed parts of the world don't have enough manufacturing jobs ready for all these men and women to take. They also are producing more new babies in both rural and urban settings. Birthrates in less developed countries are not declining as they did in the West.

Acquiring the funds just to meet the current demands on the urban infrastructure in most developing countries has proven all but impossible. Administering such funds in a manner that actually produces useful outcomes for people has also been a singular challenge for city leaders in less developed countries. Probably no more or less corrupt than their 19th century American counterparts, municipal officials haven't had nearly enough money to make a profitable career out of government service *and* meet all the demands put to them.

People in less developed countries have also made some of the social changes that new and established residents of Western cities made in order to settle in more securely. Other changes they have not made or the changes haven't taken hold widely enough to catch the attention of social scientists and anthropologists.

Prominent among the omissions so far, it would seem, is much explicit attention on the part of city leaders that they need to do more to address the dramatically different life chances that poorer people and persons burdened with some sort of social stigmata have. The predictable and understandable pushback on this issue, of course, would be that leaders are overwhelmed with just trying to build their city's infrastructure to the point that people can get basic services. Efforts to draw people from different social classes, religious affiliations, and ethnic or tribal backgrounds together in something approximating an effective union have been even less apparent.

A class of merchants that might become the backbone of a newly emerging middle class inside cities has not been created, so far as we can tell. If one has been growing, it would not seem to be so large and muscular that anyone has noticed. *What has been observed, on the other hand, is a growing collection of middle-class people who work in government or as professionals in the service sector of their economy.* This situation is comparable to the one seen in the United States. A robust, articulate, but decidedly nonentrepreneurial Black middle class here has been built on the back of professionally trained men and women who have made good careers for themselves working in nonprofit organizations and government.

Importantly, as Amos Hawley noted decades ago, these aren't people who are practiced in the kind of risk-taking or playing in the rough-and-tumble world that business people operate in every day. Nor are they the kind of people who are in a good position to create a host of private organizations through which merchants in the West developed a common view of their world and how they wanted to shape it (Monti, 1999).

Ethnic groups have emerged and they have helped migrants settle into their new surroundings. It is not clear yet, however, how much these ethnic groups have managed to bring together persons from the same background but different social classes into an effective and lasting social union. Differences among people based on their religion and tribal or ethnic background still matter a great deal when it comes to how these people treat each other in the political and larger public arena. On the other hand, other important institutions such as the family and schools have changed in ways that are helping their members adapt to the urban world they've inherited and shape it to meet their needs.

This picture of the urban world, like many others, isn't as full or clear as we might like. Given the speed at which urbanization has taken hold in less developed parts of the world, however, we probably should be surprised and pleased at how quickly people in these cities have adapted. Like previous migrants who made the tough transition to full-time urban residents in the 19th and 20th centuries, contemporary migrants in developing countries are learning to adapt and doing so under less than optimal conditions.

QUESTIONS FOR STUDY AND DISCUSSION

1. Cities in more and less developed countries emerged under quite different economic and political circumstances. What are some of the more important differences?

2. In what ways have cities and urban areas in less developed countries begun to copy the pattern of development evidenced in Western societies?

3. Do cities and urban areas in the West show some of the signs of overurbanization and "urban primacy" apparent in less developed countries?

4. What kinds of social roles and groups have emerged in the cities of less developed countries to facilitate the adaptation of people there to their new urban surroundings?

5. Are there parallels between the ways urban dwellers in the West and in less developed countries have organized themselves socially?

6. Is there a distinctive "urban way of life" and to the extent that there is, what are its main features?

INTERNET MATERIALS

http://www.thedialogue.org/PublicationFiles/central%20american%20htas%20report.pdf

http://press.princeton.edu/chapters/i7295.html

http://www.historycooperative.org/cgi-bin/justtop.cgi?act justtop&url http://www.historycooperative.org/journals/ahr/109.1/br_104.html

http://www.democracy-asia.org/countryteam/krishna/Civil%20Society%20and%20Political%20Participation.pdf

http://www.asiapacificphilanthropy.org/f/backgrounder_india.pdf

http://www.springerlink.com/content/1228x11m4551585r/

http://perl.psc.isr.umich.edu/papers/voluntary.pdf

http://www.asianbarometer.org/newenglish/publications/
    workingpapers/no.38.pdf

http://ipsnews.net/news.asp?idnews 46452

http://www.dfid.gov.uk/R4D//PDF/Outputs/
    CentreOnCitizenship/ResSumOct08.pdf

http://siteresources.worldbank.org/INTCPR/
    Resources/WP36_web.pdf

http://academicjournals.org/AJPSIR/PDF/Pdf2009/
    Feb/Hassan.pdf

http://www.postcolonialweb.org/africa/ronning2.html

http://muse.jhu.edu/login?uri   /journals/journal_of_
    democracy/v019/19.1khrouz.pdf

http://www.nai.uu.se/research/areas/collective_
    organisation_a/

NOTES

1   http://www.mckinsey.com/Insights/MGI/Research/
    Urbanization/Building_competitive_cities_key_to_
    Latin_American_growth, p. 1.
2   http://www.docstoc.com/docs/52718861/Urban-
    Quality-of-Life-More-Than-Bricks-and-Mortar,
    p. 178.
3   McKinsey, op. cit., p. 26.
4   Ibid., pp. 24–25.
5   Ibid., p. 36.
6   See "India's Cities Buckle Under the Strain of
    New Arrivals" in the December 1, 2010, edition of
    The New York Times for further evidence of the
    problems faced by rural migrants to Indian cities.
    One of the more intriguing and disturbing features
    of life in some of India's regional urban centers
    like Mumbai is that they have become centers of
    political corruption in ways oddly reminiscent of
    what happened in some bigger U.S. cities after the
    Civil War. The upper-caste people who once ran
    these cities no longer did. The political empower-
    ment of lower-caste people had a surprising and
    disturbing effect on the quality of life in these
    places. It turns out that people still voted on the
    basis of their caste, and the diminished power
    of upper-caste elites and professionals who had
    benefited from government corruption in the past

were replaced by lower-caste crooks and political
hacks. Upper-caste families lost more than their
political clout, however. They also lost control
over their daily lives. Lower-caste politicians and
criminals, often one in the same, have run "kidnapping rings" that "targeted mostly affluent, largely
upper-caste neighborhoods." The first families hit
were those of business people. Later, as business
people bought off politicians and hired more
guards, the targets became professionals such as
doctors, teachers, and engineers. Kidnapping them
declined only when other members of their important professions refused to work unless victims
were released (Witsoe, 2010, pp. 270–272).

7   Rapid urbanization in China as in most countries
    has compelled people to change the way they
    thought about each other and treated each other.
    In the presence of so many new people they
    didn't know personally or even in terms of where
    they'd come from and their social class, formerly
    polite interactions with one's neighbors were
    replaced by "indifference." "Neighborhood obli-
    gations," Janowiak (2010, p. 267) has observed,
    have been discarded in favor of other forms of
    connectivity" including ties based on school
    affiliation, "work contacts, association with
    places of origin, friendship bonds, and close fam-
    ily relationships." Secret societies, guilds, and
    "common ethnic and/or religious affiliation"
    have also become more important. "Taken
    together, ethnicity, religion, and native place
    associations serve as essential bases for the forma-
    tion of social connection or kinship ties" in con-
    temporary China (Jankowiak, 2010, pp. 260–261).
    Urban "kinship" ties have become more elabo-
    rate in Chinese cities. "Individuals who are out-
    side the formal (e.g., bilateral or patrilineal)
    genealogical systems are frequently transformed
    from casual friends into close quasi-kin,"
    Jankowiak (2010, p. 262) argues. Bilateral grand-
    parent ties also have become more important as
    China's one-child policy took hold and more
    parents needed help with child-rearing duties.
    However, the emerging "bilateral multigenera-
    tional family is a fragile institution" (Jankowiak,
    2010, pp. 265–266).

3

HOW THE UNITED
STATES BECAME URBAN

The urbanization of the United States, like that of Canada, was built on the back of England's mercantilist muscle and successful competition with other European societies for colonial supremacy in North America. The populating of Australia and the eventual ascendance of its four main cities was a necessary concession to the hard stop that those same colonial impulses came to with England's failure to rein in American colonists' own mercantilist ambitions. And the key to this country's expansion and development as a preeminent world power today was the town that would be a city.

Americans are prolific town and city builders. Indeed, the whole idea behind England's push to colonize the Americas in the 17th century was to build towns that would be a commercial success for their financial backers. The cumulative effect of the 400 years' worth of continuous and sometimes frenzied town and city building since then can be summarized simply but its significance can't be overstated. The United States today has an array of small, medium-sized, and bigger urban settlements that are linked through one or more regional commercial networks. All the larger cities and even a number of the medium-sized ones are directly involved in commercial exchanges at the national and international levels

as well. Their trading and investing are made easier by a complex communication and transportation system that rivals anything found in the most developed countries of the world.

This is admittedly a big claim. But the story of how America became urban offers compelling evidence of how popular and effective urban settlements are as population centers and sites of economic and political activity. We will present an abbreviated version of this story in the present chapter. Before we do that, however, and to provide the reader with an idea of just how big an accomplishment making America urban really was, we will lay out in a general way what the current urban and metropolitan landscape in the United States looked like 10 years into the 21st century.

Nearly 80% of Americans live in urban settlements today, a figure that is a little greater than average for countries in the West, but not dramatically so. Cities in different parts of the United States took turns growing more quickly, but it wasn't until 1920 or so that the country's population as a whole became mostly urban. That statistic and year shouldn't make anyone's eyebrows rise except for what happened to the United States on either side of that date: the Civil War and World War I at the front end and a crippling economic depression followed by the Second World War on the back end.

Table 3.1 Number of Urban and Rural Places of Different Sizes, 1790–2000

Year	2000	1990	1970	1950	1930	1910	1890	1870	1850	1830	1810	1790
Urban Places >2,500	9,063	8,510	6,433	4,307	3,183	2,266	1,348	663	237	90	46	24
1 million or more	9	8	6	5	5	3	3					
500,000–999,999	20	15	20	13	8	5	1	2	1			
250,000–499,999	38	41	30	23	24	11	7	5				
100,000–249,999	178	136	100	66	57	31	17	7	5	1		
50,000–99,999	419	355	240	126	98	60	30	11	4	3	2	
25,000–49,999	838	741	520	253	186	119	66	27	17	3	2	2
2,500–24,999	7,561	7,214	5,517	3,821	2,805	2,037	1,224	611	210	83	42	22
Rural Places <2,500	21,044	14,925	14,334	13,279	13,468	11,843	6,495					

Population and Housing Counts, U.S. Census Bureau. Data derived from Table 4, Population by Urban and Rural and Size of Place: 2000, and Table 8, Population by Urban and Rural and Size of Place. Based on the 1950–1990 definition of urban places for the 1950–1990 period and the pre-1950 definition of urban places for the 1790–1950 period.

The Great Depression and World War II only managed to slow down the rate of urban growth but certainly didn't stop it. The country's urban population actually saw two of its bigger growth spurts in the decades on either side of the American Civil War. Indeed, the impulse to build towns and cities in the United States was so strong that it could withstand the effects of two world wars, an economic meltdown that spanned continents, and a civil war that could have ended the country.

Creating and maintaining cities is a big and expensive enterprise under the best of circumstances, and one would think that economic downturns and wars hardly qualify as factors that would make city building more likely. The irony, however, is that *the viability of the country's rural areas holds the key to understanding how city building was able to be sustained under difficult circumstances.* Increases to the country's urban population over the last two hundred years could only be sustained because farmers were able to produce, store, and ship more food for people in their own country and have plenty left over to sell overseas as well. At one of the receiving ends of this chain were American cities whose economies were robust enough to absorb displaced agricultural workers not only from the United States but from a great many foreign countries as well.

Another important part of the urbanization story in the United States has been the degree to which different parts of the country over the years have become urbanized. Every region of the country today has more than 70% of its residents living in urban settlements. That is surely a big portion of America's population. We know from the experiences of countries in less developed parts of the world, however, that achieving this kind of regional balance is difficult.

It wasn't easy to accomplish in the United States, either. The Northeast, which was settled earlier than other parts of the country, has over 84% of its people living in urban places today. It passed the 50% threshold by 1880. The Midwest, which was aggressively settled and developed by people from the Northeast, has nearly 75% of its people in urban settlements. It passed the 50% threshold in 1920, the same year the population of the United States as a whole was officially declared to have become more urban than rural. The South, historically the least urbanized region of the country, today has nearly 73% of its people living in urban places. The West, in the meantime, was the last region of the country to be developed but made up for its late start by urbanizing more quickly than the other three regions. Today nearly 87% of its people live in urban settlements. Like the South, it passed the 50% threshold in 1920.[1]

The run-up to something approximating urban parity among the four regions of the country produced, as we noted above, an array of settlements of different sizes. None of our nine largest cities approaches the size of Mexico City, Cairo, New Delhi, or Beijing. *What urbanization in the United States has left us with instead are many more urban places—smaller cities that serve more regional markets, larger and smaller suburban municipalities, and even modestly sized towns—than countries in less developed parts of the world have.* As the data presented in Table 2.2 show, our urban population is distributed generously across the full array of those bigger, medium-sized, and smaller places.[2] Our communities are integrated into a national system of cities, suburbs, and towns.

This unprecedented accomplishment wasn't planned, but it wasn't an accident, either. Some cities grew and prospered in the interior of the country in areas that didn't have access to major

bodies of water or particularly congenial climates. Other places with seemingly more going for them and aspirations of someday becoming a city ended up folding or didn't grow much beyond a good-sized town. Luck, timing, and no small measure of outright chicanery and fraud played a part in determining which places made it and which ones didn't. What both the winners and losers had in common was this: boosters and builders expanded the country and colonized every new part added to it on the back of the town that would be a city.

CITIES IN THE PROTO-INDUSTRIAL/ COLONIAL PERIOD (1600–1780)

European explorers found urban settlements and the remnants of preindustrial cities when they arrived. These places belonged to native peoples whose great misfortune was to be in the way of successive waves of European immigrants who invaded and then settled these territories as if they were their own. The cities built by indigenous peoples, like the Indian mounds of Cahokia, Illinois, just outside St. Louis, do not figure prominently in the story of American urbanization except as relics. Their fate also foreshadowed what would happen to native peoples in Africa and Asia when Europeans showed up on their territorial doorsteps in the 18th and 19th centuries.

American colonization and settlement came late in the proto-industrial period. Despite the wealth and power of the European capitals that carved up all of North America and Mexico, urban settlements in 17th and 18th century America went through the same ups and downs that proto-industrial urban settlements in Europe experienced. Towns and cities may have been crucial pieces in the colonial chess game played primarily by England, France, and Spain. But the fact that these pieces were traded rather than taken off the board didn't make their rise any easier for the people who had settled there first.

It was Spanish colonizers who overthrew Indian empires in the West and Southwest,

Table 3.2 Percentage of Population in Urban and Rural Places of Different Sizes, 1790–2000

Year	2000	1990	1970	1950	1930	1910	1890	1870	1850	1830	1810	1790
Urban Places >2,500	79	68.50	65.60	59.60	56.10	45.60	35.10	25.70	15.40	8.80	7.30	5.10
1 million or more	8.20	8.00	9.20	11.50	12.20	9.20	5.80					
500,000–999,999	4.60	4.10	6.40	6.10	4.70	3.30	1.30	4.20	2.20			
250,000–499,999	4.90	5.90	5.10	5.40	6.50	4.30	3.90	4.00				
100,000–249,999	9.40	7.90	7.00	6.60	6.20	5.20	4.40	2.60	2.80	1.60		
50,000–99,999	10.10	9.70	8.20	6.00	5.30	4.60	3.20	2.00	1.20	1.70	2.10	
25,000–49,999	10.30	10.30	8.80	6.50	5.20	4.40	3.60	2.40	2.80	0.80	1.10	1.60
2,500–24,999	22.40	22.70	20.90	20.30	16.10	14.60	12.90	10.50	6.40	4.70	4.10	3.50
Rural Places <2,500	21	31.50	34.40	40.40	43.90	54.40	64.90	74.30	84.60	91.20	92.70	94.90

Population and Housing Counts, U.S. Census Bureau. Data derived from Table 4, Population by Urban and Rural and Size of Place: 2000, and Table 8, Population by Urban and Rural and Size of Place. Based on the 1950–1990 definition of urban places for the 1950–1990 period and the pre-1950 definition of urban places for the 1790–1950 period. Percentages in the "Urban Places" row match the sum of the total of places with populations more than (>) 2,500 in each column.

empires that had built cities populated by tens of thousands of people. The Spanish promoted urban planning in their earliest towns by introducing ideas like rectangular grid-patterned streets surrounding a central plaza. Their versions of early American cities combined commerce, religious, and military functions. French explorers and adventurers founded commercial centers along the waterways of colonial North America's perimeter. These urban outposts provided the foundation for what would eventually become America's Midwestern cities.

Towns built along the Eastern Seaboard by English explorers were intended to promote social and religious harmony under the economic banner of mercantilism. English colonists were encouraged "to organize towns and to arrange their farming and extractive industries around these towns" (Glaab & Brown, 1976, p. 1). They were supposed to turn a profit. Everything they didn't need to sustain themselves was supposed to be sent back to England where it was rendered into products sold at home and back to the colonists. A kind of "corporate communalism" marked the commercial and administrative approach to town building promoted by the English in the territories they settled or took over from people such as the Dutch in what had been New Amsterdam and was quickly renamed New York.

English port towns soon developed a system of trading among themselves and with the Caribbean that complemented trading that was officially sanctioned with the homeland. This promoted competition among the port towns, a competition that was crucial to their subsequent development and that of the nation as a whole. Well tied to their rural hinterlands and positioned to take advantage of their natural resources and agricultural surplus, early American towns did not grow to the size of contemporary Mexico City and Lima, Peru, both of which at the time had in excess of 50,000 residents and were primarily political and administrative centers. The English town that would soon enough become the basis for an American city certainly served the political and administrative needs of their colonial overseers. But, as we noted at the start of this chapter, they were first and foremost entrepreneurial ventures designed for commerce and intended to be a long-term investment that would pay off their financial backers handsomely.

Early town leaders in the American colonies emerged from the commercial class of artisans and merchants, just as they had begun to do in European cities. From them came a host of deals—public–private partnerships involving both business people and politicians—that provided capital and muscle for the development of everything from the town's infrastructure to the provision of social services (e.g., sewage, bridge and road construction, building codes, fire protection, and attempts to deal with epidemics). All of these activities were inspired by the growth of a place that looked increasingly like a city and the problems engendered by urban growth.

Commercial and political leaders had a hard time acquiring public financing for services and building schemes with property taxes, which would have provided more predictable revenue streams than licensing fees and fines. But city leaders have always found state legislatures unsympathetic to their pleas for the right to tax their citizens and businesses. What they did instead was borrow money from investors in the form of publicly guaranteed bonds so they could keep building the city. Or, they undertook the aforementioned public–private partnerships that allowed developers to do projects that would make them money and serve the public good by helping the city to grow.

These weren't the only steps that early city leaders took in order to grow their settlements. They also organized courts and constabularies with the intention of keeping life orderly and promoting trade. When things didn't go their way with their colonial overseers or later on when they found newer settlers not to their liking, these same "gentlemen of property and standing" could also be found at the head of local mobs, just as they were during the American Revolution (Richards, 1970).

It's not a coincidence that early town leaders made an explicit connection between political liberty and economic freedom and were willing to fight to make their point stick. Unable to pursue their own material interests and their town's development, they had felt compelled to promote many illegal trading arrangements both in the Caribbean and westward in deals that at times even involved their French enemies. These illicit exchanges became the foundation of America's commercial empire.

Colonial American leaders may not have liked all the people that tried to settle in their city, but they quickly learned that limitations on immigration were unworkable and frustrated growth. The result was that long-term residents made a self-conscious effort to open their towns up to more people and to a more heterogeneous population even as they tried to control and "guide" the newcomers so that they would be less disagreeable. People who subscribed to different religions, who came from countries the original settlers didn't like, people whose professions were too much like those already held by too many current residents or whose social pedigree was somehow suspect, all of them eventually made it in. And just like their European counterparts had done, American colonial town leaders gradually opened the door to full citizenship for more of these newcomers.

Colonial towns may not have had a landholding aristocracy to lead the way, but local business leaders weren't shy about standing in as a substitute. They developed a complex and stiffly hierarchical system of social classes that made it clear to everyone exactly where they stood in the city's pecking order. Although there was mobility within and between classes, differences in wealth tended to widen during this period. The resulting differences in the life chances of more- and less-well-to-do people were played out in the way space was set aside for certain activities and people but not others. It also was apparent in the kinds of buildings that were put on some streets but kept off of others.

This system of economic and social stratification was also rigid enough so as to encourage people to move on and populate even newer towns farther west. This option wasn't available for women, children, and slaves who were among the most marginal, poorest, and least mobile members of the community. Their social status and economic situation wouldn't begin to improve for at least another century and even today still lags behind that of many other people who live around them. In the meantime, city leaders worked hard to make less reputable and accomplished residents act better than they might have otherwise been inclined to do.

Townsfolk developed a set of customs and organizations more varied than those available in rural places. Many of these customs reinforced distinctions in rank and accomplishment. There were moments, however, when people from different levels of society were in each other's presence as equals. While men and women occupied fairly well-defined and different social spheres, women did acquire more property rights and had greater political and economic options than women in nonurban settlements. Taverns were not only a popular site for recreating and social intercourse but some were also distinctly "democratic" in that they invited members of all social classes to share the facilities. Even slaves, especially those in more northern towns, had fewer and more flexible rules and customs to deal with than their counterparts did in smaller townships.

Despite their comparatively robust social and cultural life and some early commercial successes, some places succeeded and others did not. New York and Boston would grow and become rich enough so that people there were able to invest sizable sums in ventures in the Midwest and South. Urban settlements like New Haven, Connecticut, and London Town, Maryland, ultimately wouldn't do nearly as well. The difference between success and failure was determined in no small part by how well a particular town's merchants were hooked into international trading networks, many of which had been illegal under the mercantilist rules laid down by England prior to the American Revolution.

Some portion of the profits that early American city leaders made from commerce also went to building monuments to the merchants' success and to subsidize early manufacturing facilities in their own and nearby cities. A good portion of their discretionary investments well into the 19th century also went to infrastructure improvement, construction, and real estate projects. These activities were more in keeping with their commercial interests.

Regional differences in urbanization showed up before the American Revolution. The more agrarian South, for instance, made fewer and smaller urban settlements. They relied on Northern financing to keep their farms and plantations going and Northern manufacturers for many of the finished products they used. Notwithstanding such regional differences, the connection between rural and urban areas was already well in place before the end of this period. So, too, was the development of a system of smaller and larger town and urban settlements linked in regionally-inspired trading relationships and competition with each other.

CITIES IN THE LATE PROTO-INDUSTRIAL AND EARLY INDUSTRIAL PERIOD (1780–1870)

The late proto-industrial period ultimately was one of substantial growth for a number of urban settlements. Early on, however, these places had found it hard just to maintain their current population, much less make it grow. That's because many would-be settlers didn't stay long. People passed through established urban settlements on their way to someplace newer and more inviting. Nevertheless, by the early 19th century, the rate of population growth in American cities was outstripping the overall growth in the U.S. population.

Inter-city competition along the Atlantic Seaboard had resulted in the proliferation of new towns that would be cities in the American interior. Places like St. Louis, Louisville, Cincinnati, and Pittsburgh had already been established by the end of the 18th century. Additional towns began to take hold, spurred on by advances in long-distance transportation such as the steamboat and, somewhat later, the railroad. Until comparable advances were made in short-distance transportation, however, the hinterlands that surrounded cities were left relatively underdeveloped, if not undeveloped. *Town and city building took on a leap-frog pattern in which large empty spaces were left between bigger urban settlements.* This arrangement of urban places became the foundation of a network of full-grown cities and up-and-coming towns that would cover the whole country by the first third of the 19th century.

A pattern of triangular trade among England, coastal towns, and parts of the Caribbean had developed early on in America's colonial history. That pattern was now copied in trading relationships that developed among river cities in the American interior, New Orleans at the bottom of the Mississippi River and close to the Gulf of Mexico, and East Coast cities like Boston and New York. Interior cities continued to take migrants, public investments in the form of military garrisons, investment capital, and finished goods from the East Coast. Unlike the smaller and less numerous cities in the South, they also quickly developed trading territories of their own farther west and a modest manufacturing base.

Important as western expansion was to East Coast cities, most of the trading conducted by coastal cities was done with each other. Southern

cities traded comparatively little with each other, because they all were growing the same crops. They relied on trade with Midwestern cities and products and financing from Northern cities for most of what they needed or wanted in the way of luxury goods. This left the regional network of cities in the South relatively underdeveloped. Other cities like St. Louis, Cincinnati, and Louisville that remained tied to river or canal trade instead of becoming early railroad centers would eventually see their growth eclipsed, too.

The social and class system of interior cities was, except for slaves, relatively more open and flexible than that of Eastern cities. This was part of the reason so many persons had moved west instead of trying to make a go of it in places like New York, Boston, and Philadelphia. *In the towns and cities of the interior, merchants and persons with "professional" training but less wealth occupied the highest levels of the city's social ladder.* Beneath them were wage earners with varied jobs who constituted most of town's resident population and whose economic situation varied depending in part on whether they were skilled or unskilled.

Immigrants swelled the number of semi-skilled and unskilled persons living in Midwestern cities. Many became engaged in the social life of the city, joining organizations and churches with the rest of the people who'd live there longer. Some of these people, like their counterparts back east, needed at least occasional help from local charities and were less well integrated in the city's organizational life. Slaves and transients, like the boatmen and people who drove wagons, were at the bottom of the social ladder. They also were thought to be behind most of the vice and violence that took place in cities of this era.

Notwithstanding cleavages between different classes, *there were parts of urban life in the interior that brought different kinds of people together.* "All classes," Richard Wade (1976, p. 129) wrote, "mingled in churches, schools, and a large variety of civic organizations. In addition, the men, at least, shared the same amusements—horse racing, billiards, drinking, and even the theater being great levelers." Schools and libraries also played a part in the "co-mingling" that took place among persons of different social ranks.

In Eastern cities before the Civil War, those at the top of their city's economic pyramid were seemingly preoccupied with solidifying their position and wealth and reinforcing their social standing. They accomplished this by joining only certain kinds of organizations, by acquiring larger houses, and by using personal items that were clearly more expensive than those used by persons socially beneath them. These persons did something else that was important and distinctive. They diversified their wealth and holdings, as we already noted, by moving into manufacturing, building railroads, and underwriting ever more ambitious real estate and construction projects both in their immediate area and elsewhere in the country.

Members of middle and lower classes might acquire property and move into better jobs, but maintaining their position was hard and their fortunes could be easily reversed. Working-class families couldn't manage with just one wage earner, given the rising cost of durable and nondurable goods. Women and children from these families found that they had to take jobs away from their residence to enable their families to survive. By comparison, women from better-off families became revered figures. Separate social spheres for women and men were actually more apparent at that level than in the working and lower classes. Persons with less money simply couldn't afford the luxury of having lots of space where they could make and keep something like a private life.

More rigid social and legal lines were maintained for slave and free Black persons. But Northern Blacks were better able to develop organizations that paralleled those of White people and achieve a modicum of economic stability. In this, they behaved very much like more recent migrants to cities not just in the United States but in developing countries today, too.

The growth and diversification of the urban population taxed and challenged established public and private leaders. There were increases in crime, gangs, and mob violence that went well beyond those seen in colonial times. *Managing these social tensions and reducing the level of physical privation apparent in less-well-to-do parts of the city became a pressing matter for the rest of the century.* Indeed, by the end of the first third of the 19th century, better-off people had begun initiating a series of moral and social reform crusades that were intended to address these kinds of problems, if not reduce the level of material inequality that marked each of the city's several social classes.

The geographic breadth of their reform programs and the number of persons affected grew substantially over the course of the 19th century and well into the 20th century. In fact, the funding for reform efforts had to shift from private to public sources simply because wealthy people didn't have enough money to satisfy all the demands for assistance being put to them. The organizations undertaking reform efforts grew as well, and the professionalism of program administrators increased. It should be noted that this was also a period in which municipal police departments and public school systems became established and much larger. Repairing urban places and reforming urban people, as we shall see later in the book, became undertakings that required the work of organizations almost as large and complex as those manufacturing all the goods that urban people were buying.

A "positive environmentalist" movement was launched during this period as well. Its backers focused on how changes to the built environment (e.g., better roads, parks, buildings, and improvements to the city's infrastructure) might enhance the moral and social lives of city residents. The earliest innovations and additions to the city's infrastructure may have been brought first to business areas and neighborhoods with more well-to-do people in them. Eventually, however, many infrastructural advances make their way down to people living in poorer parts of the city. It's important to note that less-well-to-do urban residents in U.S. cities had earlier and greater access to improvements in their city's infrastructure than their European counterparts did

(Teaford, 1984). At the same time, these improvements greatly increased a city's level of public debt and the extent to which urban politics was practiced corruptly.

URBANIZATION IN THE MID- TO LATE INDUSTRIAL PERIOD (1870–1920s)

The industrial period is associated with the largest and most sustained growth in American urban settlements in U.S. history. Every decade between 1860 and 1910 the percentage of the population residing in cities grew at least 36% and on two occasions grew by more than 50%. The number of smaller and medium-sized cities also increased substantially.

These places became connected through a national system of railroads that was eventually supplemented and expanded by a national system of highways and air traffic. Cities like Omaha, Seattle, and San Francisco, which had already been transit hubs, gained in prominence as a result of railroad expansion. Others like Portland, Salt Lake City, and Butte also saw their fortunes and populations rise as a result of the railroads and the presence of manufacturing.

It was the largest cities, cities that had already gained prominence as commercial centers, however, that added the most heavy industries to their economic base and remained the best connected urban places in the country. Cities in the South grew, too, but the region still lagged behind other parts of the country in its overall rate of urbanization. Its level of urban growth didn't exceed that of the rest of the country until 1920 which, as we already noted, was the year that America officially became a predominantly urban nation.

Migrants from rural parts of the United States and from overseas were responsible for most of the population increases that American cities experienced. A quarter to a third of the rural migrants came from the United States, where there was a marked decline in the number of farms and agricultural workers after the Civil War. Most of the migrants, however, came from foreign countries, probably for some of the same reasons rural migrants from inside the United States moved to cities. Blacks moving from the South constituted the single largest bloc of rural-to-urban migrants in the years between the two world wars. Unlike Whites, however, they did not stop at smaller or medium-sized cities before reaching their ultimate destination. Foreign immigrants, too, were more likely to stop at cities that already were large and had more industrial employment opportunities.

These industrial cities would change in many unexpected ways because of the immigrants' presence. *The grid design in many cities, especially outside the Northeast, had to be amended. Cities no longer interspersed people with certain kinds of land uses. The physical closeness of different classes and groups that had been occasioned by living in a compact city also became less prevalent.*

What changed most, however, was the center or downtown area of the biggest cities. "The new downtown," Goldfield and Brownell (1990, p. 268) have argued, "expanded out and up, pushing lingering residential uses out of the center and creating a skyline of tall monuments to business and finance. And the center included different districts—retail, corporate, and entertainment—each appealing to different segments of the urban population." These were the central business districts we know best and the ones that continued to spread outward (and upward) through the remainder of the 20th century.

Technological advances in construction and infrastructure (e.g., steel girders, better bridges, elevators, central heating, and plate glass windows, telephone, lighting, paving, water purification and the removal of waste) and short-distance transportation (e.g., ferries, trolleys, subways, and streetcars) enabled cities to expand both upward, outward, and even beneath the ground at the same time. *The cramming together of workplaces closer to the city center and the piling up of working-class and immigrant peoples on blocks closer to the city center, however, also alerted city leaders to the necessity of creating more restful and attractive places for everyday people to enjoy, lest they behave poorly.*

Population densities probably reached their highest levels in the most industrialized cities in the late 19th century. Though widespread suburbanization was still decades away, some middle-class workers were already commuting from the closest-in suburbs. Working-class persons and even some people who would have been considered poor were able to live away from downtown and industrial areas, too. These complementary movements spurred on the development of secondary business districts outside of the downtown area and helped to decentralize the population.

Granted, there was still a lot of shoulder rubbing going on in cities. Yet *residential enclaves based on ethnicity, class, and color also became a more important fact of residential life inside American cities.* The arrival of so many foreign immigrants and the growing distance between where many people lived and where they worked produced a level of physical separation among different populations that had not previously been seen.

The end result of all this filtering and separating was the kind of physically and socially fragmented city that 19th century reformers worried about but seemed incapable or unwilling to stop from being built. Whatever else one might say about these cities, this much seems clear. *Social separation and segregation reached their practical and legal limits inside cities during the late industrial period.*

Black people may have been forced into segregated quarters more than other newly arrived migrants to the city, but they would eventually find other areas inside cities to reside. In the meantime, White people, even those whose material wealth may have been just marginally better than some of their fellow ethnics, began to move to the outer edges of cities and in a few cases to the inner ring of suburbs surrounding cities as well. The result was that the practical and legal limits of segregation in the suburbs to which so many persons relocated and fled would only be tested in the postindustrial period.

As far as the social engagement and involvement of migrants in the city were concerned, immigrant populations and enclaves had stretched the capacity of native institutions to accommodate them. *Blocked from becoming involved in many native organizations, especially those populated by more prosperous residents, immigrants developed their own parallel set of organizations to further their adaptation.* Newspapers, ethnic organizations, churches, lodges, clubs, banks, philanthropic associations, shops, and other businesses catering to their particular and peculiar tastes were all part of the mix.

Many families took in boarders of unrelated fellow countrymen, and this, too, helped to relieve the strain of becoming better integrated into American society. Immigrants also sought out and acquired much formal training in schools, often at night.

Governance became a full-time occupation during the industrial period. Municipal governments were increasingly run by persons who took management on as career-minded professionals rather than as part-time volunteers. Some of them eventually were trained and certified as experts over one or another of the technical operations that cities needed in order to operate smoothly.

Even with all the upgrading that was occurring in city systems and the growing professionalism of its workers, governments were not up to the task of managing the great growth their cities were experiencing. They still lacked the formal power to tax and spend revenues in a way that enabled them to respond to growth more effectively. As a response to these problems in governance, *political machines of varying size and permanence tried to balance the needs of a larger population with the limitations imposed by state legislatures* which worked hard to limit the amount of public money the "bosses" could acquire and steal. The clients of political bosses and their cronies weren't all poor, and they weren't only ethnic immigrants who were clamoring for more and better services. They were also businessmen who wanted to get a piece of all the public building and services being provided by local governments.

A counter movement by so-called "reformers" or "Progressives" later sought to dampen the power of these political machines by central-izing control of local government in a chief executive and agency heads, cutting back on the patronage that lower-class and immigrant people exchanged for their political support, and making the awarding of contracts far more efficient and honest. That wasn't the only thing reformers tried to accomplish. They focused on making philanthropic and planning efforts better organized as well. Reformers advocated for "scientific management" principles and data and pushed for the delivery of modern services through, among other things, public ownership of utilities. They also worked to introduce new technologies and approaches to reform, especially in public health, education, and housing. *This broad package of reforms was pushed as a way to improve the physical appearance of their city and to reduce the chances of disorder by mitigating the effects of poverty.*

Perhaps the most immediate beneficiaries of Progressive Era reforms, however, were the city's first "technocrats." These were the people who actually ran all the public agencies that were created during this period. Their expertise and bureaucratic base made them relatively immune to partisan attack, but this didn't keep them from learning the political game or becoming effective players in it.

Local politics and government worked differently in the South, because its cities "never really experienced as powerfully the three factors that had underwritten political machines—immigration, industrialization, and the widespread franchise" (Monkkonen, 1990, p. 120). The border city of Memphis may have been an exception with its Boss Crump. In general, however, southern cities kept their commercial and landowning political leaders into the mid-20th century.

The political history of smaller cities and growing suburban towns was different from that of larger and midsize cities. It challenged the general progression outside the South of commercial elites giving up power to professional politicians. These smaller places didn't have enough immigrants and public money coming in to support a political machine. Furthermore,

leaders in these communities retained ideas reminiscent of an earlier time when the "unity of business and city interests" was clearer and more often articulated (Monkkonen, 1990, p. 125).

Bigger cities, which had already grown fat by serving other cities in their immediate area, found their business leaders expanding their horizons to other regions and even to foreign nations. Big businesses were no longer as tied to the economic fortunes of their home city. Hence, they were far more likely to indulge in the luxury of letting others guide the political fortunes of their headquarters city. As we noted in the first chapter, the seeds for today's "global cities" were planted in the industrial era.

The federal government's role in city building changed during this period. It had once been implicated only in the founding of many cities through its support of harbor and river dredging, supplying military garrisons, and its subsidization of railroad expansion. The federal government would take a much bigger and more direct hand in local government activities during the Great Depression. Since then, federal programs and funding to local governments for a variety of purposes has grown to become a permanent part of municipal budgets. We mention this now to underscore just how little outside assistance local governments could count on in the absence of continued growth and the additional revenues that growth brought in the way of increased tax revenues.

Local municipal expenditures from the 17th through the 19th centuries had focused on capital investments in infrastructure (e.g., marketplaces, docks, streets) and aid to the poor. Budgets became larger and expenditures more varied throughout the 19th century (e.g., fire, police, schools, public health, utilities, government building, and welfare) as local governments moved from being regulators to service providers. Given the serious limitations on their ability to raise new tax revenues, local governments depended a great deal on borrowing money to finance projects. In this, they acted a lot like corporations chartered in one state but borrowing and lending in others. Limits on municipal debt weren't even introduced until the late 19th century, and as a result municipal debt increased substantially throughout the industrial era.

City government was never particularly efficient and too easily corrupted. As the century progressed, however, city aldermen found their say over budgetary matters and making municipal policy diminish. These were primarily small businessmen, part-timers who didn't serve long enough to develop much citywide clout and often fought among themselves. On the other hand, they also were the persons in government to whom residents turned for favors and to get their wishes granted.

The creation and implementation of citywide policy increasingly fell to executive leaders (i.e., mayor, comptroller, and department heads the mayor controlled) and appointed commissions and boards that oversaw one or another important quasi-public activity. The leaders of bigger businesses and wealthy people were sometimes appointed by the state to oversee the work of these bodies. Even when they were appointed by local officials, however, they had an annoying tendency to act independently of local politicians when it came to watching over the parks, libraries, schools, police, and the investment of municipal funds.

Local control of municipal affairs was further undermined by state representatives and senators who weren't from cities. To be sure, these men could be nudged, encouraged, and bribed into deferring to their city counterparts on many matters involving special legislation affecting cities. But city delegations, which weren't composed of saloon keepers or the biggest businessmen but from some place between these two classes, weren't an especially talented or effective lot. State-enforced home rule petitions and administrative oversight boards further eroded the ability of urban legislators to get bills passed in the state legislature.

All of this builds to the following point. With the growing sophistication of new technologies and science, the ascension of well-trained experts to actually run programs and determine the content of policies was unavoidable. They are granted independent authority to make decisions and run increasingly complex public institutions.

Other nongovernmental experts (e.g., doctors, sculptors, fire underwriters, builders, architects, real estate developers) and better organized but decidedly less well-positioned collections of residents (e.g., labor unions, streetcar and utility companies) also tried to influence policy through their professional organizations.

Despite all the confusion, continuous poor financing, and corruption, American cities still had more services and more modern services than comparable European cities of the era. Upscale areas, as we noted earlier, might acquire these services first. But less-wealthy neighborhoods eventually got them, too. This is part of the reason so many suburbs allowed themselves to be absorbed by cities well into the 19th century. They simply had better services (Teaford, 1984, pp. 217–281).

URBANIZATION IN THE LATE INDUSTRIAL AND POSTINDUSTRIAL PERIODS (1920S–2010)

The 20th century saw the emergence of great metropolitan areas spanning hundreds of square miles and covering many counties. The overall effect on cities was that many of the empty spaces between the large roads and train lines that had led city residents out to fairly distant suburbs now were being filled. Advances in short-distance transportation; the bleeding of manufacturing, retail, and wholesale jobs into suburban areas; and the availability of more credit and relatively cheap long-term mortgages for home buyers surely played a big role in making city dwellers into suburban residents. However, the proliferation of communication, finance, management, clerical and professional service jobs in the central city also pushed cities into emptying out and refitting some of their most prized downtown real estate.

While suburbanization in the United States had been a feature of urban life well before the 20th century, an overall shift in the balance between city and suburban population growth didn't become dramatic until after World War II. The shift happened so quickly that the share of the population held by cities in the 20 largest metro areas in 1950 dropped from 58% to 49% in one decade. During this same period, automobile registrations were growing by 180% (Teaford, 1993, pp. 98–99). Changes in the relative fortunes of cities and suburbs enabled less urbanized parts of the country, especially in the South, perhaps, to catch up in the contest to become better connected to other municipalities in their region and also to other parts of the United States.

Central cities took advantage of the opportunity to rebuild and redefine themselves in different ways. Cities and suburbs in the Northeast and Midwest took one path and urban areas in the South and West took another. The age of a metropolitan area became a determining factor in the relations between cities and suburbs. *Older cities in the Northeast and Midwest couldn't annex additional territory, and their suburbs became marked by distinctive racial, economic, and ethnic lines. Newer cities in the South and West continued to absorb territory, even as people and jobs moved farther away from the urban core.*

The expanding federal role in municipal and metropolitan affairs became fully apparent during this period. "Federal intervention in the wartime economy [had] encouraged local migration in the direction of suburbs and national migration to the Sunbelt." During and after World War II, federal construction had the effect of "regionalizing" the national economy as well. This was accomplished by locating military installations and the aircraft industry in such a way as to benefit Southern and Western cities. In the meantime, debts due to capital investments that "northern cities had bought for themselves in earlier decades" were still being paid off as so-called "Sunbelt" cities were enjoying an unprecedented influx of federal dollars (Chudacoff & Smith, 1988, pp. 262–263).

Almost $2.5 billion in additional federal dollars were spent during the Depression by the Public Works Administration and went to construct bridges, airports, public buildings, and water and sewer facilities. When paired with highway construction monies and federally insured mortgages after the Second World War, the federal role in subsidizing suburbanization became undeniable. This proved to be especially true in cities in the South and West that didn't experience their most rapid growth until after the automobile became an effective means of traveling short distances inside metropolitan areas.

One notable result of all these expenditures and the inducements to relocate in suburbs was that central cities lost many of their White residents. While minority persons eventually followed Whites into the suburbs and are making these places more integrated today, they also have become the predominant population in many cities. Influxes of foreign immigrants in the late 20th century and first decade of the 21st century helped to push at least some of those cities even closer to becoming majority-minority cities.

Even as minority people were becoming a bigger part of the residential population of many cities, the central business district and nearby neighborhoods were being redeveloped and updated in ways that were supposed to attract modern corporations and lure middle-class Whites back. The "renewal" and expansion of downtown areas was supported by politicians, builders, labor unions, and major "business interests." The idea was to reinvigorate the commercial heart of older central cities and attract a different class of people to become full-time city residents.

Some neighborhoods were cleared of many older buildings and residents, people who usually were minorities and never were wealthy. These large parcels of land often remained vacant for many years waiting for private developers to do something. Meanwhile, displaced residents and businesses got little help in finding suitable places to relocate and poorer minority residents were often moved into high-rise public housing sites on the outskirts of the downtown area. These early urban renewal initiatives had devastating effects on many neighborhoods, which often were a great deal more viable than the bureaucrats and politicians pushing to clear them out had made them out to be.

In the end, downtown areas did become home to more corporations, fancy hotels, shopping malls, sports venues, and convention centers.

They also acquired many of the middle-class and upper-middle-class residents that the backers of redevelopment hoped to entice back downtown. Later attempts to improve and rebuild parts of many inner cities focused on rehabilitating structures rather than knocking them down and in keeping at least some of the longer-term residents.

Some researchers have referred to the years between 1992 and 2007 as a "new urban renewal" period. This one involved the demolition of high-rise public housing sites and the further displacement of low-income minority people from neighborhoods that were ripe for redevelopment (Hyra, 2012). Many of these neighborhoods actually had a long history as Black residential enclaves and were redeveloped with that idea in mind. They became "gentrified" by more well-off Black persons and centers of Black cultural celebration and tourism.

In light of all the changes that metropolitan areas across the country have experienced in the last half-century, there are several questions about the future of cities and metropolitan areas that would be wise for us to consider.

ARE CITIES COMING BACK?

As with many questions related to urbanization in this country, the short answer is, "It depends." It depends on what region you're talking about. It also depends on how one defines what a "comeback" would look like for cities in different parts of the country.

It bears noting at the outset that the United States is beginning to see the development of large "megapolitan" areas not unlike those we have said are beginning to emerge in Latin America and Asia. The most prominent one in the United States will run from coastal Maine to the southern end of Virginia and include all of the major cities in New England and the Mid-Atlantic States. Others will cover parts of the Carolinas and Georgia, Florida, and the upper Midwest. There will be three in Texas alone, another two giant ones in California, and one running along the Oregon and Washington coast. Colorado, Nevada, and Arizona will each have one as well. Some states with notable cities in the Midwest, South, and Southwest will not be part of these "urban corridors" (Nelson & Lang, 2011). The point to be taken from this is that the United States will have more of these "megapolitan" areas than developing regions will have, and they will be better connected with secondary urban centers than the ones in Latin America and Asia will be.

Some cities have been growing a little faster than their companion suburbs (i.e., from 0.1% to as much as 3% faster between 2010 and 2011). Other cities have been growing a little slower than their surrounding suburbs (i.e., 0.1% to 0.9%).[3] For reasons described below, rates of urban and suburban growth have slowed down generally.

In general, *metropolitan areas in the West and South (especially in Texas) are growing at a much faster rate than those in the Midwest and Northeast.* Larger and medium-sized central cities (i.e., cities with more than 200,000 persons and between 100,000 and 200,000 persons, respectively) in the West and South are growing at a fast rate (i.e., plus-10%). Cities in the West are growing even faster than that.

Some portion of the growth in the South and West has undoubtedly been fed by annexing new territories and their populations. That is why central city populations in the West, especially, are growing even faster than the population of the whole metropolitan area. In the Midwest, metropolitan growth has been smaller (i.e., less than 10%) and their cities have grown even more modestly, probably 3% to 5% or less. Both the larger and medium-sized cities in the Northeast are losing population. *In general, places that were more dependent on manufacturing grew less, while those with more literate workforces and larger immigrant populations did better.*

Older industrial cities, almost all of them in the Northeast and Midwest, did bounce back a bit in the 1990s. Or the speed at which they were losing residents slowed down. Even cities such as St. Louis, for instance, which has only managed to slow its population losses to a trickle, have managed to gain full-time residents in their downtown areas.

The picture of growth and decline was complex even in the South and West, where the overall population in big and medium-sized cities was still growing. The downtown areas in larger southern and western cities lost population and so, too, did downtown areas in midsize western cities. By comparison, the downtown populations of larger and medium-sized central cities in the Northeast actually grew, even as those in both bigger and medium-sized central cities in the Midwest shrunk. In general, *the parts of central cities that tended to grow most in the last decade have been the neighborhoods encircling the downtown areas of central cities.*

Populations in the largest metropolitan areas and the cities in them shifted from majority White to "majority-minority" between 1990 and 2010. Faster-growing areas saw increases in their Black population especially in the South. The Asian and Hispanic populations grew faster in the West. Slower-growing areas saw decreases in their White and sometimes in their Black populations. Minority growth was predictably greater in areas that had little or no growth and might be called "declining."

In general, the amount of racial separation in American urban areas has been shrinking in recent decades. Edward Glaser and Jacob Vigdor of the Manhattan Institute recently issued a report based on recent census data that back up this claim.[4] They found that by most standard measures of residential segregation, American cities are more desegregated today, if not yet fully mixed and socially integrated, than they were a century ago (Pfeiffer, 2012). The number of urban and suburban neighborhoods that are exclusively White has decreased dramatically in recent decades. And the number of all-Black urban neighborhoods continues to shrink.

Glaeser and Vigdor have hastened to add that the end of segregation hasn't brought about the end of economic inequality. Indeed, there are census tracts in all U.S. cities that continue to have high rates of population loss and concentrated poverty. Many of these have predominantly Black residential populations. At the same time, large influxes of Hispanic migrants in many cities have also led to increased rates of poverty in census tracts where they tend to predominate. Whatever improvements U.S. cities have seen in terms of economic expansion and redevelopment have yet to touch these residential areas. Many suburbs have achieved levels of concentrated poverty that were once expected to be found only in inner-city slums. Moving poor people to areas where they might have expected to do better economically hasn't worked as well as reformers expected (Sampson, 2012).

The number of households with married couples and children increased in the South and West, while declining in the Midwest and Northeast. In a surprising turn of events, however, *suburbs now contain more non-family households than they do married couples with children.* Cities in metropolitan areas with many immigrants are acquiring this same "suburban household" pattern, while suburbs in slower-growing areas are becoming more "urban" in their household pattern.

Downtown areas became even more dominated by single persons, unrelated individuals living together, and childless families. The number of young adults and college-educated adults also increased in downtown areas. Homeownership rates and racial and ethnic diversity increased in all downtown areas as well. *The number of wealthier and poorer households in downtown areas has also grown.*

Residential movement in the U.S. generally is down to around 3.5%, owing no doubt to the lingering effects of a bad economic recession (Frey, 2011). As a point of comparison, "between 1995 and 2000, 46% of U.S. residents changed address" (Berube, Katz, & Lang, 2005, pp. 5–6). The number of new foreign residents is down as well. Among those who did enter the United States, however, they tended to head for larger coastal metropolitan areas. Domestic migrants were more likely to move to Sunbelt locations. In areas that attracted both kinds of movers, immigrants moved to the urban core while domestic migrants generally settled in more outlying suburban areas. More recently, foreign immigrants have headed to newer "gateway" cities in the South, metropolitan areas that had relatively small immigrant populations until recently, and to suburban locales as well. Domestic Black migrants, too, have been moving back to southern cities.

ARE ALL SUBURBS GROWING?

In general, yes, *suburban areas across the country are growing, but that growth is not occurring evenly and some suburbs are actually losing population.* Suburbs in the South grew three times as fast as their central cities did. Suburbs in the West kept pace with their central cities. Suburbs with cities declining in population had growth one third that of suburbs attached to quickly growing cities. This means that suburbs in the Northeast and Midwest aren't growing nearly as quickly as those in the South and West.

Only about two thirds of the suburban communities in the 35 largest metropolitan areas grew between 1990 and 2000. Population growth was highest in unincorporated areas and in newer suburbs. Suburbs losing population were most often located in metropolitan areas in the Northeast and Midwest and located closer to the central city. Suburban losses in the South and West were less numerous and spread across the metropolitan area.

Among the most notable expressions of suburban growth since 1990 are places popularly known as "edge cities" (Garreau, 1991) and "Boomburbs" (Lang & Simmons, 2001). Exactly how much overlap there is between the two is difficult to gauge. However, both terms refer to suburban areas that have grown large enough (i.e., often with 100,000 or more residents) to qualify as a central city in their own right. Owing their existence to the automobile, they are located some distance from the major central city of the metropolitan area in which they've emerged. They have no dense urban core and are built around highway intersections, big malls, and office complexes.

Only one of the 53 nationally recognized "Boomburbs" isn't in the South or West. Virtually all have grown at double-digit rates for the past few decades. Most still are growing at that pace, but growth in several has begun to slow down. The ones whose growth seems to be slowing down are landlocked and cannot continue to spread out or have become centers of immigrant settlement. Among the "Boomburbs" still growing are ones that are more like planned communities in that they share some of the social and economic features of gated communities. This means they're pretty exclusive residential enclaves that don't have many minority residents and few if any poor or moderate-income residents.

"Edge cities" can be found in more parts of the country and are anything but planned. Their most notable feature is probably the highway interchange around which they've sprung. Although they lack anything remotely comparable to the downtown commercial centers of traditional cities, edge cities have lots of office and retail space and attract shopping malls the same way trailer parks seem to draw tornados. Indeed, edge cities may have more jobs than they do full-time residents. With their office towers, shopping malls, and large surface parking areas surrounded by spread-out residential areas accessible only by car.

Exactly how many minority persons have settled in Boomburbs and edge cities is difficult to say. However, *minority people have become a much more prominent feature in the residential populations of American suburbs in the last couple of decades.* This turn of events, needless to say, caught a great many experts by surprise and inspired a lot of popular attention in the media (Medina, 2013).

In the 102 most populous metropolitan areas, racial and ethnic minorities made up 27% of the suburban population in 2000. This figure was 19% in 1990. Indeed, minorities constituted the bulk of suburban population gains. Among all minorities, Asians are the most fully suburbanized. Approximately half of Hispanics now are and upward of 40% of Blacks have become suburbanites, too

Metropolitan areas in the South and West have the highest levels of minority suburbanization in part because they exhibit lower-density suburban-style development patterns. There are few White-only census tracts in the suburban sections of metropolitan areas in the South and West. During the 1990s the level of segregation decreased in more than 270 of the 291 metropolitan areas followed by the census bureau by more than 5%. Segregation levels tend to be higher in the Midwest and Northeast but have decreased with time. The shift has come primarily from Blacks moving into formerly all-White areas.

Areas that have seen steep increases in Hispanic and Asian populations have actually become more segregated, especially in the 10 largest metropolitan areas where by 2000 "42 percent of Hispanics and 30 percent of Asians lived in neighborhoods in which they made up at least 50 percent of the population (and Blacks no more than 10 percent)" (Fasenfest, Booza, & Metzger, 2006, p. 110). *Minority segregation has actually increased in the suburbs, even as more minorities have moved into and reduced the overall amount of residential segregation in the United States.* This means that minorities, particularly non-Black minorities, tended to move into suburbs more recently populated by people from their backgrounds. There has been a corresponding increase in the number of suburbs with neighborhoods that have poor people living there (Brookings Institution, March 7, 2012; Johnston, Poulsen, & Forrest, 2007).

The most striking spatial mismatch between where people live and where jobs are remains for Black people. Though there was a modest 3.2 % decline in the spatial-mismatch gap between Blacks and Whites between 1990 and 2000, still one of every two Black persons would have to move in order for them to have equal access to areas where jobs could be found. Whites have the lowest mismatch, and only one of every four or five White persons would have to move for them to have equal access to where jobs are located. Hispanics and Asians fall somewhere between Whites and Blacks.

Blacks in the Northeast and Midwest are more physically isolated from jobs. They are least isolated in the South. Metropolitan areas with less residential separation between Blacks and Whites have lower rates of job mismatch for Blacks. If the mismatch were less for better-educated Blacks or Black people with better jobs, however, then the physical isolation of less-well-to-do Blacks would be even more severe (Raphael & Stoll, 2006, p. 135).

ARE CITIES AND SUBURBS BECOMING MORE ALIKE?

Although the income gap between cities and suburbs has stabilized nationally, the gaps in the Midwest and Northeast are wide and continue to grow. Smaller gaps in Southern and Western metropolitan areas, on the other hand, are shrinking. More people live in middle-income suburban tracts today, but their share of the population is shrinking because even more people are living in particularly wealthier and poorer tracts. The growing gap between the top and bottom tracts "owes not to the poorest suburbs falling further down the income scale but to wealthy suburbs pulling farther away from the others" and in particular the number of middle-income suburbs that have become more affluent (Swanstrom, Dreier, Casey, & Flack, 2006, pp. 155, 157).

Cities still have double the poverty rate of suburbs, but the number of poor people in cities and suburbs has become nearly identical. Poverty rates increased in the Northeast and Midwest, while they declined in the South and West. "After doubling in the 1970s and 1980s, the share of poor individuals living in high-poverty neighborhoods (where the poverty rate exceeds 40%) declined by nearly one quarter in the 1990s—most dramatically in inner cities in the

Midwest and South" Swanstrom et al., 2006, p. 155). Poverty is becoming more concentrated in western cities and suburbs, especially the inner-most suburbs and among Hispanics.

How suburban communities whose populations have become more economically and racially mixed will manage this kind of change is anyone's guess. The impact these people will have on the municipality's tax base and schools, for example, is likely to be substantial. The economic recession and burst housing bubble that came in 2008 will further compound whatever problems these close-in suburbs will have in the short run. There may be a rather big and long-term silver lining in this cloud, however. If even some of the people who moved farther out to get away from central cities and the people who lived there now find it advisable to move back toward the urban core, inner-ring suburbs may come to enjoy a bit of the renaissance that older central cities experienced in the 1990s.

These changes are not likely to change the face of residential areas any time soon. To be sure, *there has been a modest but nonetheless real trend away from residential separation between Whites and Blacks in the last couple of decades. It has not been matched, however, by comparable reductions in the separation of Whites and Hispanics or Whites and Asians.* If anything, these populations have grown a little more apart as the number of Hispanic and Asian immigrants became more concentrated in central cities and suburbs.

At the same time, *there's also been an increase in the residential separation of people with more education and more income from people with less of these important resources* (Rothwell & Domina, 2009, pp. 87–88). William Julius Wilson (1980) may have been right when he said that the social class of Black people was becoming a more important determinant of their life chances than their color. But this change is happening slowly and looks at this point as if it's being complemented by some signs of increasing residential separation between well-off

people and people who are anything but well-off (Adleman, 2004).

A FINAL LOOK AT URBANIZATION IN THE UNITED STATES AND LESS DEVELOPED COUNTRIES

In assessing the relative strengths and weaknesses of urbanization in a Western society like the United States, we should recall the ways it has differed from the process of city building in less developed countries. Urbanization in such countries until recently has been characterized by the absence of a system of smaller and medium-sized urban settlements. They have agricultural systems that can't feed their own people much less export food. Their manufacturing sectors may be growing manufacturing but are still not large enough to accommodate all their unskilled workers. Finally, governments that don't have funds to keep up with the most pressing needs of their people much less modernize their urban infrastructure. Whatever shortcomings and imbalances urbanization in the United States may exhibit, they pale in significance when compared to this list of problems.

Cities in the Northeast and Midwest that have suffered substantial losses in their manufacturing base and populations have some features that look suspiciously like those we expect to see in societies that are "over-urbanized." They can't adequately house or employ large numbers of their residents. The life chances of more socially and economically marginal women, children, and minorities appear every bit as problematic today as they were a century ago. And municipal governments seem unable to meet the needs of their most chronically at-risk residents. It may be that cities in Western societies such as the United States will never have the resources to improve the life chances of all these people. If that is the case, then our failure to do so should serve as yet another cautionary lesson in what may be possible to achieve in the cities of less developed countries and what may not be possible.

QUESTIONS FOR STUDY AND DISCUSSION

1. What similarities and differences are there in the way cities and metropolitan areas have developed in the Northeast and Midwest as compared to the South and West?

2. Cities have always captured a society's excess wealth and then used that wealth to celebrate the kinds of people and ways of life found in these places. In light of this fact, are American suburbs the greatest accomplishment or failure of American city building?

3. American cities experienced big population losses and economic disinvestment in the second half of the 20th century as a result of their de-industrialization. What can you say about the future economic success of American cities by looking back to a time when they weren't industrial centers?

4. Describe the ways in which different levels of government have influenced the process of city building and suburbanization in the United States.

NOTES

1. Table 18: Population by Urban and Rural: Earliest Census to 2000. Population and Housing Counts. U.S. Census Bureau, 2000.

2. Table 4: Population by Urban and Rural and Size of Place: 2000 and Table 8: Population by Urban and Rural and Size of Place Based on 1950–90 Urban Definition: 1950–1990; and Pre-1950 Urban Definition: 1790–1950. Population and Housing Counts, U.S. Census Bureau.

3. http://www.theatlanticcities.com/neighbor hoods/2012/06/urban-or-suburban-growth-us-metros/2419/

4. http://www.theatlanticcities.com/neighbor hoods/2012/06/watch-these-us-cities-segregate-even-they-diversify/2346/; http://www.theatlantic cities.com/housing/2012/07/how-suburbs-gave-birth-americas-most-diverse-neighborhoods/2647/#

4

THE SEEDS OF URBAN THEORY

Classic Statements About Cities and Communities

The earliest cities in Europe and North America looked very different than they do today. Things that we tend to associate with cities—like skyscrapers and subways, and even paved streets—became part of city life in the 20th century. Yet we shouldn't assume that our cities today are totally different from those of the past. As we noted in the first three chapters, the seeds of today's cities were planted centuries ago. Cities have grown so much in the past 150 years that they almost seem natural as if these seeds are more literal than figurative, as if the Eiffel Tower in Paris, the Empire State Building in New York, or the Burj Khalifa in Dubai were inevitable results of the dreams of early urban pioneers. But these cities have not grown according to a predetermined or natural plan. They have been built by people, people with varying levels of power, people affected by their social situation and the economic and political resources they have to work with. How and why such people built cities the way they did and live in cities the way they do are the larger questions we will be addressing in the next two chapters.

Though the buildings and other physical structures have changed, many of the social dynamics of city life that emerged in the 19th century are familiar to us today. Others have changed a great deal. Luckily for us, skilled observers took note of 19th century urban life and often theorized about the potential outcomes of the grand changes their cities were experiencing and they were living through. We will see later in the book that many of the issues that concerned these early urban theorists are still at the forefront of our inquiries about cities, suburbs, and towns.

Observers and theorists of the growing cities in the 19th century were primarily concerned with the ways that the new urban world would be different from the rural traditions that many of them held dear. There was a good bit of fear about these growing urban centers that seemed to overwhelm them and nostalgia for the rural way of life. We will see in the next chapter that the pessimistic and antiurban views of the early theorists were woven so tightly into the fabric of the discipline that many of its threads still remain intact. Cities had their supporters, to be sure. Our job here is to uncover and lay out both theoretical orientations in greater detail (Lees, 1985). We don't intend to replace pessimism with a new brand of wide-eyed optimism. The goal, as this book attests, is to help students of city life paint the clearest, though not necessarily the brightest, picture of cities and their surrounding settlements.

The 19th and early-20th century theorists tended to agree on a few things about cities. The shift from one form of social organization to another (e.g., rural to urban; totalitarian to democratic; feudal to capitalist; religious to secular; simple to complex) was inevitable, *evolutionary*, and, for better *and* for worse, disruptive. Their observations and interpretations gave us some of our first tools to begin understanding the social life of a still relatively new but rapidly growing urban world.

ALEXIS DE TOCQUEVILLE (1805–1859): OBSERVATIONS OF CULTURE AND COMMUNITY

Alexis de Tocqueville was an aristocrat in post-revolutionary France who played multiple roles throughout his life—historian, politician, traveler, and social observer—but is most often considered a political theorist. As such, he is regularly quoted by political thinkers holding a variety of liberal as well as conservative points of view. His ideas have also influenced contemporary studies of communities in cities, suburbs, and small towns (e.g., Monti, 1999, 2012; McLean, Schultz, and Steger, 2002; Macgregor, 2010).

Tocqueville is included here as a classical urbanist primarily because he considered 19th century society, with its growth of urban settlements, as a new form of human organization. His relevance to urban sociology derives from at least two distinguishing and influential features of his thinking: his keen-eyed observation of everyday life and institutions and his ability to compare and contrast these social inventions in different cultural settings such as France, Britain, Algeria, and the United States. He was a master of what sociologists refer to as a *historical and comparative* approach to understanding society and social arrangements.

Looking for patterns within, between, and across nations, Tocqueville identified new forms of authority and social institutions, such as

democracy, and identified their consequences for human values such as freedom and community. Like many of his contemporaries, he was ambivalent about cities and their influence on individual autonomy and people's ability to govern themselves. His hot-and-cold assessment of cities and urban life at the time is summed up nicely in the following observation he made after visiting Manchester, England:

> From the foul drain the greatest stream of human industry flows out to fertilize the whole world. From this filthy sewer pure gold flows. Here humanity attains the most complete development and its most brutish, here civilization works its miracles and civilized man is turned almost into a savage. (Tocqueville, 1982, p. 306)

Tocqueville, like many theorists, is clearly of two minds about the city: "Foul drain[s]" and "filthy sewer[s]" somehow create and emit "the greatest stream of human industry" and "pure gold." Notice how urban dwellers are *both* "civilized" *and* "savage."

But Tocqueville has more to offer the contemporary student of cities, suburbs, and towns than poetic and pithy aphorisms. By connecting his detailed firsthand observations with his knowledge of the ebbs and flows of history, Tocqueville provides us with useful ways of understanding and addressing culture and community.

Tocqueville's most known and oft-quoted work is *Democracy in America*, which was written after his travels throughout the young nation in the early 1830s with his confidant Gustave de Beaumont. Though their original intention was to study the American penal system, their travels took them into about 50 of the new cities and towns that were growing under this "new" state defined by its democratic principles, if not always by democratic practices. Within the pages of *Democracy in America*'s two volumes, Tocqueville provides an implicit theory about the role of culture in the emergence and maintenance of institutions and personal autonomy or "individuality." He paid particular attention to three elements of culture.

I have thought that all the causes tending to the maintenance of a democratic republic in the United States can be reduced to three: The particular and accidental situation in which Providence has placed the Americans forms the first; the second comes from the laws; the third flows from habits and mores. (Tocqueville, 1982, p. 77)

Tocqueville argues that specific cultural habits, dispositions, and beliefs are absolutely necessary in causing and maintaining a society's institutions and that those institutions, once established, in turn shape the beliefs of its inhabitants.

Applied to urban life, we can see that Tocqueville argued that the spatial arrangements, governance, and culture of people ultimately determine the "social health" of society. Perhaps most importantly for Tocqueville, a people's culture, in the form of habits, customs, and convictions, affects individuals' way of being in the world and interacting with one another.

One of the "habits" that Tocqueville viewed as an important way of living in a democratic society was that of joining groups. He described the United States as a nation of "joiners," with a tendency to form associations of different sizes and purposes in order to serve the common good. Instead of retreating into their own individualized private worlds, a potential danger of an egalitarian society, Tocqueville saw that many Americans became members of voluntary *civic associations*. These groups were spontaneously arranged by varying interests and goals. They could be intellectual groups like a book club you may be a part of or even the class for which you're reading this book. They could be religious groups or congregations or political organizations like the Young Democrats or Young Republicans at your school. Despite the fact that these groups had, and have, different interests and "calls to duty," the underlying practice of joining taught Tocqueville, and us, an important lesson: *When past social ties break, individuals tend to find new ways to connect and commune with others.*

The fear that the new urban world would sever the traditional bonds between people influenced Tocqueville and the other classic urban theorists who you'll read about below. Civic associations are at least one way that individuals learned to create new types of connections and a new egalitarian way of life that is closely tied to the development of both democracies and cities. Tocqueville shows the ways that civic associations encourage bonding between the individuals who are directly involved but also build bridges to the wider society. In many ways, Tocqueville's observations anticipate the rise of urban subcultures and ethnic enclaves, both of which can be and have been labeled as "urban villages" (see Gans, 1962; Monti, 1999). At the same time, he also identified how some organizations could facilitate contacts between more homogeneous groups and people in the larger society who were ethnically or racially different or held different points of view and customs.

As you will see, others saw the creation of new "interest groups" as evidence of fragmentation, alienation, and conflict. For both Karl Marx and Friedrich Engels, such groups were defined by their *economic* and *material* interests above all else. As such, they were necessarily pitted against one another under the conditions and logic of industrial capitalism. Despite the social and physical ills this created, these conflicts weren't necessarily bad when interpreted from a macroscopic view of history. Marx and Engels tell us why.

KARL MARX (1818–1883) AND FRIEDRICH ENGELS (1820–1895): FEARS OF CAPITALISM AND THE WORKING CLASS

Karl Marx, the man who famously—or infamously—urged us to not just interpret the world but to change it, remains one of the most widely discussed thinkers in many disciplines across academia over 150 years since his major works were published. He remains an inspirational figure to some urban sociologists because of his acute description of the processes that drove 19th century capitalism. He is also known for his prescriptions for dealing with the inequalities associated with capitalism and ultimately toppling the political and economic regimes that built and ran the growing cities of 19th century Europe. For others, Marx and his followers represent a dogmatic and ultimately failed way of thinking about social and political change. Regardless, we can all agree that Marx's emphasis on class relations were products of the social changes he witnessed in burgeoning 19th century industrialized European cities. Of note, however, is that Marxian analysis of city life didn't become popular until the 1960s. For now, let's dive into Marx's ideas and then into those of his "comrade," Friedrich Engels.

For Marx, the rise of capitalism and the growth of cities go hand in hand. Capitalism—the dominant mode of production industrializing regions—relies on the accumulation of capital whereas urbanization relies on the accumulation of people. The capitalist mode of production, according to Marx, develops when human labor becomes a commodity, when rural peasants can no longer work for themselves but have to sell their time and effort to someone else. They receive money to survive (sometimes barely) in return for their work (i.e., their labor power).

Marx labels those who sell their labor power the *proletariat* and those who pay people to work the *bourgeoisie*. The bourgeoisie typically own the land and technology necessary to produce goods to sell on the open market. Due to the logic of capitalism, the bourgeois class took advantage of the difference between the price of the labor required to produce commodities and the value they could get for those products in the marketplace. Marx observed that in almost all successful—that is, profitable—industries the price of labor was lower than the price of the manufactured goods. This difference is called "surplus value" and is essentially the source of the capitalist's profit that could then be reinvested in new technologies and produce new commodities that required more workers. As such, while industries—the same ones that helped build cities on a mass scale—and profits would grow, so to would the number of exploited workers.

According to Marx's theory, *social relationships between people become relations between things. Workers simply become cogs in the machine.* (See Charlie Chaplin's silent film *Modern Times* for a stark visual representation of this metaphor.) Workers become alienated and estranged from the products of their labor. The products that workers made were not theirs; they belonged to the owners of the means of production. Workers don't own anything—neither the tools nor the finished product. For Marx, the human ability to create and build things is the essence of human nature. Furthermore, due to continued specialization of tasks in the new factories, they were alienated from other workers. So, in the end, workers are alienated from the products they work on, from themselves, and from other people. They were also alienated from their former way of life. Many of the workers on the assembly lines of the new factories were former rural dwellers. They became dependent on urban markets and industries to sell their wares and, ultimately, to leave their villages and become industrial laborers themselves.

What is noteworthy about Marx's thinking is that the ensuing tensions that were crucial to the rise of conflict between these different classes were based in cities. As the industrial city grew, the bourgeoisie began to produce goods for the marketplace and make money for nothing else than money itself. As workers figuratively morphed into things themselves, people would eventually and inevitably, according to Marx, become less than human. This leads to the most devastating changes in social relations and relationships as rural life is devoured by industrial cities.

Constant revolutionizing of production, uninterrupted disturbance of social conditions, everlasting uncertainty and agitation, distinguish the bourgeois epoch from earlier ones. All fixed, fast-frozen relations, with their train of ancient and venerable prejudices are swept away; all new-formed ones become antiquated before they can ossify. *All that is solid melts into air, all that is holy is profaned, and man is at last compelled to face with sober senses, his real conditions of life, and his relations with his kind* [emphasis added]. (Marx & Engels, 1848/1978, p. 476)

It is easy to recognize Marx's distaste for the industrializing cities. But, in a somewhat contradictory way, Marx actually welcomed urbanization *for* the troubles it created. Instead of being scattered in the hinterlands, workers were now concentrated in cities where they could mobilize against the bourgeoisie by forming trade unions first and then, Marx hoped, as a mass ready to revolt against the ruling capitalist class. Of course, modern history didn't play out this way, though unions have played an important role in fighting for and supporting the rights of workers (e.g., minimum wage laws, child labor laws, work environment/building codes) and buffering the "maximize profits, minimize costs" logic of capitalism.

Much of Marx's writings about cities are implicit and often quite abstract. Marx wrote about the evils of industrial capitalism rather than the cities where the logic of industrial capitalism was unfolding most obviously and painfully. His comrade, sometimes co-author, and financial supporter, Friedrich Engels, fleshed out what Marx had left implicit in much of his writing. He provided rich and detailed descriptions of the harsh relationship between capitalism and city life.

Engels, himself the son of an industrialist, conducted his "fieldwork" in Manchester, England, because it had grown at the same time that capitalism had spread throughout the United Kingdom. His commentary highlights the uses and abuses of urban space and residential segregation

If anyone wishes to see in how little space a human being can move, how little air—and such air—he can breathe, how little of civilization he may share and yet live, it is only necessary to travel hither. True, this is the Old Town, and the people of Manchester emphasize the fact whenever anyone mentions to the frightful condition of this Hell on Earth; but what does that prove? Everything which here arouses horror and indignation is of recent origin, belongs to the industrial epoch. (Engels, 1845/1999, p. 67)

Engels argued that all the newly born industrial cities had a strikingly similar pattern and social relations that worked according to a predictable logic. He observed the radical difference in the working and living conditions of the affluent and the poor. He credited these disparities to the capitalist mode of production that needed concentrated pools of dispensable laborers to call on and cast off. Underpaid workers (who we now call the "working poor") lived in dismal tenements. They were often kept out of sight from the upper- and middle-class bourgeoisie as they traveled between the central commercial districts, where they owned and managed businesses and warehouses, and the often lush houses and garden villas, where they lived on the outskirts of the city. (You will be reminded of this type of zone-like patterning when you read about Ernest Burgess and the Chicago school's "urban ecology" model in the next chapter.)

Every great city has one more slums, where the working class is crowded together. . . . In general, a separate territory has been assigned to it, where removed from sight of the happier classes, it may struggle along as it can. These slums are equally arranged in all the great towns of England, the worst houses in the worst quarter of the towns. . . the streets are generally unpaved, rough, dirty, filled with vegetable and animal refuse, without sewers or gutters, but supplied with foul, stagnant pools instead. Moreover, ventilation is impeded by the bad, confused method of building the whole quarter. (Engels, 1845/1999, pp. 70–71)

The last line from the quote above seems to imply that Engels would support new urban-planning techniques to fix these housing problems. That, however, is not the case. Engels believed that the only way to answer the "housing question" was to release the properties from the bourgeois landowners who would ultimately benefit from the improved conditions. The improvements would (a) satiate the working class and (b) increase the cost of the land, eventually pricing the poor out of their refurbished dwellings.

Though Engels feared that the city made the masses increasingly vulnerable to exploitation by their employers and diseases from their poor working and living conditions, he did, however, see a silver lining. Like Marx, he believed that the growing population of exploited workers would eventually revolt. He also recognized the liberating potential of mechanized labor. New technologies could lighten the workload, shorten the working day, and free up time for workers to develop and pursue intellectual endeavors. And this could lead to a prosperous and vibrant modern urban culture (Merrifield, 2002, p. 44). The key word, however, is "could," which is usually followed by "if." Spending too much time on "coulds" and "ifs" creates a void between theories about the urban world and the world itself.

Mostly, *Marx and Engels argue that cities create a distinctive way of life defined by alienation and conflict between distinctive social classes. For them, the only way to cure the "urban ills" that were increasingly present in the new industrial cities was to replace capitalism with a new mode of production, namely, socialism.* Both Marx's and Engel's answers to the important theoretical questions of the time are filled with hopeful wishes. These hopeful wishes about a different urban future were, in part, influenced by an emotional reaction to city life as a more complex and therefore more destructive way of life than had been experienced in rural villages. They were not alone in seeing a strong division between urban and rural life fueled by a romantic nostalgia for the past. Ferdinand Tönnies constructed perhaps the most enduring dichotomy, one that still influences students of communities, despite his fairly explicit nostalgic mourning for the inevitable loss of community in the modern urban world.

Ferdinand Tönnies (1855–1936): The Consequences of the Rural/Urban Divide

Marx and Engels—in both their solo-authored and co-authored works—were disgusted by

what they saw in cities, sought to explain where the troubles came from, and presented alternative versions of what our urban future could look like. Ferdinand Tönnies took a different yet perhaps equally pessimistic approach from his fellow Germans. He was primarily interested in defining the consequences of the mass migration away from the village toward the city. Like Tocqueville, Tönnies was concerned about social relations within the new and expanding urban social order. He was, however, much more nostalgic than Tocqueville. Yet, and perhaps more importantly, Tönnies was more systematic in his analysis. Tönnies offered a typology that remains a source of inspiration and debate for students of social relations in cities, suburbs, and towns.

The idea that the modern city represented the antithesis of traditional rural life is most associated with Tönnies's work *Gemeinschaft und Gesellschaft* (1887) where he outlines two basic organizing principles of social relationships and institutions. He ties them to the kind of place (i.e., a town and city) where they would be found. (Recall this distinction in our later discussion of "physical determinism" and the way urban planners use a variation of this idea when describing how to fix cities.)

Tönnies's typology can be understood as an evolutionary theory that lays out the development of human society from one stage to another. The first stage is the **Gemeinschaft** or "communal association." This is the traditional, small community where everybody knows your name and business. With an obvious nod to the popular 1980s sitcom *Cheers*, we like to call this the "Norm norm" (Borer & Monti, 2006). Relationships are intimate and enduring in small towns and villages where people work together for the common good, united by kinship and family ties. The neighborhood and the church were dominant institutions that helped maintain social control, as was a common language.

On the other end of the spectrum, or the next stage in human social development, is the **Gesellschaft** or "society association." This is the modern city, characterized by rampant individualism that trumps community interests. Relationships are less about personal ties and more about calculated business exchanges that are constrained by common laws rather than common morals. Tönnies's distinction between *Gemeinschaft* and *Gesellschaft* societies conflates the preindustrial/industrial divide with the rural/urban one. The twin forces of industrialization and urbanization were linked to diminished social bonds and the changing nature of the family. *For Tönnies, the family unit is the most important foundation of a healthy society. Tönnies decried the effects of child labor and women entering the labor force. Both were common in industrial cities. And both had the potential to weaken the power and importance of the family.*

The shift from *Gemeinschaft* to *Gesellschaft* societies was a result of the increase in industrialization and the rise of capitalism. The new social rules of the city served the interests of merchants who sold their commodities on the basis of contracts rather than kinship or friendship ties. When the majority of transactions between individuals are based on the impersonal exchange of money, human interactions become impersonal. Tönnies feared that this would put individuals' self-interest above concern or care for the common good.

Tönnies's characterization of the village and the city shares common themes with both Marx's and Engel's views. Yet Tönnies yearned for a romanticized past rather than a future changed by revolutionary acts. His pro-rural/antiurban sentiment, however, remains a recurring theme throughout much of the 20th century and into the 21st century. But there are more dissenters today than there were in the 19th century. We will meet one of those early dissenters next in the work of Emile Durkheim. Durkheim constructed his own dichotomy of contrasting types of social order that shared some things in common with Tönnies's. But, for Tönnies, one type of social order was necessarily better than the other. *Gemeinschaft* was seen as natural, while *Gesellschaft* was artificial. For Durkheim, both types were natural forms of social organization,

each with their own problems and advantages. The issue, then, is to figure out how each type of social organization works and, perhaps, to try to make it serve the most people in the best possible way.

EMILE DURKHEIM (1858–1917): FROM THE DIVISION OF LABOR TO URBAN IMAGERY

The idea that healthy communities cannot exist in cities and can only be found in rural villages depends on what we mean by healthy. As we will argue here and elsewhere throughout this book, healthy comes in many forms, some that exist outside of Tönnies traditional *Gemeinschaft* environment. Emile Durkheim was interested in the same transformations as Tönnies, but developed a model of contrasting social order that posits a different conclusion. In his seminal work, *The Division of Labor in Society* (1893/1947), Durkheim sets out to show the ways that changes in society—specifically, occupational specialization—affect social cohesion and solidarity. During a time when industrialization forced specialization of workers' skills and interests, highlighting the negative consequences such as alienation was in vogue. Durkheim offered a unique counterinterpretation.

> The question that Durkheim raised in regard to this issue centered on whether there was any moral function in specialization. Contemporaries of his, such as Tönnies, argued that specialization contributed to the disintegration of the larger social order. Durkheim's response was that that which is moral contributes to both solidarity and the healthy continuity of society. For him, the division of labor had this function. (Karp, Stone, & Yoels, 1991, p. 13)

Durkheim argues that one type of social solidarity is not necessarily better than the other. Instead, they are simply different and, consequently, have different conditions for creating social bonds.

Traditional, rural life offered a specific form of social cohesion based on homogeneity that Durkheim labeled *mechanical solidarity*. *Social bonds are based on common beliefs, customs, rituals, routines, and symbols. Social cohesion is a result of individuals engaging in similar activities and shared responsibilities. Individuals are connected to one another because their tasks and commitments overlap with one another*. It might seem odd and a bit backward to describe small-scale, preindustrial societies as being "mechanical." But Durkheim used the term to suggest that since most people were alike, they were, in effect, like interchangeable parts of a machine.

In the modern industrial city, heterogeneity rules. Individuals are often quite different from each other. They come in all shapes and sizes and have different religious beliefs, political affiliations, ethnic backgrounds, and racial makeups. They perform different sorts of labor and so have very different day-to-day lives and even conflicting interests. The list is large and so are the social consequences of having so many different kinds of people living and working in the same place. Rather than declaring that there wasn't any type of cohesion between these urban dwellers, however, Durkheim argued that a new type of social bonding emerged that he labeled organic solidarity.

People's differences didn't tear them apart or make them act purely on the basis of self-interest. Instead, individuals were actually held together by their differences and the need for each others' specialized skills and abilities. Urbanites' social bonds were based on specialization and mutual interdependence. In a paradoxical way, a society characterized by **organic solidarity** has *both* more unity *and* more individuality. This is reflected in the organization of your college or university. Go to your school's website and take a look at all of the different administrative offices and the different departments programs. Then look at the faculty profiles. The division of labor creates not only specialized tasks for individuals, but specialized knowledge as well. Each employee relies on others to do their jobs. Look at your classroom.

No one sitting to the right or left of you built those seats or desks. Your professor definitely didn't construct the building you entered and the doors you opened to get to your classroom, nor does he or she teach chemistry or literature if his or her specialty is sociology. The complex division of labor that is necessary to help your school meet its core mission of educating students is emblematic of the type of solidarity we find in modern, urban societies dependent on a high degree of specialized skills and knowledge.

Durkheim called this type of solidarity "organic"—despite its existence in and emergence from the industrial city—because he equated the interdependence of specialized individuals to those of the parts of a living organism. The use of biological metaphors for understanding urban life has been, as we will see in the next chapter, an important yet contentious theme in the development of urban theory.

For Durkheim, both mechanical solidarity and organic solidarity are natural forms of social organization. Social cohesion exists in each, but by different means. *The unity promoted by the shared morality of rural villages and towns evolves over time. It is replaced by a new for type of social cohesion that comes from the interdependence of specialization in industrialized cities*. It should be noted, however, that Durkheim—showing his own moralism—believed that the moral value of specialization was not, in fact, realized in modern cities. Durkheim concluded that this had less do with the division of labor itself and more to do with unequal opportunities to specialize in certain types of labor. Some people—the poor—lacked the resources to pursue the specializations they would have liked.

Most scholars tend to see Durkheim's distinction between mechanical and organic solidarity as his only contribution to urban theory. His interests in morality lead to his study of religious beliefs, most notably in the *Elementary Forms of the Religious Life* (1912/1965). Durkheim's ideas about the divisions that people make between the sacred and the profane are useful for understanding the ways that people related to different places in various cities, suburbs, and towns. Some places are treated with more value than others as if they have "sacred" qualities. Of course, what is considered sacred for one group is not necessarily sacred for another. This is why there are often heated debates over which buildings should be preserved and which should be demolished (Borer, 2008).

Moreover, Durkheim's discussion of totems as "symbolic representations" of particular populations and places can be used to show the significance of urban imagery. People often connect cities to particular images—the New York skyline or the Las Vegas Strip—which can have consequences on the ways people understand social relations in particular cities. This can influence everyday life as well as policy making and social reform. We will discuss the importance of urban imagery in Chapter 5. For now, we are going to move on to discuss another theorist, Max Weber. Unlike Durkheim, Weber wrote a classic essay about urbanization, appropriately though not necessarily creatively entitled, *The City*. As we will see, Weber's ideas place him between his fellow Germans (i.e., Karl Marx and Georg Simmel) because of his attention to both structural issues, like the market, and everyday life issues like meanings that individuals connect to their social actions and interactions.

MAX WEBER (1864–1920): THE NATURE OF THE CITY AND ITS INSTITUTIONS

Max Weber's contributions to the field of sociology are enormous. Urban scholars have used his not-specifically urban ideas to understand the various elements of city life. His most direct discussion of cities is less about urbanism and more about urbanization. He uses a *comparative framework*—discussing the wide variety of cities beyond the Western world and across various time periods—to make an argument about "the nature of the city." *Weber shows us that cities cannot be defined by one characteristic—such as population—since there were plenty of towns in the Middle Ages that had plenty of inhabitants but still lacked sufficient economic and political autonomy. A city, then, as Weber argues, is recognized as a settlement embedded with strong economic and political institutions.*

Placing a heavy emphasis on a city's marketplace and its governance, Weber (1958), puts forth his own criteria for a settlement to earn the title of "city."

> To constitute a full urban community a settlement must display a relative predominance of trade-commercial relations with the settlement as a whole displaying the following features: 1) a fortification; 2) a market; 3) a court of its own and at least partially autonomous law; 4) a related form of association; and 5) at least partial autonomy. . . thus also an administration by authorities in the election of whom the burghers participated. (pp. 80–81)

There are a few important insights that we can take away from this quote as they relate to Weber's theories of modernity and to others' ideas about city life.

First, the city is a multidimensional settlement. That is, a city is a collection of autonomous institutions. It has a rich and extensive local market place for both production and consumption. The city's "inhabitants live primarily from commerce and the trades rather than from agriculture" (Weber, 1958, p. 66). The city must also have a strong political, legal, and administrative body that maintains its own armed guards (read: police force).

Urban economics and politics are both based on rational laws and rules determined by depersonalized bureaucratic principles that contrast greatly with the "traditional" authority of "Lordly manors." The increased use of rationality as a necessary feature of urbanization and urbanism is a reoccurring theme throughout Weber's ideas about modernity. The influence of rationality, however, varied across the world. The process of "rationalization" had more steam in the Western world than it did in the East. According to Weber, "the Orient" was too immersed in "magical beliefs" to benefit from the rationality that was necessary for the development of autonomous institutions as well as creating connections between those institutions. Of note, is the section entitled "Magical Barrier to Oriental Civic Development" (Weber, 1958, p. 99). "Weber's study of the city is as central to his investigation of the development of capitalism as his work on religion" (Mellor, 1977, p. 191). Weber's analysis of the rise of industrialized cities and the decline of religion are both linked to the process of rationalization and demystification in the modern world.

Second, Weber uses the term "urban community," which seems like he disagrees with Tönnies who would be shocked by the connection of these two terms. On further inspection, however, Weber's ideas are actually aligned with Tönnies's. The type of *urban* community that Weber describes is not like *Gemeinschaften* collections of individuals connected by common traditions, bloodlines, and kinship ties. This new form of community is more like a "network" (a term that's become popular in contemporary urban studies). And this network consists of individuals, as well as collectivities like guilds, companies, or "civic associations" connected to one another by the laws of the city and the state.

The city itself, then, is an open association where individuals—though still not *all* individuals—can choose to participate. The new political community, with its democratic forms of association, depends on the presence of a new class: the urban bourgeoisie. The city is dominated by the bourgeoisie whose economic interest is preserved by the secular, rational, individualist, and market-oriented community formations that emerged in medieval cities. Economic independence of individual households resulted in the emergence of the new class of merchants and craftsmen. *The development of rational legal institutions enabled the individuals to be free from traditional group memberships, and, in turn, to develop their own individuality.*

In new civic creations, burghers [middle-class merchants] joined the citizenry as single persons. The oath of citizenship was taken by the individual. Personal membership, not that of kin groups or tribe, in the local association of the city supplied the guarantee of the individual's personal legal position as a burgher. (Weber, 1958, p. 102)

Unlike Marx's and Engels's intensely negative views of the bourgeoisie, Weber saw the importance of the activities of this new class—and their roles as both producers and consumers—for the development of a sustainable urban culture that encouraged innovation and individuality. Yet as Weber recognized, individuality has its dark side too.

The lack of traditional identity status markers had profoundly ambivalent consequences for urbanites. As noted above, the city was a liberating space because it allowed urbanites to escape from the traditional bonds that often condemned them to particular social roles and identities. Cutting these bonds, coupled with the sense of anonymity, had its dangers.

Weber wrote that a city is a "dense settlement of dwellings forming a colony so extensive *that personal reciprocal acquaintance of the inhabitants is lacking*" [emphasis added] (1958, p. 65). This observation is reminiscent of Marx's ideas about alienation and, as we'll see in the next section, Georg Simmel's account of urban social psychology. Though Weber mostly wrote about the institutional structure of the city, he recognized that the lack of "personal reciprocal acquaintance" could lead to a sense of loneliness and detachment. Weber read and was familiar with Simmel's writings that offered a detailed analysis of the experience of the city and how it impacts subjective feelings and social interaction.

GEORG SIMMEL (1858–1916): THE EXPERIENCE OF CITY LIFE

Of all the theorists we discuss, Georg Simmel is probably the one most dedicated to writing about urban life. He deserves this declaration because he wrote about an eclectic variety of subjects: the psychology of urbanites, art, food, fashion, the senses, sex, and even yodeling. Many of these topics have developed into subfields of sociology in recent decades (though no one has developed a sociology of yodeling, yet).

Simmel's interpretations of urban life are particularly instructive for students interested in the everyday life encounters in cities' shared places and spaces. The starting point for Simmel is that people in cities must interact with strangers. In cities, thousands of individuals are physically close to one another, yet remain emotional and culturally distant. Think of a trip on a crowded commuter bus or train. Passengers share very close physical proximity and yet may not even make eye contact with one another, never mind share any sort of a more meaningful bond. In Simmel's words, "It is the synthesis of nearness and distance which constitutes the formal position of the stranger" (1971b, p. 404). As such, a city's strangers are near and far at the same time, creating an interesting social dynamic that could be problematic to those accustomed to rural villages and small towns.

The frequent interaction with strangers creates a unique problem for urban dwellers. In his seminal work originally published in 1903, usually translated as "The Metropolis and the Mental Life," Simmel argues that the sheer size of the city and the numbers of strangers who live there mean that individuals must protect themselves against potential sensory overload. Such mental adaptations were unnecessary before the advent of the city. In rural environments the pace of life was slower and interactions were rhythmic and habitual. The city, however, with its "swift and continuous shift of external and internal stimuli" (1971a, p. 325), requires individuals to psychologically adapt to the urban environment. And these adaptations have a profound impact on the ways that people relate to one another in the modern urban world.

Simmel suggests that modern cities generate conditions that predispose individuals (i.e., "the metropolitan type") to become reserved in their relationships with one another.

Thus the metropolitan type—which naturally takes on a thousand individual modifications – creates a protective organ for itself against the profound disruption with which the fluctuations and discontinuities of the external milieu threaten it. Instead of reacting emotionally, the metropolitan type reacts primarily in a rational manner, thus creating a mental predominance through the intensification of consciousness, which in turn is caused by it. (1971a, p. 326)

In order to filter out the varied stimuli that an individual encounters in the city, he or she must approach the city's social and built environment by engaging in a process of *intellectualization*. Similar to Tocqueville's observations of a shift from the "habits of the heart" to those of the mind, individuals are forced to adopt a calculating and calculated mentality in their interactions with others. The process is connected to three important characteristic of a distinctive urban way of life.

First, the "protective organ" is enacted by the development of a "blasé attitude," an indifference to others and the cacophony of sights, sounds, and smells that constitute the urban environment. The "blasé attitude," according to Simmel, is necessary because it would be impossible to take in, interpret, and respond to all of the stimuli one encounters. Try to remember or imagine yourself walking down a busy city street. Imagine trying to say "hello" or even making eye contact with everyone who passes you. Impossible! It would be psychologically exhausting and you would never get to where you're going or get to the business that brought you there in the first place. Perhaps most importantly, in some parts of some cities, you might end up eating a knuckle sandwich.

Second, adopting a rational, calculated, and impersonal demeanor toward others is a cause and a result of an economy based on the exchange of money. No longer is bartering an effective and efficient way of doing business. Such traditions have been replaced by a depersonalized "money economy" that influences all forms of social relations. Everything, including people, is measured in dollars and cents (or the nationally specific denomination of currency). In this sense, people are continually evaluating others in term of their economic worth, which consequently pits strangers against each other. Moreover, the calculating mind of "the metropolitan type" is dependent on a defined schedule that coordinates time and timed activities. Punctuality takes on heightened importance in the city. As Simmel writes, "If all the watches in Berlin suddenly went wrong in different ways even only as much as an hour, its entire economic and commercial life would be derailed for some time" (1971a, p. 328). Simmel is implying, then, that even though it may be more impersonal, the rational actions of individuals create a form of social order that combats the potential chaos of the metropolis.

Third, the impersonal, calculating mentality leads to more individuality in cities than in traditional villages and small towns. Simmel shows a healthy degree of ambivalence about the freedoms of urban dwellers. The severing of traditional emotional bonds, combined with the presumably cold and indifferent reactions to others, can lead to feelings of alienation and a lack of self-worth. "Under certain circumstances, one never feels as lonely and as deserted as in this metropolitan crush of persons" (1971a, p. 334). For those who are able to adapt to the urban condition, the city's lack of traditional social control can lead to an increase individuality and creativity. Simmel follows Durkheim's interpretation of the positive consequences of a complex and specialized division of labor birthed in modern cities. In order to avoid being swept away by the crowd and "making oneself noticeable" (1971a, p. 336), individuals must call upon their own creative imaginations. Taken together, these creative acts make the city a potential locus of innovation and social change.

It should be clear at this point that Simmel had a keen eye on the characteristics of a distinctive urban way of life. He also tells us that traditional forms of interaction are usurped by a rational and calculating mentality that, in his estimation, is necessary for survival in the modern city. Though Simmel has a direct influence on the Chicago school because Robert E. Park had attended Simmel's lectures in Germany (more about this in the next chapter), he was almost forgotten by most urban sociologists until the 1990s. As an *urbane* urban scholar, his writings deserve greater attention than they have been given throughout the past century or so. The same can be said about W. E. B. Du Bois, except for the fact that his ideas were ignored by fellow sociologists in his day. Du Bois was, in fact, a victim of the very subject he studied: racism.

W. E. B. Du Bois (1868–1963): The Structure and Experience of Race

Mostly known as an essayist, poet, and activist, W. E. B. Du Bois was a towering intellectual figure. He was the first African American to graduate with a doctorate in sociology from Harvard University. His dissertation, "The Suppression of the African Slave Trade in the United States of America, 1638–1870," was published by Harvard in 1896, and he published 15 more books, two autobiographies, three historical novels, and two other works of fiction during his lifetime. For better and for worse, his lyrical writings—such as *The Souls of Black Folk* (1903/2007)—have outshined his presence as a pioneer of classical urban sociology. But another culprit has kept him out of urban sociology textbooks for over a century. As Lawrence Bobo contends, "Had not racism so thoroughly excluded him from placement in the center of the academy, he might arguably have come to rank with Max Weber or Emile Durkheim in stature" (2000, p. 187). Like Weber and Durkheim, as well as the other theorists we've discussed, Du Bois was concerned about the ways that modern urban life differed from traditional rural life. Yet in many ways Du Bois's study of Philadelphia's African American community is more than an extension of European urban theory. Rather, *The Philadelphia Negro* (1899) is the starting point of American urban sociology.

Though it didn't have the influence on either urban sociology or urban policy that it probably should have, Du Bois's *The Philadelphia Negro* (1899/1996) anticipates some of the most important developments in the ways that scholars investigate and interpret cities and race relations. His work was motivated by his belief that knowledge has power. He believed that precise scientific knowledge about African Americans could "cure" the problems imposed upon them by outsiders (i.e., White capitalists) and reinforced by negative self-images that remained from years of servitude. His goal was to conduct a social scientific analysis that would upend the dominant theories of race at the end of the 19th century, such as eugenics or craniometry (see Gould, 1981), that tended to view a person's lower social position as a result of his or her inferior biological and hereditary traits.

Du Bois set out to understand the plight of the "Negroes," asking why this particular population had such a difficult time "assimilating" into the mainstream culture of Philadelphia and other major American cities.

> This in itself is not all together unusual; there are other unassimilated groups: Jews, Italians, even Americans; and yet in the case of the Negroes the segregation is more conspicuous, more patent to the eye, and so intertwined with a long historic evolution, with peculiarly pressing social problems of ignorance, crime, and labor, that the Negro problem far surpasses in scientific interest and social gravity most of the other race or class questions. (Du Bois, 1996, p. 5)

In order to provide answers to the questions he asked about "the Negro Problem," Du Bois used a variety of methods to explore the condition and dynamics of the Philadelphia's African American population, predominantly located in the Seventh Ward.

His empirical study combines urban ecology and urban ethnography (both of which became the primary modes of analysis of the Chicago school) in a creative way. He used both descriptive statistics and information from interviews he conducted with almost 10,000 individuals who lived in the area. Census data helped him identify broad general trends and a self-designed survey of the Seventh Ward provided more precise information about residents' geographic origins, marital status and family structure, education, employment (or lack thereof), the role of the church, housing conditions, and political beliefs and political actions (e.g., voting behavior). Du Bois collected ethnographic data to fill in the gaps about criminal activities and experiences of prejudice and discrimination. *The Philadelphia Negro* provides a "think description" and detailed portrait of African American culture in an influential American city.

Du Bois's theoretical breadth is remarkable for its time, and, if conducted today, would certainly garner accolades from scholars wed to differing theoretical paradigms. He was able to connect structural issues—what some today call "institutional racism"—to the experiential or social psychological issues of discrimination and prejudice. Instead of viewing these as separate realms of urban life, Du Bois saw how they were intimately related. Poverty, crime, and prejudice were intricately linked to both social structure and social interactions.

In his discussions of occupations and employment, Du Bois discusses the difficulties that many African Americans face when trying to obtain and then keep their jobs. If hired, they were often relegated to the lowest status position and were the first to be fired. There were two important consequences of this situation, and both tended to reinforce the social inequalities in the city.

First, Du Bois saw business owners as potential reformers by training and employing African Americans who, without opportunities for "legitimate" work, often turned to criminal activities to support themselves and their families. Of note, Du Bois, like most classic theorists, only discusses male workers. According to Du Bois, "A Negro woman has but three careers open to her in this city: domestic service, sewing, or married life" (1996, p. 322). The situation for African American males, however, was not much better. Du Bois thought that White employers would benefit from better-trained and healthier African American workers. This seemed like the rational option with a rational capitalist economy. What Du Bois found, however, was that irrational beliefs (e.g., racism) could still exist in a supposedly rational environment.

> If now a benevolent despot had seen the development [of the effects of race prejudice on Africa American employment], he would immediately have sought to remedy the real weakness of the Negro's position, i.e., his lack of training; and he would have swept away any discrimination that compelled men to support as criminals those who might support themselves as workmen. He would have made special effort to train Negro boys for industrial life and given them a chance to compete on equal terms with the best White workmen; arguing that in the long run this would be best for all concerned, since by raising the skill and standard of living of the Negroes he would make them effective workmen and competitors who would maintain a decent level of wages. He would have sternly suppressed organized or covert opposition to Negro workmen. *There was, however, no benevolent despot, no philanthropist, no far-seeing captain of industry to prevent the Negro from losing even the skill he had learned or to inspire him by opportunities to learn more* [emphasis added]. (1996, p. 127)

Without a "benevolent despot" to save the day, African American employment was low. Even when African Americans were hired, they were distrusted and treated poorly by White workers. Poor race relations thwarted worker solidarity that led to extended forms of alienation. In Du Bois's account of Philadelphia, the irrationality of racism trumps both "class consciousness" and economic self-interest.

The other important consequence of the linkage between structural racism and experienced discrimination is that it led to more alienation *within* the African American community. The Seventh Ward was not uniform. Instead, Du Bois uncovered a fairly rigid status hierarchy between the blocks of the neighborhood. Though they often corresponded with social class, race—or more precisely "color"—was a more influential

factor. Du Bois presented the distinctions as Grades 1 through 4 (often indicating lightest skin color to darkest):

> Grade 1: respectable families earning enough income to live well
>
> Grade 2: respectable working class with steady paying work
>
> Grade 3: the poor without a steady income
>
> Grade 4: criminals, prostitutes, and "loafers"

Du Bois argued that the "upper class" of African Americans had responsibility to "pull up" those beneath them, a clear allusion to how ethnic groups in the modern world are composed of people from different levels of society or social classes (Smith, 1985). Du Bois, as we saw above, believed the same about the relationship between Whites and African Americans. In the end, Du Bois points his finger at both communities and calls on them to work together to eradicate prejudice and discrimination. As Du Bois declares, "Surely here lies the first duty of a civilized city" (1996, p. 396). Du Bois's hopes for "a civilized city" are still alive today as witnessed by nonprofits, community organizations, and politically minded social movements.

CONCLUSION

As you have seen, the most important classical theorists and observers of city life were all concerned with the ways that this emerging form of human settlement and organization affected and would continue to affect social relations. Though a general pessimism about the city—whatever city—can easily be discerned for their respective writings, there were also some differences regarding how they saw the future, and the past. Figure 4.1 is an attempt to map each theorist's disposition (pessimistic versus optimistic) and their focus (urbanization versus urbanism).

Tocqueville saw the promise of cities borne of democratic values but only if their residents could replace older kinds of association with

Figure 4.1 Classical Theorists' Feelings About the Growth and Culture of Cities

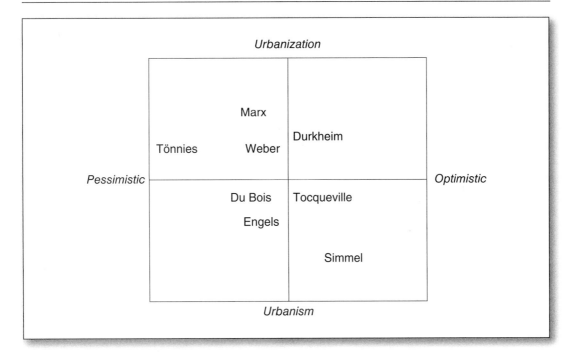

new ones. Though Marx is the grand theorist par excellence of capitalism's influence on the growth and experience of modern industrial cities, it was his comrade Engels who helped reveal Marx's insights through careful empirical analysis of urban social class relations and encounters. Both Marx and Engels recognized the problems with city life but welcomed them because of the potential roles that a concentrated mass of alienated workers could play to bring forth the revolution they desired. Tönnies also focused on the problems of the city, but instead of revolution to move things forward, he hoped for a revolution or at least a series of reforms that would halt urbanization and allow individuals to live more traditional, rural-like lives based on homogeneity rather than the heterogeneity of the urban populations. Durkheim embraced heterogeneity, seeing the importance of specialized labor and interests that could lead to new forms of association based on interdependence. Simmel feared what the city's environment might do to the way

that people think and act toward others, yet he greeted the potential liberating forces of urbanization that could lead to individual freedoms and creativity. Du Bois's analysis of city life shared some things with Simmel's since both attempted to connect the social structure to the lived experiences of urbanites. Du Bois, however, focused heavily on social problems connecting racial and ethnic divisions. Still, he saw the possibility that, if able to voice their concerns in a democratic and egalitarian manner, even the most downtrodden could shed their stigmatized social statuses and take part in the promises a city could offer.

The ways that these theorists—as well as many of their contemporaries who students might be interested in, from scholars like Sir Henry Sumner Maine and Gustave Le Bon to poets and novelists like Walt Whitman and Charles Dickens—interpreted city life was connected to the way they saw the past and the imagined future. As George Herbert Mead (1932) rightfully noted, "Every conception of the past is construed from the standpoint of the concerns and needs of the present" (p. 32). As such, it's important to recognize that all social theories are themselves embedded within specific historical, social and cultural contexts. It is important, then, for you to connect their classic statements about cities, suburbs, and towns to the histories of urbanization and urbanism discussed in previous chapters. The same goes for theorists and "schools of thought" presented in Chapter 5. We will see how theories and theorists in the 20th century and 21st century build on the foundations of the classic thinkers and how their ideas are responses to the growing and changing conditions of cities and the desires and demographics of their populations.

QUESTIONS FOR STUDY AND DISCUSSION

1. For each theorist presented in this chapter, imagine what they might say about contemporary cities like Los Angeles or Las Vegas. How might theses cities change their interpretations and how might they support them?

2. From what you've read about the classical theorists, what theoretical "seeds" or empirical questions have they provided for current and future scholars of cities, suburbs, and towns? Which ones are you most interested in and why?

3. Read a biography of one of these scholars. In your opinion, how did both the personal lives and the social context they were living in affect their interpretation of cities and communities?

5

THE FRUITS OF URBAN THEORY

Contemporary Perspectives on Cities and Communities

If the foundation of sociology was laid in the 19th century, the newly constructed discipline was more like a downtown apartment building than a single-family house in the "burbs." Sociology was built out of the same bricks and mortar that created cities. Due to the transformative processes of industrialization and urbanization, sociology was, at its core, a distinctly "urban" enterprise. Urban sociology became its own distinct subfield, inhabiting its own floor in that grand tenement of the discipline. But the urban focus of so many of the concerns addressed by people in the discipline as a whole is unmistakable and strong.

The main tenants on the urban sociology floor have changed over the course of the past century. Each owner has redecorated the hallways, stairwells, and elevators, and made renovations to the apartments on its floor. The 19th century theorists discussed in the last chapter were all concerned with questions about the transition from one form of social settlement (i.e., the traditional, homogenous, rural village or small town) to another (i.e., the modern, heterogeneous, industrialized city). Both literally and metaphorically, these theorists wandered into the city by themselves and, like many of those they found there, felt lost in the crowd. Alienation ruled the roost.

By the 20th century, the city had become a fact of life in the United States. Though cities were still growing and changing, they were here to stay. Schools of thought—rather than important individual thinkers—emerged to describe and make sense of the city, and they occupied different parts of the urban sociology floor. Like the people whose lives they sought to describe, they didn't necessarily get along and at times all but refused to recognize each other. The one thing they had in common, however, was their generally negative or pessimistic view of the city and its people.

The members of each school still call upon the 19th century theorists, though in varying ways and with different emphases, in order to tell their part of the urban story and investigate the social pathologies associated with urban life. These contemporary theorists added their own particular twist to the story and sometimes denied the importance of the other schools. As the size and influence of cities grew through the 20th century, new theories attempted to supplant older ones because new times need new theories. Yet, each new theory or school of thought still reached back in time to cull the seeds of the classical urbanists. That is why these schools turn out looking and sounding a great deal more like each other than they suppose or would care to acknowledge. In urban theory, as with many other elements of our lives, "everything new is old again." We build on the past rather than reject it.

This chapter outlines the dominant theoretical paradigms that have influenced urban and community research in the 20th century. Specifically, we will address the time-honored Chicago school, the neo-Marxian or Urban Political Economy approach, the postmodernist Los Angeles School, and the Urban Cultural Perspective. Though each "school" makes distinct contributions by building on and renovating the ideas that came before their own, the first three schools tend to look at the city and see "social disorganization" as its organizing principle and interpretive framework. Whether they describe the city as "a mosaic of social worlds" (Park, 1925/1967), residentially and racially "hypersegregated" (Massey & Denton, 1993), or a Keno-like collage (Dear, 2002) does not matter. They all see the city as fractured and fragmented, perhaps inevitably so. As such, we will see that many of the scholars that have studied urban and community life have followed the tenor of their European predecessors. The Urban Culturalist perspective—admittedly our preferred approach—draws upon the earlier theoretical schools but is not bound by their pinched view of cities and urban life. It is a more inductive and ultimately more optimistic approach that allows for both theoretical and methodological flexibility (Borer, 2006).

We contend that paying too much attention to "social disorganization"—which often comes from a general misunderstanding of the relationship between cities, suburbs, and towns—seems to tell only one type of story about contemporary urban social relations. Not telling other stories doesn't do justice to the people whose everyday lives become the most important plots for us to uncover. Though the floor where urban sociologists reside is in need of some major renovation, we nevertheless pay homage to those who built the load-bearing walls atop the settled yet shifting foundation laid down over a century ago.

THE CHICAGO SCHOOL OF URBAN SOCIOLOGY

Established in 1892 by Albion Small, the Department of Sociology at the University of Chicago was the first sociology department in the United States. Under the early guidance of Small and W. I. Thomas—whose call to study social actors' point of view or "definition of the situation" remains one of our most important dictums—the Chicago sociologists adopted a "progressive"/ "reformist" stance in response to the perceived injustices and inequities of the city they were living in and investigating. The notion of the city as a research laboratory emerged from their in-depth studies of different Chicago neighborhoods, social settings like dance halls, and classes of people. It is not too far-fetched to say that Chicago is probably the most well documented city in the contemporary world.

The numbers alone made the city a great lab. Chicago's population skyrocketed from about 500,000 in 1880 to about 2 million by 1910. Such a boom in population brought both European immigrants and rural American migrants who were unfamiliar with the newly burgeoning urban cultural ways of life into contact with one another.

Given such drastic changes within a relatively short period of time, it is not surprising that ideas about instability, alienation, and "anomie" would influence their studies. As Maurice Stein (1964) has written:

> Durkheim's analysis of suicide, in which he showed how social differentiation releases men from group ties and moral constraints on to leave them isolated and without values that confer meaning on life, underlies much of the theorizing of the urban sociologists. . . . Small wonder that the Chicago sociologists focused on the absence of established institutional patterns in so many regions of the city, stressing that the neighborhood grew and changed so rapidly that sometimes the only constant feature appeared to be mobility... and why "disorganization" accompanied "mobility." (pp. 16, 18)

The type and frequency of mobility they saw taking place in front of them was in stark contrast to the geographic stability of traditional rural life that some of them experienced as children or heard stories about from their families and from their intellectual ancestors, the 19th century theorists.

Critical of "armchair theorizing," the Chicago sociologists set out to provide empirically based ways to observe and understand city life. While some set out to uncover the stories of the immigrants and migrants, others sought to outline the overarching ecological structure of the city by the way people populated and used the land. An early member of the Chicago school, Robert Park—a former journalist and former part-time student of Georg Simmel—understood the importance of firsthand observations and experiences of and within the urban environment. He pushed his students, and colleagues, to explore the city as a social laboratory:

> You have been told to go grubbing in the library, thereby accumulating a mass of notes and a liberal coating of grime. You have been told to choose problems where you can find musty stacks of routine records based on trivial schedules prepared by bureaucrats and filled out by reluctant applicants for aid or fussy do-gooders or indifferent clerks. This is called "getting your hands dirty in real research." Those who counsel you are wise and honorable; the reasons they offer are of great value. But one more thing is needful; firsthand observation. Go and sit in the lounges of luxury hotels and on the doorsteps of the flophouses; sit on the Gold Coast settees and on the slum shakedowns; sit in the Orchestra Hall and in the Star and Garter Burlesque. In short, gentlemen, go and get the seat of your pants dirty in real research. (quoted in McKinney, 1966, p. 71)

Motivated by this intellectual "call to arms," Park, his colleagues, and his students set out to uncover the intricacies of their city. Collectively, they investigated urbanism—the ways of life in cities—via ethnographic field work. They also sought to uncover the forces of urbanization—the development and growth of the city—via quantitative data and ecological suppositions. Together, they hoped to reveal both the unique

details of Chicago's urban mosaic and the outer frame that holds that "natural" parts together.

Regardless of their individual interests, *the Chicago school members' studies were based on the assumption that the city functioned like a living organism*. This organism was made up of two separate levels that "mutually interact in characteristic ways to mold and modify one another" (Park, 1925/1967, p. 4). The two levels are the "biotic" and the "cultural." The biotic, or symbiotic, level determined the structure of the city resulting from inhabitants' competition for scarce resources. The cultural level was driven by communication and consensus. Culture, then, was as an adaptive response to the changes that were happening at around them. The structural changes at the biotic level, like population growth, were forcing cultures to change and adjust to the new social environment of the city. We will address their two ways of thinking and investigating urban life separately in the next two sections. It bears noting, however, that in the language of science, culture in this scheme was a "dependent variable" not an "independent variable." It was an effect rather than a cause of the larger economic and population changes occurring around people, changes over which they seemingly had little control.

URBAN ETHNOGRAPHY: URBANISM AS A WAY OF LIFE

Members of the Chicago school who focused on urbanism followed a general rule that the many parts (i.e., neighborhoods, enclaves, subcultures) that made up the whole of the city needed to be described and explained. There was no single overarching way of life or culture to which everyone or most people, classes, races, and so forth would subscribe to or embrace as their own. Instead, there were different "subcultures." Each "subculture" was unique.

These ethnographers took to the streets to investigate the varying adaptive responses to urban environment that resided with these separate social worlds. *Separated by the dominant attributes of ethnicity, race, and class, each social world offered its own lessons on urban survival. Moreover, because the city was dependent upon a highly specialized division of labor, various occupations were studied to show the variety of ways people had learned to make a living in what was often viewed as harsh and cutthroat setting.* Park (1925/1967) offered the following list of both mainstream and "deviant" vocations for urban ethnographers to investigate:

> The effects of the division of labor as a discipline, i.e., as mean of molding character, may therefore be best studied in the vocational types it has produced. Among the types which it would be interesting to study are: the shopgirl, the policeman, the peddler, the cabman, the night watchman, the clairvoyant, the vaudeville performer, the quack doctor, the bartender, the ward boss, the strikebreaker, the labor agitator, the school teacher, the reporter, the stockbroker, the pawnbroker; *all of these are characteristic products of the conditions of the city, each with its special experience, insight, and point of view determines for each vocational group and for the city as a whole its individuality* [emphasis added]. (p. 14)

We can already see here *the development of a theory of cultural adaptation as well as a theory about the influence of a city's divisions of labor on its culture.* The little worlds that make up the city's mosaic—each with their own forms of adaptation and vocational specializations—added to the overall diversity of the city. Again, each one was worthy of investigation.

Park's colleagues and students took this task seriously. The Chicago school produced an immense amount of firsthand accounts of the city's various social worlds from the beginning of the 1920s and into the next couple of decades. Some of the social worlds, like those you might find in an ethnic enclave, were bound by location and proximity. Others addressed specific "social pathologies" related to various vocational types and social positions like gamblers and taxi hall dancers. Along with the abundance of dissertations and theses produced during that

period, a number of books were published (all by the venerable University of Chicago Press). These became instant classics of urban sociology as well as other subfields like criminology, deviance, and ethnic and race relations. A sampling of publications reveals the array of topics available for study in Chicago:

> Nels Anderson's *The Hobo* (1923); Frederick M. Thrasher's *The Gang* (1927); Louis Wirth's *The [Jewish] Ghetto*; Ruth S. Cavan's *Suicide* (1928); Clifford S. Shaw's *The Jack-Roller* (1930); Harvey W. Zorbaugh's *The Gold Coast and the Slum* (1929); E. Franklin Frazier's *The Negro Family in Chicago* (1932); Paul G. Cressey's *The Taxi-Dance Hall* (1932); Walter C. Reckless's *Vice in Chicago* (1933); Norman Hayner's *Hotel Life* (1936); and St. Clair Drake and Horace R. Cayton's *Black Metropolis* (1945).

While each study examined "a distinct world, with its own way of acting, talking, and thinking" (Cressey, 1969, p. 31), when viewed together, they provide important insights about the diversity of Chicago's growing population. Ulf Hannerz (1980) called the Chicago ethnographers' collection of studies a "cooperative ethnography . . . [an] achievement worth noting because it has scarcely been paralleled elsewhere" (p. 54). These studies all support Park's (1925/1967) seminal claim that the city is "a mosaic of social worlds which touch but do not interpenetrate" (p. 40). Though the lack of overlap and connection between social worlds was overstated by the Chicago school, these studies provide a wealth of evidence about the heterogeneous nature of city life.

Heterogeneity became a staple for defining the demographic structure of a city. In his seminal essay, "Urbanism as a Way of Life," the most explicit statement of the Chicago school's urban theory of social disorganization, Louis Wirth (1938) argues that heterogeneity, along with size and density, are the three most important determining factors of city life.

> The central problem of the sociologist of the city is to discover the forms of social action and organization that typically emerge in relatively

permanent, compact settlements of large numbers of heterogeneous individuals. We must also infer that urbanism will assume its most characteristic and extreme form in the measure in which the conditions with which it is congruent are present. Thus the larger, the more densely populated, and the more heterogeneous a community, the more accentuated the characteristics associated with urbanism will be. (p. 9)

For Wirth, these independent variables—size, density, and heterogeneity—*determine*, or automatically produce, the ways that people act, talk, and think in cities. And, according to Wirth, those ways had a uniformly bad impact for both individual psyches and social relationships.

Wirth offered a number of propositions based on these three determining variables to show how a distinct culture emerges from the city. But Wirth's interpretation of urbanism is based on a pessimism inherited from past theorists' writings. Most notably, Wirth takes Simmel's ideas about urban anonymity and puts them at the center of his depiction of urbanism, arguing that the move from primary (e.g., family ties) to secondary social relations (e.g., labor unions and large-scale corporations) is inherently destructive to human affairs. Though Wirth provides a succinct and generalizable definition of the city with propositions that have been tested (and, for the most part, have been found untrue), he failed to show exactly how urbanism, as "as a way of life," worked. This criticism, however, could be pointed toward the Chicago school's more "macro" minded scholars of urbanization. To their credit, however, they were not trying to understand the ways people act, talk, and think in cities. Instead, they sought to develop a view of the totality of the city in order to understand how it functioned as singular, living, and barely breathing entity.

URBAN ECOLOGY: OF PEOPLE AND PLANTS

While the Chicago ethnographers were getting their hands dirty and shoes scuffed in all the enclaves and subcultures that they studied, their ecologist brethren were asking other questions about the structure and form of the city. The answers to those questions, however, provided an overarching rationale for the ethnographers' studies of the distinct social worlds located across the divided terrain of the city's natural areas. The ecologists wanted to understand the *natural* forces behind the city's growth and diverse population. They were interested in uncovering the *natural* laws of population distribution and the *natural* processes that determined the winners and losers of successful adaptation to the urban environment. Note that *natural* has been italicized to highlight the emphasis that the Chicago school put on the analogous connection of people and plants. They believed that the city was a superorganism where competition for space was relegated to the "fittest." This, of course, dismisses the importance of other factors ranging from the tangible (like wealth) to the intangible (like feelings). But let's first lay out the "urban ecological" perspective before we begin dissecting it, for there is some merit to using a biological metaphor, though mostly as a heuristic device or conceptual stand-in for more precise or appropriate terminology.

Beginning with the writings of Roderick McKenzie and then fully elaborated by Ernest Burgess and Amos Hawley, the urban ecologists promoted the view that human community life functioned like other biological communities. Like any other organism, human beings must adapt to their surroundings and fend off potential dangers. The biological battle for existence was correlated with the economic competition for space. Those who couldn't compete were relegated to the bowels of history or, more to the point, the bowels of the city. The most successful communities and people would take over the "best" areas of the city and have a higher survival rate. Chicago ecologists also paid attention to the ways that urban dwellers cooperated for the sake of mutual survival and defense against successive waves, or "invasions," of newcomers and migrants. Emphasizing *natural* competition and cooperation suggested that the city's spatial structure was a result of *natural* processes that were out of reach of human participation and engineering.

One of the most enduring legacies of the Chicago school ecologists was the construction of an idealized urban model intended to visually depict the biological processes that created the city and the divisions within it. Ernest Burgess's "concentric-zone model" (1925, pp. 47–62) showed how patterns of land use reflect successive phases of invasion and occupation. The outcome was a series of concentric circles or zones with the central business district (CBD) placed firmly in the center. This was the hub of and for the city's economic activity. The highest land values were in this zone. Moving outward, the CBD was surrounded by a "zone of transition" that was perpetually under threat of being invaded by businesses and industries with growing commercial interests. Those who could leave this vulnerable area did. But those who couldn't, those who couldn't afford to move, were forced to stay in this area. As such, this zone contained marginal populations, from immigrants to criminals to the mentally ill, and became an area known for poverty and vice. This is where the Jewish ghetto, Little Sicily, Chinatown, and parts of the Black Belt were located.

The next zone was for the assimilated and upwardly mobile, like the children of immigrants. Burgess called this the "zone of working-men's homes." The second generation immigrants and the factory laborers who lived there weren't poor but they weren't wealthy enough to own land or their own apartments. The "residential zone," instead, was populated by the middle class, mostly white-collar employees and small business owners and managers. They lived in newer, or at least renovated, apartments and single-family homes. Crime rates were significantly lower in this zone than the working class's *natural area*, which was less crime-ridden than the "zone of transition" just outside the CBD. The last and farthest-away zone was what most would recognize as the suburbs. This was the "commuters' zone," filled with residents who were dependent upon the city for their jobs but

economically successful enough to live in the safer periphery of the city.

With some notable artistic license necessary in order to deal with Lake Michigan (which cut the zones in half down a north–south line) Burgess's model was a pretty accurate description of the residential segregation of Chicago. But *it was intended to do more than describe Chicago; the goal was to show the social patterns one would expect to find in all industrial cities*. Because Burgess painted in broad strokes when making his model, it was easily susceptible to criticisms that led others—including his own colleagues—to offer their own modified layouts of the city.

Most notable were Homer Hoyt's "sector model" (1939) and Chauncy Harris and Edward Ullman's "multiple nuclei model" (1945). Hoyt's "sector model" was based on the idea that cities' growth patterns depended on their main lines of transportation. Transport corridors would produce patterns of intense competition for land and real estate around them. Instead of concentric zones, "the city was pictured more like a starfish or a spoked wheel" (Karp et al., 1991, p. 55). Harris and Ullman disagreed with both configurations. Their "multiple nuclei model" de-emphasized the CBD in favor of a more de-centralized vision of the city. Their model suggests that multiple nuclei develop in areas that have a specific concentration of specialized activities and facilities, like manufacturing, shopping, or education.

Models like these continue to be criticized because of their reliance on biological analogies or their attempt to depict complex social realities in grossly simplified forms. Many of the critiques based on empirical research are valid (i.e., cities aren't arranged in exactly the same way). At the same time, they often underestimate the ingenuity of the model builders who, for the first time in history, tried to present and explain the patterned spatial divisions of cities through visual means. The pedagogical and heuristic value of these models remains high, even if one disagrees with the ecologists' one-size-fits-all modeling of a complex urban form.

One of the major problems with the Chicago school's ethnographic and ecological studies is the lack of attention to culture as a productive force. Culture was often assumed to be only reactionary (the dependent variable referred to earlier). Larger natural forces emerging over the competition for land shaped human relations. As such, human agency, or human action, is underdeveloped in their analyses.

If human agency isn't part of a model or theory of urban life, then how can social reform be possible? The Urban Political Economists try to answer this question and amend the lack of agency in urban theory by focusing on the political and economic interests of powerful players. However, they also look at culture as something of lesser importance. For now, let's see how the Urban Political Economy perspective challenged and subsequently usurped the Chicago school's dominant point of view in urban sociology.

URBAN POLITICAL ECONOMY AND THE "NEW" URBAN SOCIOLOGY

In the late 1960s and early 1970s, social and political unrest in urban areas grew, in part, from increased racial polarization and restrictive government policies. Urban scholars were prompted to find new ways for understanding these emerging realities of city life (Walton 1993, p. 302, Kleniewski, 1997, p. 35). New forms of urban analysis drew upon Max Weber's writing and the rediscovered ideas of Karl Marx (and to a lesser extent Friedrich Engels) in order to explain what the Chicago school's biologically deterministic theories couldn't. Developed under a few different names, this newly emerging perspective was tied together by few base assumptions that directly challenged the Chicago school's approach (Kleniewski, 1997, p. 37). Of particular importance is the idea that *a city's form and growth are not the result of "natural processes," but come from decisions made by people and organizations that control wealth and other key resources.* As such, powerful decision makers were responsible for the conditions of cities

rather than some abstract evolutionary principles. Due to its emphasis on powerful actors, this perspective—generally recognized as the Urban Political Economy approach—quickly became, and perhaps still remains, the dominant theoretical paradigm of urban sociology.

People were more powerful than the Chicago school allowed, and the power that some people yielded could be used to help some while hurting others. Weber's ideas about the ways that key actors influence the distribution of social goods provided theoretical and historical weight sociologists to explore how such actors controlled urban assets and land markets. Such individuals and organizations included real estate investors and agents, urban planners, housing managers, police, policy makers, mortgage lenders, and financiers. It was argued that these individual and collective actors could determine which social groups and populations could gain access to particular property markets.

In one of the first books to adopt this new perspective and address these issues, *Whose City? and Other Essays on Sociology and Planning*, Ray Pahl (1970) argues that

> a truly urban sociology should be concerned with the social and spatial constraints on access to scarce urban resources and facilities as dependent variables and managers or controllers of the urban system, which I take as the independent variable. (p. 221)

Human agency is intricately connected to conflicts over the distribution of resources that, in turn, have consequences on urban forms and social arrangements. Focusing on this type of inequality dispelled any notion that housing and land markets were in any way open to "free" market competition or biological cooperation. But it also pigeonholed those who adopt this paradigm into an economic determinism. Solidarity and cooperation are impossible because the city forces people to view others only as players of segmented roles or cogs within the urban "growth machine" (Logan & Molotch, 1987; Gottdeiner & Feagin, 1988). As such, social solidarity is viewed as an unachievable goal and not a reality under the conditions of cities dependent upon capitalism for growth and sustenance.

The "new" urban sociology, then, sought to explain cities as part of larger story about class conflict, capital accumulation, and ideological control. Urban theorists directly inspired by the Marxian theories—like David Harvey, Manuel Castells, and Henri Lefebvre—transformed general theories about the "evil and avaricious capitalist system" (Harvey, 1973, p. 133) into explanations about the struggle for urban space.

Harvey argues that the continual redevelopment of certain areas of cities (i.e., *not* the areas that with the most need) is a consequence of profit-motivated capitalists. Speculators and developers are given the freedom to invest in what, whom, and where they want without interference from, and sometimes with the help of, the local and federal government. According to Harvey, this tends to benefit affluent Whites and hurts poor African Americans and other minorities who have trouble obtaining loans to buy houses. From this vantage point, Harvey (1973) stresses the role of the built environment as commodity and as a source of profit and loss.

> Under capitalism there is a perpetual struggle in which capital builds a physical landscape appropriate to its own condition at a particular moment in time, only to have to destroy it, usually in the course of a crisis, at a subsequent point in time. The temporal and geographical ebb and flow of investment in the built environment can be understood only in the terms of such a process. The effects of the internal contradictions of capitalism, when projected into the specific context of fixed and immobile investment in the built environment, are thus writ large in the historical geography of the landscape that results. (p. 124)

The urban landscape is subject to the contradictory impulses of investment and disinvestment by the power elite pushed by a desire to divide upper-class and working-class residential areas in order to avoid potential confrontation. This type of residential segregation, in turn, creates an unevenly developed environment differentiated by high and low land values that benefit the capitalist class at the expense of the "underclass."

From the Urban Political Economy perspective, the city is viewed as a profit-making machine that is fed by the reconstruction and redevelopment of the built environment, basically wherever revenue can be generated. Manuel Castells (1977) connected Marxist theories to the city by interpreting the dual roles of the city as a unit of production (similar to Harvey's ideas) and a locus of social reproduction. Uneven and unequal social relations are reproduced by both individuals' consumption of things like food and clothing and their collective consumption of things like housing and other social services (e.g., hospitals, schools, and parks). Castells argues that the state is a tool for the wealthy. Therefore, cities are organized so that the state provides minimal social services and facilities needed to reproduce and maintain a flexible, somewhat educated, and a mostly healthy workforce at the lowest cost possible. This includes the provision of often cheaply and poorly built government subsidized housing. Castells deemed such housing inadequate.

Castells stresses that the spatial form of the city reproduces the contradictions of capitalism that Marx outlined long ago for cities that exhibited great disparities in wealth. For Castells (2000), capitalism reinforced the idea that "spatial transformation must be understood in the broader context of social transformation: *space does not reflect society, it expresses it, it is a fundamental dimension of society*" (p. 293, emphasis added). As such, he criticized the Chicago School as well as other scholars who unrealistically approached the city as a distinct ecology that was somehow independent of the larger capitalist system that stretched well beyond the city's, borders. Castells (1977) outlined the need for so-called "structural" readings of the city:

> It is a question of going beyond the description of mechanisms of interaction between activities and locations, in order to *discover the structural laws of the production and functioning of the spatial*

forms studied. . . . There is not specific theory of space, but quite simply a deployment and specification of the theory of social structure, in order to account for the characteristics of the particular social form, space, and its articulation with other historically given forms and processes [emphasis added]. (p. 124)

Castells's structural take on cities is intended to correct the idea that urban space was shaped by the knowledge and action of those who live, work, and play in them. This supposed corrective, however, thrusts Castells—as well as other Marxist-oriented theorists—to the other extreme whereby *the spatial forms of the city are determined by forces outside of the control of everyday people.*

By answering the question—"is there an urban sociology?"—with a negative response, Castells continued a long tradition of seeking out the basic defining features and contours of the city. Castells's radical take on the "urban question" sent a shock wave throughout urban studies with his insistence that the social processes that produced the city were not distinctly urban but, rather, endemic to capitalist society.

Discussing Castells pivotal role in the development of a "new" urban sociology, one explicitly linked to Marxist critiques of capitalism, John Walton (1993) writes:

In brief, Castells argued that urban sociology had no "real" or concrete object because "urban" referred only vaguely to things not rural than to some specific phenomenon. Rather, urban sociology (or "ideology") was concerned with certain activities such as social groups that formed communities, created a subculture, and avoided anomie, none of them intrinsically urban. . . . Castells's mock "astonishment" at the lack of a uniquely urban theoretical object, and his consequent characterization of the field as "ideological," was no more than a forceful rhetorical device for arguing, as others have before and since, that urban sociology would gain more coherence by focusing on a particular set of problems that lend themselves to explanation from a preferred theoretical orientation. (pp. 304–305).

Just like the Chicago School which took Park's "call to arms" seriously and went out and hit the streets to explore the distinct social worlds of the city, a new generation of urban scholars influenced by Castells set out to study the processes and effects of the most dominant institutions that shape cities: economics and politics. The foundational assumption for these scholars is the idea that *cities are products of the forces of capitalism and are therefore influenced by and are a part of a global political economy.* Such a claim has led to a vast amount of research on world-systems theory (Wallerstein, 1979; Smith & Timberlake, 1995), globalization (Short, 2004), and "global cities" (Sassen 2001, 2002, 2010).

Many studies by Urban Political Economists provide a fresh viewpoint by unhinging the city from its territorial boundaries and looking at it within a broader global context. These studies are a far cry from the Chicago school's attempt to uncover the intimate details of a city's varied and unique social worlds. Yet, they still tend to favor the idea that "social disorganization" is the ruling principle of city life regardless of its existence as single entity or as a node in an expanding cross-national network. Urban Political Economists dismiss traditional Chicago-style urban sociology while still maintaining the belief in "social disorganization." A similar coupling of older and newer ideas about urban life is part of the so-called postmodern approach. We will see how this plays out in the next section during our brief trip to Los Angeles.

POSTMODERNISM AND THE LOS ANGELES SCHOOL

As cities, and the world around them, changed during the last quarter of the 20th century, theorists sought new ways to understand urban life. Across many fields and disciplines, postmodernism became very trendy and gained momentum in the 1980s because it is a purposefully fragmented point of view. Since the world is fragmented and unstable and therefore unable to be understood by one single "grand narrative," so too are postmodern theories. Drawing from multiple sources across historical periods and disciplinary borders, postmodern urban theories reflect the hodgepodge and mismatched spatial forms of the supposed postmodern city. Where the modern city was defined by industrialization and production, the postmodern city is defined by consumption, simulation, and the "thrill of spectacle" (Hannigan, 1998, p. 4). Social life in the postmodern city is dictated by the whims of consumers who, as Sharon Zukin (1991) claims, desire to be pacified by the imaginary fantasy land of Disney. Postmodern urbanists argue that "rampant consumption and instant gratification are the leitmotif of life in postmodern cities" (Borer, 2006, p. 178), and the place that embodies those beliefs to the fullest degree is Los Angeles.

Geographer Edward Soja (1989) was the first to label LA the quintessential postmodern city and harbinger of what cities are today and will be tomorrow. "Los Angeles is the place where 'it all comes together'. . . . One might call the sprawling urban region a paradigmatic place" (p. 191). His description of the multiple worlds merged together in LA's downtown area provides some indicators of the newly developing forms of fragmentation in the city.

> There is a dazzling array of sites in the compartmentalized corona of the inner city: the Vietnamese and Hong Kong housing of a redeveloping Chinatown; the Big Tokyo finance modernization; the induced pseudo-SoHo of artists' lofts and galleries . . . the strangely anachronistic wholesale markets . . . the capital of urban homelessness in the Skid Row district; the enormous muralled barrio stretching eastward toward East Los Angeles . . . the intentionally yuppifying South Park redevelopment zone hard by the slightly seedy Convention Center, the revenue-milked towers and fortresses of Bunker Hill. (pp. 239–240)

If you find Soja's portrayal of LA is confusing and disorienting, then he's actually done his job well because he wants the reader to *feel* what LA *feels* like when they read about it.

Believers and participants in postmodernism are devoted to using purposely imprecise and metaphorical language for analyzing contemporary urban life. Of course, the use of metaphors is an effective, and sometimes necessary, rhetorical device for deciphering complex problems. And metaphors have played important roles in the ways urban sociologists view and discuss cities: "the city" as a bazaar, a jungle, an organism, a machine, etc. (see Langer, 1984). But postmodernists' metaphors, purposefully, never refer back to anything socially or morally substantial because, so the argument goes, the "real" is only a representation that "bears no relation to any reality whatsoever: it is its own pure simulacrum" (Baudrillard, 1983, p. 11). Janet Wolff claims that postmodern urban studies are intended to disrupt and demolish the boundaries between "the real city" and "the discursive city" in irreparable ways (p. 553). From this point of view, there is no difference between what we talk about and our talking about it.

In order to talk about the fractured nature of postmodern cities like Los Angeles, Michael Dear, along with a few co-authors of various "manifesto"-like articles, has tried to develop a new language for discussing postmodern urbanism. For example, the term "Keno capitalism" (Dear & Flusty, 1998; Dear, 2002) is used to describe the random, lotto-like patterning of the spatial structure of Los Angeles, which looks a lot different from traditional modernist cities like Chicago. A new language and a new model were devised to depict new urban realities connected to technological advancements in transportation and communication. Dear and Flusty (1998) introduce some of the new language in connection to the supposedly new social conditions of postmoderntiy:

> Urban process is driven by global restructuring that is permeated and balkanized by a series of interdictory networks; whose populations are social and culturally heterogeneous, but politically and economically polarized; whose residents are educated and persuaded to the consumption of dreamscapes even as the poorest are consigned to carceral cities; whose built environment, reflective of these processes, consists of edge cities, privatopias, and the like, and whose natural environment, also reflective of these processes, is being erased to the point of unlivability. (pp. 59–60)

The so-called LA school—which seems to exist in name only because, in part, it is admittedly "pathologically antileaderhsip" (Dear & Flusty, 2002, p. 11)—purposely presents a model at odds with the Chicago school's ecological models.

Yet all of the talk about fragmentation is, in the end, simply a reiteration of the "social disorganization" thesis that originated in Chicago. Moreover, no matter how much Dear and others appear to embrace postmodernism's abhorrence of grand narratives (i.e., macro-structural explanations of human behavior), they fall back on the assumptions that underpinned explanations of the modernist cities (e.g., economic determinism). Addressing urban sociology's "postmodern challenge," Kevin Fox Gotham (2001) correctly detects the similarity between the LA school and the political economists. "Despite [the postmodernists'] different analyses and conclusions, their work remains rooted in Marxian theory, highlighting the centrality of economic and material processes in cultural analysis" (p. 66). As such, it's hard to find what is new here. This is a shame because Los Angeles and other western "Sun Belt" cities such as Phoenix, Houston, and Las Vegas are different from Chicago. The main point is that these cities are not so radically different that new words need to be invented to make sense of them.

Once stripped of their neologisms, abstruse references, and images of dystopian gloom (see Davis, 1998, 2002.), the city and the people within it are hard to find. Barred by the trappings of postmodernism's "architectural determinism" (Lees, 1994, p. 446), the LA school forgot to include the most important part of urban studies: the people who live, work, and play in the cities we study. In response to Dear and Flusty (1998), Peter Jackson (1999) correctly spotted the LA school's "ethnographic void." He found "no ethnographic component to Dear and Flusty's review of current work on Los Angeles and no reference to such work in the agenda outlined for future research. Instead, their prose is populated with the cool abstractions of social polarization and fragmentation" (p. 401). As such, they have no way of knowing how people practice urbanism and thereby are unable to evaluate how well their practices work.

Even though the Chicago school had a strong ethnographic agenda that brought researchers into the distinct social worlds of Chicago, they still saw culture as *reactive* rather than *proactive* (i.e., a dependent variable rather than an independent variable). Individuals and groups are forced to respond to the large ecological processes that pushed and pulled them in and out of different areas of the city. The Urban Political Economists agreed, but contended the pushing and pulling wasn't "natural" but a response to decision made by powerful elites in pursuit of business interests. The postmodernists share the same view, but with no good end in sight. In many ways, they're Marxists without the revolution. As such, all three schools lack a sufficient and thorough understanding or appreciation of culture and the work that people do to maintain and/or reconstruct their urban worlds. Gerald Suttles's (1984, p. 283) remark that "practically everyone seems to give local sentiments and culture passing attention, but that is usually the end of it" still rings true almost 30 years later.

Ignoring culture has left us with a diminished understanding of urbanism and the everyday experiences of people in the city. Our approach—presented in brief in the next section and exemplified throughout this book—focuses on the connection between urbanization and urbanism. We give urbanism—the ways people construct and practice urban culture and community—its long overdue day in the sun.

THE URBAN CULTURALIST PERSPECTIVE

Influenced by symbolic interactionist writings on everyday life in cities (e.g., Karp, Stone, & Yoels, 1991; Lofland, 1998) and cultural sociology's imperative to analyze "meaning-making" (e.g., Spillman, 2002), the Urban Culturalist perspective focuses attention on the practices and processes of culture and community-building in cities. Urban Culturalists explicitly investigate the symbolic relationship between people and places and the ways that places are given meaning and value. The development and redevelopment of the urban-built environment is viewed as a means for understanding cultural values, ideas, and practices (e.g., Monti, 1990; Bridger, 1996; Lofland, 1998; Milligan, 1998; 2003; Borer, 2008). The overarching goal is to understand the ways the people contribute, in varying degrees and with varying reasons, to the social life of cities. The city, therefore, is viewed as a collective accomplishment.

The Urban Culturalist perspective is *place*-based, but it is not *city*-based. That is, one city is not viewed as *the* city that absolutely exemplifies the 21st century urbanism in the way that Los Angeles, as well as Miami (Nijman, 2000) or New York (Halle, 2003; Halle & Beveridge, 2011), has been presented by contemporary scholars. City-based theories are problematic because they not only lack sticking points for making comparisons between cities (and between cities, suburbs, and towns) but, as Robert Beauregard (2003, 2011) successfully argues, they tend to favor particular cities and schools where scholars reside. Beauregard (2011) is skeptical of city-based theories because they tend to be exclusionary and consequently damaging to the utility of urban studies.

> In addition, by fueling radical uniqueness, a proliferation of city-based theories diminishes what cities have in common and often denies that an "ordinary" city can add value to urban theory. Instead the claim is that some cities have theoretical value and other cities do not. The latter receive theory; the former create it. Thus, what is needed is not an acceptance of city-based urban theories but a critical spirit that fosters skepticism. (p. 199)

The Urban Culturalist perspective adheres to this skepticism. With the exception of a few seminal works that address intra-urban phenomena such as civic culture (Monti, 1999, 2012), interactions in public places (Lofland, 1998), and gentrification (Brown-Saracino, 2009), much of the work that comes from this perspective is based on specific case studies. Regardless, these scholars

are keenly aware of the ways that certain places become unique or, for that matter, ordinary. In fact, "place making" becomes an object of inquiry (Borer, 2010).

Most urban sociologists begin with a social problem or phenomenon then seek out places in the city or cities they're investigating where that problem or phenomenon happens or happened. The Urban Culturalist perspective prompts scholars to begin with a place and ask an open and inductive question: "what happens or happened here?" Starting from a place, *then* moving outward can yield important and unexpected findings. This provides opportunities for researchers to build new ideas and theories from the ground up instead of making and then "testing" assumptions. This does not mean that researchers shouldn't be aware of past theories or past research on the area and population they're studying. Elijah Anderson (2002) made this point well:

> The ethnographer should enter the field armed with a certain sociological sophistication, even a theoretical perspective that, as the fieldwork proceeds, helps to formulate questions concerning the social organization of the subjects and their settings. The orienting questions should emerge from the local knowledge the researcher gains from the field setting, not just from his or her intellectual preconceptions. . . . In fact, the most penetrating ethnographic questions often result from a fusion of concerns that reflect both the ethnographer's engagement of the social setting as well as his or her own sociological orientation. (pp. 1536–1537)

Anderson is critical of what he calls the "ideologically driven" studies conducted by, in particular, urban sociologists who adopt a Marxian or Urban Political Economy approach (e.g., Wacquant, 2002). Instead of letting theories drive the research, it is important, if not necessary, to let the community's "local knowledge" dictate the direction of the research. That is, we need to allow community members to speak about what matters to them and allow them to reveal the realities of their life to us, rather than the other way around.

Even while allowing "local knowledge" to play a central role, Urban Culturalists still bring certain theories and "sensitizing concepts" with them into the field. There are six keys areas of theoretical and empirical concern that Urban Culturalists have contributed to and continue to cultivate: (1) images and representations of the city; (2) urban community and civic culture; (3) place-based myths, narratives, and collective memories; (4) sentiment and meaning *of* and *for* places; (5) urban identities and lifestyles; and (6) interaction places and practices. This can be used in a comparative framework for studying the similarities and distinctions between types of places and the people who use and inhabit them.

"Cities are the largest thing human beings have built that actually work," wrote Daniel Monti (1999, p. 18). Because of a city's physical size, as well as the large number of people within it, it is impossible for individuals to understand "the city" in its totality. We tend to see only parts of it. And those parts tend to signify the rest of the city, for better and for worse. In their seminal essay, "Symbolic Representations and the Urban Milieu" (1958), R. Richard Wohl and Anselm Strauss were concerned with the ways that urbanites construct symbolic images of the city in order to avoid an "anomic" breakdown in the face of the vast metropolis. In some ways, they echo Simmel's concerns, showing that the creation of symbolic representations of the city is a coping mechanism, like the blasé attitude (Simmel, 1971a; Wirth, 1938), necessary for dealing with the city's potentially overwhelming physicality.

Because the city is so large, these representations are essential for urban living. They become the foundation for a common language within the city and between other cities and regions. Wohl and Strauss showed that people attach these representations to both natural and artificial objects. Artifacts located throughout the city (e.g., trees, rivers, parks, buildings, street corners, and neighborhoods) can all become symbolic markers. Some of these become synonymous with the city itself.

Thus the delicate and majestic sweep of the Golden Gate Bridge stands for San Francisco, a brief close-up of the French Quarter identifies New Orleans, and . . . a view of the New York skyline from the Battery is the standing equivalent for the city. So well understood is this symbol that a movie can establish its locale by doing no more than flashing a picture of (New York's) skyscrapers on the screen for a moment and then directing the camera into the opening episode of the film. This coded, shorthand expression is at once understood by the audience. (Wohl & Strauss, 1958, p. 526)

These objects, these places, help groups identify the city and also provide a means for personal identification with the city. Viewers see these widely known images in movies and on television and are able to situate the characters in their appropriate context.

Symbolic representations are potentially open to all, inside and outside the city. Symbolic representations can provide, at least minimally, a semblance of order by providing a means into an *inclusive* urban community. Such images or representations can create "common referents" as part of a common "cultural literacy" for urban dwellers and visitors (Demerath & Levinger, 2003, p. 221). Acting as common reference points, they allow for the possibility of dialogue between groups within the city.

Gerald Suttles called attention to various cities' respective "urban iconography" by clarifying the physical and spatial objects that are deemed meaningful in cities. He sought to make the analysis of cultural meanings objectively accessible and empirically observable by focusing on urbanites' "collective representations." In order to detect the "cumulative texture of local culture," Suttles (1984) directs our attention toward the things that people put in museums (i.e., high culture) and what they put on their car bumpers and T-shirts (i.e., popular culture) "because these objective artifacts give local culture much of its stability and continuing appeal" (p. 284) are both given and passed down by "expert" culture makers and workers (e.g., novelists, journalists, architects, museum curators, and archivists) *and* acted upon and reworked by both residents and visitors.

Recent works by Urban Culturalists have highlighted the dynamic and grounded social processes behind the construction of place identities, characters, and images. They have shown how the meanings of specific places, like blues clubs in Chicago (Grazian, 2003), sidewalks in New York (Duneier, 1999), and Fenway Park in Boston (Borer, 2008), are constructed by the people who use these places but are also indebted, for better or for worse, to the overall "symbolic representation" of the city. These places, in turn, help create and foster the overall image of the city as well. Boston's Fenway Park is the oldest active ballpark in major league baseball. Images of the ol' ballpark are used in corporate and tourism advertisements and they are also used by everyday people in and outside of Boston as a symbol of Boston. Certain meanings about the history of Fenway Park vary between and within groups, which lead to heated debates in the late 1990s and early-2000s over whether or not the ballpark should be torn down in favor of a freshly built one. Yet certain features that remain constant, such as the outer red brick facade, the towering left-field wall (a.k.a., the Green Monster), and the bright lights that shine during home games and other events, signify the ballpark's visual relationship to the city.

The images of cities are often connected to the stories that people tell about the city and the places they've been to within it for work and for play. People create connections to places through the stories they tell about them. Think of a time when you traveled to a new city, or tried out a new restaurant. Actually, think about what you did after your trip. You probably told someone about it. And if you told your story by showing someone pictures of your trip—either in person or through social media such as Facebook—you probably already understand the connection between images, narratives, and places . . . at least intuitively.

Such narratives are worthy objects of study for urban scholars. But we must always keep in mind that place narratives are never filled with complete, unadulterated facts. Varying emphases on certain characters and plot lines offer multiple interpretations of similar events that affect the telling and retelling of stories about places. These stories are not any less real than the raw data of facts. The factual accuracy of a story is often less important than the purpose of the story or the way that it is used. Nevertheless, collective memories can favor powerful groups, those who chose which stories to commemorate or conceal, over those who accept such stories as a verifiable and irrefutable history (Walton, 2001).

Published in 1959, W. Lloyd Warner's *The Living and the Dead: A Study of Symbolic Life of Americans* is a landmark study of public commemorations and the consecration of local and national characters and places through the presentation and performance of symbolic civic narratives. Warner (1959) examined "Yankee City" in the days before, during, and after its 300th-year anniversary celebration.

> Five days were devoted to historical processions and parades, to games, religious ceremonies, and sermons and speeches by the great and the near great. At the grand climax a huge audience assembled to watch the townsmen march together "as one people" in a grand historical procession. . . . Those who watched saw past events portrayed with symbolic choice and emphasis in dramatic scenes of the tableaux that passed before them. At that moment in their long history the people of Yankee City as a collectivity asked and answered these questions: Who are we? How do we feel about ourselves? Why are we what we are? Through the symbols publicly displayed at this time with near and distant kin collected, the city told its story. (p. 107)

The telling and retelling of the city's history, however selected, provided means for communal, familial, and personal identification with Yankee City, even for those whose social positions existed outside of the images rendered by the dominant local business elites.

S. Elizabeth Bird (2002, p. 526) has shown "local narratives are less about 'history' and more about how people construct their sense of place and cultural identity. . . [they] are not just about the site itself but about the particular concerns of the people who tell the legends." Even though place narratives are selective history, it would be a mistake to assume that the dominant narrative about a place is the only narrative that exists or the only one that counts.

Jonathan Wynn's (2010a) work on urban "tour guides" provides a useful example. He borrows the term "urban alchemists" from Jack Katz (2009) to describe the city guides who provide walking tour for both tourists and residents. The guides use a mixture of personal reflections, local folklore, and historical anecdotes in order to create new narratives about their city (in this case, New York) and as an "attempt to transform their participants into 'better' New Yorkers" (Wynn, 2010b, p. 150). In many ways, these guides attempt to re-enchant the urban environment by showing others the little treasures that exist along New York's less traveled paths.

Urban alchemy is a cultural practice that can be seen on the level of local, street culture—from tour guides to graffiti artists to homeless recyclers—but it can also be seen on a larger scale. Norton Long, a political scientist who was interested in the ways that cultural practices influenced the social life of cities, was interested in "urban alchemy" when he discussed the city as an "ecology of games" (1958). He contended that while each social grouping or "game" has its different rules and roles for its "players," no game within the city is so isolated that it would not come into contact with another or, for that matter, does not need to come in contact with another. Instead of Park's understanding of the city as a mosaic whose social worlds do not interpenetrate, Long argued that often proximity was enough to foster at least weak civic bonds between presumably incompatible interest groups. As Long (1958) describes it, "sharing a common territorial field and collaborating for different and particular ends in the achievement of overall social functions, the players in one game make use of the players in another and are, in turn, made use of by them" (p. 255). Interdependence is necessary between specialized occupations and lifestyles.

While the games have their own places to be played, they also occur in places that are commonly shared. Such places are often referred to as "third places." Ray Oldenburg (1989, p. 16) defines "third places" as "public places that host the regular, voluntary, informal, and happily anticipated gatherings of individuals beyond the realms of home and work." Coffee shops, pubs, and other small businesses (Oldenburg, 1989; Milligan, 1998; Borer & Monti, 2006; Macgregor, 2010) provide settings for the "games" played by business men and women (the owners, managers, and employees), patrons (playing leisure "games"), and other groups who use the sites for gatherings and displaying information for various causes, retail opportunities, and local events.

Because individuals in cities utilize many different places within their city, urban inhabitants learn multiple ways of *practicing* urban culture and community (i.e., they learn and are capable of playing by the rules to multiple "games"). And the rules of these games usually involve a hodgepodge of liberal and conservative values. In Monti's (1999) historical analysis of civic culture in American cities, liberal and conservative thinkers see the world very differently, in theory. But, everyday people reconcile these different and theoretically irreconcilable points of view in their everyday routines. The type of civic culture that has been built and continues to be built in American cities, as well as other cities around the world, is neither liberal nor conservative. It is a hybrid culture made up of individuals and groups that think and act in a variety of liberal and conservative ways.

Even though communities are collective accomplishments, not everyone plays an equal role in making those decisions or practices them exactly the same way all the time. Urban dwellers can change their ways of thinking and acting, but only tend do so within tolerable limits. This hybrid mixing is at the heart of what Monti calls the "paradoxical community." Because the cultural influence of cities stretches beyond their physical borders, the same kinds of "paradoxical community" practices can be found in suburbs and small towns (see Macgregor, 2010).

Paradoxical or not, communities in cities are packed with meaning and emotional attachments, even if those allegiances waver between significant territories and significant people. Like most things, it's not a matter of either/or.

The sociology of emotions has developed as a strong subfield over the course of the last 30 years. Its roots, especially in regard to cities, go back much further. In 1945, Firey published a study on the sentimental value attached to certain areas in Boston and the way that land had been used throughout the city. In an essay entitled "Sentiment and Symbolism as Ecological Variables," he showed that large areas of land in downtown Boston were not only reserved for noneconomic uses, but were also left "undeveloped" because they had been collectively endowed with symbolic meaning. These areas could not be fitted into a model predicated on concentric circles, zones, or nuclei.

Boston's "sacred sites," the parks, cemeteries, and the 48-acre area in the center of the city that formed the original "commons" of the community, had never been developed (Firey, 1945, p. 140). Furthermore, Beacon Hill, an upper-class residential neighborhood near the center of the city, was not taken over by the CBD and continues to maintain its privileged position inside the city.

Beacon Hill survives not merely because the people who live there share a common ecological space that serves a set of rational economic functions. Rather, the community's existence and environment is *caused* by their cultural values, the sentiment they attached to their territory. According to Firey (1945), the residents of Beacon Hill could have lived in less-expensive districts with an "equally accessible location and even superior housing conditions. There is thus a noneconomic aspect to land use on Beacon Hill, one which is in some respects actually diseconomic in its consequences" (p. 144). "Sentiment" and "symbolism," which affect a range of related variables from social prestige to ethnic or racial prejudice, are therefore important ecological factors that influence spatial distribution and patterns of development and redevelopment. Firey's study has lasting impact by showing how cultural factors can affect political agendas related to land-use decisions (Maines & Bridger, 1992; Borer, 2008, 2010).

"Sentiment" and "symbolism" are key elements in the ways that individuals and groups construct their identities. Questions concerning the types of identities that arise within the city have been a part of both literary and sociological discourse since the late 19th and early 20th centuries. Urban sociologists have succeeded in identifying many of the nuanced ways that identities are both constructed and maintained in cities.

Gregory Stone's "City Shoppers and Urban Identification," published in 1954, provides a useful analysis for linking identities to places and to other people in publicly shared places. Stone (1954, p. 37) shows "the possibility that some urbanites, as a consequence of the relationships they establish with personnel of retail stores manage to form identifications which bind them to the larger community." Stone found that many urban residents develop meaningful and valuable relationships with clerks and other personnel at the places they shop. Rather than treating the retail store employees as dehumanized automatons or utilitarian cogs in their own consumption machines, "customers injected elements of primary group relationships into what were 'supposed' to be purely secondary relationships" (Lofland, 1998, p. 3).

Of particular importance are "the personalizing consumer" and his or her relationship to and with the store as a meaningful place. Stone's informants who had developed strong attachments to stores they frequented often talked about these places as *their* store. Everyday places become important loci for the development of urban identities and relationships. Can you think of places that you frequent that you might refer to as *yours*?

Claude Fischer's (1975, 1976) "subcultural theory" deals with urban culture and identity explicitly and supports claims that culture has *analytic* autonomy apart from economics and politics. In order to explain the lack of "anomic" psychological disorders in the city, evidence that opposes one of Wirth's key propositions, Fischer found that individuals sought out similar types of people based on strong identity markers like ethnicity, race, class, lifestyle, or profession, or some combination of these attributes. Instead of spawning only impersonal and superficial relationships, the city was home to many close-knit social networks. Fischer claimed that urban areas allow for the creation and maintenance of new subcultures that mold the tastes of the city's diverse population. Only cities with large populations contain enough people to provide the critical mass necessary for such groups to emerge and evolve (Fisher, 1976, p. 37)

Diverse identity and lifestyle groups supply the city with a variety of relatively available leisure, recreation, and entertainment activities. One of the remarkable aspects of city life is that it affords residents and visitors opportunities to try on different hats, so to speak, and be a part of more than one social circle or "scene" (Irwin, 1977). David Grazian (2003, pp. 21–22) makes the distinction between an individual's daytime self and their "nocturnal self," which he defines as "a special kind of presentation of self associated with consuming urban nightlife." The places where people go at night for leisure and pleasure, the places that define a city's nightlife, are important sites for the enactment and reconfiguration of personal and collective identities and fantasies. As part of their identities, the places people go to live out their fantasies are no less real than other status/identity markers that sociologists tend to favor (e.g., income, political affiliation, gender). By forging a nocturnal self in the city's bars, nightclubs, restaurants, and cafes, late-night revelers achieve a very personal kind of satisfaction that cannot simply be reduced to social status gain; the self-esteem generated by their successful negotiations of the city's entertainment options seems to represent the fulfillment of a dream. Grazian shows how people can, and often do, internalize the meaning, character, or status of the places they patronize.

Individuals' identities are never constructions of their own making. Other people are necessary. As such, it is necessary to acknowledge the roles that social interactions between people in places play in the construction of those identities,

regardless of their stability. To study places as sites of interaction and social gatherings, we must consider the range of places, in regard to scales, style, and utility, and "ask what these places . . . have in common and how they differ" (Gieryn, 2000, p. 464). Addressing the similarities and differences between places provides a way to study one culture or compare separate cultures. For instance, there are noticeable and seemingly obvious differences between the ways individuals act toward others in their homes and in their workplaces. These behaviors are intricately connected to both the way we see ourselves and the way others see us. As such, deciding which places to go and which scenes to participate in, and, for that matter, how to participate in them, often requires a good deal of deliberation. Urbanites need to acquire the meanings and skills to act aptly. Lyn Lofland (1973) discusses "urban learning," as an achievement of modern cultures. She acknowledges the importance of both cultural institutions (e.g., the mass media) and personal interactions as means for making the city manageable and meaningful.

With varying indebtedness to Gregory Stone, Erving Goffman, Jane Jacobs, and William H. Whyte, Lofland (1998) constructs a useful vocabulary for recognizing face-to-face interactions in public as well as the visually, physically, and emotionally enticing elements of urban places. These attributes consist of a mixture of "esthetic pleasures" that are influenced by the design of places and "interactional pleasures" that come from the people who occupy such places. These qualities can affect the types of interactions and the pleasures derived from them. For instance, "people watching," which is one of the pleasures that Lofland identifies, is dependent on, most obviously, the presence of crowds or at least a flow of people. To "people watch," certain architectural or structural elements of the site must be present, such as clear lines of visibility, proper placement or mobility of seating, and enough space for action to ensue and entice. Though individuals are motivated to "people watch" for different reasons, the common act of "people watching" is a key element of the negotiated order of public places.

Melinda Milligan's (1998, 2003) analysis of changes to a local coffee house's physical traits (i.e., their layout, atmosphere, and positioning in relation to nearby sites) points us toward important factors that influence social behavior and the practice of culture. The physical structure of a place, however, does not determine action, but it can influence behavior. Conversely, actors can appropriate or change, to varying degrees, the physical layout of a place to suit their individual and collective needs. Such adaptations are easily observed in public places, like open parks, where people add to the setting by bringing their own blankets and chairs, or in coffee shops where seats and tables are often moved and rearranged to accommodate patrons' social needs.

CONCLUSION

The main schools of thought in urban sociology are presented here to give you an understanding of the varied ways that scholars look at cities, suburbs, and towns and the people and places that populate them. The ways that a scholar chooses to look at a city, or any place for that matter, depends largely on the questions they have about the growth or culture of particular cities or the connections between particular settlements. Those interested in the economics and politics of urban land use will tend to draw upon the models and insights from urban ecology, political economy, and postmodern approaches. And those interested in the culture and everyday life of cities will tend to draw upon the models and insights stemming from the Chicago ethnographic tradition or some combination of symbolic interactions or urban culturalism.

Of course, there is room to connect the insights from multiple schools. Good scholarship, like any other type of work, is dependent on using the right tools for the right job. Scholars are not immune, however, from the whims and trends of both past and current scholarship. Nor are they completely immune from their own personal sentiments and feelings about urban life. Figure 5.1 maps where these schools stand regarding such

Figure 5.1   Contemporary Theorists' Feelings About the Growth and Culture of Cities

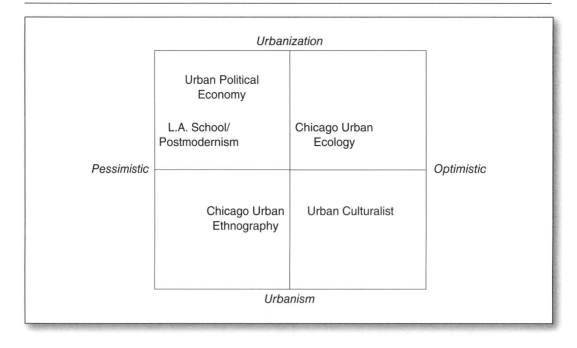

sentiments (pessimistic vs. optimistic) and their focus (urbanization vs. urbanism). Make sure to compare this map to Figure 4.1 in the last chapter. You can easily see how the seeds of classical theorists influenced the fruits of contemporary schools of thought.

This wealth of perspectives highlights how rich cities, suburbs, and towns are as sites of inquiry. This chapter only highlights the most dominant schools of thought due to issues of both clarity and space constraint. As you delve deeper into urban studies, you will see that other theories exist that critique and support those presented here. Though no theory is perfect, in part, because social life is dynamic and privy to change, we recommend that students of cities use whatever theory suits their empirical questions but not let the theories cloud their analysis. As the saying goes, there's nothing like a little data to ruin a perfectly good theory. Perhaps the best way, then, to think about theories is to think about them as tools for coming up with good questions and tools to help you makes sense of the data that will help you answer those questions. Regardless of the tools you choose, we

implore the novice and the veteran alike to pay attention to both urbanization and urbanism and to avoid assuming a one-way, linear connection between these two rich, fascinating, and often baffling social phenomena.

QUESTIONS FOR STUDY AND DISCUSSION

1. What are the similarities and differences between the schools of thought presented in this chapter? How do scholars from each school answer the following question: What is a city?

2. Urban sociology grew out of Chicago. As such, Chicago was and still remains the most studied city and the most available muse for urban theorizing. Contemporary scholars have offered interpretations of newer cities as more appropriate muses for theories of contemporary urban life (e.g., Los Angeles, New York, Miami, Las Vegas). What city do you think best symbolizes the contemporary urban condition, and why?

3. Why and how does urban culture matter? Why do you think that scholars have tended to ignore questions about culture in favor of questions about the economy or politics?

6

CIVIC CULTURE AND THE POLITICS OF COMMUNITY

For students of urban life, no questions matter more than these: What is a "community" and do urban-dwelling Americans have any?

Questions about communities—what they are, how they work, and whether or not they work well—have been a central focus for sociology since its earliest days. But long before we social scientists asked these questions, generations of social philosophers, religious and popular writers, business leaders and politicians, and would-be city builders wondered aloud and often with grave reservation about the social foundations of the new urban world they were making. For a number of reasons that will be outlined below, Americans have worried a great deal about these questions as they relate to cities, perhaps even more than residents of other developed countries have.

Because this is an urban sociology textbook, this chapter focuses primarily on the kinds of communities we associate with places: places as big as metropolitan areas or as small as neighborhoods or blocks. As the reader will recall from Chapter 4, a great deal of early sociological theorizing was motivated by concerns arising from the shift from more traditional forms of communal living to more urban ways of life. The impulse to study communities sociologically

came from the same set of changing social conditions that motivated the emergence of sociology as a discipline. As a result, we can't really understand where the study of community came from, or why people wanted to study it, without remembering that sociology emerged in the latter part of the 19th century in response to social and political changes that upended what people viewed as more traditional and relatively stable social arrangements.

As you probably recall from history classes, the American, French, and even to some extent the ultimately unsuccessful English Revolutions were premised on the aims of overturning traditional social orders based primarily on hereditary hierarchies. That is, prior to these revolutions, one's place in society was determined by the luck of one's birth. One's standing in society was determined by features of one's background over which the individual had little control. These fairly rigid, hierarchical systems determined not just individuals' life chances, but also dictated how members of society ought to interact with one another—these systems provided rules for day-to-day social life. Each position in the hierarchy came attached to a set of privileges and obligations (many more obligations than privileges for most) with regard to your treatment of and the treatment you could expect from other people. That treatment again depended on an individual's ascribed status rather than on any achievements on an individual's part.

These systems were, of course, replaced with ones that insisted, at least in principle, that each individual should be the master of his or her own destiny. To be sure, not every individual had equal control over his or her destiny right away. Women and people of color would have to wait even longer for this belief to be applied to them. In principle, however, one's social position was no longer governed by one's parents' standing. What did that mean for determining how to interact with others? To whom did one have obligations? Over whom could one assume a privileged status? If everyone was equal, who would take charge of providing the infrastructure and services that a society needed to run smoothly? No one knew. Suddenly, the rules of social deference seemed pretty hazy, and human beings as a species are generally not fans of uncertainty. This upending of the old order made things seem pretty chaotic for a while.

The other big change taking place was the process of industrialization, which in turn precipitated massive shifts in populations. In the late 1800s and the beginning of the 1900s, Western Europe and the United States had been industrializing for a while. The growth of employment opportunities in factories caused a shift in the populations of these countries. Many moved from being primarily composed of rural residents, to being largely urban for the first time. Europeans had never seen cities of this scale before, so no one quite knew what to do about the problems arising in them. And the problems were horrendous. As in the case with much work-related migration, the people who were willing to move to cities to look for jobs were the people most desperate for them. They were poor, uneducated, and untrained in machine work.

Cities at this time were extremely densely populated places with very high concentrations of poverty. Many urban dwellers lived in terribly overcrowded conditions in very poor structures without adequate waste removal technology. Large parts of industrial cities were truly squalid.

There were neighborhoods where wealthier folks lived in homes of better quality, but even these neighborhoods lacked amenities like good sewers and clean water that we associate with decent living standards.

What does this have to do with the thinking about communities and community-making at the time? Cities and city neighborhoods seemed like very troubled places compared to what people began to think they recalled of days past, where most people lived in rural areas and even the poor had access to gardens in which to produce their own food, the assistance of neighbors, and fresh air, and other such idyllic features of rural life. Rural dwellers of the past had, in theory, also been able to count on a modicum of *noblesse oblige*, the sense of moral responsibility that demanded that their social betters care for them or at least protect them. Instead, it seemed to many observers that people now lived in run-down, dirty, and unhealthy places where everyone had to fend for him or herself. Would it ever be possible to return to a more cooperative way of life under such miserable conditions?

Finally, we need to talk about a third change that is related to these first two. Partly because of the shift in the changing nature of social relations, and because of the need to be able to organize larger numbers of people to complete various tasks, bureaucratic forms of organization had begun to be more prevalent, especially in cities. Bureaucracies rely on written sets of rules and procedures and divide tasks so that anyone can be plugged into a role and get it done. Anyone's role in a bureaucracy is (at least in theory) not one they have because of who they are, but because of their qualifications.

How might bureaucratization impact community life according to early observers? On the one hand, bureaucracy offers a model that anyone can follow no matter what sort of organization one is forming or what the goals of that organization might be. But while it might provide a handy blueprint for getting things done together as a group, if all decisions are based on rules and policies and following proper procedures, what might happen to people's relationships with one another? Would there be any room for affect, for compassion, familial obligation, or love? As we saw in statements like Toennies's and Wirth's, observers of urban life worried that increased reliance on rationalized, instrumental relationships like those apparently demanded by urban life would squeeze out more emotionally rich and intimate ties.

In the United States, questions about social cohesion and community have been of particular concern for two additional reasons: the legacies of slavery and immigration. Would it be possible for people from many different national, ethnic, linguistic, religious, or racial backgrounds to forge ties and work together? Or would "Americans" of different stripes form ties primarily with others like themselves?

American history in towns, suburbs and cities provides examples of both sorts of community-making and others besides. This chapter examines this history of thinking about community and community-building as it has unfolded both in and outside of sociology. Of course, since sociologists frame their research to answer pressing questions of the day, it is no surprise that there is significant overlap between sociological and popular thinking about these questions. In addition, when we examine the history of civic culture and community-making in the United States, we find persistent questions about the impact of technological advances on our ability to create community. In other words, Americans have continuously worried about whether we had any community, and if we did, was it being eroded or undermined as new-fangled contraptions such as cars, telephones, and the Internet changed our patterns of behavior.

VOLUNTARY ASSOCIATION, CIVIC CULTURE, AND SOCIAL CAPITAL

Questions about community-making and its importance for democracy stretch back to Classical Greece, but in the United States, the importance in America of voluntary engagement in civil society was described in the 1830s by

Alexis de Tocqueville, a young Frenchman who traveled the new nation to avoid military service. Tocqueville was struck by the contrast between America and the older, more aristocratic European societies he knew. In England, he argued, if something needed doing, a well-placed member of the nobility might be in a position to just go ahead and do it. In France, the monarchy could get things done as it saw fit. But in the United States, a society in which people were ostensibly more equal, who had the responsibility to provide needed infrastructure or services wasn't at all clear. No single individual had sufficient authority to decide where a road should go and come up with the money to have it built, for example. Furthermore, in a society where people were more equal, had someone attempted to do so, his efforts would have been viewed as an illegitimate assertion of power.

The problem, as Tocqueville saw it, was that in an individualistic society, submitting to the projects of some uppity individual seems like a relegation of one's independence. Things could only get done when individuals worked together to complete them. The solution in America was for people "of all ages, all stations of life, and all types of disposition" to form associations. In democratic countries, he observed, "knowledge of how to combine is the mother of all other forms of knowledge; on its progress depends that of all the others" (Tocqueville, 1840/1863, p. 129).

According to Tocqueville, associations served four key functions. The first was to meet needs that the government could not or would not satisfy. Where the young government did not help the poor, for example, religious and secular charitable organizations formed to provide assistance. The second major function of voluntary associations was to provide training for democratic citizenship. Tocqueville observed that in voluntary organizations, members learned concrete skills such as running meetings, drawing up bylaws, and working through conflicts within the group to solve a collective problem. These skills were then transferable, he believed, to the public arena, both for those who might run for elected office and for constituents. Third, when a project could be accomplished by private citizens through a voluntary association, it had a legitimacy it would not have had otherwise. Finally and perhaps most importantly in Tocqueville's view, voluntary associations helped Americans overcome their tendency toward isolation that might otherwise have taken hold in an individualistic culture. Thus, in voluntary associations, "feelings and opinions are recruited, the heart is enlarged, and the human mind is developed only by the reciprocal action of men upon each other" (Tocqueville, 1840/1863, p. 132).

The realm of voluntary association Tocqueville had described is frequently referred to as *civil society. Very broadly, civil society is the realm of voluntary activity that lies between the state and the market, including the family, community and other nongovernmental associations, and extra-economic institutions.* Though they vary in their definitions of civil society and their theories of how it works best, sociologists generally agree that civil society, or a healthy civic culture, is essential to a vibrant democracy. The basic argument is that civil society needs to be free of the state so that the state can't control what is happening in it; the kinds of organizations and institutions in civil society need autonomy from the government in order to remain critical of it. It is in civil society that groups of citizens can express grievances with the state and act as watchdogs. If all the institutions in civil society were sucked into the political process, their independence, the argument goes, would be lost. For similar reasons, civil society is supposed to remain independent of market interests.

In practice, the relationship between the state, the market, and civil society can be quite complicated. There is more overlap than there is gap between these three institutional sectors (Monti, 2012). For instance, some groups in civil society exist for the purpose of influencing politics. We sometimes refer to these as "special interest groups." Organizations large and small ostensibly formed for nonpolitical purposes, the promotion of cancer research for example, hire lobbyists

and contribute funds to parties and candidates for office they believe will support their causes.

There are also segments of civil society that have little if anything to do with the state—the average bowling league, lodge, or poetry reading group, for example. As we will see, advocates of social capital theory like Robert Putnam argue, however, that these kinds of groups are still important to democracy for other reasons insofar as they promote neighborliness and communication among people and provide opportunities to build social trust. It is in "soccer clubs and singing groups," Putnam argues, that the ultimate success of a democracy lies (Putnam 1993a).

Businesses, even bigger corporations, often act as civic associations or do things that have a serious impact on the civic lives of their employees and everyone else in the community, too. One expects them to provide good products and services at a fair price, to be sure, or not harm the environment and their customers, issues typically included in discussions over the role that "social responsibility" plays in business affairs. But businesses and the people who own and run them also assist the communities of which they are a part by promoting good causes or encouraging their employees to do so, just like your typical club, lodge, or run-of-the-mill civic association would. Their presence in communities can help to solidify the identity of the place and the people in it as belonging to a particular group and, importantly, not to other groups (Silverman, 1999; Boyd, 2000; Vallejo, 2009; Zukin, 2009). Businesses also bring together in the workplace different kinds of people who might not otherwise have occasion to associate with each other or see each other as equals. That is just one of the reasons why arguments over affirmative action have proven so contentious and important. The point is that much of the social good that businesses routinely do is routinely overlooked precisely because it is so commonplace (Monti, 1999, pp. 240–278; Borer & Monti, 2006, pp. 39–62; Brush, Monti, Ryan, & Gannon, 2007, pp. 155–176).

The phrase **civic engagement** *generally refers to all the ways people in a democratic society* *exercise their rights and fulfill their responsibilities.* Included among the ways people civically engage are voting, standing for elected office, jury service, participating in extra-governmental organizations, and making monetary contributions to parties, candidates for office, and charitable organizations. Community engagement also includes involvement in a broader array of informal activities, such as neighboring, participating in groups of people with similar recreational interests and, increasingly, in virtual networks.

The well of positive fellow-feeling and good-will Tocqueville ascribed to the strong tradition of voluntary association continues to lie at the center of our thinking about community-making and social cohesion in the United States. As a culture that values the individual and promotes the idea that good comes of individuals pursuing their own best interests, how can we expect to be able to work together when collective action is needed, especially when individuals' interests seem frequently to be at odds? One of the principle concepts available for exploring this basic question is that of *social capital*. In urban and community sociology, *social capital refers to the value of social networks, that is, to the potential to get things done together that comes of peoples' relationships with one another.* Most basically, "social capital refers to those stocks of social trust, norms and networks that people can draw upon to solve common problems" (http://www.cpn.org/tools/dictionary/capital.html, March 10, 2010). Social capital is important, according to many theorists, because it enables people to cooperate and coordinate their actions and thereby "enhances the benefits of investment in physical and human capital" (Putnam, 1993a, pp. 35–36).

Social networks, in theory, promote cooperation among community members in several ways. First, they promote *norms of reciprocity and mutual trust*. That is, members of the community share the expectation that when an individual does a favor for someone else, the good they do will be returned at some point in the future. Second, *social networks* can promote exchanges of information allowing people to coordinate their actions and to verify the trustworthiness of other individuals and groups. Third, sites of social capital and the reciprocity it produces can provide examples of past successes that can be templates for new endeavors. Finally, a community with a well-developed stock of social capital and dense social networks can provide an informal system of social checks that can deter those who might act in ways that could damage the community, by preventing those individuals from sharing in collective goods in the future (Sirianni & Friedland, 2001 These beneficial norms can be supported in a variety of ways (Coleman, 1988)—in mundane neighborliness, in the formation of groups and institutions that find success getting things done together, in collaboration among such groups, and even in the stories that residents tell that reinforce their shared view of the community's history or a shared vision for its future. Just as easily, however, social capital can be undermined by factionalism, a lack of communication among actors or groups, or a collective sense of failure or defeat that makes residents believe it is not worth investing their time, energy, or money in the community. Social capital matters. Without it, the investments individuals or small groups make in a community (e.g., commercial, philanthropic, or otherwise) cannot effectively be put to use. That is because a community would lack the collective traditions that enable it to take full advantage of those investments in ways that generate big returns on them (Putnam, 1993a; Flora & Flora, 2008).

Social capital can operate in two ways. *Bridging social capital* connects diverse people and interests within a community or to people or organizations outside the immediate community. Bridging ties may be weak (Granovetter, 1973) and instrumental. That is, they need not include deep, personal connections or feelings of affection. People with bridging ties may not know a great deal about each other beyond what they know in the context of the one tie they share with one another. For example, members of a town's chamber of commerce may know each other only as fellow business people who share a desire to improve the community's economic outlook. They need not know each other in deeply personal ways to work together to accomplish the goals they share as chamber of commerce members.

On the other hand, *bonding social capital* describes the connections among people who believe they share a similar background or characteristic. Such ties may be based on shared kinship, religion, or ethnic background, for example. Bonding social capital is strongest when individuals have contact with one another in a variety of settings or social roles, as in the example of residents of a neighborhood who share an ethnic or national heritage, patronize one another's businesses, and have overlapping memberships in other kinds of organizations.[1]

Bridging and bonding social capital are not mutually exclusive. It is not hard to imagine that a relationship that begins as a bridging tie can become more like a bonding tie over time. However, in theory, these two modes of social capital building offer different benefits and constraints. *Bridging ties are especially useful in creating new possibilities for sharing information but may be too superficial or fleeting to support sustained collective action. Bonding social capital can create networks on which members can rely when they need assistance, but deeply bonded groups can also be insular and exclusive.*

Theories of social capital and civic engagement have become a cornerstone of sociological studies of community life. These concepts are appealing, but also controversial. One argument in favor of the importance of voluntary associations is that they provide the basis for engagement in a democracy's political life, in part by providing arenas in which group members can discuss and debate political issues. However, some researchers have found that, instead, such voluntary organizations are sites where members actively avoid politically relevant topics because they view politics as an anathema to the recreational purposes of the group, and any exchange about politically relevant topics, to the extent they happened at all, are relegated to more private, "backstage" interactions (Eliasoph, 1998). Lichterman (1996) found that even in environmental groups in which one might assume politics would be a central focus, some people construed their activism so narrowly as to deliberately shy away from controversies members feared would be unpleasant or damaging to the group's sense of cohesion. *In other words, there is no guarantee that the voluntary organizations of civil society somehow "naturally" connect citizens to democratic processes or responsibilities.*

It is also important to remember that there is a second side to the social capital coin. Voluntary organizations and other kinds of groups may help bring individuals together, but as we just mentioned, they also have an exclusive quality. Social capital obliges group members to help police the group's boundaries to exclude people, groups, or behaviors that are contrary to the group's shared sense of itself (Bourdieu, 1986). Bonding social capital in particular, while "undoubtedly provid[ing] opportunities to those who belong . . . also reinforce pre-existing social stratification, prevent mobility of excluded groups, minorities, poor people, and become the basis of corruption and co-optation of power by the dominant social groups" (Narayan, 1999, p. 13). Narayan argued that bridging (or crosscutting) ties are more valuable for helping those with less privilege access new information and resources that might lead to increased opportunity.

Nancy Fraser (1992), on the other hand, argued for the importance of bonding social capital among marginalized people in a community (though without using the language of social capital[2]). Because of the extreme difficulty marginalized individuals will have in gaining access even to bridging ties with members of more socially powerful groups, a society's minorities instead need venues in which they can come to understand their situation in the context of existing social structure, as opposed to seeing their marginalization as the result of individual failings. Sites she calls "subaltern counterpublics" from which more privileged members of a community are excluded allow those with less privilege to begin to articulate a shared sense of their social position, the first step in beginning to work collectively to change their situation. We will see a dramatic example of such venues in the discussion of Black churches in the civil rights movement below.

In addition, a number of sociologists have levied a variety of more specific empirical critiques against the research finding social capital on the decline. Whereas Putnam (2000) argued in his widely read book, *Bowling Alone*, that Americans are spending less and less time engaged in voluntary associations because more and more of our time is taken up by increased work hours, by longer commutes, and in private entertainment (such as TV and computer use), others have argued that Putnam is simply capturing shifts in the ways Americans find to interact with each other (Monti, Butler, Curley, Tilney, & Weiner, 2003), not true declines.

So what can we learn from the debates about social ties in the United States? First, it is clear that whether or not voluntary organizations create the kind of social capital Putnam and others believe, they have long been an important part of the lives of American communities. More importantly, if we take culture seriously, we must look beyond the veracity of claims about social capital and individualism, and ask what the persistence of these debates tells us about ourselves. The longevity of these debates reveals a cultural ambivalence if not an outright anxiety about how we are to strike a balance between the importance we place on individualism and self-reliance and the reality of our need to work together much of the time. They also highlight the tension in our culture between creating an effective sort of pluralism that admits (or at least tolerates) all, and the frequent desire to spend time among those with whom we frequently feel most comfortable—people like ourselves.

Empirically, researchers adopting a cultural perspective on these questions can step outside the terms set by these debates and ask another type of question altogether. It might be more fruitful not to ask which types of social capital or associational form are most beneficial but to ask what opportunities or constraints are afforded by different modes or "styles" (Lichterman, 2006) of civic engagement or community-making. We can also suspend theoretically driven questions about community-making, and ask instead what practices people use to make community in everyday life (Macgregor, 2010). Approaching research this way allows us to recognize novel forms of community-making that existing theories might not prepare us to see.

The connection between bridging and bonding forms of social capital has been explored in a variety of urban contexts, mostly in the United States but also in other parts of the world. The findings are consistent across different cultural settings (Andrews, 2009; Anjaria, 2009; Dekker, Volker, Lelieveldt, & Torenvlied, 2010; Orum, Bata, Shumei, Jewei, Yang, & Trung, 2009; Pares, Bonet-Marti, & Marti-Costa, 2012; Roberts, 2011). These different kinds of social capital are mutually reinforcing rather than contradictory or in tension with each other. The concern over maintaining or increasing the level of social capital in different community settings may resonate most strongly with middle-class persons. But the skills that go into building more social capital into particular communities can be shared across different social class lines or be used to exclude persons with less status and money (Boyd, 2008; Brisson & Usher, 2007; Britton, 2011; Chaskin, 2010; Curley, 2010; Freeman, 2008; Hipp & Perin, 2009; Hyra, 2006; Manturuk, Lindblad, & Quercia, 2012; Mesch & Levanon, 2003; Moore 2005). The latter appears more likely to happen when an area is being "upgraded" in terms of the social class of the persons moving into it. But persons with less wealth and social status can draw on their particular brand of ethnic or racial social capital in order to build a community in which they fit, can feel welcomed, and behave competently (Chiswick & Miller, 2005; Portes, Haller, & Guarnizo, 2002). As resources go, social capital has proven to be as fungible as money.

The following section of this chapter provides a cursory history of civic culture in the United

States primarily as it applies particularly to cities and the kinds of collective efforts and ties to which urban dwellers have turned to try to make life in cities better. Frequently, these efforts are aimed at improving the provision of services like housing, sanitation services, education, and transportation (Castells, 1983). However, just as frequently, urban voluntary associations and organizations have tried to tackle the problems of urban living conditions by reforming urban residents. As we will see, the shift to predominantly urban life changed the way that Americans engaged with one another, but the communal forms that people brought with them to cities also helped to shape and alter urban life. We will also see that as social, economic, and technological changes unfold, Americans continuously find new and creative ways to manage the tensions between individualism and community, pluralism and homogeneity.

HISTORY OF URBAN CIVIC CULTURE IN THE UNITED STATES

Voluntary associations have always been a part of urban life in the United States. Indeed, voluntary associations are often viewed as having their roots in the emergence of the Protestant Reformation (Singleton, 1975), and it is possible to view the history of colonial America as a story of such associations. Protestantism encouraged believers for the first time to view themselves as equal members in churches to which they freely belonged, as opposed to followers in top-down hierarchies to which everyone was obliged. The settlers that arrived in Jamestown and in Plymouth colony were members of voluntary organizations: religious groups hoping to form societies according to their religious ideals. Additional associations formed quickly even in colonial cities and included firefighting societies, mutual aid and insurance groups, libraries, charity organizations, boosters, and lodges. Free Masonry was especially popular, and because Masonic Temples existed in many cities, members moving to a new city or traveling away

from home could easily make social and business connections using their Masonic credentials.

The connection between religious affiliation and religiously inspired social activism is deeply rooted in American history generally but in American cities especially. For that is where all the tensions and possibilities inherent in building a society filled with many different kinds of people were played out most obviously and sometimes violently (Porterfield, 2012; Boyer, 2012; Roof, 2012). The paradoxical qualities of religious bodies as places that could separate different groups *and* provide new venues for outsiders and newcomers to become more actively engaged in the life of the cities where they lived is very clear in U.S. history.

The middle and upper classes were especially active in voluntary organizations, particularly those with a religious foundation or that were religiously inspired. Voluntary organizations gave women, barred from entering public life through voting or holding public office, one of their few means of participating in public life. Women ran and staffed countless charitable, service, and religious organizations, almost exclusively with volunteer labor. The tie between Protestantism and the rise of middle class women's (religious) voluntary organizations in cities of the early 1800s continued into the Victorian era (Chudacoff & Smith, 2004). In cities with larger populations of free African Americans, Blacks formed churches, mutual assistance societies, and newspapers, analogous to those formed in White society. They were often given names signifying African connections, setting them apart from White institutions. In some cities like Philadelphia, Blacks had a richer and more diverse organizational life than lower-class whites (Chudacoff & Smith, 2004).

Less formal types of communal life were invaluable for integrating newcomers to cities—both newcomers from rural parts of the United States and new immigrants from outside the United States Kin networks were very important for socializing newcomers. High housing costs and housing shortages meant that newcomers frequently had to live with extended family or other migrants from their former homes. Despite the unpleasantness of overcrowding in these situations, the arrangements benefited both parties. Newcomers had assistance getting on their feet in the city, and the hosting family had someone to help pay rent. Middle and upper-class reformers did not always recognize the value in these arrangements, and instead saw in them urban crowding and a lifestyle that was antithetical to the ideal of the nuclear family in a detached family home. Their formalized urban reform organizations ostensibly aimed at assisting the urban poor frequently overlooked the importance of informal social networks to so many newcomers.

In the late 1800s we begin to see evidence of the tensions between the benefits that some kinds of voluntary organizations afforded members, while reinforcing inequalities for nonmembers. Labor organizing began to take hold, providing some real benefits to union members. However, unions excluded women and non-Whites, preventing them access to certain kinds of jobs altogether. They also excluded unskilled workers, who could not get access to the benefits unions were protecting for their own members. In addition, large waves of immigration typically precipitated the formation of nativist organizations, such as the American Protective Organization and the American Patriotic League in the late 1800s. Also in this era, business elites in many cities, alarmed by the dominance of urban political machines controlled by immigrant leaders and supported by the working class, began forming chambers of commerce and "good government" leagues in hopes of returning control of municipal governments to the hands of the "better" classes. Municipal reformers pushed for nonpartisan, city-wide elections that undermined machine bosses and their associates' ability to retain elected positions.

At the end of the 1800s, several cultural shifts occurred that created the conditions that gave rise to large scale social reform efforts and organizations. Business elites tended to view the running of a city as similar to running businesses, and were often able to make some inroads when

it came to reducing corruption and the cost of urban government. While they continued to try to address urban problems like substandard housing conditions and education, they were also beginning to find avenues to try to tackle additional problems, such as unemployment. Men wanting to push for these kinds of social reform found that official government arenas were frequently not the places to do so. As some men began to turn to channels outside political ones to take up these issues, they found themselves suddenly working side by side with the women's voluntary organizations that had been working to address these problems all along.

The emerging native-born professional classes at the turn of the 20th century believed there were practical solutions to urban social problems and further that the tools of the emerging social sciences could inform their interventions. Social scientists' descriptions of urban problems together with sensational journalistic exposés popular at the time combined to fuel the expansion of social reform organizations. In addition, the growth of the Social Gospel movement added religious legitimacy to many social reform efforts.

Many reform efforts of this era were really aimed at moral reform, and anti-vice organizations formed in many cities, particularly those in which native-born middle classes were most concerned about what they viewed as the unruly behavior of large numbers of immigrants (Beisel, 1997). Middle-class men and women in cities worked to outlaw behaviors ranging from prostitution to gambling to drinking alcohol. In the minds of these reformers, the improvement of individual morals was inextricably tied to the success of cities and the improvement of urban conditions. Lazy, immoral, and poor residents were not the kinds of citizens who would improve cities. Cities would improve only when such people abandoned their slovenly ways and acted more like their middle class betters. The rise of the Social Gospel movement created the opportunity for progressives and religious leaders to develop bridging ties based on these shared beliefs that changing the urban environment and reforming individuals were essential one and the same project.

As the nation's urban population expanded rapidly at the end of the 19th century due in large measure to immigration, middle and upper-class residents were dismayed by the large numbers of urban poor. Though state and municipal governments were slowly beginning to assume small amounts of responsibility for assisting the destitute, private charities were growing to serve these purposes. Charitable groups followed the trend toward increasingly bureaucratic organizational forms in all areas of life, and began to organize themselves into larger structures. By 1900, most major cities had a Charity Organization Society that facilitated communication and activities among charitable groups (Chudacoff & Smith, 2004).

Also in this era, the Settlement House movement aimed at changing urban conditions by forging new kinds of social ties. Educated young "settlers" moved into urban neighborhoods among working classes with the idea that their presence would be mutually beneficial. The idea was to create social ties between reformers and working classes that would be mutually improving (though mostly improving to the poor). Voluntary associations grew tremendously in the 1920s as new middle- and working-class urban dwellers looked for ways to bring a sense of community to their urban lives. Sports leagues, community chests, and groups like the Kiwanis, Lions, Elks, and women's clubs were extremely popular during this time.

Much urban organizing in the first half of the 1900s that was aimed at addressing urban ills had a distinctly top-down flavor. This continued to be true into the 1940s and 1950s, but by the 1940s, some changes were evident. Beginning the 1940s until his death in 1972, activist Saul Alinsky applied a model of labor organizing to poverty-stricken urban neighborhoods, beginning with the Back of the Yards Neighborhood Council in Chicago. This new model of grassroots neighborhood organizing influenced urban organizing for the foreseeable future. Unlike the urban reform organizations run by members of the middle or upper classes, Alinsky's model for organizing was based on the idea that the poor themselves should direct the changes they wanted in their neighborhoods.

The irony is that while cities were often viewed as isolating, they are also act as sites of communal possibility that do not exist elsewhere. Because of their larger populations, cities have always offered opportunities for minority group members to find each other (Fisher, 1982). It is in these sites where they do so that we can begin to see the possibilities for Fraser's "subaltern counterpublics." As early as the 1940s, for example, meeting places for homosexuals emerged in many of the country's larger cities. On one hand, such places provided relative safety in numbers for their patrons. On the other, once known to the public they were frequently targeted by law enforcement for raids. However, these sites, and the collective anger about the raids on them, are frequently credited with providing the seeds of the gay rights movement in the late 1960s.

Another example in which urban sites promoted bonding capital that had a tremendous impact on the nation is that of Black churches and their importance for the civil rights movement. Churches and other institutions in the Jim Crow South were of course strictly segregated. According to one logic of social capital, the argument would be that if White churches had allowed African Americans in, it would have become a more effective site of civil society by virtue of becoming more diverse—a site where bridging capital could be built. But Fraser, in a sense, argued that by being barred from White churches, and having to have their own congregations, African Americans got something just as important and maybe even more important. According to Fraser's logic, had Blacks and Whites been able to join institutions like churches as ostensible equals, it would have allowed congregations, Black and White, to gloss the ongoing discrimination Blacks faced outside the church. In fact, inequality would have become impossible to talk about, because if congregants are all equal in the organization, it becomes tough to see ourselves or others as people who experience systematic inequality.

What happened instead was that Black congregations came to be central crucibles of the civil rights movements. Congregants could talk among themselves as African Americans, and these opportunities allowed them to develop a collective consciousness, a sense of themselves, that felt angry about their unequal status and could begin to talk about ways to address the problem. African American college campuses were also important places where this happened. To use the language of social capital theory, churches provided sites where bonding capital could be generated and put to use in the coordination of collective action.

Churches also provided places that were relatively safe physically. We value church-going in our culture, so churches were less likely to be bombed or raided by police than other kinds of buildings. They also provided a variety of other important resources that facilitated bonding and collective action: They could provide meeting spaces for large groups and even provide supplies. Churches continue to be important community centers in some African American communities (Patillo-McCoy, 1998). In poor neighborhoods that have suffered disinvestment by other kinds of institutions, churches continue to provide services and even experiment with becoming investors themselves, as in the case of the Abyssinian Baptist Church Development Corporation in Harlem, which has redeveloped a number of residential properties for rent and sale (http://www.adcorp.org/), with the larger goals of shoring up Harlem's economic future.

From the earliest urban settlements in the United States, business organizations have had a tremendous impact on what contemporary cities look like due to their influence at local, state and federal levels of government. Even in preindustrial cities, wealthier residents, particularly merchants and professionals, collaborated to improve roads and build sidewalks, perhaps less out of some sense of social obligation than to ensure that materials, goods, and customers could move to and from their places of business

(Orum, 1995). Especially in the era of urban redevelopment/renewal in the 1950s and 1960s, when real estate and business coalitions influenced housing policy (Housing Act of 1949) at the federal level and municipal officials to effect "slum clearance" and redevelop large sections of many cities including Boston, Richmond, New York, and New Orleans, these initiatives replaced low-rent and public housing with business structures like high-rise office buildings, luxury hotels, convention centers, and the like. On occasion, corporations and major institutions also took a more direct role in redeveloping the neighborhood around them (Monti, 1990). Of course, the persons displaced by such efforts still required places to live. Efforts to house as many of those people as efficiently as possible spurred the building of the massive, high-rise public housing projects that were built in cities around the country.

Business owners and organizations play an important role in smaller communities as well. Sociologists Jan Flora and Jeff Sharp found that in Aurora, Nebraska, the development corporation founded in the 1960s that included all the town's major commercial interests and worked to groom new generations of business owners for civic leadership had largely set in motion a culture in which this town of about 4,000 has been able to raise local money to provide state-of-the-art public institutions such as its library and education center, which in turn has been a draw allowing them to attract new industries to town, some from much larger cities (Flora & Flora, 2008).

Many of the similarities in the forms of voluntary and civic association in rural and urban areas stretch well back in American history. Despite a general sense that life in America's cities and rural areas are quite different, we find that rural areas were affected by the same social and historical forces that shaped urban areas, and rural citizens found ways to get things done together nevertheless, just as urban ones did. At the same time that industrialization and factories became more important in cities, mechanization was changing agricultural methods and the processing of agricultural products. Though the term "factory farm" was still many decades from use, farmers were finding that they had to invest more money in tractors and machines to remain viable, and the high cost of these investments meant that many made formal and informal arrangements with neighbors to share machinery, or trade work. The work of processing agricultural goods into value-added products began to move out of homes and into small "factories," which typically employed a handful of people engaged in a task such as turning milk into cheese. Such operations were frequently owned by a cooperative of farmers who all brought their products there to be processed (McMurry, 1995). Though small compared to urban factories that might employ hundreds of people, rural cooperatives still increasingly relied on more bureaucratized ways of getting things done just as urban manufacturers did.

The associational forms that sprang up in cities were quickly exported to more rural parts of the United States. Even in associations typically associated with rural life, we find urban roots. Perhaps the best example of the urban influence on rural associational life is in the history of the National Grange of the Order of Patrons of Husbandry, better known as the Grange. The Grange is the country's oldest association of farmers and was formed in large part through the initiative of an adviser to President Andrew Johnson.

After the Civil War, Johnson sent Oliver Hudson Kelley to the South to collect agricultural data. Kelley initially found that Southerners viewed him with suspicion. However, his membership in the Freemasons opened doors for him in the South (Nordin, 2007). Kelley felt that rural farmers could benefit from an organization modeled on the Freemasons that would represent their interests, and the first Grange Hall opened in Washington, D.C. in 1867 (http://www.nationalgrange.org/about/history.html May 28, 2011). At the local level, Granges focus on community service and the formation of farmer cooperatives. The organization immediately became influential in state and national politics, influencing issues as diverse as railroad regulation, the formation of extension services, rural mail delivery, temperance, and women's suffrage. Though its membership has declined from its peak in the Progressive Era of the 1920s, the Grange still boasts over 300,000 members.

DECLINING COMMUNITY?

Social capital theory places heavy emphasis on sites in civil society in which residents have face-to-face contact with one another. Organizations like many of those described above, such as lodges and the Grange, fit nicely with social capital theory. They typically bring members into face-to-face contact at the local level, while fostering extra-local contact by virtue of being chapters of larger regional and national organizations. *There is no question that membership in some kinds of organizations has declined since the 1960s (Skocpol, 2004, Putnam, 1999), and some argue that American voluntary organizations now more frequently operate on the model of therapeutic self-help, focusing attention on individuals rather than on community engagement (Wuthnow, 1996).* Does this mean that civil society in the United States is eroding? According to such arguments, Americans' time for such organizations has declined due to increased commuting time, hours spent at work and in private forms of entertainment, such as watching television and using the Internet. In addition, the rise of so-called tertiary organizations, large membership organizations which one joins simply by giving money (such as the American Association of Retired Persons or the World Wild Life Fund) do not demand much, if any, face-to-face contact among members. Any sense of belonging to such organizations, they argue, is purely superficial.

The first important point to keep in mind about these arguments about declines in the kind of rich communal forms that are essential for democracy is that they are not at all new. Thomas Bender (1993) traces the history of such arguments as they wax and wane throughout America's cultural history. In addition, we can consider the substance of these arguments, and the evidence that membership in formal voluntary organizations looks more like the ebbing and flowing of tides (Skocpol, 2004) rather than the steady decline that some fear.

We can also consider, as we did above, the veracity of some of the underlying assumptions made about those voluntary associations. For example, Moose Lodges and the like did bring group members into face-to-face contact with one another, possibly allowing them opportunities to forge important personal ties and undertake projects that benefited their communities. At the same time, such organizations often had features diametrically opposed to democratic ideals. Many excluded persons of particular races, religions, or economic statuses. Women's participation was frequently limited to support roles, such as providing meals for meetings and the like. In addition, when membership in exclusive voluntary associations overlapped with a community's business and political leadership, decisions and deals were struck in sites from which many were excluded.

TECHNOLOGY, COMMUNITY AND CIVIC CULTURE

Another source of concern for Putnam and other critics particularly worried about the potential decline of voluntary associations and civil society is the effect of technologies that may remove community members from face-to-face contact with one another. They cite data indicating that the more hours Americans spend online and watching television in the privacy of their own dwellings, the less time they spend in face-to-face contact with others. They also cite the evidence of the decline in face-to-face membership organizations. Private and virtual entertainment, they argue, are eroding traditional venues of recreation and thereby social capital and community building.

However, when we examine the impact of new technologies on community-making in the United States as we do below, we find that

Americans make very creative uses of new technologies, invariably using them to connect with one another in ways their inventors never imagined. Like other concerns about declines in the amount or quality of American community, worries about the impact of technology on our ability to connect with one another are not at all new. For each new innovation that has appeared over the last 250 years, some observers of social life have found reasons to worry that community-making will be damaged. The urban reform efforts of the early 1900s, for example, were facilitated by the increasing ease of communications using the telephone and telegraph. These inventions (along with the reformers' confidence in their ability to tackle urban problems with professional expertise) facilitated communication across cities and spurred the growth of local movements into the national progressive movement (Chudacoff & Smith, 2005). These technologies made possible the growth of organizations like the National Municipal League, which began as a network of civic reformers, and the National Child Labor Committee, which was able to bring the issue of child labor to national attention. Similarly, networks of churches formed the Federal Council of Churches of Christ, which epitomized the values of the Social Gospel movement, calling for equal rights, improved housing and working conditions, and educational reforms. The advent of such regional and national organizations would have been much more difficult were it not for easier communication across long distances.

Again, the advent of the phone induced fear that people would spend less time interacting face to face, but spawned a whole variety of ways for people to interact that telephone companies had not intended. It was imagined that typical phone users would be urban businessmen. However, it quickly proved a boon for the middle- and upper-class women whose gender expectations limited their opportunities for engagement outside the home, and for rural dwellers who found the phone could help bridge the miles between themselves and their nearest neighbors (Fisher, 1994).

Though phone service providers initially imagined that urban dwellers would be their primary customers, rural residents who lived far from their nearest neighbors were desperate for phone service in their communities. Many rural communities formed a new kind of voluntary organizations—the telephone cooperative—to provide themselves service rather than wait for larger companies to bring service to rural communities. Some so-called farmer telephone co-ops saved money on infrastructure by stringing phone lines from farm to farm along fence posts. Rural communities used party telephone lines to issue community news and weather broadcasts and even as a means to broadcast musical performances (Fisher, 1994).

Public discussions about the Internet have unfolded in a manner very much like discussions about the innovations discussed above. What does it mean for the social cohesion of neighborhoods and other place-based communities if people may increasingly opt to invest their time in more diffuse "portable" communities instead (Chayko, 2008). It should be noted that the Internet is not the first technological innovation to enable individuals spread across great geographic areas to imagine themselves as part of a shared community. As Benedict Anderson (1983) argues, the advent of the book played a vital role in creating the possibility of nationalism, in which people who would never meet each other could nonetheless begin to belong to "imagined communities" of fellow countrymen. More recently, some observers have worried that increased use of computer-based communication would undermine face-to-face socializing and draw individuals' time and energies away from the kinds of place-based communities with which they were more familiar (Putnam, 1995, 2000), while others heralded it as the basis of an almost perfect community-building tool. Of course, neither of these extreme views has been completely borne out. Just as the developers of telephone service imagined people using that new technology in a limited number of ways, the Internet was initially imagined as a tool primarily for the military and elite researchers, and

possibly to facilitate communications among colleagues in business settings. However, as soon as the Internet became more widely available in the 1980s, people began to use it in a variety of new forms of community-making. As early as the mid-80s research was showing that users who ostensibly joined newsgroups and other online networks ostensibly to access information, were instead using these forums primarily for sociable chat, and that online communication was supplementing face-to-face ties in a variety of ways (Wellman, 1996).

As the reader can certainly guess, contemporary research suggests that online and other forms of digital communication are not a drain on community life, but are in fact impacting it in some interesting and important ways. In their study of a new Canadian subdivision, Hampton and Wellman found that access to the neighborhood's electronic message boards and email indeed changed neighbors' interactions with one another. Residents in the homes which lacked Internet access got to know their geographical neighbors better than those who used the Internet, but those who used the Internet and community message boards and LISTSERVs came to know more fellow residents throughout the neighborhood, not just their immediate neighbors (Hampton & Wellman, 2003).

Organizations in civil society are rapidly finding new ways to appropriate contemporary technologies. In the last few years, increasing numbers of organizations from the Red Cross to the Brooklyn Public Library have turned to text messaging to raise money. In addition, while critics of the way the Internet may further encourage superficial kinds of social belonging, some researchers find that face-to-face groups make extensive use of the Internet through websites and chat rooms to cement bonding ties, and that these technologies facilitate deep relationships among diverse individuals who might not have had a chance to meet face to face (Chayko, 2008).

Today one of the chief concerns remaining about digital communications, at least in the context of online chat rooms and the like, is that the opportunities it provides for anonymous communication allow individuals to say anything—including things that might be unfounded or simply rude—because they are not subject to the social pressures toward civility that operate in communications in which parties cannot hide their identities. As such, critics argue, what veneer of civility that held our public fabric together is deteriorating. The balance of the evidence suggests that technology does change the ways we build and manage community. However, rather than simply draining community as people often fear, the new novel opportunities afforded by changing technology come with novel kinds of constraints. Wuthnow (2002, 2005) and others suggest that rapid communications increasingly mean that contemporary civil society requires groups to form loose networks and alliances with other groups to be effective, and be prepared for greater flexibility than was required of them in the past.

CONCLUSION

Americans are endlessly innovative when it comes to finding ways to connect with one another—both with people like themselves and with people they believe are different. Though their forms have evolved over time, we continue to rely very heavily on voluntary associations and informal civic ties that can be sustained in or beyond geographical locations. The fact that we continue to worry about whether or how well we can get things done together reflects the continued tension in our culture about how to strike a balance between the individualism we value and the interdependence we need. Fortunately, urban residents seem to have come up with ways to bring individuals together (i.e., through the government by making better citizens or the marketplace and the way it brings us into complex groups of shoppers and investors) and better organized groups (i.e., primarily through collections of like-minded commercial leaders and ethnic people who act in concert) in a workable mix of community-building strategies (Monti, 1999).

QUESTIONS FOR STUDY AND DISCUSSION

1. Why were people afraid of cities and the way of life they were thought to create?

2. What is "social capital" and how does it figure into the creation of voluntary associations?

3. Do modern technology and leisure pursuits enhance or undermine efforts to sustain a community?

4. What is the relationship among the governmental (public), market place (private), and voluntary (nonprofit) arenas in American civic life?

5. Is community life in America on the decline?

6. Does *more* civil society necessarily make for a *better* civil society?

NOTES

1. The constructs of bonding and bridging social capital can be usefully viewed as restatements of Toennies's *Gemeinschaft/Gesellschaft* distinction, and also of Durkheim's organic/mechanical solidarity.

2. Nancy Fraser's work more properly belongs to the body of literature on the public sphere, which theorizes the opportunities citizens in any society have to engage each other in particular kinds of dialogue that may be important for maintaining a democracy. Readers who are interested in this set of theories should begin by reading Jurgen Habermas's work in this area and the many responses to it, such as Fraser's. Fraser is introduced here because her concept of the subaltern counterpublic offers such a useful way of thinking about how different types of social capital might offer different kinds of opportunities and constraints.

7

AMONG KIN, FRIENDS, AND STRANGERS

Social Control in Cities, Suburbs, and Towns

Social philosophers, would-be reformers and scientists, business leaders, and public officials fretted about the prospect of making a community out of all the different kinds of people who were moving into cities in the 18th and 19th centuries. *The people who most kept them up nights worrying about how to create and maintain effective communities were "strangers" to the city. And the scariest strangers, not just in the United States but also across most of Europe, were unattached young people, transients, and aliens or foreigners.* Now, the fact is that *Western societies have done a superb job of transforming many and perhaps even most of these strangers into culturally familiar and economically productive students, tourists, commuters, and members of distinctive ethnic groups* (Monti, 2012). But no one in the late 18th century or throughout the 19th century knew that was going to happen and many observers thought that newcomers and outsiders were turning their cities into unmanageable hell holes. In this chapter we will find out why.

We will have to do some housecleaning and first describe the ways in which theoreticians and observers talked about (and still do talk about) all the "strangers" in our midst. To our thinking, the best person to lead us through this intellectual thicket is the sociologist Lyn Lofland. She's been writing on this subject for a long time and knows more about it than just about anyone on the planet. Here's what she says about the way in which the connection between *strangers* and city life has been imagined: "The city, because of its size, is the locus of a peculiar social situation: the people to be found within its boundaries at any given moment know nothing personally about the vast *majority* of others with whom they share this space" (Lofland, 1973, p. 3). The city is filled with people who don't know much, if anything, about each other, where they came from, or who their families and friends are. They are strangers in a *biographical* sense. But many theorists, reformers, and community leaders also imagined that city dwellers—especially the newcomers, outsiders, and passersby—also are *cultural* strangers. That is, they do not know or share each other's values, customs, and views about what passes for acceptable behavior, especially when they're in public and can't avoid each other.

In case you missed it the first time, here's the point they were making. *People in cities don't know each other personally and can't be counted on to hold the same expectations and values and practice being in the world in the same way. As a result, it is most unlikely and probably impossible for people living in cities to create a meaningful way of life that most of them can embrace as good and depend on to bring some continuity and predictability into their otherwise chaotic lives.* That's it.

Now, it doesn't take much imagination to see how contemporary thinkers identified with this argument and used it in their work. The human ecologists and reform-minded scholars of the Chicago School hoped new institutions like large corporations and school systems and more geographically inclusive forms of metropolitan government would give people new and better ways to relate to each other. The conflict-minded Marxists and postmodernists figured people would either fight their way to a new and better world or be reduced to hiding behind the walls of the smaller parts of the city where others like them could avoid "those other people" and find a measure of peace and quiet.

Whatever validity their ideas may have, Lofland points out, the condition they talked about was a relatively new one. For most of human history, people lived in communities in which there was little or no anonymity and the arrival of strangers was a comparatively rare occurrence. In the late 18th century and early 19th century, newspapers in many cities still published the names of people who were visiting and where they were staying. That practice was quickly abandoned as cities grew and widespread immigration began to take hold sometime after 1820.

As we have seen, the transition to life among large numbers of strangers deeply troubled observers of early urbanization and we continue to be troubled by the apparent puzzle of how to form meaningful or at least effective ties with others. This is why classical theorists like Durkheim and Simmel used terms like "anomie" and "strangers" to describe the mental and social

states of people who filled the industrial cities of 19th century Europe and America. It's also why theorists like Gustav LeBon worried about "crowds" and Marx expected the "proletariat masses" to rise up against their capitalist overlords. People were expected to act in a disruptive manner because their contacts with others were superficial and unconstrained by convention.

One of the most compelling themes in 19th and 20th century thinking about cities and urban life revolved around how people could possibly get along and, in effect, manage and control their own and each other's behavior. The dense population concentrations in urban areas offer interesting trade-offs: possibilities for anonymity, potential to locate people similar to oneself, but also questions of how to control large numbers of people who do not have personal ties to one another. And no one, it seemed, had very good or satisfying answers to these questions.

In smaller communities such as villages or small towns, social control is easier to understand and execute. It is largely a matter of the personal knowledge residents have of one another and their familiarity with a well-established way of life. In theory, because individuals are likely to know one another personally and everyone's behavior is highly visible to everyone else, it is easy for a small community to have an explicit set of standards and to be able to enforce them. Strangers are easier to manage because they are so few in number and so highly visible. In large, densely populated communities, such controls cannot be effective, or so it was thought.

If most of the people one encounters on a daily basis are strangers, how were they to avoid a Hobbesian "war of all against all?" How could urban residents possibly count on one another to enact at least a modicum of decent, civil behavior? As we saw in the chapter on classical statements about urban life, one of the chief concerns classical theorists dealt with was that of how societies composed largely of a wide variety of people who did not know each other would cohere.

This chapter examines how urban dwellers and municipalities manage strangers and newcomers, both as groups, as in cases in which large numbers of new people arrive in a city at once, and as individuals on a daily basis. Controls can be formal, that is, according to established laws or procedures, or informal, exerted according to tacit norms or mores. Urban dwellers around the world solve problems of social control in ways that reflect overarching cultural values. In the United States, questions about balancing need for social control are often weighed against our cultural belief in individual freedom and privacy.

We will look first at issues related to groups of newcomers or strangers in cities and the ways that U.S. cities have responded particularly in periods of high levels of immigration, both internal and international. We then turn our attention to the kinds of mundane ways that urban dwellers exert control on each other to behave in socially acceptable ways and even forge meaningful social connections in such a "world of strangers" (Lofland, 1973). As we will see, city residents have a variety of ways to connect with one another without completely compromising their privacy and ways of working together to promote social cohesion that don't depend on personal connections. Where this is not possible, they also develop skills that help them to avoid situations or people that might be dangerous. Underscoring all these discussions are questions about the nature of public space available in a city and the ways that the built urban environment influences the interactions that take place there.

SOCIAL CONTROL OF GROUPS

Lyn Lofland (1973) argues that one of the most astonishing features of preindustrial urban life to someone from the 21st century would be the very public and violent methods that were used to control peoples' behavior. Public torture, amputations, hangings, stonings, burnings, and beheadings were among the techniques that were used. Such punishments were usually carried out in the busiest public spaces of the city such as markets, and onlookers frequently became enthusiastic audiences and, in some cases, participants. The bodies of the executed were frequently left to rot in full public view as an added inducement to others not to engage in the crimes that would result in such a fate.

In the colonial era of the United States, leaders continued to rely on such highly personal and very public mechanisms of social control to manage behavior they deemed unacceptable. Among the problems and violations people included on this list were various forms of vice (everything from adultery to public drunkenness), poverty, and indebtedness. Some methods to deal with such matters were less violent, like impounding the property and livestock of debtors and placing impoverished or ill persons with relatives or in the homes of other citizens willing to care for them. But physical punishments were still meted out. "'Sinners' were frequently pilloried and subjected to public ridicule. Colonial Boston, for instance, had three well-patronized whipping posts, and whipping was one of the more popular spectator sports in America at the time" (Lofland, 1973, p. 35).

By the early 1800s, urban areas in the United States were already too large and too densely populated for such shaming methods to be effective and public punishment was becoming less acceptable. At the same time, American cities were about to experience rapid growth in the years preceding the Civil War and their populations would include larger numbers of transient workers, young single men with no particular investment in the community, and after 1840 large numbers of immigrants. In this same period, most cities experienced an increase in property and violent crimes. Middle-class business leaders who counted on a modicum of social order to encourage commercial activity and members of the middle and upper classes who were less concerned about business but more about morality had to find new ways to control growing urban populations.

Many of the public institutions we take for granted today—not just the police and schools but organizations like the YMCA and Girl

Scouts—were created to solve problems related to social order and control. At the same time, a cultural tension between the need for social control and a deep belief in individual rights was evident even in America's earliest urban history. For example, as urban populations grew dramatically in the mid-1800s, middle and upper classes (and particularly people in the business community) who feared increases in social disorder began to advocate the creation of professional police forces. But there was significant nervousness about the idea of a formal institution of social control, mostly because the oppressive nature of British control remained so fresh in the public consciousness. As a result, policing advocates had to overcome popular distrust of military-like authorities, and early police weren't even allowed to wear uniforms or carry firearms. In addition, cities were growing so quickly that it was impossible to hire adequate numbers of police. Wealthy citizens and business elites were able to demand that officers' attention be concentrated on the neighborhoods that mattered most to them, leaving crime unchecked in working-class and poor neighborhoods. The irony of this policy, of course, was that the lack of policing in such neighborhoods increased elites' perception of them and their residents as dangerous (Chudacoff & Smith, 2005).

These "dangerous classes" presented an additional challenge for urban elites. In the first half of the 19th century, middle-class reformers placed the poor and delinquent in almshouses, workhouses, and penitentiaries. These institutions, consistent with prevailing Protestant ideals, were meant to provide deviants with a steady and stable organizational backdrop that would facilitate their conversion if not to firm Christian beliefs then at least to more socially acceptable behavior. The added benefit to the middle and upper classes, of course, was that those whose behavior or condition they found offensive were simply removed from view (Rothman, 1971). Reformers were acutely aware that such institutions would never be adequate to solve the social problems of growing cities and worried that these undesirables might wreak social havoc at

any time. The institution of free, tax-supported schools (and later mandatory school attendance laws) resulted in part from reformers' belief that schools could assimilate the children of immigrants and inculcate acceptable values in the children of the poor. Boston led the nation in school reforms, opening public elementary schools in 1818. By the 1850s, most of the country's growing urban areas had some publicly funded schools.

Unattached women constituted another category of people moving to cities in this era. According to the prevailing morality of many elites, unmarried young women were, at best, vulnerable to the pull of vices like drinking and prostitution. At worst, they were already morally compromised by the time they arrived. Women moving to cities alone in the late 1800s included native-born Whites from rural areas, African Americans from the South, and children of European immigrants. Burgeoning urban areas drew young women principally because of the opportunities for wage employment in factories. Jobs in factories or as domestic workers gave single women their first opportunities to earn money of their own and enjoy independence. However, women's wages in factories or as domestic workers were not sufficient to maintain individual households, so many lived in boarding houses or in institutions such as the YWCA where they could pool financial resources and provide each other with the support to avoid some of the urban dangers to which single women might be exposed and succumb.

The next challenge to urban social cohesion in the United States came in the form of massive immigration beginning in the late 1800s and continuing into the first quarter of the 1900s. As we saw in the last chapter, urban elites feared immigrants in part because so many were poverty stricken and helped to swell cities' populations of poor residents. In addition, many newcomers had lifestyles, habits, and hobbies that seemed antithetical to middle- and upper-class residents' beliefs about the behaviors required to make and keep their city orderly. The native-born working classes frequently feared what the influx of new work-hungry migrants meant for their own job security.

On one hand, urban areas needed the new residents they attracted. These newcomers were the laborers, the customers, and the tenants that made urban growth possible. However, cities did not always manage the arrival of newcomers gracefully. Due to the large numbers of newcomers in this era, most cities periodically experienced violence among groups who believed their interests, particularly their economic interests, were being threatened by new arrivals. The number of riots, violent strikes, and brawls among the city's different social classes, races, and ethnic and religious groups grew during the 19th century and probably peaked in the latter decades of that century and the early decades of the 20th century (Davis, 1986; Ryan, 1997).

Attempts to control large populations of newcomers in America's growing cities did not come only from other city dwellers. At turn of the 20th century (and during period of rapid urban growth preceding it), rural Americans often viewed the interests of those in urban areas as opposed to their own. They saw their own social (that is, moral) and political influence fading. They launched a series of moral and political crusades of their own, many of which were intended to reassert what they considered "traditional" American values.

Some historians view the national temperance movement as the last gasp of rural dominance in the United States. While it is true that rural religious figures were leaders in promoting Prohibition, the movement also represented the beginnings of ties among rural leaders and urban middle-class leaders (primarily Protestants). Rural fear and distrust of cities and the social changes they seemed to exemplify and foment also gave rise to the resurgence of the Ku Klux Klan in the second and third decades of the 20th century. The KKK became especially influential in rural areas where it was easy to imagine that the nation's problems were being caused by the non-Whites, Catholics, immigrants, Jews, and feminists concentrated in cities.

Violence was not the only way that urbanites attempted to control newcomers. One option for dealing with newcomers or people whose color, lifestyle, or behavior residents found distasteful was to avoid them altogether. Those who faced the most discrimination were newcomers who were non-White. By the turn of the 20th century, many cities had ordinances that prevented African Americans, Asians, and Latinos from buying land in certain areas or locating businesses in certain neighborhoods. So while White immigrants ultimately dispersed throughout urban areas and into suburbs, non-Whites remained concentrated in the neighborhoods available to them, limiting their business and educational opportunities.

Such ordinances were only one of a number of reasons that many newcomers to U.S. cities ended up living in *enclaves* with others like themselves. *Enclaves emerged in part because of attempts of native-born populations to control newcomers, but also allowed groups of newcomers to manage some of the risks inherent in moving to a new city.*

An enclave has some characteristics of a subculture, in which a group of people shares common traditions and values that are ordinarily maintained by a high rate of interaction within the group. The Hasidic community in Brooklyn, New York, is a good example of how people sharing an ethnic and religious identity can support each other and develop an effective enclave. However, this kind of community also can insulate its people from criticism when they behave in ways that outsiders would condemn. That same Hasidic community, for example, has been opened to criticism because it refused to share information about child abuse with local authorities, and some members of the community found themselves ostracized for speaking out (Otterman & Riviera, 2012).

An enclave differs from a subculture in that it is generally understood to be bound to a particular place—a neighborhood for example. They are characterized by the proliferation of commercial establishments and other institutions particularly suited to serving the needs of the resident group (Abrahamson, 2006). Another good contemporary example would be the shops, churches, and travel agencies that all serve the Chinese American community in any of the Chinatowns in major urban centers. But not all subcultures have ties to places that would make us refer to them as living in an enclave. For example, the contemporary European Romany population is highly mobile, moving back and forth within countries like Spain, or even across borders to see relatives and to celebrate Romany holidays.

At one time ethnic enclaves existed primarily in central cities, though in particular regions of the country where there were large numbers of settlers coming from particular areas, rural enclaves often formed. Enclaves grow by becoming magnets that attract new members of the group, who, in the case of enclaves based on ethnicity or national identity, might be kin of residents already there. Traditionally, enclaves were differentiated from ghettos by a relatively high degree of commercial self-sufficiency— they were basically economically self-contained.

Enclaves formed in places they did for a variety of reasons. Closeness to places of work associated with members of the distinctive group is often one reason the settlers chose a particular residential area. In some cases, such as the concentration of Norwegian immigrants in sections of Brooklyn near the East River, recent immigrants lived close to their jobs in the nearby shipyards and docks. In addition, however, living near the water seemed to make these Norwegians feel at home (Jonassen, 1949). In other cases, enclaves develop because of patterns in real estate markets. Wealthier people who can afford to live in the most desirable parts of a city give rise to upper-class enclaves, such as Boston's Beacon Hill. Less well-off newcomers must live where they can afford to and so concentrate in areas that are affordable and available. Enclaves continue to grow because they then attract other people who share the same significant quality as the pioneers. New members are recruited through social networks and attracted to the enclave by its unique amenities.

Enclaves may offer those who fear newcomers a sense that such a group is safely contained in a particular area of a city. However, an enclave also offers newcomers safety in numbers and access to innumerable social and economic resources. A good contemporary example of this is the Iranian enclave in Houston. For those who follow traditional Muslim practices in arranging and negotiating marriages, observing communal religious holidays, enclaves offer important resources, because the rest of society is not set up to make such observances possible. For example, the proper traditional response to death in a Persian Muslim community involves assembling mourners in a mosque for a prayer service, ritual washing of the corpse, burial in an exclusively Muslim graveyard, digging the grave exactly to a prescribed depth, and making sure that the deceased faces Mecca. Even within the enclave it is difficult enough to find the technical skills and communal cooperation that are needed for such tasks. Outside the enclave, it is all but impossible.

Despite violence and sometimes legal attempts to manage them, newcomers to cities don't always remain outsiders for long, especially when there are large numbers of them. While elites of this era believed they had an interest in managing the newcomers they saw as undesirable, the newcomers themselves were finding a variety of ways to manage their lives and experiences in their new homes. Ethnic enclaves provided important loci in which this could happen. As immigrant groups began to represent larger proportions of many urban populations, they leveraged the networks and internal social capital created in enclaves to increase their economic and political opportunities, first among themselves, then beyond those groups. Not all of these efforts relied on completely legal means, creating a new set of challenges to urban social control. In the late 1800s, as cities expanded too rapidly for municipal governments to keep up with the burgeoning needs for infrastructure and poor relief, neighborhood or enclave "business" leaders sometimes began to take on these responsibilities. In so doing, they cultivated loyalty through their use of political *patronage*, providing loans, jobs, and other services to those who needed them for the price of recipients' fealty.

At the same time, nascent municipal governments were generally in a state of flux, as municipal leaders struggled to retain control of their cities and, in their view, protect municipal control from encroachments by growing state governments. The combination of deep urban needs and barely controlled chaos in municipal governments and leadership allowed successful enclave business leaders to step into key roles in city governments, ushering in the era of urban machine politics. The immigrants and sons of immigrants who often became city machine bosses were intimately familiar with the needs of the populations they served. They governed cities the way they controlled neighborhoods: by granting personal services and favors to individuals (e.g., public sector jobs as police officers, teachers, clerks, and inspectors) and neighborhoods (such as parks, sanitation, or road improvements). In exchange, their constituents and erstwhile clients provided the leaders with the loyalty the machine's political personnel needed to maintain control of public offices, returning the favors they had received with financial contributions at campaign time and their votes at the polls.

The stereotypical machine boss of the era was a first- or second-generation Irish immigrant. Perhaps the most prominent example is the Tammany Hall machine that controlled New York City for several decades. Like other immigrant organizations that ultimately become more political in nature, the Society of St. Tammany began primarily as a fraternal order with "wigwams" in the major cities of the Northeast. In Manhattan, its leaders, primarily businessmen, drew on their tight connections with Irish immigrants to influence the outcomes of local elections through the influence of patronage and occasionally through outright violence at the polls.

On one hand, machine politics and systems of patronage created social order. Bosses created clear systems of hierarchy and social deference in urban societies that lacked them before and often provided genuinely needed infrastructure and services. In doing so, they had to work closely with business people who wanted to build and serve the growing urban population.

On the other hand, such systems frequently relied on financial corruption and at least the threat of violence. Municipal indebtedness increased dramatically during this period.

In many cities, native-born elites responded to the rise of machine politics with municipal reform movements. One way to undermine urban machines was to try to limit voting rights to property owners, thereby excluding large numbers of the immigrants and working-class residents whose votes had supported urban machines. The rationale, of course, was that those who owned property (and paid property taxes) were those who properly understood the city's best interests. (Similar rationales were used in southern cities such as Memphis to limit the franchise of Blacks and poor Whites.) In cities where limiting suffrage was not politically feasible, reformers worked to make municipal elections nonpartisan and to rationalize and bureaucratize municipal offices and functions to remove from the equation the personal loyalties on which patronage systems depended.

Social deference, at least in matters of government, was shifted to deference to formal rules and structures based on qualifications or expertise rather than deference to powerful individuals to whom one was connected by virtue of common national origin. Such reform efforts represented a push back against ethnic minorities by native-born elites. Nonetheless, lawmakers still depended largely on ethnic working-class constituencies to be elected. In this way, ethnic minorities and their representatives slowly moved from machine-style means of leveraging municipal control to retaining control through sheer voting power. This led to the passage of Progressive Era reforms including regulations regarding housing, working conditions, and pensions in nearly all U.S. cities. Despite native-born Americans' attempts to rein in immigrants and their influence, immigrants made their marks on the cultures of the cities where they located. In Milwaukee, for example, the large number of German immigrants gave the city a distinctly German feel (Orum, 1995), and the city retains marks of its German heritage today.

As we have seen, enclaves have traditionally formed around racial or ethnic identities. But industrial-era cities were famous for other kinds of voluntary and sometimes legally enforced "enclaves" created around their residents' wealth or religion too. Beacon Hill and Back Bay Boston are two such upscale enclaves. So, too, were the gated and very exclusive neighborhoods at the western edge of St. Louis that were built for that city's wealthy commercial and industrial leaders at the end of the 19th century. Early suburbs had some of the same trappings of exclusivity.

Of late, we've expanded the understanding of identities that can be the basis of enclaves to include other kinds of groups, such as the gay enclave in the Castro neighborhood of San Francisco, which began to emerge in the 1960s. We can even imagine groups based on some other commonality like wealth, occupation, lifestyle, or some combination thereof. What remains the same is that in general an enclave involves a special relationship between a distinctive group of people and a particular place; the question today is what kind of place. Today there are enclaves even in suburbs—inner-ring suburbs are now often home to very recent immigrant enclaves—groups that once would have been found in central cities.

While we probably wouldn't say that they are completely self-contained today, we can still see that enclaves have sets of institutions and commercial establishments aimed at the population that exists there: churches, therapists, and clinics that specialize in treating members of the population; grocery stores and restaurants with particular kinds of foods; and clothing stores that sell specialty clothing. In San Francisco, the Gay Yellow Pages directory is comparable to other cities' Chinese Yellow Pages, or the Hispanic Yellow Pages.

One contemporary example of a suburban enclave is Orange County, California's Little Saigon, reputedly the home to the highest concentration of ethnic Vietnamese people outside of Vietnam itself. A visitor to any of the several municipalities, including the cities of Westminster and Yorba Linda, finds innumerable Vietnamese restaurants, grocery stores, and shops carrying the specialized traditional clothing for Vietnamese wedding ceremonies. At the heart of the consumer experience in Little Saigon is the Asian Garden Mall, a prime example of the way that newcomers to U.S. cities both shape and are shaped by the communities and institutions they enter. Though the indoor shopping mall has become a hallmark of U.S. suburban life, the Asian Garden Mall is interesting because it has been designed around several features of Vietnamese culture that are quite different from the dominant commercial culture in the United States. The developer, himself a Vietnamese American, designed the mall recognizing the importance of shopping areas in Vietnam for adult socialization, and to that end, put the food court type area at the right at the main entrance. Because haggling is a part of Vietnamese shopping culture, stores that sell similar items (for example, all the mall's jewelry stores) are grouped together rather than placed at opposite ends of the mall to facilitate shoppers' ability to bargain with merchants.

One way to deal with the multitudes in urban settings is to try to escape them. Suburban developments, as we just noted, were a crucial tool in keeping people apart who weren't supposed to be able to live together congenially or were disinclined to try. In Europe, suburbs, as an area outside the city to which wealthier residents could retreat, have a long history dating all the way back even to the Middle Ages (McDonnell, 1978). In the days before mechanized transportation, these areas were on the fringes of cities. By the late 19th century, British planners were designing planned towns nestled into the outskirts of cities like Manchester and London for middle-class families (Porter, 1994; Corden, 1977). As we saw in Chapter 3, housing and lending policies in post–World War II America encouraged the rapid expansion of suburbs; new developments were available primarily to White, middle-class residents. Developers and neighborhood associations used racial covenants to keep middle-class African American families from purchasing homes in new suburban developments (Massey & Denton, 1993).

Day-To-Day Stranger Management

Not all stranger management involves keeping different kinds of people apart in ghettos or enclaves or is as dramatic and frightening as the large-scale episodes of urban violence described above. Sociologists have also examined the myriad methods that urban dwellers use to exact respectable behavior from one another (most of the time). Some of these means are formal, legal mechanisms, and many more are informal. Some of the solutions offered, as we will see later in the book, have focused on changing peoples' behavior by making changes to the physical urban environment.

Consider, for example, that an estimated 38 million people visit New York's Central Park each year (http://www.centralparknyc.org/visit/general-info/faq/), or that on an average weekday, about 38,000 people pass along the sidewalk of just one New York City block (Whyte, 1974). Needless to say, few of these people know each other and many of the individuals use these spaces for different purposes. Even early statements about urban life were very concerned about what it would mean to live among and share public spaces with strangers. Wirth, for example, argued that living among strangers would force people to change how they related to others in some fundamental ways. In particular, they would have to rely far more heavily on thinking categorically about the people around them—that is, relating to people as members of groups rather than as individuals.

More recently, Lyn Lofland (1973) has argued that there are two ways to make sense of strangers, both based on visual cues, either from their appearances and/or according to spatial information about the kind of people likely to be found in some part of the city. Prior to the advent of ready-to-wear clothing, for instance, what one wore was more narrowly determined by one's status or occupation than it is today, and elites in

preindustrial cities at times created new ways to distinguish themselves from the "meaner" classes so that there would be no confusion about who was deserving of social deference.

Another worry that has persisted since it was first articulated by observers such as Simmel is that living so much among strangers would have an alienating effect on the human psyche, which would undermine peoples' willingness or ability to behave civilly toward each other. Recall from Chapter 4 Simmel's concern that urban dwellers would become blasé or completely indifferent to others' needs. This same fear is frequently revisited at moments when the media brings an incident to light where a shocking degree of uncaring behavior has taken place. One particularly infamous case was the 1964 murder of Kitty Genovese in Kew Gardens, Brooklyn, when it seemed that many people must have heard the assault as it was happening yet did nothing to stop it or even called the police. And yet, such incidents of apparent urban chaos are rare, suggesting that most of the time, urbanites can count on each other to behave in relatively orderly ways. What principles order everyday behavior in the public spaces city dwellers share?

As we saw in the classical theorists' statements on urbanism, many pointed out that urban life would require increased reliance on formal social control mechanisms. Some viewed this change negatively, imagining that the loss of interactions based on personal knowledge associated with premodern life was truly that—a loss. But if we take culture seriously as we do in this textbook, it makes more sense to think about the different opportunities and constraints that may be available in different kinds of relationships. For example, when formal rules govern an impersonal interaction, participants may not have as much discretion as would be useful. However, when personal considerations are the bases of interactions, there may be pressure for participants to avoid resolving situations in ways that include negative consequences. Some research bears out concerns about avoidance of formal consequences in smaller communities where law enforcement officials know those in their communities well. Some researchers estimate that incidents of domestic violence are highly underreported in rural areas, as police who know both perpetrators and victims well look to try to get the parties to resolve the situation informally rather than make a formal arrest (Van Hightower & Gorton, 2002).

As leaders in rapidly growing and industrializing cities attempted to grapple with the needs of their many new residents, cities developed reputations as unhealthy, alienating, and immoral places to live. Those assumptions, as we will see later in the book, translated into approaches to planning and designing cities that tried to bring little bits of solitude and nature into cities. Perhaps this was not a bad idea in theory—planners wanted to give people a break from congestion and the stress of constant stranger management by providing arrangements of housing and parks that afforded quiet and privacy. In other words, prevailing planning models of the day attempted to bring a little bit of small-town life to the city.

Jane Jacobs (1961) argued against these models of planning vigorously. Why? Because she thought that what makes cities fundamentally different from small towns and suburbs is the way that strangers must work together to maintain social control. In small towns or communities, residents can use informal social pressures that can only be brought to bear among people who know each other personally. For example, residents of a small community may feel pressure to treat others reasonably well to avoid damage to their own reputations.

Like the classical social theorists who worried about social cohesion in growing cities, Jacobs argues that such personal types of social control are ineffective in cities. Residents and planners can't solve urban problems, she says, using solutions that work in other kinds of places. Jacobs argues that what makes urban life dangerous at times is not the simple fact that people don't know each other. Urban spaces are dangerous when the built environment or daily practices offer no effective way to manage strangers—no casual sources of social control. You have to make use of the kinds of social control that work

well when you have lots of strangers around. So arguing against the dominant planning philosophies of her day, Jacobs disagreed with the idea that urban dwellers needed public spaces that promoted solitude. She also was skeptical of urban redevelopment projects that did not promote eyes upon the street or integrate housing with other kinds of buildings.

A safe city street doesn't have to be pretty, Jacobs argues, it just has to be populated. She offers the example of Boston's North End, which was one of the safest neighborhoods in the city even though most of the people living there were not at all well-to-do (Jacobs, 1961; Whyte, 1966). Sometimes neighborhoods are better if they aren't pretty, according to Jacobs. She tended to associate gentrification with people who aren't invested in keeping eyes on the street. At the same time, she said that bars get a bad rap in neighborhoods because they bring in strangers and encourage unruly behavior. But the strangers in and of themselves aren't the problem. Neither, in principle, are the bars, especially when they serve a clientele that is largely local or "from the neighborhood."

Jacobs argued that one of the principal features of a safe city street was that it was busy so that people were watching it at all times. The eyes may belong to people that make some city dwellers uncomfortable, such as homeless people or street vendors viewed by some as nuisances. Jacobs argued that such people can provide the kind of vigilance no one else can. As if to prove Jacobs's point, street vendors were the first to see and report the attempted car bombing in Times Square in May 2010. And as further evidence of just how small and un-strange urban life can be, one of our co-authors, who lives in St. Louis, knows one of the two men credited with alerting the authorities.

One of the principal changes to urban public spaces over time has been a trend toward increasing specialization in the way that different kinds of spaces are used. Urban public spaces were once more frequently mixed use, bringing many sorts of people together for many purposes, all in one area. In preindustrial cities, for example, public spaces were filled with all kinds of people doing many different things—vendors selling goods and customers buying them, public punishment of wrongdoers, begging, disposal of refuse, and general hanging about. The trend over time has been for municipalities to increasingly limit the number of legitimate uses of particular areas. Usually the motive is to cut down on behaviors that people find offensive, such as relieving oneself of bodily wastes, panhandling, and sexual solicitation.

A person's social status has a tremendous impact on one's access to public spaces. Lofland argues (2002), for example, that *"public" space has been increasingly "commodified." That is, a space that once was used by different kinds of people was taken over by a private business or select group of people for their personal use, even to the point that they might make money off its use.* As a result, the owners of such spaces have been able to limit the access of certain undesirable persons like the homeless and panhandlers. In their study of street vendors in Greenwich Village, Duneier, Carter, and Hasan (1999) provide another example of how this process works. He found that because he was White, he was frequently allowed to use nearby restaurant or shop restrooms. The African American vendors with whom he worked were denied access to these restrooms and had to relieve themselves in public, which made them vulnerable to citation and arrest in ways that Whites were not.

City sidewalks are public places in which many strangers encounter each other in the course of their daily activities. In the same study mentioned above, Duneier (1999) also investigated the ways that people using city sidewalks worked to manage other persons' behavior. For example, while pedestrians frequently tried to avoid street vendors and particularly panhandlers who tried to entangle pedestrians in conversation, panhandlers engaged pedestrians' pets and children to draw reluctant adults into conversation.

Ray Oldenburg (1999) provides another important way of articulating key features of places that allow urban dwellers to connect safely with strangers. He calls these places *"third places."* Shops that invite or allow different kinds of people to gain entrance and share time together would be good examples. They are public but at the same time they ironically give people some privacy too by enabling residents to have some control over how much involvement they have with people they meet there.

Such sites have long been important parts of urban life. By the mid-1700s, taverns and coffee shops in colonial American cities like Boston and New York had come to serve as places of trade, leisure, and politics, places where men of a variety of social classes gathered. Ultimately, they served as crucibles for the Revolution (Chudacoff & Smith, 2005). At the end of the 19th century, saloons continued to serve as gathering places especially for young, unattached (mostly working-class) men. Saloons frequently offered free food, served as informal banks where men could cash checks or borrow small amounts of money from the owner, provided places where they could leave messages for one another, and were places where information about jobs, labor organizing, and many other activities could be shared.

These are places like coffee shops, bars, cafes, or even hair salons or barbershops where patrons spend more time than it actually takes to eat a meal or get a haircut. They are places where people can hang out and talk to each other at least casually. They get to know others who hang out there but can still control how much information about themselves they choose to share, and connect with others without becoming obligated to invite others into their private spaces (their homes), unless they so choose. The prevailing social norms that develop in such places define minimal levels of acceptable social behavior, so that it is clear when a patron is violating shared standards of courtesy.

Ideally, a "third place" should provide a space where people set aside status differences, moodiness, and petty personal concerns. Oldenburg also distinguishes third places from some of the civic and other kinds of organizations discussed in the previous chapter—clubs like the Elks, the VFW, sports clubs, or religious groups. He argues that third places need to be open to everyone, while groups based on shared status (like a club open only to veterans, in the case of the VFW, for example), beliefs (as in the case of a church), or interests (like a hockey club) by nature attract a narrower segment of the population rather than a broader one.

A "third place" has a number of characteristics that allow strangers to safely connect with each other without becoming socially entangled in undesired ways. They provide a neutral ground on which people may gather and serve as leveling places where people are not judged strictly by class, occupational, or other types of status. The principal activity in a "third place" is talk, and the opportunity to talk with others both familiar and strange is primarily what draws people into such a place. These places must be open often, so as to be accessible to people at many hours of the day and night. They are characterized by the presence of a core of regular customers who set the behavioral tone of the place. They tend to be places with a low profile rather than fashionable places (that may fall out of fashion at any moment) and places where the mood inside is consistently playful. Finally, they provide an atmosphere similar to a home away from home, especially for regulars. Though we usually think of third places as sites that serve an area like a block or neighborhood, Borer (2008) found that a landmark gathering place like Fenway Park can come to function as something like a "third place" not just for an entire city but even for a large geographical region.

Several researchers have argued that "third places" do not necessarily produce the broader, more socially inclusive contacts that Oldenburg and others ascribe to them. The introduction of certain kinds of boutique shops and restaurants (as compared to those owned by big retail chains) and more upscale coffee houses and reclaimed parks sometimes mark the coming of neighborhood "gentrification" (Hyra, 2006; Zukin, 2009; Madden, 2010; Carroll & Torfason,

2011; Papachristos, Smith, Scherer, & Fugiero, 2011; Tissot, 2011). In more exclusive communities, like upscale suburbs, these same shops and spaces serve an equally important integrative purpose for the people who live there. The connections made there, however, are more like those that happen when similar people develop what is called "bonding" social capital. The "bridging" social capital that occurs when different kinds of people assemble does not happen.

A central problem faced by 19th and 20th century reformers was how to encourage people to identify with more of the city that way. Residents might feel good about their own small corner of the city and even be prepared to defend it when different kinds of people began to "invade" a neighborhood that "belonged" to someone else. It was hard to imagine how these kinds of "border wars" might be ended or at least softened, however, much less how the city's different races and classes might come to see the city as something in which they were all invested and felt comfortable crossing.

While images of such race- and class-infused tensions still feed our images of cities and the way different kinds of people fill them, sociologist Eli Anderson (2011) has observed how some minority persons in Philadelphia had found civility and in some cases even friendship in unaccustomed places. His characterization of the "cosmopolitan canopy" details the kinds of opportunities that arise for diverse city dwellers to enjoy one another's company. In his study of central Philadelphia, Anderson finds spaces separate from the street where the diversity of the people there is part of the attraction. These are places like the Reading Terminal, food courts, sports arenas, certain shopping areas, and parks where diversity is expected and people can let down the guardedness they must frequently maintain in other urban public spaces. These cosmopolitan canopies encourage civility, mutual curiosity, in which diverse people may develop the kinds of social competences and sophistication that allow them to get along.

One of the authors of this text (Monti, 2012) has argued that people in Boston have extended this "cosmopolitan canopy" further, even to the point that the city's whole civic culture, not just particular spots in the city, has come to be covered by it. Monti found that people in Boston, a city famous or infamous for its incivility and unwelcoming attitude toward newcomers and outsiders, have become much more welcoming and accommodating than they were in the past. The price that newcomers and outsiders have paid to become more like insiders is apparently one they are willing and able to pay. They have learned how to mimic and adopt ways of acting and talking in public that most long-term and better-established Bostonians embrace. They've also developed the sense of proprietorship for the city as a whole that 19th century reformers hoped for but didn't really believe the newcomers could acquire or execute effectively.

To be sure, not everyone in Boston or any city is equally covered by or willing to live with the obligations that come to people who have embraced comity as part of their lives. But even when they are not finding ways to connect with each other as individuals, city dwellers are continually coordinating their actions in ways that allow things to function smoothly for the most part. Lofland (1973, 1998) observes that urbanites follow a series of behaviors that allow them to maintain a "social bargain" in public—tacit agreements about their minimal obligations to protect one another so that everyone can go about their business. Urbanites must behave so that their interactions with the multitude of strangers they encounter are predictable and ensure the protection of their and others' personal privacy. Questions about how this actually happens spawned a tradition of research that carefully examines the myriad small ways that urban dwellers conduct themselves in public places.

Lofland (1971) argues that individuals first ensure order by ordering themselves to protect their own sense of self in the presence of the strangers they will encounter in public places. They do so by checking their own readiness to enter social situations, and by taking a "reading" of

a setting before entering so that they themselves may behave according to the norms in operation. Similarly, Karp (1973) found that even when people were engaged in ostensibly "deviant" behavior such as visiting the porn shops that once occupied Times Square, individuals were careful to try to maintain an appearance of normality and respectability before entering the store and then protect their own and others' privacy while inside by avoiding eye contact or conversation with other patrons.

Other research has examined the concrete techniques that urbanites use to share busy sidewalks in orderly ways, including continually scanning ahead of the pedestrian in front of them, and cooperating wordlessly with each other to coordinate passing others going the opposite direction with cues like a slight angling of the body (Wolff, 1973). Elijah Anderson (1992) points out that longtime urban dwellers also avoid possible danger by developing expertise differentiating among strangers who might be dangerous and those who are less likely to be so.

Today, urban dwellers continue to wrestle with the need to find effective ways to manage large populations of strangers. For Americans, the dilemma between the need for methods of social control that will be effective in urban areas and our cultural unease about undue surveillance and coercion continues. Consider, for example, the debates surrounding the "stop and frisk" policy adopted by New York City's police under Mayor Michael Bloomberg. The policy encourages officers to stop anyone they choose and frisk individuals with the aim of confiscating weapons. The Bloomberg administration argues that this policy has played an important role in lowering New York's violent crime and homicide rates. The possibility of being frisked and arrested for carrying a weapon, advocates of the policy argue, has decreased the number of New Yorkers carrying guns, hence, decreasing incidents of gun use. But the policy makes people at both ends of the political spectrum extremely uneasy. On one hand, gun-rights advocates claim the policy deprives individuals of rights they believe are guaranteed to them in the Constitution.

On the other hand, civil rights advocates argue that the policy is an invasion of privacy and point out that the individuals stopped are disproportionately Black and Hispanic—and that the policy is a clear case of racial profiling. Taking a step back, we can see that both groups oppose the policy for reasons having to do with underlying cultural values about the importance of individual privacy.

Urban dwellers in different nations manage the balance of social control, surveillance, and privacy in ways that reflect the tenor of these debates in their cultures. A 2006 report commissioned by the British Information Commissioner found that there were 4.2 million CCTV (closed-circuit television) cameras in use in Britain at that time.[1] Use of CCTV footage has become a routine part of police work in Britain. While some municipalities in the United States make limited use of CCTV for traffic control, for example to catch cars running red lights, it is difficult to imagine CCTV becoming so pervasive here in a culture that so deeply values personal privacy.

Some cities are also experiencing a new kind of interactional problem. The interactional problems and solutions described above are all predicated on high population densities, usually a hallmark of urban life. Today, as some "Rust Belt" city neighborhoods depopulate, residents who remain may find themselves with no immediate neighbors. Detroit, which had a population of 1.8 million people in 1950, today has a population of just over 714,000 (*Wall Street Journal*, March 23, 2011). More than a fifth of the city's housing stock is now vacant. This means that while a few neighborhoods, such as Midtown, remain populated and vibrant, many neighborhoods have few residents. Where there are few residents, there are no "eyes on the street," and the individuals (many of whom are elderly) who live in these relatively deserted areas are vulnerable to crime. The city's decline in population creates a vicious cycle in which services decline, face-to-face social controls fail, and additional residents, particularly those of the Black middle and upper classes, continue to leave the city.

Detroit is not the only city in which depopulation has depleted the ability of residents to watch out for each other. Klinenberg (2003) argued that the depopulation of some neighborhoods in Chicago contributed to the deaths in the heat wave that killed hundreds of people there in 1995. Elderly residents in particularly vulnerable neighborhoods were those who had few neighbors to check in on them or help them to safety. Though this aspect of his research has been controversial (Duneier, 2004), the point remains that in cities with declining populations, some of the face-to-face social controls residents have relied upon in the past may cease to function.

BEING ALIKE AND DIFFERENT AT THE SAME TIME

Human ecologists did everyone a great favor by pointing out how populations in modern industrial and urban societies (without much direction but a lot of coordination) manage to house, clothe, and feed most people at least passably well. Somehow these most basic tasks are accomplished every day for generations so that hundreds of thousands and sometimes millions of men, women, and children can make a living and find ways to fit in their communities. This is not to say that everyone does well or is necessarily happy with their lot in life, but that the population as a whole survives and even thrives for long periods of time.

Other theorists—notably those more attuned to all the inequities, rough spots, and holes left unfilled in these societies—were far less convinced about their overall stability and sustainability. They wondered how all the different kinds of persons living in this kind of society could possibly get along and work side by side effectively when there was so much obviously pulling them apart or keeping them from coming together in a social and cultural sense.

On one level, then, the urban world described by human ecologists, economists, demographers, and the like obviously worked. On another level, it obviously didn't or certainly didn't work well enough to keep people off each other's back and out of each other's face. *This is the urban world that social psychologists, so-called "conflict theorists" and "postmodernist" theorists, described and for which they prescribed certain social and cultural "remedies" to treat whatever it was that ailed these societies.*

The major challenge facing these societies was to keep people working from the same social and cultural script, if not always on the same page, often enough and well enough so that all the important routine tasks of feeding, housing, and clothing people could be accomplished. The reformers, thinkers, planners, business and civic leaders, and public officials who worried about this had two compelling problems: how to keep all the different puzzle pieces they were working with from flying off the table and how to assemble them into a pretty picture rather than an ugly one.

They differed and argued passionately about how equal and alike urban dwellers had to be. We still haven't come up with a good or satisfying answer to this particular question. But the broad outline of an answer is clearer today than it was back in the 19th century when the overall shape and composition of modern urban societies started to become apparent.

Research undertaken by historians, social scientists, and policy experts in the last couple of decades suggests that we are not in as bad shape culturally or socially as we have been taught to believe. Places like ethnic enclaves that we used to talk about and still point to as examples of how people put their social and cultural acts together don't appear as solid as they once did. More exclusive inner-city neighborhoods, suburbs, and gated communities aren't as impenetrable and isolated as their patrons and residents expected or wished. People have done a better-than-expected job of managing face-to-face interactions so as to deal with the problem of their "biographical" and "cultural" strangeness. Groups and organizations—some drawing more exclusively from one or another social class, ancestral, or religious collection of people and others drawing from various levels and social groupings—are dealing more effectively with

this challenge as well. The civic cultures of some cities may be becoming more open to different kinds of people as well. We will not know for sure, however, until additional researchers look or take yet another look at the way people in other cities are treating each other these days.

No one would be surprised to learn that it is hard to make residential areas that are both racially and economically mixed (Monti & Burghoff, 2012). The good news is that there are many ways to make effective communities. The homogeneity or heterogeneity of a population doesn't guarantee its success or doom it. So-called ethnic enclaves, for instance, often have a preponderance of lower-income residents and people whose English proficiency is not good (Chiswick & Miller, 2005). Michelle Boyd (2000) and Vallejo (2009) have pointed out that an enclave that has staged something of a renaissance can use its racial or ethnic legacy as a marketing tool and point of historical pride. The same circumstances might promote conflicts between members of the same race or ethnicity who have different social class statuses (Theodore & Martin, 2007; Boyd, 2008), of course. But the concerns and ill will that sometimes pop up when different races, ethnic groups, or classes live in the same neighborhood or part of town need not produce much overt conflict and can inspire people to reach out to other kinds of persons (Moore, 2005; Guest, Cover, Matsueda, & Kubrin, 2006; Brisson & Usher, 2007; Usher, 2007; Hays & Kogl, 2007; Greif, 2009; Chaskin & Joseph, 2010; Britton, 2011; Wu, Hou, & Schimmele, 2011).

The concern over "strangers" and "strangeness" repeated by so many persons over the last couple of hundred years might just as well be applied to the very institutions urban residents created to protect and insulate themselves from each other. *Institutional strangeness* occurs when the people inside one of the larger corporate entities we built to shield us from each other—public schools, large religious institution, parts or all of the government itself—are discovered behaving in ways that undermine our confidence in them (Monti, 2012). A school district might be found discriminating against many of its own students. A church might have hidden its priests' improper treatment of children. These deeds may engender shame and provoke outrage. Even when that happens, however, people find ways to change the institution (or make enough cosmetic changes to it) so that they can gradually learn to trust and count on the institution much as they had in the past (Monti 1985). Continuity rather than dramatic change, comity rather than either consensus or widespread and ongoing conflict would appear to be the hallmarks of an urban way of life today.

SUBURBAN "SOCIETY"

American suburbs, until recently at least, were nothing like the "third places" described by Oldenburg. They were not places where different kinds of persons were supposed to be able to find and become comfortable with each other. Originally, suburbs were only places for the wealthy, as only the wealthiest city dwellers could afford the high transportation costs associated with living even what we now consider short distances from workplaces (Jackson, 1985). People's faith in greener spaces was predicated in part on the idea as sites of tranquility and morality. They weren't cities. They also held enough trees, gardens, open areas, clean air, and water to remind people of calmer, more countrified, if not rural, places. However exaggerated and romanticized, this was part of the narrative that drew people to the suburbs.

By the 1920s, model communities like Sunnyside in Queens, New York, and Radburn, New Jersey, were being offered as alternatives to dreary inner-city apartments and high-rise living. It wasn't until later, particularly after World War II, that many more modest suburban developments were built so that they were affordable to more working-class Americans. Epitomized by the Levittown developments, these are usually what we think of when we think of the suburban boom years.

Historian Kenneth Jackson (1985, pp. 234–245) has said that post-WWII suburbs shared several traits. They were built on the periphery of large central cities and, at least in comparison to their European counterparts, had a low population density. Suburban tract housing also was comparatively cheap because buyers could secure low-interest loans. That made it attractive to would-be home buyers, even if the style of the housing did not.

Suburbs grew rapidly in part because they seemed to offer a number of opportunities consistent with cultural goods that Americans value. Among these are the American value of smaller rather than larger communities, of detached housing, and perhaps most importantly of homeownership. By 1970, more Americans lived in suburbs than in urban or rural areas. Industry and services followed. So much so that by 1980 the modal type of commute in the United States was from suburb to suburb (Pisarki, 1987).

Two other features of the new suburbs made them as socially distinctive as they were architecturally uninspiring. First, they sorted people according to their social class and race. New suburbs reflected the pattern of social separation and even outright segregation that had become so prevalent in American cities of the industrial era. Second, the people who moved there were active socializers and joiners.

William H. Whyte found much to criticize in the suburbanites' penchant for conformity and what he called "group think" in his 1956 book about Park Forest, Illinois, entitled *Organization Man* (1956). But historian Becky Nicolaides (in press) correctly notes that what Whyte described really was a pattern of "vibrant community engagement." People looked for and found many neighborly pursuits and groups in which they could become involved.

It was a pattern that would not persist, however. Within a generation, Nicolaides observed, sociologist M.P. Baumgartner was describing a much different picture of suburban sociability and civic engagement in her book *The Moral Order of a Suburb*. Based on field work she undertook in a suburb outside of New York City,

Baumgartner found a local culture of tolerance but also of indifference and at times outright avoidance. The suburb Baumgartner describes lacked "social integration." Nicolaides (in press) suggests that the apparent lack of "community" was inspired by some of the very attributes that Baumgartner "believed characterized suburban living generally: the 'privatism' of families; the high mobility of homeowners; and the compartmentalizing of social life—all things also present in Park Forest."

The speed with which Americans' social lives and civic engagements shrunk in the last quarter of the 20th century has been the subject of much speculation by commentators like Robert Putnam and not confined to suburbs. But Nicolaides is particularly interested in the suburbanization of social disengagement and chronicled it in her study of Pasadena, California.

She summarizes her observations this way.

In its broadest outlines, the history of associational life in Pasadena comports with the idea that diversity strains the process of community cohesion and engagement. On the simplest level, it appears the town diversified and overall participation declined. Yet on closer examination, evidence suggests that an inclusive strategy could prove successful with diligent, persistent effort. Groups like the Junior League, Altadena Baptist Church, and the Interracial Women's Club showed how a conscientious commitment to diversity could generate robust engagement and social capital in a transformed postwar world. These groups represented organizational expressions of a more inclusive suburban ideal. In the process, though, residents kept things at arm's distance. The suburban home was increasingly closed off from gatherings. A more crisp division between public and private worlds was drawn. (Nicolaides, in press)

For a sizable number of businesses and individuals the suburbs offered little more than an escape from tighter municipal regulations and higher urban taxes. Affluent suburbs could keep taxes lower than central cities that had to allocate large portions of revenue for social welfare programs. But the suburbs also helped to defuse some of the historical animosities that had grown between different classes and races in at least two ways. On the one hand, they provided *individual persons* with similar class and racial traits a place they could move and not be bothered by people they didn't necessarily like (Sampson, 2011). They were every bit as exclusive, perhaps even more exclusive, than many city neighborhoods had been. On the other hand, many suburbs apparently and unexpectedly became sites where *voluntary associations* (e.g., local organizations) and *institutions* (e.g., the public schools) pursued more tolerant ideas and promoted more inclusive practices.

There is some evidence from social surveys to support this hypothesis. It would seem that Americans have become a bit more exclusive in terms of whom they hang out with even as they were becoming a little more inclusive in their group memberships (Monti, Butler, Curley, Tilney, & Weiner 2003). There are lots of people who join exclusive organizations or acquire a diverse set of friends and acquaintances. But a slightly larger number of us today are doing what Nicolaides says the people of Pasadena have been doing. *They have been turning inward toward people more like themselves for their more intimate social contacts and outward when it comes to the groups they join or the ideas they practice in public.*

People may be becoming less enthusiastic joiners and socializers not because they are unsociable and disengaged but because they have grown more confident and secure about the places they live and the people who surround them. They can afford the luxury of pursuing their private interests, likes, and dislikes today because they're more certain that the larger and more open public spaces around them aren't filled with untrustworthy strangers.

Sociologists have long agreed that capitalism (or "privatism," to use the term of Warner, 1968) played a pivotal role in shaping the emergence and defining the shape of Western and particularly of American cities (Tilly, 1990)—and not in a good way. We can also think about the ways that capitalism played a similar role outside cities in suburbs and towns. Even prior to industrialization, wealthier residents of both cities and towns lived closest to the center of towns where they ran businesses and frequently in neighborhoods on hills overlooking the rest of the town. The same residents held many elected offices in their new communities and as a result they were in a good position to see that land in their towns was used as they saw fit.

Over time, the suburbs have become more open or inclusive both in terms of who lives there and how people conduct their public business. The way of life practiced there has become more "urban," just as observers have been speculating and fretting for the last half-century. The results aren't quite what people expected. But they are far from the awful ones that contemporary social commentators and scientists predicted.

CONCLUSION

The days of public corporal punishments being meted out in city squares are long gone. Cities today rely on a variety of formal social controls such as laws and police forces to maintain order. Individual city residents also employ a variety of informal practices to protect their own and others' privacy and remain relatively safe even though many of the others with whom they come into contact are strangers. Americans have not always managed each other and particularly newcomers peacefully, but as cities in the United States have faced a variety of challenges—sometimes real and sometimes imagined—to maintaining social order in times when large numbers of newcomers have arrived at once, and have, for the most part, found ways to accommodate large and diverse populations individually in "third places" and collectively under a "cosmopolitan canopy." As many American suburbs have become increasingly diverse, residents have found ways to manage one another and, for the most part, to live together with "relative" strangers.

QUESTIONS FOR STUDY AND DISCUSSION

1. Lyn Lofland describes how individuals in urban areas can be "biographical" and "cultural" strangers. Does the preponderance of evidence provided by historians and social scientists support her ideas?

2. How much does the physical layout of a place contribute to making people strangers or helping them to become less strange to each other?

3. What social inventions have urban people made in order to reduce or at least manage the impact of strangers?

4. Did the suburbs inoculate people from becoming strangers or do a better job at making strangers into passable acquaintances and friends?

NOTE

1. http://news.bbc.co.uk/2/shared/bsp/hi/pdfs/02_11_06_surveillance.pdf.

8

How Social Scientists, Planners, and Reformers Figure Out What's Going On and What Needs Fixing

This book is filled with references to research and theories about the development of cities, suburbs, and towns and how people in these places live. We described our preferred way to look at all that information and make sense of it (i.e., our so-called "cultural perspective"). Mindful that writers representing other schools of thought can look at the same evidence and come up with a much different take on what's going on, however, we also reviewed their approaches to studying urban phenomena. Fair as we tried to be, of course, there's a good chance that people who don't share our point of view will say we didn't offer a treatment of their ideas that was as thorough and balanced as it should have been. In effect, we stacked the deck to favor the approach we like and downplayed the value of their perspective.

Disagreements of this sort arise all the time among the practitioners of academic disciplines. Our research is reviewed by knowledgeable persons before it's published and frequently provokes spirited debate among specialists on the subject being studied. Sometimes the argument is over the data that were analyzed or the kinds of statistical manipulation to which they were subjected. On other occasions, the argument may be about how our findings were interpreted and the appropriateness of one theory over another in helping us make sense of those findings. It is how we test the limits of what we know and refine the questions we ask.

Apart from standing toe-to-toe and screaming at each other, which sometimes happens at conferences and on the pages of the journals where our work is published, there's really only one good way to determine whose approach actually works better. Put them to some kind of empirical test. Make them compete in much the way athletic teams do on the field. Look at a body of evidence and see which approach does a better job at explaining how urban places develop and people behave.

Such testing is an important part of what researchers do. It's also a distinguishing feature of any discipline that wants to pose as a science.

For these reasons alone, we need to consider how researchers go about the business of studying urban places and people.

Here we will introduce some of the more important protocols researchers use to collect, examine, and talk about the information they gather. Social scientists would call this a "methods chapter." But it's more accurate to say that it's a chapter on the "sociology of knowledge" pertaining to urban places and people. *We're not just interested in how researchers study urban phenomena but in how their methods affect the way they imagine and talk about these places and people.*

The questions researchers ask and answer are connected to the kinds of evidence available to them and how they've been trained to analyze data. All the information at their disposal and the insights gleaned from it are used by more than scholars and students, however. They also are used by people who want to fix what they think isn't working well in these places and change the way people live and work there. Policy makers and reformers can have strong opinions on these matters, and their opinions also shape the questions researchers ask and the answers we come up with.

By now you should have a pretty good feel for the kinds of problems that scientists, planners, and reformers worry about and study. Clearly, there are lots of gaps in what we know. Good research will fill some of these holes and help us determine which ones we should go after next. Even after we've given it our best shot, however, the chances are small that any one perspective will provide all the answers to how people build and live in something as big as a city or metropolitan area.

Research is also expensive to do and time consuming. Not many countries have the resources and trained personnel to conduct research much less the means to put it to good use. Even when we have the money and personnel to conduct research, however, the fact is that sometimes we know what we're looking for and sometimes we don't. On those occasions when we have hypotheses or good hunches about what's going on, the data we acquire can help us figure out which of those hunches is more plausible and which ones we can probably set aside. There are many occasions, though, when our research is a bit more speculative. It looks more like we're poking around in the dark for anything that will help us describe and understand a little better what we knew very little about before. We call this work "exploratory" in the hope that no one will notice how much we didn't know about the question or problem that drove us to get the information we pulled together and analyzed.

As with many human endeavors, it's not the questions we ask that get us into trouble but the ones we *don't* ask. One of the strengths of exploratory research is that it helps us come up with new and better questions to ask. Unfortunately, this kind of research may not be picked up by scientists who test hypotheses or may not be easily translated into testable propositions. Then there's this: *even when we think we've come up with a pretty clear picture about what's going on there's no guarantee that our hard work will be put to good use.* Reformers and policy makers may push ahead with changes based on their own explanations about what's happening and bothering them. Or they may not use the information that scientists pull together in order to determine whether any of the solutions they've been trying out actually make much difference.

There's more than intellectual modesty at work in this admission. Policy makers, agency officials, professional reformers, and part-time activists all have an interest in using research, if only to make the point that they were right all along and anyone who disagrees with them completely missed the boat. They are advocates, not dispassionate observers. They don't have the luxury or inclination to wait for researchers to get all the information that might be desirable to have or think is needed in order to address a problem that should have been taken care of yesterday. And a lot of the time, as we just acknowledged, researchers can't really say what's going on with a great deal of certainty, or that what is going on in one setting will apply equally in other places.

Those of us who fancy ourselves scientists also may have a preference for one of the policy positions being argued over and tip our analysis or choose our words in a way that favors the side we favor. Our error may be inadvertent. But sometimes it isn't. For evidence of both, one need look no further than some of our most ardent arguments over race and ethnic relations in this country. Steven Jay Gould's (1981) reanalysis of IQ research tests showed how the data used in many studies had been manipulated and fudged in order to show that some people—immigrants, Blacks, and women—had lower IQs than White males. More recently, scholars who were invested in the idea that racial segregation was persisting ignored signs that Blacks, especially middle-class Blacks, and Whites were finding more racially mixed (often suburban) settings in which to live (Massey & Denton, 1993; Dawkins 2005; Glaeser & Vigdor 2012).

The lesson to be taken from this is clear enough. You have to be a careful and smart consumer of the research that social scientists produce and planners and policy makers use. We don't always play fair or fight nice. So, the only way you're going to know what information you can trust is to have some understanding of what it is we actually do. By the time you finish this chapter, you might not find our research any more convincing than you did at the outset. But you will have concluded one thing about our work that may surprise you. Research isn't for sissies.

NUMBERS, PICTURES, AND WORDS

Research on urban settlements and people is based on artifacts, pictures, words, and numbers. Obviously, there is less information available the further back in time one looks. Archaeologists literally piece together a picture of early settlements and the people who occupied them from the bones, shards of pottery, pieces of rock and metal, wall paintings, and the remnants of building sites they uncover. The pictures and pieces of their lives that people leave behind become more

numerous, detailed, and available for study when one focuses on more recent settlements. More importantly, people also put down more about themselves in words. Early on they might have left diaries, letters, and stories. Later they would add whole books, newspapers and magazines, and many formal accounts of their business dealings and government records. Today, you can include all the materials stored on the Internet, too. All these sources can be mined for evidence of how urban settlements and people operate.

Key to any scientific endeavor is the systematic collection of information. You can't say much if you only have a little information, aren't sure about where it came from or how it was collected, and, importantly, don't have a clue about how to organize or think about the evidence in front of you. More detailed and accurate information allows us to make increasingly finer and more precise comparisons of urban settlements and the kinds of people who occupied these places. Ultimately, it also allows us to make better sense of how they lived.

Most people equate science with rigorous research that is based on numbers, the more the better. Whether one is dealing with more information from a small number of sites and people or less information taken from a great many settlements and people, numbers are the gold standard by which most research is judged. They allow one to subject comparisons to statistical manipulation and determine with some precision just how much alike or different these settlements and people are from each other. If similar reports were available in the past, you also can begin to put together a picture of how these places and people changed over time.

Equally rigorous but less easily generalized to other settlements, people, and times are studies based on information drawn from as few as one settlement and the records people left or the ones we collected by observing them or talking to them. The information may be detailed, but there simply isn't enough of it to count. These case studies can offer tantalizing hints about how settlements were put together and people lived but not enough information to reach anything like a definitive conclusion about what goes on in other places. However, as examples of exploratory research, case studies can suggest new questions that should be asked as new cases are studied and added to the ever-growing body of research.

Both kinds of studies—the more *quantitative* type where there are lots of numbers from one or more sites and the more *qualitative* pieces usually featured in case studies—are used in research on how urban settlements develop as well as on how urban dwellers live. Archaeologists, anthropologists, and historians study contemporary settlements and people, but their work is the only work we have on places and people from earlier times and hard-to-reach places.[1] Social scientists—sociologists, political scientists, psychologists, and economists—do most of their work on more modern settlements and people. That's largely because their disciplines didn't emerge as respectable pursuits until the middle and late-19th century when people were desperate to make better sense of industrial-era cities and the people who were flocking to them. It also has something to do with the kinds of information they like to collect—numbers—and the way they like their research to be taken—as scientific.

Numbers produced by government agencies are commonly used in studies of *urbanization.* Governments track everything from the number and kinds of people who occupy a given municipality and records of industrial output and jobs to public accountings of public expenditures and taxes. Census data, for instance, are often used to tell the story of how settlements in the United States have grown for all or part of the time since we began collecting that kind of information nationally in 1790. They also can tell us something about the kinds of people that lived and worked there (and by implication which ones didn't), how well or poorly they were faring, and whether they'd done better or less well in the past. Data on public expenditures and taxes help show us what mattered to governments, the problems they faced, and how their priorities changed over time. Information from government records in more recent times is sometimes supplemented

with numbers collected by business organizations, foundations, and nonprofit institutions that were made available to the public at some point.

Researchers who write about the history of different kinds of settlements in the United States before 1790 have to rely on other kinds of documentary evidence. There are maps, drawings, paintings, and, later in the 19th century, photographs. There also were people around who wrote and kept records about how their settlement was doing. Assuming there were persons like them in different settlements and they kept similar records, then historians and social scientists can begin to piece together a more complete picture of how settlements were doing at that time. Newspapers, magazines, and records collected by businesses and organizations such as churches also provide valuable information when they are published or can be retrieved. Much of this written material, however, is better used or used more often in the study of *urbanism* or how people actually lived in particular places and times.

David Tyack and Elisabeth Hansot (1990), for example, used documentary evidence going back several hundred years to trace the evolution of our larger public debates over coeducation in American schools. They consulted school records and changes in curricular offerings for boys and girls, histories written about individual schools, arguments over the up and down sides of coeducation that were published in formal reports and the popular press, pictures of children in different school settings, among many other pieces of documentary evidence to make their case. Beyond the fresh perspective brought to our conversation about the place of girls in schools, this work contributed to an even bigger discussion about the ways in which women's civic roles had changed in American cities. We were able to see how much larger their civic engagement was, how much earlier it started than we might have known, and the historical origins of agitation on behalf of women's rights that took place in the 1970s and 1980s.

Historical and archaeological evidence even older than this was drawn on in the first three chapters of the book where we learned about the origins of city life and the development of cities in different parts of the world, including the United States. You can go back and better assess now how much we were able to glean about the development of cities and suburbs from this kind of material. You'll be reminded that the view of older urban settlements revealed through these records is from something like 30,000 feet and centuries ago rather than the last couple of years and on the ground where individual persons actually lived.

Research with numbers also is found in studies on *urbanism*. Social surveys and polling data are particularly helpful in this regard. They provide us with a snapshot of what persons were thinking and doing in one place or from different settlements just as census research can. The real strength of this research is that social surveyors get a lot more information from the people who are interviewed than census takers do. They acquire a broad but superficial picture of people's lives, what they believed, their attitudes, their affiliations with others, membership in different organizations, and anything you can imagine a researcher might want to know about them. If the sample of interview subjects is large and varied, then what these people said is taken to indicate what their neighbors were probably thinking and doing at the time. Apart from the fact that social surveys can only skim the surface of peoples' thoughts and deeds, nobody was doing large-scale social surveys much before the mid-20th century. The insights afforded by survey research, therefore, go back only a generation or two.

This is where historians can be helpful again. The written materials and pictures that people from the 17th, 18th, and 19th centuries left behind about American towns and cities provide us with a great deal of information. The problem is that the picture of everyday life that one often gets from historians comes from people who weren't average, run-of-the-mill men and women. They were more likely able to read and write and from someplace higher on their community's social and economic ladder than most of the persons they wrote about. Less well-to-do

persons sometimes left clues to how they lived, mostly from artifacts found in the ground beneath where they lived or worked. But most of what was written about their daily lives comes from people who were decidedly better off than they were. There's much more material being provided directly by less well-to-do people today. But all manner of historians and social scientists have been chronicling how these people lived since the mid-19th century.

Among the earliest and most detailed social surveys conducted *before* the advent of the computer and rigorous sampling procedures was carried out by Henry Mayhew (1861/1968) and his associates in mid-19th century London. The richly-detailed sketches of the city's working poor and "street people" captured their everyday lives and struggles, the kinds of jobs they held, where they hung out and slept at night. There were beggars and prostitutes among the people whose stories were told to be sure. But there were many more people who struggled in sweatshops and whatever "casual" employment and part-time work they could find. Mayhew accumulated their stories and summarized them in several volumes that showed how precarious an existence these people led and how very little money they earned for all the work they did. Mayhew's research and writing painted an unromantic picture of life in the most prominent and richest city of his time and helped to lay the groundwork for modern welfare and work relief programs. It also helped to validate some of the studies that were beginning to be produced at the tail end of the 19th century by the early demographers and epidemiologists of their day.

Apart from studies based on things like census data and in more contemporary types of social surveys, most research into urban settlements and people comes out as case studies. Case studies have been a staple in sociology, political science, anthropology, and history since their inception. Often equated with "community" studies in sociology and political science, the unit of analysis or subject is usually neighborhood-sized when the researcher is attempting to study and describe the way of life or culture of the people occupying a specific place. Such a study also might be used to describe the "culture" of an organization or institution, but most of the work focused on the way people lived.

Little or no attention may be paid in case studies to how what's learned about a particular community can be applied to the city as a whole or how the community might have changed over time. That connection is left for the reader to make. The study is generalized only to other "communities" like it, such as an ethnic enclave or village, and only for the period in which the study was carried out. It might focus on a particular element of life in that community, as would be the case in a study focusing on how social class or gender relations play out there. In this case, the author may suggest how class, gender, or ethnic relations in that place or among those people may be connected to class, gender, or ethnic relations in society as a whole.

Entire cities can be the subject of case studies by social scientists, too, but rarely are (Monti 2013). The focus of these works typically is on the way the city's economy, population, and/or political system is organized or has changed over time. Historians and anthropologists are much more likely to describe the culture of a place or people as a whole, reasoning that the events and ideas they see practiced or in play tell us something about the way people generally thought and acted in that era. They also may seize on a particular element of life or event as revealing some underlying truth about the way of life practiced by people in a particular community or society (Boorstin 1974; Fischer 1989).

Historians Susan Davis (1986) and Mary Ryan (1997) showed just how turbulent 19th-century American cities were through their studies of rowdy street celebrations and popular uprisings, parades, and demonstrations. But they also used their careful description of "public life" back then to make a point about contemporary Americans' civic habits. Both scholars effectively acknowledged that contemporary life isn't nearly as rowdy as it used to be. Davis talked about the growth of malls and the erosion of "public spaces" available to people with something on their mind to say.

Ryan (1997, p. 312) used her analysis to raise questions about whether "the pragmatics of making public policy through civil war" may have reached "a point of diminishing returns."

Needless to say, authors working in different disciplines borrow each other's ideas and use complementary approaches to conduct their studies. There is more than a little overlap in their respective approaches and some of their theoretical ideas. Still, historians are far more likely to use their case studies to make a more expansive statement about the times in which the people they study lived.[2]

Social scientists don't look at the world the same way most historians do. You can see just how differently by picking up a couple of social science and history journals and reading some of the articles published in them. Naturally, it would be helpful if the subject matter deals with urban settlements, metropolitan areas, or people who live in these kinds of places. But it need not. In the case of the social science articles, don't worry if you can't follow all the sophisticated statistical analyses that the author presents. Just look at the way the argument is set up and delivered. Do the same for the history articles.

You probably won't have to read more than three or four before a pattern begins to emerge. You'll find that much social science research is built around or delivered through numbers. It also talks about social phenomena using words like "independent" and "dependent variables." Independent variables are presumed to "cause" or are used to account for differences in dependent variables. The size of a city's population or the kinds of people that live there, for instance, might be used to account for how many of the residents commit crimes, how long they are likely to stay in school, or how much money they make. For instance, we might hypothesize that more crime is committed per capita in bigger cities than smaller ones or that bigger cities have more wealthy and poor people but comparatively fewer middle-class people than smaller places have.

Independent variables often deal with big things like the size of a city or something relatively permanent about a person like his color and gender, something that's out of the person's control to change. Independent variables also can include something that people might change about themselves like how many years they go to school, their marriage status, or job. More often than not, however, what people do or say is treated as a dependent variable. Researchers are hoping to determine why so many persons do this and not that, say one thing and not another, and hold views different from the ones that people in other parts of town or other communities hold.

What much social science research about cities and other sorts of communities has in common is the tendency to focus on conditions or behaviors that researchers view as problematic. Bigger places or places with more minority residents, for instance, might be looked at to see if they have more divorced people, delinquency, drug use, people who are poor, belong to fewer clubs, and so forth. Rarely, if ever, would we look to see how many books city dwellers read, how many little old ladies they help across the street, or how often local businesses do things that help their customers but reduce the profit they make. The focus on social problems is in large measure a function of researchers' perceived need to collect information that we think will help understand and ultimately solve those pressing problems. However, the assumption implicit in much social research on cities is that people in bigger and more crowded places or places that have more different kinds of people living there have more problems and more people exhibiting problematic behavior.[3]

Even when it turns out that people in urban settlements are no more likely than village dwellers to have problems we're still left with the impression that the best that big-city people can do is react to changes or adjust to conditions over which they have little control (Fischer 1976). Sociological research sometimes seems to suggest that individual people in cities don't make things happen. Things happen to people, and their response to the conditions they face is often problematic. In other words, it can sometimes emphasize "social conditions" and "structures" at the expense of individual agency.

Research in history journals doesn't always present people as winning or being nice to each other, but they're rarely portrayed as ineffectual. History writers are much more likely to show human beings acting on the world rather than always reacting or being victimized by it. Men and women may not make big things happen. They may even fail. But historical research typically depicts even people who lose as having put up a fight. On the other hand, historians sometimes downplay the way that larger systemic forces influence the range of actions available to those individuals.

To argue that there's something suspect about a discipline whose practitioners have a particular way of looking at the world misses the point. Researchers are trained inside what some people like to refer to as academic "silos." There's a sociological silo and way of looking at the world, just as there is a psychological silo or an economic silo and way of making sense of the world. To make matters even more confusing, there are researchers in each of these "silos" who have different takes on what the people in their own silo should be looking at and how to make sense of the information they tend to collect. It can all be very confusing at times, even to the people inside the silo. But all professionals have a particular way of looking at the world. It's how they bring some order to all the information they collect. Indeed, if they didn't already have these silos, they would have had to invent them just to give their research and writing some organization and direction.

Their differences notwithstanding, there are similar or common themes that cut across the work done by the people in these different silos. None of us can avoid the social and political context in which we conduct our research and write, for instance. Intellectual tastes and prejudices change, though often slower than we'd like. The organizations that underwrite our work have certain priorities and questions they want addressed. It's not a big leap to conclude that they probably have answers they'd be happier to receive and others they'd rather not. Under these circumstances one would be surprised if researchers produced results that were way out of line with what their peers and audience expected. That's why all the different professionals who looked at urban settlements and people in the 19th century came up with remarkably similar pictures of how troubled these places and people were (Lees, 1985). It's also why some kinds of people were thought to be inherently less capable than others and why Black and White people were shown to still be living separately when there were already many signs that this barrier was beginning to break down.

For instance, public and private leaders in the late 19th and early 20th centuries who were trying to understand urban problems were desperate to figure out how different kinds of people were going to fit into cities that were growing very quickly and in ways no one had seen before. *They worked exceedingly hard to find new ideas and ways for all the residents of big cities to come together or act in concert, new ways that would transform a seemingly chaotic mass of strangers into something approximating a self-conscious "people" and effective "community."* Such leaders tended to come from cities' White, native-born elite and were predisposed to believe in their own positive qualities.

It certainly wasn't a coincidence, then, that 19th and 20th century researchers consistently found that White people had higher IQ scores than Black people, men had higher scores than women, and long-time Americans had better scores than immigrants. Research of the sort that showed certain kinds of people being better qualified to fit in had predictable and important consequences for everyday life in American cities and for national policies. Women and Black people were denied access to schooling altogether or were educated less well and not as long as White males were. They also could be directed to fill jobs—in the home and outside the home—befitting their "innate" abilities and temperament. Restrictions on immigration were justified in part because research showed what so many "native" Americans already took for granted: Foreign people would be hard to fit in and were only good for some kinds of neighborhoods and jobs.

Reanalyzing the IQ data that 19th and early 20th century researchers had worked with, Stephen Jay Gould (1996) and his assistants discovered that earlier scientists had tweaked their samples and analyses in such a way so as to make drawing patently racist and sexist conclusions all but inevitable. When previously omitted data were included, Gould found a great deal more overlap than gap in the IQ scores of these persons. He argued that the original researchers had looked at their evidence through White male American lenses. They'd conducted their work at a time when people assumed that White people, men, and American-born persons were inherently smarter and better than Black people, women, and foreigners. No one, least of all the scientists, was surprised when the data came out the way they did.

Gould also found much-publicized contemporary research on the alleged gap between IQ and other test scores for these populations that was every bit as biased as the earlier work he'd studied. It would seem that bad scientific habits are as difficult to break as some bad personal habits are. One of the important lessons coming out of his research, however, was that science also could correct what early scientists had got wrong. The biggest mistake that earlier researchers made had come well before information they collected was analyzed. It was logical or ideological in nature rather than numerical.

Many researchers today, including the authors of this book, would like to think they have some built-in immunity to the bias bug. We don't believe, for instance, that White males are inherently smarter or better than Black persons, women, and immigrants. Nor are we likely to support policies and programs that would restrict anyone's opportunities on the basis of color and gender or keep foreigners from coming into the country and treat them badly once they arrived simply because they were, well, *foreign*. We all want to think that our progressive-minded colleagues can be counted on to treat people fairly, no matter what they look like or where they come from.

The world is more complex than we think. We are as likely to bring our "progressive" bias into the science we preach as reactionary professionals were to bring racism and sexism into the science they practiced. Social psychologist Jonathan Haidt has argued, for instance, that left-wing scholars constitute a "tribal-moral community" just like the one reactionary scholars once had (Tierney, 2011). The roots of this "community" are to be found in the "fight for civil rights and against racism" in the 1960s and 1970s. It "became the sacred cause unifying the left within the academy" and has stayed that way for nearly five decades at this point.

One result is that an overwhelming number of today's university faculty hold very progressive or socially liberal views. Their "sacred values" blind them to the hostile intellectual climate they've created and held over the heads of conservative thinkers since the 1960s. The left-leaning social science tribe has also become self-perpetuating. People who supported those values were drawn to the social sciences. People who held different values chose different careers.

It's not hard to find evidence that the kinds of questions and answers left-leaning people come up with are every bit as biased as the ones conservatives prefer. Sociologist Scott Cummings (2011) recently assembled census data outlining homeownership rates by race for 1990 and 2000. Predictably, Whites had the highest ownership rates at just over 68%. Blacks and Hispanics, at 43% and 42% respectively, had much lower rates of ownership. American Indians and persons of Asian descent, at 54% and 52%, fell somewhere in between. Except for the American Indian data, perhaps, no one would be surprised by these findings or by the conclusion that as of 2000 it looked like Black and Hispanic people still were being discouraged from purchasing a house.

When Cummings broke down these rates according to the nationality (or tribal ancestry) of Whites, Blacks, Hispanics, Asians, and Native Americans something interesting happened. Not all White persons were equally likely to own a house. Persons of Slovenian descent had the highest rates (i.e., around 85%). Whites of Salvadoran descent had relatively low rates of home ownership (i.e., 23%). The

same proved true for different kinds of Black, Hispanic, Asian, and Native American people. Blacks who traced their ancestry to South America had ownership rates at about 53%, but only about 14.5% of Black people of Dominican descent owned homes. Among Hispanics almost 48% of West Indians owned their own houses, while only about 14.5% of Panamanian Hispanics did. Nearly 77% of Asian people of Taiwanese descent owned a house, but only a bit more than 12% of Hmong did. Finally, and perhaps most surprisingly, ownership rates among Native Americans went from about 77% for Lumbee Indians to 38% for persons of Cheyenne descent.

People of different races have different rates of homeownership. No card-carrying social scientist would be surprised by that. Nor would they think that on the basis of such evidence government programs to help people from "races" that have been discriminated against in the past should be ended.

It's not clear what they would say about Cummings's other major finding. That's because we've been trained to expect White people to be better treated or do better than minority people and that something needs to be done to undo the effects of *racial* discrimination. It doesn't even enter our mind to worry about *ethnic* discrimination, and there are no laws singling out individuals from different ethnic groups for privileged treatment like there are for people of a particular "race" or gender. Yet the fact is that there are greater differences in rates of homeownership among ethnic people of the same race than there are between persons of different races. Persons who claim to be politically liberal may have some difficulty reconciling their values with these facts.

Based on these data, for instance, it would be pretty hard to argue that "Blacks" or "Hispanics" as such are being discriminated against today. Are there still gaps between Whites and non-Whites? Yes, there are. At the same time, some Black people have rates of homeownership greater than those of some White people. The gap is either closing or was never as great as we made it out to be. As it happens, rates of homeownership for Black people come closest to matching those of Whites whose ancestors are from Central and South America. This means, of course, that White people from Central and South America have the lowest rates of home-ownership among Whites. We'll come back to this point momentarily.

The picture of homeownership afforded by these data certainly doesn't tell us everything we'd want to know about whether and how we should amend public policies intended to increase home ownership among minority persons. It does suggest, however, that we need to revisit them and think a lot harder about who really needs help and who doesn't.

One could argue, for instance, that rates of Black homeownership will eventually rise to levels achieved by some White groups as more recent Black immigrants from Central and South America gain a stronger foothold in the economy. That would be a good thing, no doubt about it, if only because we wouldn't need to offer public subsidies to "Black people" much longer. This assumes, however, that recent Black immigrants should be included in our policy calculations when they haven't experienced the history of discrimination that Black Americans have. Ignoring that problem for the time being, a better and fairer measure of how much Black people are still being discriminated against today would come from comparing rates of homeownership for Black people from Central and South America to those of White people from Central and South America. Of course, it might take a decade or two before changes that large showed up in census data.

In the meantime, many persons, especially those who think of themselves as being socially progressive and politically liberal, still believe that "Blacks" are victimized by widespread and systematic discrimination. They probably would take strong exception to any effort to diminish the help Black people get to buy a house, no mat-ter how long they've lived in this country. To sustain that argument, however, one would have to show that ethnic differences among persons of the same race don't matter when it's patently obvious they do. One also would have to argue that no White person deserves special consider-ation and assistance even though some could clearly use it and their ancestors have lived here for generations. Given the results of Cummings's analysis, it's actually far more likely that self-respecting liberals would argue that these Whites also should receive assistance to buy a house.

If nothing else, this evidence suggests that our national discussion about race and homeowner-ship policies can't be boiled down to an easy black and white answer. On the other hand, maybe it can. The most provocative aspect of these findings is that they mirror what Gould found when he took a harder and more complete look at the IQ scores of different kinds of per-sons. Namely, there were greater differences among Whites and among Blacks than there were *between* Whites and Blacks, greater differ-ences among men and among women than there were *between* men and women, and greater dif-ferences among native-born persons and among immigrants than there were *between* native-born persons and immigrants.

That evidence pointed to a reduction in the gap between better treated or better liked catego-ries of persons and those less well thought of and treated in the United States. Or it might have been taken to mean that there had never been a sizable gap, much less one that was genetically rooted, in the scores of Whites and Blacks, men and women, or native-born and immigrant Americans. Whatever the source of the overlap in their IQ scores, differential treatment on the basis of one's color, gender, and nativity was not justified. There was no good moral basis, much less a biologically based justification, for treat-ing men better than women, Whites better than Blacks, and native-born Americans better than immigrants.

The important policy issue raised by Cummings's research is that differential treat-ment *favoring* Black people or Hispanic people on the basis of their color might not be justified in the area of homeownership. Even if we were able to come to some agreement on this very sensitive point, it is unlikely that there would be much push to dismantle all the programs set up to encourage homeownership by minority people or that such pushing would succeed. To the extent that is so, we would be acting on a bias no less real and indefensible than the one once used and still used sometimes today to discriminate against American citizens who are Black and Hispanic.

Researchers might help shed light on how big a problem Black and Hispanic Americans still have. Since academic researchers apparently are disposed toward favoring policies that expand the number of claimants for assistance, however, any evidence they bring to bear on this question is likely to be discounted or at least looked at skeptically. As Gould's research shows us, facts don't speak for themselves. They are framed in a way and nudged into saying what people want them to say, maybe especially when sensitive or contentious matters are being discussed.

What often happens in public policy disputes where there are strong differences of opinion like the one involving minority homeownership is that we effectively elect to have it both ways. We might formally accept responsibility for causing harm to a particular class of persons. But it's more likely that we'll simply acknowledge that harm has been done. Our struggle then is to find a way to undo the damage or at least soften its effects on the aggrieved class. The problem, as we've seen in the case of race and homeownership, is that not all members of an aggrieved class (i.e., Blacks and Hispanics) may actually have a grievance and the persons who get assistance may not be the ones who need it most (Monti, 1997). This may be one of the reasons why policy-related research so often shows that reforms make some difference in people's lives but not as big a difference as its proponents had hoped for or its detractors feared. A good example of this phenomenon is apparent in the modest-to-disappointing results exhibited by minority people who participated in the "movement to opportunity" relocation experiment tried out on public housing tenants in Chicago and several other cities in the 1990s. A review of the impact that moving had on tenants showed that the

dramatic improvements hoped for either didn't happen or were a lot more limited than the backers of the experiment had predicted. Part of the reason why the relocated people didn't do better than expected was that they either didn't move far from their old neighborhood or moved into an area very much like the one they'd just left. The ones who did better moved out of Chicago or to a different country (Sampson 2012; Sharkey 2013). Another obvious answer to what happened (or didn't happen), these authors think, is this. The effects of poverty may be a lot harder and take a lot longer to undo than researchers have the time to study or reformers have the luxury and patience of waiting for.

The effect of reforms, one that is unexpectedly captured by researchers, is that we crawl toward changes we aren't as thrilled about—or dead set against making—as we made ourselves out to be. The biggest contribution of research to this policy-making ritual may be that it familiarizes us with persons and places we know precious little about but who have become impossible to ignore. We inform and educate our fellow citizens a little more and a little better about these people and places. Our work is usually better at laying out how big a problem there is than at showing how to solve it or why our reforms aren't working as we'd expected. But that doesn't diminish the broader cultural service rendered by all the studying and writing that researchers do. Indeed, as the history of moral reform crusades in this country demonstrates, our best work chronicles the conditions of peoples' lives, how they deal with the situations they face, and how all their deal making and accommodating plays out over time (Boyer, 1978). It doesn't settle arguments about what should or shouldn't be done. It sets the table we sit around and argue over better.

The fight Gould picked with contemporary researchers who still insist there's a genetic basis for differences in "intelligence" or educational accomplishment, for instance, didn't change how we fund education or treat minority children. What our scholarly intramural spat did accomplish in this instance may have been even more important in the long run. It altered the shape and affected the content of our current disputes over race by reminding us how much louder, strident, meaner, and absurd our table-clearing our arguments used to be. It held the mirror of our own history in front of our faces where we couldn't ignore it. Good research won't necessarily make us smarter or keep us from making mistakes. What good research does best sometimes is keep the light focused on stupid so we can push it off the table or put it under a napkin and get down to talking about what's really bothering us and what we can do about it.

How We Came to Study What We Study

When it comes to arguments over what kind of research is better or needed more to help us get to that point, some of us favor the fragmented, partial but otherwise rich views of life in urban settlements that are found in case studies. Others favor the broader, more representative, but not especially deep view of life and conditions revealed in surveys and census data. The truth is there's actually more than enough space on the table for both kinds of research. As with anything else people consume, however, we have definite preferences for the kind of research we like to set out and think everyone else should take first and eat most.

Antecedents to the quantitative and qualitative research done today were fashioned in mid-19th century Europe. Henry Mayhew's thumbnail sketches of laborers and poor people in East London may have been prompted by fear of the "dangerous classes," but the evidence he assembled made it difficult to paint these people as the cause of their own misery. The cumulative effect of the stories he and his assistants gathered was to show that illness, old age, death, and accidents—notably, conditions over which the poor had little control—made it all but impossible for people to lead a healthy life. The kinds of jobs these people had once filled were gone. Men and women had been compelled to find more casual and temporary sources of employment wherever they could. Displaced artisans had become day laborers, and day laborers became part of a chronically underemployed and frequently unemployed mass of displaced workers crammed together in the slums of London.

John Snow's less dramatic but equally compelling interviews of London's Soho residents in 1854 allowed him to pinpoint which public pump was fouled and thus the source of the cholera epidemic that had broken out that year. Snow's map showed a pattern in the outbreak that had eluded officials. He also was able to track the contaminated water back to the waterworks companies that had been drawing drinking water from parts of the Thames River polluted by raw sewage. His use of maps and statistics presaged the development of public health and epidemiology as research-driven enterprises. The work such people did in tracking and analyzing the spread of contagious diseases and the prevalence of health conditions in certain populations established these types of social research as legitimate scientific endeavors.

American researchers would soon use the same techniques to describe and understand conditions in their own cities. Widespread concern about immigrants, for example, prompted a dramatic expansion in the number and variety of question posed by interviewers for the 1920 census. You might recall that 1920 was the year in which the U.S. population was officially declared to be "urban." In any case, items like the number of rooms each household had and the availability of toilets were introduced so as to provide officials with an overview of immigrants' living conditions.

Analyses based on census data complemented more detailed descriptions of everyday life in American cities. These were stories of the sort Henry Mayhew might have collected or been composed by Dickens (Woods, 1898/1970; Sinclair, 1905/1960; Steffens, 1904/1969; Woods & Kennedy, 1914/1962). The research was often undertaken by settlement house workers and volunteers working on behalf of organizations that were trying to help the poor and immigrants by studying where and how they lived. Their findings were compiled into reports that went to a variety of public and private leaders who needed to know what was going on in certain parts of the city before initiating campaigns to clean them up and save the local residents from themselves (Boyer, 1978; Du Bois, 1899/1996; Lees, 1985).

There's still a strong reformist edge or point to a great deal of social science research dealing with urban places and people. Much of the research done in urban areas or that focused on urban residents in the post–World War II era, for instance, had the twin goals of diagnosing and understanding urban ills and fixing urban places and people. Among the more important topics dealt with have been the redevelopment of older central cities, the consequences of suburbanization and urban sprawl, the rise of newer metropolitan areas in so-called "Sunbelt" states, and the impact these changes had on poor and minority people with few good job prospects who were left behind in rundown inner-city areas.

No small part of this research, much of it *quantitative* and based on census data or social surveys, explored the extent to which minorities, especially Blacks, had access to the same kinds of jobs, housing, and educational opportunities as White people did. Concern about the conditions faced by minorities in general was replaced by a growing chorus of researchers who chronicled the conditions under which persistently poor people live. This was especially apparent in studies of the poorest Black Americans, inner-city residents whose situation was so desperate that it was hard to imagine how it could ever change (Sampson 2012; Sharkey, 2013).

Many *qualitative* pieces of research followed the pattern of case studies conducted by University of Chicago faculty in the early 20th century. This was especially true of work that chronicled the lives of various "denizens" of the inner city or suburbs including gays, street people, the homeless (e.g., Liebow, 1967; Humphreys, 1975; Baumgartner, 1988; Anderson, 1999; Duneier, 1999), and gang members (e.g., Moore, 1978; Padilla, 1992; Monti, 1994; Miller, 2001). A second stream of case studies focused on community

change and the redevelopment of inner-city neighborhoods (e.g., Suttles, 1968; Kornblum, 1974; Susser, 1982; Anderson, 1990; Monti, 1990; Cummings, 1998; Small, 2004).

The specific issues raised in each of these books may have been different. Unlike the work undertaken in quantitative studies, social scientists who write case studies and specialize in qualitative pieces of research like to explore new questions. They're not inclined to revisit other scientists' research sites in order to check out the finer points of their analysis. The authors' assessments of what was going on in their respective research venues, therefore, don't necessarily coincide. Nevertheless, their work reached back to important ideas that researchers from the University of Chicago had brought out in their pioneering work earlier in the 20th century. They were likely to make a connection, for instance, between the physical state of the locale they were studying (e.g., rundown and fragmented versus cleaned up and put together well) and the social and moral worlds of the people who live and work there (e.g., socially disorganized and tough to manage versus orderly and congenial). Gangs were more likely to take root and be nastier in rougher parts of a city or suburban municipalities, for example. On the other hand, neighborhood change and redevelopment would produce better looking and more socially congenial results in areas where institutional and corporate landholders and community people were seen having a bigger stake in the outcome.

The familiarity of the researcher with his community or subjects is a crucial feature in all these studies. Firsthand observations and revealing interviews provide an intimate picture of life in the communities where the research was undertaken. At the same time, they give critics many chances to read their own values into the stories the researcher has chosen to tell about the people and places he studied. Critics have ample opportunity to pick apart the researcher's methods and conclusions and not infrequently impugn his motives in ways that researchers working with lots of numbers usually manage to avoid.

Laud Humphrey's (1975) book detailing the lives of men who had homosexual relations in public restrooms touched a number of these raw nerve ends. It was provocative for both its subject matter and the methods he used to get personal information about the men he observed. The finding that these men were living otherwise conventional, even conservative, lives was overwhelmed by concern over, among other things, the way Humphrey tracked these men to their homes by taking down their license plate numbers and getting their addresses from driving registration records. His subsequent interviews with them at their homes under the guise of an unrelated and notably federally funded survey raised additional concerns. On top of that, the fact that a number of his subjects were employees of a hospital affiliated with his university didn't make senior officials of his university happy. Indeed, the intramural fight inside his university became a much-publicized dispute in the academy generally and was instrumental in the effort to compel researchers to take their human subjects' rights seriously. It also contributed to the eventual closing of the sociology department at his university. Students still read his work, if only to learn how *not* to do fieldwork and research in which the observer also becomes a participant in the site or group he's studying.

Mitch Duneier's (1999) work on sidewalk vendors provided a detailed picture of how these men made a living, the moral and legal lines they crossed, and where they fit into the larger economy. Elijah Anderson (1999) chronicled relations between "street people" and more conventional families in a Philadelphia ghetto. And Katherine Newman (1999) described how the "working poor" of Harlem embraced standards of personal morality usually subscribed to more secure and well-off middle-class persons. Applauded by many reviewers, these works provoked a feverish backlash against both the works *and* the authors for the sanitized and even romantic way in which they had allegedly presented their subjects. Criticized, too, was the way they'd supposedly downplayed or ignored the

woeful political and class conditions that laid at the root of all the problems the authors either danced around or inadvertently embraced by their renderings of contemporary race relations (Wacquant, 2002).

As is the custom in such debates, the original authors were given an opportunity to respond. But the effect of a public and professional spanking of the sort experienced by these authors for messages they never penned or intended to be pulled from between the lines of the stories they related undoubtedly left a bitter aftertaste. It's impossible to know whether other researchers took the cue and didn't pursue the lines of inquiry laid down by these researchers. However, the kind of intellectual reining back into the leftist fold intended by such an attack wasn't missed by anyone.

One of the authors of this book had his own public brush with infamy as a result of his study of school desegregation in the St. Louis area (Monti, 1985). Heralded one day in a lead editorial in *The New York Times* soon after it was published, the work and its author were excoriated on the pages of the same newspaper a few days later by the NAACP's chief counsel who came as close to calling the author a racist as one can without actually using the word. The author's sin was real enough in the eyes of some people who were staunch advocates of the reform and enmeshed in the industry that had sprung up around school desegregation research and programs. He was the first researcher to point out that both the defenders and critics of desegregation were engaged in a loud but well-choreographed dance that created only the appearance of change in the lives of the children the reform was supposed to help. The ritualistically prescribed crises and reforms he described may be vital to the maintenance of the culture and help people adjust to changes in smaller digestible pieces. However, the idea that desegregation enabled school officials to run their districts in much the same way they always had didn't go over well with civil rights advocates who were implicated as "enablers" if not collaborators in this process.

The moral to be taken from these brief stories is that *researchers who delve into sensitive topics are likely to provoke both interest and outrage from people with a stake in the outcome of how these issues play out in the public arena.* This is particularly true of research on topics that agitate policy makers and challenge important institutional caretakers like police departments and public school systems. Much as we might wish it otherwise, researchers aren't in control of the message people take from their work and the political ends it is used to serve. The fact that these books had received awards or some measure of public recognition didn't stop them from being lambasted. Indeed, it probably increased the scrutiny to which they were subjected. The effect of the lessons each of these authors learned, as we noted earlier, was that researchers need to have thick skin when delivering unwelcomed and unexpected news.

In addition to the reformist tradition built into much of our work, there's a second and equally strong tradition among urban researchers to describe and measure everything about their subjects better than we measured it in the past. This more "scientific" part of what researchers do is supposed to help them come up with findings that can be generalized to more settings or groups of people. It is most often captured in arguments over the way we "measure" things by people whose stock-in-trade is presented in the language of statistics. However, it's driven by the same impulse to discover orderly principles in the apparent chaos of city life that pushes reformers to do the work they do.

The primary objective of number-crunching urban researchers, of course, is to come up with principles that describe how these places and people are set up and operate. If someone can figure out how to put all their science to good use, that's even better. But the scientist's interest in patterns doesn't necessarily translate into policies and programs intended to make the urban world prettier or nicer. It's enough for the scientist to have figured out the big picture.

The biggest-picture scientists in urban research are the human ecologists. The information they collect and analyze allows them to describe how towns in Western societies grew into cities and how cities became part of much larger metropolitan areas surrounded by many smaller places. It also enables them to explain why cities in many non-Western societies *didn't* grow that way. Given the right data, more mathematically inclined scientists would generate diagrams and equations that captured how these patterns unfold. The diagram and equation for one city or urban region would be compared with diagrams and numbers from other cities and regions until we have a pretty clear idea of what the overall picture of urban development looks like.

As it happens, two physicists, Geoffrey West and Luis Bettencourt, announced in 2010 that they'd produced just these kinds of equations and done the equivalent of cracking the city's underlying DNA code or structure (Lehrer, 2010). They reportedly did it by scouring "libraries and government Web sites for relevant statistics . . . downloaded huge files from the Census Bureau, learned about the intricacies of German infrastructure and . . . looked at a dizzying array of variables, from the total amount of electrical wire in Frankfurt to the number of college graduates in Boise. They amassed stats on gas stations and personal income, flu outbreaks and homicides, coffee shops and the walking speed of pedestrians."

After two years of analysis, they discovered that "all of these urban variables could be described by a few exquisitely simple equations." According to the researchers, what was represented in these equations were "laws that automatically emerge" whenever people live in cities. For instance, the scientists concluded that cities rather than small towns are "the real centers of sustainability." Their statistics showed that cities are more efficient than smaller places, and not by just a little. "People who live in densely populated places require less heat in the winter and need fewer miles of asphalt per capita."

The physicists also found that cities "facilitate human interactions." Urban dwellers exchange more ideas and collaborate more than people in other kinds of settlements do. Their creativity spawns further inventions and efficiencies that enable people there to live better than they would elsewhere. Mind you, West and Bettencourt don't claim that everyone in cities is well-off and happy about their situation. It's just that the urban population as a whole is better off for having lived in a city than someplace that isn't a city.

As interesting as it must have been to see huge datasets reduced to a few equations, the insights the physicists drew from all their number crunching are anything but new. Economists, historians, the aforementioned human ecologists, and even the spare urban planner or two have used almost identical words to describe the "economies of scale" or efficiencies that cities create. They also have long commented on the inventions city dwellers come up with that enable so many people to be crammed into the same small space without life in the city coming to a screeching halt.

West and Bettencourt may have been too enamored with their numbers and equations, but they did provide a measure of substantiation for ideas about city life that have been around for a long time. This was not a small accomplishment. You'll recall that we noted earlier in this chapter that there are many statements scholars make about urban places and people that are based on good research but not enough data for them to say anything definitive. Their ideas aren't easily translated into testable propositions. West and Bettencourt took the time and had the resources to look at data that effectively put these ideas to a more rigorous statistical test, even if they didn't realize it at the time. They reaffirmed that cities work relatively well and, indeed, a great deal better than their critics have long argued.

As one might expect, there are researchers who have challenged West and Bettencourt's findings and conclusions. Their analysis, one critic observed, did not take into consideration changes that haven't yet made it into data sets of the sort the physicists used. For instance, the suburban "Boomburbs" and edge cities we talked about in the second chapter have been producing many more jobs than central cities in the last

decade or so. The physicists' findings apparently don't reflect that fact. In rebuttal, West and Bettencourt shrug their shoulders and note that scientists still don't have all the bugs worked out in their equations about how planets move. The smaller details of how cities work will be worked out later. Those of us watching these arguments unfold from the sidelines can only nod our heads in agreement with both sides. This is the way we do science.

The other numbers frequently used in urban research come from social surveys. Researchers interview persons and ask them questions about what they do or think about a range of topics. The sample of people being interviewed has to be big enough and representative of the kinds of people the researcher was looking to interview (e.g., elderly people, teenagers, middle-class divorcées) before the findings are taken seriously. If the sample and questions were well designed, then whatever these people say probably applies to all persons who are like them but weren't interviewed. If the samples and questions weren't well designed, then the research can't be taken seriously.

The amount of published research based on social surveys is substantial and covers a large array of questions. What people are asked depends on what researchers think is important and what the people looking to use what researchers find want to learn. Among the first topics urban researchers put through this kind of empirical testing were ideas suggested by sociologist Louis Wirth. His classic essay "Urbanism as a Way of Life" (discussed in Chapter 5) laid out a series of hypotheses about how the size, density, and heterogeneity of big-city populations affected the way people thought and acted. Wirth and most writers of his era expected that people wouldn't react well to living in such populous and compact places surrounded by lots of different kinds of people.

The research inspired by his paper in the decades following its publication showed quite the opposite (Fischer, 1976). Urban dwellers ultimately were not shown to be particularly "alienated" or as prone to acting poorly as traditional theories about modern urban society would have us believe. They certainly have their issues and problems, but perhaps no more so than men and women living in much smaller, spread-out places or people who had the presumed advantage of living alongside others who were a lot like them.

This was a good example of how careful research based on social surveys could contradict what had passed as conventional wisdom for a long time. Wirth's essay is no less revered today as a classic piece of social science writing on the city than when it was first published in 1938. In fact, ideas laid out in it still find their way into our public deliberations about cities and the way people allegedly live in them. The difference today is that there's a lot of research to counter the impression that cities are places where people with problems are likely to congregate and/or otherwise sober and sane people become intemperate and wacky simply because they live there.

Another interesting feature of Wirth's essay is that it built on work he had done on behalf of the National Resources Committee on Urbanism in 1937, the first presidential commission looking into the conditions of American cities. Wirth was its chief researcher and the primary author of the report. Completed during the height of the Great Depression, the report laid out the condition of U.S. cities and the problems they faced. Wirth's essay the following year in the *American Journal of Sociology* summarized what observers had long thought about the impact that cities had on their residents and the poor way people reacted to city life. It certainly wasn't the first time that researchers and writers had expressed their concerns about city life. It was notable, however, for its systematic treatment of that subject and for being published at a time when so many people were out of work and national leaders were worried about the possibility of mass uprisings and political agitation inside cities.

Concern about cities and the ability of people to lead productive and civilized lives there didn't end with the Great Depression. In some ways, it actually grew in the post–World War II era with the onset of mass suburbanization, the loss of unskilled and semi-skilled jobs in cities, and the increasing presence of minority persons—mostly Black, relatively recently arrived, and not yet well integrated into regular economic and social routines—in many American cities. As we noted earlier, a whole generation of academic researchers responded to these issues with an unprecedented outpouring of books and scholarly journal articles on one or another troubling urban problem or problematic urban population.

Another wave of research on the state of America's urban areas and the integration of people into ongoing community routines came in the 1990s. This period was marked by cities completing a marked transition away from manufacturing to professional and technical industries. There also was a dramatic increase in immigration from parts of the world that hadn't sent many immigrants to the United States before and the movement of Black and other minorities into the suburbs. The response by American researchers to all these changes had the same hand-wringing sense of urgency that research during the civil rights era and Great Depression had exhibited.

We'll focus on two different but complementary research debates that arose during this period, both of which built on concerns that Louis Wirth and generations of observers have expressed about urban places and people. The first debate was over the idea that the persons who find their way to urban areas are somehow different from people who don't end up in cities. The second debate revolved around the question of how well people respond to the pressure of living in an urban world today. Both discussions, at their foundation, have an even longer pedigree in the social sciences, one that reaches back to the work of Ferdinand Tönnies (as you will recall from Chapter 4) who distinguished urban societies (i.e., so-called *Gesellschaften* societies) from pre-urban societies (i.e., characterized as *Gemeinschaften* societies).

It should be noted that by the end of the 20th century, researchers were working under the assumption that the better part of the United States was effectively "urban" in character. Every region of the country was heavily urbanized by then. City people and big-city ways were now part of the "metropolitan" landscape, so much so that many suburbanites could no longer escape the everyday realities and problems familiar to people who lived in big cities. More important for our discussion, the ways that researchers once talked and theorized about cities and worried about the people who lived and worked there were now being appropriated to describe American society as a whole and Americans generally.

With regard to the kinds of persons who reside in urban areas, Richard Florida (2002, 2005) has asserted that places with high concentrations of artistic people, immigrants, and gays do better economically than places with fewer of these persons. Modern urban societies (i.e., the *Gesellschaften* societies) thrive when they have more members of this "creative class" because the culture of these places is open to new ideas and people. Now, you'll recall that's what physicists West and Bettencourt concluded and many other scholars have been saying for a long time about what makes urban societies different. But Florida was celebrated as a kind of latter-day prophet and got a lot of credit for opening peoples' eyes to the advantages of attracting a more diverse and creative workforce to urban areas. His pitch was that if you acquired more people like this, your moribund economy would undoubtedly rebound. Cities all over the country bent over backward trying to portray themselves as somehow being more creative than their neighbors. Their clamoring was expensive, but it helped elevate Florida to the status of a noted public intellectual.

The problem with Florida's argument, apart from the fact that scholars had been saying the same thing for a long time, was that the evidence he adduced to support it actually showed how unfounded his conclusions were. He converted his counts and percentages of "creative people" into a simple ranking system and reported those figures. This let him say that one place had more or less creativity going for it because it had more or fewer gays, artistic types, and immigrants.

Florida didn't specify (for good reasons it turns out) "how much" better or what might "count" as a big or little difference in the "creativity" of the local population. If we assume that having more of these persons actually matters, when you looked at the actual percentages of these persons in all the urban areas Florida studied, three things are immediately apparent. First, all urban areas had a lot of people who would have qualified for membership in Florida's "creative class." Any statistical comparison of these figures would have shown the differences among urban areas to be trivial. Second, some places such as Dayton, Ohio, which has seen little in the way of growth, have higher percentages of creative people than a city such as Tucson, Arizona, which has been growing dramatically in the last couple of decades. Third, other factors such as public expenditures on education or military installations might have been more strongly correlated to an area's economic development. In short, Florida had a lot of numbers but his findings just didn't add up.

A second area of research and debate revolves around the strength and quality of the social ties Americans share with each other. Like the research and writing that prompted Florida to look at the data he assembled, this area of research stretches back to the classical social theorists' concerns about how people in cities would get along. This debate about the quality of Americans' relationships with one another was reignited by Robert Putnam's 2000 book *Bowling Alone*. Putnam's analysis of surveys showing changes in Americans' organizational memberships and civic habits over the course of several decades revealed that people weren't joining face-to-face organizations as much and weren't as communally engaged as they'd been in the past. Traditional patterns of engagement and social ties like those that were supposed to be common in *Gemeinschaften* societies have fallen off or into disfavor as we moved into a more *Gesellschaften* kind of urban society. He argued that this apparent erosion in peoples' sociability and civic mindedness was pervasive and serious. Putnam attributes it to changing economic conditions (e.g., more of us are working longer hours) and social habits (e.g., more of us are engaged in more solitary pursuits like watching television).

His argument is consistent with the idea that modern society has wiped out or seriously diminished many of the better parts of life that people knew in earlier times when we weren't as rushed or self-absorbed.

There were problems with Putnam's analysis that other researchers pointed out almost immediately. Basically, there was a great deal of information already in the public domain that contradicted his assessment that people had greatly diminished levels of "civic capital" and "social capital." He didn't take into consideration evidence that didn't fit the view of the world he was offering his readers. A reanalysis of some of the data he worked with indicated that the changes he described weren't as big as he made them sound when he wrote about them.

On at least one occasion he even left out information from a table that would have confounded his analysis. His book shows that people who went to church a great deal donated blood more often. A fuller examination of the data would have shown that people who didn't go to church at all also donated blood often. The omission of non-churchgoers from the published data allowed the author's view of how Americans were changing their commitments and sensibilities to stand (Monti, Butler, Curley, Tilney, & Weiner, 2003; Monti, 2007). In short, the numbers came out the way he wanted them to come out. Evidence that would have contradicted his point of view was not reported. It's very much like the situation Gould found when he revisited some of the research done on IQ test scores. The lesson bears repeating. Researchers can be so committed to a point of view that they skew their analysis and come up with results showing what they expected or wanted to find.

We said earlier in the chapter that research isn't carried out in a social or political vacuum. Putnam's and Florida's respective research are no different. The process and procedures of science are supposed to insulate our work from these polluting influences but can't, certainly not entirely and sometimes not at all. Can we learn anything about our cities or how to make them better? We can certainly learn something about the culture and policy environment in which we ask and answer social questions. The questions we ask or are commissioned to ask are usually framed around what people are worried about today. The way we answer those questions is influenced, sometimes subtly and sometimes not, by what people are expecting to hear and in words familiar to them or likely to make more sense to them.

The political or intellectual bubble social scientists work in has been characterized as "liberal" or "left of center" for a while now. To be sure, there are lots of people inside that bubble who have trained newcomers in ways that reinforced a more liberal or leftist view of the world. Some of the people outside that bubble supported that approach. Other people who don't share that point of view try to push the bubble so that it will go in a different direction. Much as we might like thinking that we work in a bubble that fits our liberal sensitivities and we resist conservative values we don't share, this view ignores just how conservative some of our social scientific sensibilities really are.

The work of Florida and Putnam clearly fell into line with liberal sensibilities in one sense. They were both trying to understand how all the different kinds of people in this country could be made comfortable and more effective. After all, if America is to be an inclusive country, then room has to be made for these different people and they have to figure out how to get along with each other. Liberals like that kind of talk.

In another sense, however, the research these particular men did took us back to a time when public and private leaders worried about keeping all the new people in line and how that might be accomplished. Recall the earlier discussion about civic leaders and reformers at the beginning of the 20th century and their concerns about whether rapidly growing cities could function, given their large numbers of new residents that included both migrants from within the United States and large numbers of immigrants from other countries. We hear echoes of these debates in Florida and Putnam. How accountable all Americans were to each other and how closely they followed the rules and precedents laid down by people who were here first were questions a lot more conservative in their origins than contemporary social scientists recognize or like to talk about today. And there's little doubt that both Florida and Putnam were worried about how closely different kinds of people would follow old rules or make up their own rules and how they'd manage to work together in the meantime.

We'll see in the next chapter how reformers, planners, and policy makers use the science at their disposal to repair urban places and people. In the process, we'll also learn how they try to blend the forward-looking and backward-looking ideas talked about by researchers into a workable program of action. The inescapable conclusion of our review will be that their programs and policies are very much works in progress. This isn't a bad conclusion. It only suggests that the problems people are dealing with are every bit as complex and nuanced as the ideas are for how we can leave urban places and people better than the way we found them.

Questions for Study and Discussion

1. What questions are more likely to be addressed using quantitative data? Which ones are more likely addressed using qualitative data?

2. What kinds of answers would qualify as "liberal" and "conservative" in urban research?

3. Consider any urban problem and outline the evidence it would take for you to be convinced that it had been "fixed" and that we could comfortably move on to address other problems.

4. What are the political and scientific advantages of not being able to say that we had solved a particular urban problem?

Notes

1. Good examples of archaeological and historical studies of ancient cities would include the following:

Max Weber, *The City* (The Free Press, 1958); Gideon Sjoberg, *The Preindustrial City* (New York, NY: The Free Press, 1960); Lewis Mumford, *The City in History* (New York: Harcourt, Brace & World, 1961); Spiro Kostof, *The City Assembled: The Elements of Urban Form Through History* (Boston, MA: Little, Brown, 1992); Sir Peter Hall, *Cities in Civilization* (New York, NY: Pantheon Books, 1998).

2. Listed below are books that deal exclusively with cities, suburbs, and towns in the United States. We've taken the rather unorthodox step of listing some of the case studies we know best, if only to drive home the point that this kind of research has provided scholars with a partial and fragmented but at the same time an especially rich look into community life in the United States. A good sample of books authored by social scientists working in this tradition might include the following: Herbert Gans, *The Urban Villagers: Group and Class in the Life of Italian-Americans* (New York, NY: The Free Press, 1962); Gerald Suttles, *The Social Order of the Slum: Ethnicity and Territory in the Inner City* (Chicago, IL: University of Chicago Press, 1968); William Kornblum, *Blue Collar Community* (Chicago, IL: University of Chicago Press, 1974); Ira Katznelson, *City Trenches: Urban Politics and the Patterning of Class in the United States* (Chicago, IL: University of Chicago Press, 1981); John Mollenkopf, *The Contested City* (Princeton, NJ: Princeton University Press, 1983); M. P. Baumgartner, *The Moral Order of a Suburb* (New York, NY: Oxford University Press, 1988); Elijah Anderson, *StreetWise: Race, Class, and Change in an Urban Community* (Chicago, IL: University of Chicago Press, 1990); Daniel Monti, *The American City* (Malden, MA: Blackwell Publishers, 1999); Mario Luis Small, *Villa Victoria: The Transformation of Social Capital in a Boston Barrio* (Chicago, IL: University of Chicago Press, 2004); Michael Ian Borer, *Faithful to Fenway: Believing in Boston, Baseball, and America's Most Beloved Ballpark* (New York: New York University Press, 2008); and Lyn Macgregor, *Habits of the Heartland: Small-Town Life in Modern America* (Ithaca, NY: Cornell University Press, 2010). Here are several case studies by anthropologists that are worth reading: Sally Engle Merry, *Urban Danger: Life in a Neighborhood of Strangers* (Philadelphia, PA: Temple University Press, 1981); Ida Sussser, *Norman Street: Poverty and Politics in an Urban Neighborhood* (New York, NY: Oxford

University Press, 1982); James Acheson, *The Lobster Gangs of Maine* (Hanover, NH: University Press of New England, 1988); and Max Kirsch, *In the Wake of the Giant: Multinational Restructuring and Uneven Development in a New England Community* (Albany: State University of New York Press, 1998). Some of the best work done by urban historians was published for Oxford University Press in the 1960s and 1970s in a series edited by one the leading historians of the late 20th century, Richard Wade. Among these works are the following: Richard Wade, *Slavery in the Cities: The South, 1820–1860* (London, England: Oxford University Press, 1964); Kenneth Jackson, *The Ku Klux Klan in the City, 1915–1930* (London, England: Oxford University Press, 1967); Zane Miller, *Boss Cox's Cincinnati: Urban Politics in the Progressive Era* (London, England: Oxford University Press, 1968); Melvin Holli, *Reform in Detroit* (London, England: Oxford University Press, 1969); Humbert Nelli, *The Italians in Chicago, 1880–1930* (London, England: Oxford University Press, 1970); Roger Lotchin, *San Francisco: From Hamlet to City, 1846–1856* (London: Oxford University Press, 1974); and Thomas Lee Philpott, *The Slum and the Ghetto: Neighborhood Deterioration and Middle-Class Reform, Chicago, 1880–1930* (London, England: Oxford University Press, 1978). Also see Sam Bass Warner, *Streetcar Suburbs: The Process of Growth in Boston, 1870–1900* (Cambridge, MA: Harvard University Press, 1969); Stephan Thernstrom, *Poverty and Progress: Social Mobility in a Nineteenth Century City* (New York, NY: Atheneum, 1973); John Schneider, *Detroit and the Problem of Order, 1830–1880* (Lincoln: University of Nebraska Press, 1980); Richard Lingeman, *Small Town America: A Narrative History, 1620–the Present* (Boston: Houghton Mifflin, 1980); Roger Lane, *Roots of Violence in Black Philadelphia, 1860–1890* (Cambridge, MA: Harvard University Press, 1986); and Mary Ryan, *Civic Wars: Democracy and Public Life in the American City During the Nineteenth Century* (Berkeley: University of California Press, 1997). Bear in mind that this is just a sample of the books dealing with American towns and cities. Academic writing on these subjects can be found in a number of history and social science journals as well.

3. This hypothesis, long considered a classic among urban researchers, was first advanced by Louis Wirth in his famous essay entitled "Urbanism as a Way of Life." It was first published in 1938 in the *American Journal of Sociology*, *44*, 1–24.

9

FIXING PLACES AND PEOPLE

How Policy Makers, Planners, and Social Reformers Try to Make Cities Better

Cities are the single biggest things human beings build that actually work. At the same time, cities and the larger metropolitan areas of which they are part have many pieces that don't fit together comfortably or operate at peak efficiency. On top of that, the people who live and work there don't always get along very well.

This situation isn't peculiar to urban areas in the United States. Nor is it new. It arises whenever and wherever large numbers of different kinds of people settle in compact communities. Some of the problems, perhaps the most remediable ones, involve making changes to the physical layout and face of urban settlements. Other problems are more social in nature and involve the ability of people to get along with each other, not just informally but in terms of their willingness to collaborate on matters affecting the places where they live and work, too.

It's because large urban areas have as many inefficient parts and seemingly difficult people as they do that so much time and money is spent trying to fix them. In this chapter, we will focus on the physical and social fixes that generations of social reformers, urban planners, and public policy experts have made to the urban landscape and the people who fill it.

We can identify three overarching goals that people have had when it came to making urban places and people look better and work more effectively.

First, there were physical changes. Would-be reformers introduced every new piece of technology they could get their hands on to help the city grow and to accommodate all the people who were there. Many of these innovations but by no means all of them involved what was being built on or beneath the ground, on communication and transportation, and in seeing to it that people could conduct their affairs without being put in harm's way. There were poorly constructed buildings to fix, water and sewage systems to install or upgrade, and a variety of environmental hazards to avoid or mitigate. The story of how these kinds of changes were accomplished has been told in a number of fine works by historians and planners (e.g., Glaab and Brown, 1976; Schlessinger, 1999; Bridenbaugh, 1966, 1971; Wade, 1976; Mumford, 1961; Hall, 1998).

Second, there were social changes. Reformers wanted city people to behave better. In order to accomplish this goal, they devised spaces, moments, and programs that would separate people presumed to be incompatible. Alternatively, they came up with new ways to bring these same people together in settings and for events that might convince them that they had a lot more in common than they thought. In this way, it was reasoned, different kinds of people might learn to accept or at least tolerate each other. Some of the same historians dealt with these matters, too, but the work of social scientists and cultural anthropologists has tended to monopolize the writing on these topics (e.g., Lees, 1985; Boyer, 1978; Cummings, 1980; Lofland, 1998; Monti, 1999).

There was a second arena in which urban people worried about working together better. It was more explicitly public or governmental in nature. It involved the ways that people raised and spent money to build and maintain their municipality and eventually the whole metropolitan area or tried to empower different agencies to see that this work was done. The governance of urban regions has become increasingly complex and arguably less successfully managed than the informal relations among all the different kinds of people that live and work there.

A host of governmental and politically inspired attempts to reorganize and administer the public and private affairs of area residents and businesses have been introduced over the years. Some have worked better than others, of course. But the key to understanding both their evolution and the reasons why they haven't worked out better is that the people in charge rarely get ahead of the problems they have to address. Political scientists and some economists who have done the lion's share of work on these subjects haven't thrown up their hands in resignation, at least not yet. But, as we will see at the end of the chapter, they have chronicled many of the steps that officials have taken over the years to make all the public agencies and governments whose work they oversee work better across entire metropolitan areas.

Third, in addressing both the physical and social sides of urban development people experimented tirelessly to find a mix of publicly administered and privately inspired initiatives to make urban life more corrigible. Earlier on,

more of these initiatives came from the private arena. Over time the balance shifted in favor of more governmental solutions and answers. But there's never been a time in American history when the various schemes and collaborations used to meet the needs of an ever-changing city and metropolitan area didn't call on some kind of public–private partnership among investors, business, public officials, and reformers (e. g, Holli, 1969; Kennedy, 1992; Miller, 1968; Teaford, 1984; Wade, 1976).

Not surprisingly, work on any one of these goals often required people to think about and adjust how they worked on one or both of the other two. For instance, people in Western societies have long made a connection between the kind of local environment people lived in and the kind of culture or way of life they made inside their part of the city. The idea behind their tinkering was straightforward and found wide application in many of the reforms, planning schemes, and policies that have been adopted to repair urban places and people. Change something about the way a particular part of the city looks or how it is arranged and somehow people there would be inspired to act better. Planners sometime refer to this argument as *physical determinism*, meaning they expect people to improve because they've been given a good place or at least a better place to live and work in. A crummy physical environment was hypothesized to promote bad behavior even among persons who might otherwise be good. A good environment might inspire them to become better.

The most important tool in the urban planner and reformer's kit, as we shall see, has been housing: more of it, better built or maintained, more readily available for certain classes of people, sometimes in the central city but increasingly outside of the central city. Conditions that left too little housing or bad housing or restricted housing to certain types of persons needed to be remediated. This would be done for the sake of the people living there but also for the well-being of the city as a whole. More and better housing would make better people and neighborhoods.

Questions inevitably arose about who should be responsible for making changes or was in the best position to make them, not just in housing but to everything that would count as an improvement to the city's infrastructure. State governments have always been reluctant to grant cities much leeway in raising and spending tax revenues. As a result, city leaders had to come up with ways to lure private investors to undertake projects that allegedly served a larger public good. The resulting *public–private partnerships* accomplished a great deal for the city and usually made money for their backers. Many government-backed collaborations of this sort are still undertaken. But as we already noted, public actors and government agencies today seem to have the upper hand or are taking greater initiative in figuring out how to fix urban places and people and directing how this is to be accomplished.

The balance shifted in their favor as the 19th century wore on and public agencies and elected officials assumed more and bigger roles in fashioning social programs and building projects. The shift toward government-sponsored projects was contested in part because political leaders were skimming a great deal of money off contracts being let to businesses that wanted to work for the city. So-called "Progressives"—a coalition of traditional urban elites and their middle-class supporters—proposed a bundle of reforms in the late-19th century and early-20th century that would reduce government waste and corruption. This would be accomplished by, among other things, granting the mayor more authority and putting trained experts in charge of public agencies rather than letting neighborhood political hacks determine how public money was spent and who could be hired to work in public agencies. They also wanted to address social ills like drinking alcohol and prostitution, efforts that were part of their larger and longstanding campaign to make city residents more moral.

Several of the proposed structural reforms for city governments took hold better than the moral reforms ever did. The use of civil service exams, for example, put day-to-day control of public agencies in the hands of people who actually might have had skills appropriate for the jobs they were hired to do. This severely curtailed the machine's ability to dole out patronage jobs to its supporters.

Changes to immigration laws cut off the flow of foreigners who voted for machine-backed candidates in exchange for temporary or emergency assistance. The Depression and World War II put even bigger dents in the machine's base by inspiring the federal government to provide much more aid to a great many city residents who needed assistance and jobs for people contributing to the war effort. Machine politics persisted in some cities like Chicago and political organizations in other cities found additional ways to wield influence for extended periods of time. However, it was the very informal way that machines operated that ultimately undermined their effectiveness and shortened their life. City agencies became better organized and many city residents who needed assistance were able to receive assistance on a more consistent basis (Ross, Levine, & Stedman, 1991, p. 107–162).

Like everything else in this book, we can provide only a broad and superficial survey of how urban policy, planning, and reform have evolved in this country. As we noted at the outset, however, the United States certainly is not the only country in which people worry about how to fix cities and the people who live and work there. People in societies with cities older than our own and societies that only recently have become more urbanized also are concerned about these matters.

In the United States, we have had to manage the growth of metropolitan areas and the expansion and contraction of their central cities for only 400 or so years, if you start with the earliest colonial towns. It's only been a little more than 200 years, if you start looking around 1900 when cities as we know them began to take shape. In general, we've done a fairly good job of building and rebuilding our way into and out of problems related to the growth of urban areas. We're pretty good at stacking people up, spreading them out, moving them around, helping them make a living, and having their most basic needs met.

Some of our better technological fixes—things like improved road surfaces, telephones, and computers—found new and exciting applications in crowded urban settings. Other pieces of technology—trains that run on electricity rather than steam, steel girders, elevators, traffic lights, and water and sewage filtration systems—were basically invented for cities. All the other answers we've come up with to make urban areas work as well as they do entail managing people so that our technological fixes are used effectively and we don't get in each other's way or on each other's nerves so badly that we bring the whole metropolitan area to a screeching halt.

All the choices we've made or have had made in our name about how to address the physical and social challenges that come with living in urban settlements haven't always worked out well or been applauded by everyone. Part of the reason why has to do with the very complexity of the undertaking, the size of the place, and the sheer number of people and activities that go on in crowded urban areas every day. Part of our continuing unease with urban people and places, however, also has to do with the fact that we find it hard to agree on the best ways to address today's pressing physical and social challenges, much less guess at and plan for problems we will have to deal with decades from now.

What follows, then, are two related discussions. The first one revolves around the competing points of view that people have brought to their arguments about whether and how we should fix urban places and people. It's a discussion of ideas that have informed American social reform, urban planning, and policy making since the early-19th century and in a couple of notable instances well before the 19th century began. The second discussion involves a broad description of the kinds of innovations we've actually tried out and, more importantly, what we might have overlooked because of the way we think about urban settlements and the people we're likely to find there.

IDEAS THAT INFORM SOCIAL REFORM, PLANNING, AND POLICY MAKING

At the bottom of all reform crusades, planning schemes, and policy discussions involving urban places and people are two competing views of urban places and people. One is "optimistic" in the sense that people think much good comes from cities and the men and women who live and work there. The other view is more "pessimistic." The people who hold it are inclined to think that whatever good cities and their residents do falls short of the problems they cause. These are not new points of view. Their origin predates the founding of the kinds of cities we know today by hundreds if not several thousand years.

Though these are very different points of view, they share a common assumption about the way cities work, how the people in them behave, and what it takes to improve or fix them. Namely, *there is a connection between what a place looks like, how rundown or attractive it is, and the kinds of people who live there, the values they hold, and the way they act.* People act better when they are in nice places or places that have been fixed up. They behave poorly when they have to work in crummy conditions or live in rundown neighborhoods. This idea, which complements the concept of *physical determinism* that we introduced earlier, has shaped the way professional and casual observers alike have made sense of urban places and city dwellers for a long time. It also has a bearing on what we think can or should be done to fix urban places and people and how we explain why our repair work succeeded or failed miserably.

More optimistic social scientists, planners, and policy makers dwell on solutions that are supposed to make parts of the city look and work better, thinking this will encourage people to improve their conduct and circumstances. In this view, down-and-out individuals are relatively powerless to change the condition of their lives unless they get a lot of help. Over the years, experts and activists have talked about involving representatives of the down-and-out people in various schemes to make cities better. They run hot and cold on the question of how much and what kinds of engagement would be best. But contemporary planners and policy makers generally think that some kind of engagement is good and the right thing to do. At the same time, they have tried to downplay the idea that the improvements they help design for cities will necessarily inspire the people who use new and prettier buildings and spaces to act better. They've come to see that people often don't use the places and spaces they design in ways that urban planners expected or policy makers hoped.

More pessimistic observers are every bit as interested in making cities look and work better. They also really like the idea that people might be able to act better in the future than they've been acting so far. They're just a lot more skeptical about anything much coming of these efforts. They're even less enthusiastic about governments spending lots of money in the meantime to figure that out.

Whether one agrees with the optimists or the pessimists isn't especially important. What matters more is the way we associate bad places with down-and-out people. We view cities as a metaphor for all that's right (or wrong) with how people live in our increasingly urban society.

Cities have served as a really tough testing ground for all the next best ideas for fixing places and people that social scientists, planners, and policy makers come up with. The outcome of these experiments is all but preordained. Depending on your point of view, what experts proposed might make the city bigger and better than ever and have the effect of making the people there more civilized. Or, their failed policies and programs would have made the case for why cities should be downsized and the salvageable people living there should find a better place to reside.

Pessimists don't think the benefits of growth can compensate for the city's physical condition (which is usually declared "deteriorated" in a variety of little and big ways) or the way of life of the people who live and work there (which has been labeled as "disorganized" by most

observers over the years). For both these reasons, pessimists are skeptical about the chances of fixing what's wrong with cities and city people. Their view is that the "most intelligent and capable components of the social order were steadily losing ground to an ever-expanding proletariat." Bonds that make for "healthy and stable communities" had been "weakened." The result was that "chaos, disorder, and ugliness seemed to run rampant in the realm of cultural endeavor," because there'd been a "widespread undermining of the forces of communal control: the church, the family, and the neighborhood" (Lees, 1985, pp. 143, 152–153).

The separation of people in distinctive parts of the city that were seemingly difficult to connect as well as the movement to the suburbs by more successful people eroded the ability of the city's traditional class of leaders to accomplish their ambitious social agenda. This line of reasoning was revisited powerfully by William Julius Wilson in his 1987 book *The Truly Disadvantaged* where he spoke of the bad effect that the migration of Black middle-class persons from inner-city neighborhoods had on those Black people left behind. More generally, the men, women, and children who stay in cities or can't get out are thought to be alienated and antagonistic. They are prone to confusion, making crowds, and in general are likely to get into trouble. They also find it hard to reconcile their differing points of view or subordinating them in the name of a greater common good. At least that's what many critics and would-be reformers have believed over the years (Sampson 2012; Sharkey 2013).

That's why the idea of finding a technological fix or changing something in the physical environment is so appealing. People think (or at least they argue) that upgrading the city's physical face and infrastructure will have a softening and civilizing effect on the people who are exposed to these changes. Otherwise, pessimists have strong doubts about the long-term prospects for improving the people who live and work in cities. Their reasoning, surprisingly, complements that of optimists in some ways. They both think there are too many different kinds of people in cities. Urban people are disinclined to follow traditional rules or sources of authority, and they don't appear to be accountable to anyone but themselves (Monti, 1999, pp. 92–123). The poor social situation in cities is presumably reflected in their deteriorated physical state, especially in the most rundown neighborhoods.

You might think that people who hold more pessimistic views are dead set against anything or anyone remotely "urban." Some may be, but most probably aren't. What they would be is skeptical of any "fix" that ignores traditional sources of urban leadership and the marketplace and private arena as places to look for answers (Gopnik, 2010; Cross, 1997).

The emphasis on the private arena and market solutions to urban problems is understandable, if overblown. *Most public leaders in cities for the first couple hundred years of our history came from the private arena. They saw a direct connection between the city's economic health and improvements to the city's public infrastructure. At the same time, they also were elitists. It wouldn't have occurred to them to ask representatives of the down-and-out people to come up with solutions to problems their city was facing.* Their elitist view of the world was reinforced by professional politicians who catered to the very down-and-out people that made many traditional city leaders nervous.

That's just one of the reasons why so many well-to-do and higher-status men and women left the central cities for farther-out suburbs during the 19th century. They were escaping to places close enough to the city so they could still enjoy all the economic and cultural benefits of city living. At the same time, they thought they were moving to places that had no chance of becoming cities or attracting the kinds of people and problems increasingly found in and around the urban core. They were wrong.

Some people still subscribe to that belief and the hope that by moving farther out or into so-called "gated communities" they will not be touched by urban problems. What well-to-do city expatriates learned in the 19th century, however, is every bit as applicable to the situation faced by persons fleeing to gated communities, edge cities, and "Boomburbs" today. It's impossible to completely wall suburban enclaves off from the people who still live in cities or the problems that come from living in cities.

On the other side of this argument are people who subscribe to a more optimistic point of view. They believe that the benefits of cities and urban culture far outweigh their shortcomings. Urban problems are amenable to being fixed by all the talented people who migrate there or were born there. Planners and policy makers can facilitate the repair process by coming up with improved ways to fix urban places and engaging urban people, especially those, perhaps, who have not been part of the policy-making process in the past. A portion of these people, representatives of what Richard Florida (2002) calls the "creative classes," are expected to make a big difference by coming up with solutions to the physical and social problems people face in contemporary urban areas.

Optimists believe that people adjust to new and improved conditions by becoming more productive and by embracing more constructive civic values. It is also possible to organize people in cities in such a way as to bring different classes and groups together in common projects or at least increase their sympathy for each other. Novel answers and new ways of organizing are bound to upset some people and create some transitional problems; but people adapt and change.

People with a more optimistic perspective have evidence to back up their claims. They can point to the way that access to public resources was "democratized" over the years and in the number and variety of people who have been able to participate more fully in the life of the city. Jon Teaford's 1984 book *The Unheralded Triumph: City Government in America, 1870–1900* chronicles how local governments brought professional management to cities and vital public services to less well-to-do people during a period frequently decried for its corrupt public officials.

Such engagement can also promote a sense of "civic revival" and "civic attachment" among the city's residents (Lees, 1985, p. 227).

The "democratization" or sharing of public goods and an openness to different people's ways of socializing and conducting their civic lives makes the city's social order more inclusive and, frankly, more liberal. Other elements of reform, however, are inherently conservative and even paternalistic. Reformers imagined, for instance, that the poor would be gathered or come under the influence of "a communal banner of respectability" along with whatever material assistance they received. This would help them "escape from rootlessness and degradation." It also would have the effect of mitigating "suspicion and conflict between social classes" and help to promote new types of "cooperation and public action" (Lees, 1985, pp. 224–225, 230).

In fact, all reforms and social programs come with new rules that people have to follow, if they are to be aided. It doesn't matter how much these reforms are contested or how much they might appear to help "outsiders" act like "insiders" or at least think of themselves that way. *New reforms make the people getting assistance and the people giving it accountable to each other in ways they hadn't been before. Following rules and being accountable to others are very conservative impulses.* They are built into the policy-making process every bit as much as the liberal impulse of recognizing the legitimacy of claims made by "outsiders" is. School desegregation reforms were a good example of how people tried to help many, but by no means all, White and minority youngsters learn to get along in school if not back in their respective neighborhoods (Monti,1985).

Urban reform crusades and change programs were never intended to make all city residents equal or have them live next door to each other. What the different kinds of people living and working in cities needed was a common sense of purpose and commitment to the city as a whole. There would be moments and places where various races, ethnic people, and social classes might come together and be reminded how much they

had in common. But reducing the material differences among them to the point they became irrelevant was not part of the reformers' game plan. Reformers were driven to distraction by the apparent absence of cultural unity and the unwillingness or inability of people to live under a common set of rules and standards, not by inequality. People needed to learn how to fit in, not overcome.

The idea of reducing if not eliminating differences in the material well-being of the city's various races, ethnic groups, and social classes is a more recent invention. Pursuing something like equality, no matter how elusive and difficult that might be, represents either a fundamental misreading of the reformers' traditional urban mission or an important evolution in their game plan. The larger "structural" differences between people (how much wealth they had and where they lived) were once considered things best ignored or "left to the marketplace to work out." Reformers were out to make different people more culturally alike.

The ambition of more progressive reformers in the second half of the 20th century fundamentally changed. They were no longer satisfied with improving the metaphorical place occupied by less well-to-do and poor people and less esteemed minority populations. They wanted to change their literal place in the economic and geographic pecking order of urban areas while leaving them alone to "do their own thing" socially and culturally.

There is no small irony in the concern of more conservative leaders and opinion makers about cultural disunity in the United States today and their pleas to put the various pieces of our culture back together (Murray, 2012). We actually may be a lot closer to realizing the broad cultural goal of putting the different kinds of people in urban areas onto the same cultural script than conservative commentators are prepared to recognize and acknowledge. All those urban strangers we used to be afraid of may be looking at each other more favorably and acting more congenially in public these days (Monti, 2013). The real irony is that this growing cultural convergence would have come during a period in which differences in the wealth and well-being of various groups and classes in U.S. society have grown at least a little wider.

THE CONNECTION AMONG URBAN REFORM, PLANNING, AND POLICY MAKING

Nineteenth-century moral reform crusades, urban planning, and policy making draw on both the optimistic and pessimistic points of view. The leaders of such initiatives have generally come from the upper classes, but they've always needed the collaboration or compliance of less socially prominent persons to put their ideas into action. How deeply engaged middle-class people and working-class people were in discussing how to reform city government and their fellow citizens depended on what problems were being considered. Engaging the poorest of the poor so that they might participate in their own reclamation rarely, if ever, entered the picture.

Even today the people most deeply involved in these conversations are more likely to come from the ranks of the region's business and civic elite and middle-class persons. The professionals they hire and lay volunteers they inspire help fashion programs of action to address urban problems. *Working-class and lower-class people today are more active than they would have been at the start of the 20th century, but they remain the target of reform efforts and social programs more often than they are the creators of such initiatives.*

Louis Wirth said that an urban way of life was more prominent in places that were large, densely populated, and had many different kinds of persons living and working in close proximity. *The social part of the urban reform, planning, and policy puzzle was attributed to problems caused by the heterogeneity of urban populations.* How many people lived and worked near each other inside cities surely played a part in explaining why people found it hard to develop sympathy for each

other and a sense of loyalty to anyone or anything. *The physical face of urban problems had more to do with having large numbers of people living in settings that were severely cramped, at least by comparison to towns and villages.*

People more interested in *social* reforms and policies sought to reconnect their fellow beings to traditional institutions like religion and the family or tried to develop new rituals and institutions that urban dwellers could embrace. People more interested in the *physical* side of urban problems ended up working on projects that focused on where certain kinds of structures were built, the spaces that were made available for the public, and the way people and goods moved through the city.

Urban planning as a profession and process has always been more focused on the physical side of urban rehabilitation. Planning-like activities and policy making had been a central feature of town and city building even before the American Revolution. But the profession of urban planning was a logical extension of ongoing engineering and construction projects that helped towns grow into larger cities. Urban planning got a substantial boost from *social reform* campaigns that began during the first third of the 19th century, however. That is because people believed that the physical makeover of the city would have a salutary impact on the people who lived and worked there.

Social reforms were supposed to fix people more directly by creating new programs and organizations to provide much needed structure to the allegedly chaotic and "socially disorganized" lives of the people they were supposed to help. Early social reformers believed that most social problems were caused by the moral bankruptcy and improper training of these people. Typically, they looked at problems faced by families as the source of so much troubled or "deviant" behavior, especially the problems of children and younger unattached men and women. That's why reformers often focused on how to improve a community's organizational capacity. Only by providing institutions that drew problematic people into more conventional organizations such as schools could the mass of people in cities be shown how to overcome their own personal failings.

The idea that there was an urgent need to make urban places and people better emerged in the first third of the 19th century in response to widespread city building and immigration. By the latter half of the 19th century, one would have included industrialization as another compelling factor driving people to undertake efforts to fix urban places and people. Both urban planning and social reforms eventually qualified as *public policy* concerns, that is, as matters calling for governmental engagement and intervention. But it took the better part of the 19th century for city leaders working on these problems to reach the point where government agents and offices assumed much of the responsibility for taming and improving the city.

There was good news and bad news in this for traditional city leaders. On the one hand, upper-class people managed to engage parts of the public—their target audience—in their own reclamation. They accomplished this by having local governments take on many of the social programs these traditional leaders had pioneered. On the other hand, upper-class people turned the keys to city hall and city council chambers over to some of the very people they feared and despised most: immigrant voters and the corrupt politicians that represented them. The Progressive movement of the late-19th and early-20th centuries was an explicit reaction to the graft and enterprising criminality that local and state politicians brought to urban governance and policy making. But it also challenged all the business people from among their own ranks who cut deals with politicians in order to secure lucrative contracts to provide new and expanded public services to growing urban populations (Steffens, 1904/1969).

Early reform efforts were privately instigated, just as the late-19th century Progressive movement was. The "morality crusades" were funded by wealthy people, run by volunteers, and dedicated to "saving" poorer people and immigrants from their own bad habits. Many reform crusades were

directed toward children, since their parents were probably beyond redemption already. Part-time programs, like Sunday school, run by volunteers, eventually grew into full-day programs, like mandatory public school, run by paid professionals.

Programs for children had the dual goal of removing them from the bad influence of their parents and other neighborhood adults as often as possible and for increasing amounts of time. The most serious and permanent solution to the "child problem" came through organizations that took city children on the East Coast and had them adopted by families from small towns and farms in other parts of the country. The process of "placing out" youngsters transported on so-called "orphan trains" relocated at least 200,000 children between 1853 and 1929 (Holt, 1992). The premise of such programs was that the family structures, work practices, and natural surroundings associated with small-town life and particularly farm life could help children lead more useful and moral lives than they would have otherwise led in squalid urban settings.

Again, it's important to note that reform initiatives were never intended to reduce economic inequality in any permanent or far-reaching way. The idea behind campaigns and programs was to bring poor people and immigrants into the cultural fold, as it were, by helping them learn how to fit in better under prevailing economic conditions. In principle, *reformers were also committed to the idea of having people from different social stations and walks of life come into contact with each other, though not so much that they would actually become economic or social equals.* The presumption was that less well-to-do people and immigrants would be helped by being exposed to their social betters. Top-down, paternalistic reforms embraced principles of inclusiveness, public accountability, and piety, all of which it happens were crucial to the way that commercial leaders looked at the world (Monti, 1999, pp. 240–278).

The contemporary reformer's plan, as we have already noted, is to improve the situation faced by more troubled urban people (i.e., really poor minorities still living in isolated and rundown neighborhoods) by making a physical change in their lives such as moving them into more suburban settings. The change would occur without having the would-be beneficiaries socially prepared to take full advantage of it. Even more telling, perhaps, the loss of wealth experienced by many Black Americans in the 2008 recession was greater for them precisely because they had more of their money tied up in housing they really could not afford. Reforms that had made home buyers out of many lower-income and even moderately well-off minorities had the unintended effect of pushing them backward rather than improving their material situation.

Contemporary reformers are learning a hard lesson that 19th-century reformers found difficult to accept. The scope of the problems they faced eventually became too large and costly for wealthy individuals, foundations, and bigger businesses to handle. Indeed, one of the corollaries to changes in social reform efforts was the gradual reduction in the direct role that business people played in making reforms, instigating policies, and planning how urban places and people were to be improved. Today business people and prominent individuals are still turned to for help, especially when it comes to big rebuilding projects. But they no longer have the last word or loudest voice in fashioning or carrying out most reform initiatives. Governments do.

Over time, government agents and offices became key actors in creating policies and programs to address the ills of cities. Public agencies took over much of the hard work once initiated exclusively by voluntary organizations. Their efforts were supplemented by full-time professional "helpers" like planners, public administrators, and "social" scientists and "social" workers. These professionals helped define problems, identify potential solutions, and implement programs increasingly paid for with public funds rather than private contributions.

It actually took the better part of a century for local governments to become fully engaged in a variety of reform and improvement efforts that went beyond making more and bigger buildings or new public spaces and pieces of infrastructure.

A corollary to the government's growing role in reform programs was the gradual expansion of the geographic focus of reform and planning efforts from the warrens of the poor to the whole city. Today similar initiatives address problems on a metropolitan-wide and even regional basis. It also magnifies the problems faced in urban areas when reforms don't work by having transformed them into big public issues.

It was not until the second half of the 20th century that we found the emergence of a final innovation or theme in urban policy-making and planning initiatives: the attempt to engage the broader public affected by reforms, especially minority and less well-to-do persons, as more active participants in their own reclamation. The introduction of these people to more recent attempts to fix cities was classically "reactionary" in the sense that local people reacted poorly to initiatives like federally imposed urban renewal campaigns. Post-WWII urban renewal programs, which were first advanced in 1949 legislation, had no provision for grassroots engagement. Ultimately, they suffered many revolts against top-down plans that tore through many lower- and working-class neighborhoods. The less well-to-do people who were removed from their "slums" weren't supposed to have a voice in what happened to their neighborhood. They were part of the problem, not part of the solution.

The idea was to rebuild the areas in which they formerly lived and introduce a better class of residents whose education and professional pedigrees complemented what was going on in the updated and greatly expanded downtown area. Changing the physical face of the city required a corresponding change in the social complexion of the population. "Physical determinism" and social reform made for a powerful union when backed with federal money.

Only five years later, the 1954 federal housing act began to change the way local residents were treated and engaged. It called for "maximum feasible citizen participation" in any municipality's attempt to formulate a "workable program" for housing development. Transportation legislation in 1962 went on to call for comprehensive metropolitan-wide planning to be "collaborative." Taken together, these federal initiatives laid "the foundation for today's advocacy planning, citizen engagement, and environmental justice movements" (Birch, 2009, p. 17).

As a practical matter, however, advocacy planning of a more "progressive" sort, meaning local people were going after new rights and resources, didn't grow until the mid-1960s. That was when professional planners and would-be policy makers were inspired by the civil rights movement to involve minority persons as plan makers and program implementers. Since then, we've learned that the amount and kinds of public engagement in planning activities can vary substantially. It can range from citizen forums where ideas are solicited or reviewed to more direct involvement in actual plan-generating and decision-making bodies (Kelly & Becker, 2000). And unfortunately, we've also learned that when initiatives run into economic conditions even tougher than the ones reformers had counted on, the government becomes complicit in setting up for failure the very people they had intended to help.

URBAN AND SUBURBAN PLANNING IN THE LATE-20TH CENTURY AND EARLY-21ST CENTURY

The planning process today tends to be initiated in the public arena, makes buildings and infrastructure better, improves the environment, and, among other things, creates nicer spaces for people to use. Furthermore, and importantly, it is supposed to generate "a sustained and widespread private market reaction." This basically means *businesses take what the government starts and run with it.* There are two additional ideas about planning that are important today precisely because the government has become a bigger presence in all manner of urban reform campaigns. *First, successful physical improvements cannot be expected to solve deep-seated social problems. Second, planners should engage the general public even more in the planning process* (Garvin, 2002, pp. 1–3; Stoker. Stone, & Worgs, 2013). If nothing else, this spreads the responsibility for whatever programs are pursued and the blame when they go poorly.

The idea that making a place nicer will help address deep-seated social problems hasn't been altogether abandoned, of course. Indeed, many neighborhood revitalization projects are still designed and defended as "community development" schemes. The idea of "physical determinism" just doesn't dominate the planning profession as it once did.

The same could be said for the idea that business people need to "buy into" a rebuilding scheme, if it is to work. Important as business input is to this process, businessmen and women no longer have the only voice or final word in the development of policies, programs, and planning proposals. Other voices have emerged, including those belonging to lower-income and minority people. As we noted above, however, direct citizen engagement is a relatively recent add-on to conventional planning practices. It has been carried out in a variety of ways with more and less success and levels of commitment on the part of major institutional players.

Other signs that contemporary policy makers, planners, and reformers have scaled back their once ambitious plans are apparent. For instance, we don't talk about rebuilding whole chunks of cities or encourage people to move farther away from the urban core like we did a half-century ago and are still encouraging minority people to do. *Informed opinion these days holds that suburbanization has been pushed beyond the point of reason and produced a fragmented system of regional governance and wildly inefficient uses of space and resources. Today, sprawl and municipal fragmentation are considered bad. Concentration and regional collaboration are good.*

The popularization of terms like "sustainable development" and "smart growth" strategies speaks to these concerns. Planners today are much more likely to talk and worry about the way in which a given project affects not just the economic vibrancy of an area but also the environment and issues related to social justice or equity. They don't have a precise way to define what these terms mean, but they are sensitive to the effect that their actions have on a variety of constituents and the physical environment. Policies and practices that might be construed as promoting more "sustainable" kinds of development—energy efficiency, environmentally friendly materials, building in the city's core—are being pieced together and no doubt will continue to be called upon to justify one kind of project over another.

How much "social engineering" can be accomplished through better or more socially responsive kinds of planning is another issue that has gained a lot of attention among professionals. Contemporary experts have begun to cool, perhaps prematurely, to the idea that spreading "middle-class culture" will succeed in unifying a diverse urban population (Monti, 2013). At the same time, and a little ironically, they still believe that bringing more low-income and minority persons to live and work in the suburbs is a good thing to do. They promote such initiatives for the same reason their predecessors argued that attracting middle-class, highly educated, and White people back to the city was the way to improve both the city and the other people who lived there. Less desirable places and people would be improved by being exposed to better people and places. This is sometimes referred to as the "contact hypothesis" by people who study and write about ways to improve race relations in this country.

More modest and scaled-down visions about what might be accomplished with better designed urban and suburban places can be seen in planned New Town developments like Celebration and Seaside, both in Florida. These places were built in a way that reflected so-called "New Urbanism" principles. They were, in theory, supposed to manufacture a sense of community by bringing residents together a lot more often. The integration of private residential space with public space and the "careful design and placement of public space" promoted by "New Urbanists" were the built-in inducements to socializing that the towns' creators imagined (Talen, 2000, p. 173).

This approach actually works, up to a point. It turns out that people will hang out more in attractive, well-designed spaces and are more likely to "bump into each other" when they can walk to a shopping area that's within a couple of blocks of where they live. At the same time, building a town with such principles in mind doesn't guarantee that everyone living there is going to get along or pledge their undying loyalty to the place (Frantz & Collins 1999). The connection between creating a new place or improving an older one and fixing the people who live, work, or play there simply isn't as straightforward as reformers, policy makers, and planners have had us think.

The sense of modesty seen in contemporary planning, policy making, and reform campaigns leaves two sets of very immodest questions unanswered. First, as both a practical and principled matter, how many different kinds of people have to live and work together to create a viable community? Second, is the marketplace or government the better arena to achieve an effective measure of social mixing?

It must be said that neither of these questions can be answered easily or convincingly, given what we know today about how metropolitan areas work. What follows is more suggestive of how we might profitably begin framing new answers to them.

With regard to the first question, *there are undoubtedly instances when having a more homogeneous population is both unavoidable and makes good sense and having a more heterogeneous population produces less than optimal results.* We need look no further than the next ethnic enclave to see the constructive role that places with a more homogeneous population still play in the United States and elsewhere (Abrahamson, 1996; Aman, 2013; Stoker et al., 2013; Wang, Gleave, & Lysenko, 2013; Weck, Hanhorster, & Beiswenger, 2013).

At the same time, it's not at all clear from reforms like school desegregation that the people who went through it received as much benefit from the experience as its defenders hoped and its detractors feared (Monti, 1985). Nor is it clear that minorities who stayed in cities won't do better if and when their neighborhoods stage a comeback (Monti, 2013).

Assuming we want to encourage at least *some* mixing, however, the evidence from affirmative action programs suggests that the people who most need help in becoming better mixed with the rest of us may not be the ones who are assisted most of the time. Public policies actually may make matters worse in this regard (Monti, 1997). On the other hand, *evidence that a number of suburbs across the country have slowly become desegregated in the last few decades and that some inner-city areas have been redeveloped without pushing out all their poor and minority residents suggests that "spotty mixing" might be feasible and serve a variety of public and private interests* (Goodman & Monti, 1999; Monti & Burghoff, 2012).

Public and private leaders, whether they know it or not, wrestle with these questions every time they sit down and begin laying out the next reform or policy they want to try. Regardless of how much or little social mixing one might think is feasible or necessary to achieve in urban settlements, two things are certain. First, we still don't know what the best mix is. More importantly, perhaps, there probably are times when persons from different backgrounds, social classes, races, or genders would be better off being left alone and not pushed on each other. Second, whether and under what circumstances different kinds of persons are to be encouraged to mix probably won't be left to the people in question. Those decisions will bounce back to the public and private leaders charged with the responsibility of coming up with the next best guess about what to do with the rest of us.

We do know that low-income residents in some cities like St. Louis as early as the 1980s and Los Angeles in the early 2000s began to negotiate "Community Benefits Agreements" with local developers. The objective of these agreements, not surprisingly, was to come to an understanding about the kinds of development that might serve both the builders and the local residents (Monti, 1990; Saito, 2012). All of these activities would count as small victories in a much bigger campaign to promote the idea and practice of community-based planning.

WHAT ARE THE PROPER ROLES OF THE PUBLIC AND PRIVATE SECTORS IN SOLVING URBAN PROBLEMS?

Progressive Era reformers certainly had reason to complain about the too-cozy relation between local politicians and businessmen who were willing to lay out substantial sums of money to acquire the right to construct a new building or provide a new public service. The question of corruption aside, American cities got newer and more technological innovations put on (and beneath) the streets than their European counterparts did. To be sure, municipal debt skyrocketed. But municipal services were delivered to less wealthy residents and outside of the central business district, too.

Upper-class critics of big-city politicians and their immigrant supporters may have been pioneers when it came to fighting corrupt city hall hacks; but they weren't the only people who tried to take on public officials who tried to run over them or ignore their interests. In *Wrestling With Moses: How Jane Jacobs Took on New York's Master Builder and Transformed the American City*, Anthony Flint (2009) chronicles how Jane Jacobs beat the biggest public builder in New York City history. She had plenty of help from the press, her neighbors, and sympathetic outsiders, and she managed to stop a highway from being built through her Greenwich Village neighborhood.

Looking back at that fight and many other fights just like it requires us to take a more nuanced view of what Moses and Jacobs got right and missed. Moses may have been a monument builder who liked to tear down buildings with great historical value and replace them with highways and high-rise apartments or office towers. But he was right that monuments can serve as anchors and prompt other kinds of development to occur around them. Jacobs learned that you could take on City Hall but mobilizing the public was really hard. She also never figured out how to keep the neighborhoods she saved from gentrifying. Jacobs ended up seeing longtime residents who were less-well-to-do being displaced by more prosperous persons once the latter started moving in.

These are the kinds of issues and historical precedents that help us understand just how hard it is to come up with a definitive answer about what the right or best mix of public and private solutions is for urban problems. Some observers actually think we've come up with an answer, but we won't necessarily like it. When trying to address urban problems, the power to define the "public interest" has gradually been acquired by clones of Robert Moses. Since the 1960s, the winner of the tug-of-war between the private market and politicians has become the professional planner and agency official. These professionals, with the assistance of the courts, have grabbed more power over "increasingly intrusive development regulations, a wide variety of housing and other development subsidies, and, most controversially, [the] governmental taking of private property for purposes other than public use" (Salins, 2009, pp. 46–47). Planners' judgments have gradually replaced "the myriad individual decisions of developers and consumers" used to make in building up their part of the metropolitan area. Progressive Era reformers might have succeeded in making professional bureaucrats more powerful than they expected and maybe more than they would have preferred.

The other big winner has been the self-governing suburb. Armed with an impressive array of zoning powers, suburban municipalities were allowed to go their own way. They could limit the kinds of uses to which their land could be put, how much or how little land had to be set aside for housing, what kinds of businesses would be allowed in and kept out, and as a result, what kinds of people were welcomed and which ones weren't.

In the early 1900s, suburbs were located in "outlying neighborhoods of cities, or new communities that sprang up at the city's edge." Some eventually were absorbed into the city and "benefited from the city's planning initiatives—specifically, from the extension of municipal roads, sewers, transit systems, parks, and educational facilities." All that changed after the 1920s when people in many new suburbs in the East, South, and Midwest persuaded their state legislatures to prevent annexation and to allow them to incorporate as independent municipalities. Their "most sought-after state-delegated power . . . was the authority of regulate land use and development." Suburban leaders "looked to planning to protect the idyllic environment that had drawn them out of the cities, and to keep out most low-income and minority households that wished to follow" (Salins, 2009, pp. 47–48). The segregation that was invented in proto-industrial cities now found a home in suburbs.

This approach to modern suburban planning was facilitated by the Supreme Court's 1926 ruling that validated zoning as a means to separate "incompatible land uses" such as industry and residential; limit crowding; establish architectural consistency; and keep buildings shorter. The effect of these rules has been to yield "vast expanses of single-family homes" and strip malls along arterial roads, virtually no multifamily housing, and overly large lot sizes. The rules have put the cost of infrastructure onto developers and, eventually, allowed for the introduction of elaborate rules dictating the style, size, and accoutrements of houses in select communities (Salins, 2009, pp. 49–50).

It is within boundaries like these—limits set largely by the courts and federal and state officials—that the shape of public–private partnerships today is fashioned and their work is carried out. A brief history of how these partnerships have evolved will show us how dependent we have been on them for building and rebuilding our cities and urban areas. It also will suggest new areas where we might look for them to help.

PUBLIC–PRIVATE PARTNERSHIPS IN THE UNITED STATES

Two questions have driven reform, policy, and planning initiatives from the founding of the American colonies. First and foremost, how do we manage growth and shrinkage? Second, how do we make cities corrigible places to live and city dwellers more congenial?

Public–private partnerships have been a more obvious factor in addressing the first question. Indeed, they have been involved in every scheme to build and rebuild cities and the places people live and work outside of cities since the 17th century. In his famous book *The Urban Frontier*, first published in 1959, historian Richard Wade made it clear that several approaches to building and rebuilding cities that we talk about today have been around for a while. Higher education, for instance, was already an economic development tool by the 1830s. Building a college was not just a sign that your town or city had come of age culturally. It was a huge investment in your town or city's long-term economic well-being. Other ventures such as a railroad line, new post office, or even an asylum weren't as edifying, perhaps, but they all meant that one's town would acquire jobs and revenues and likely attract more employers. That's why city leaders fought so hard to get them and keep other cities in the region from getting them.

Local governments, Wade further observed, were always playing catch-up. They never had enough money to undertake large projects on their own and often had to ask their state legislature for the statutory authority to do something. As a result, they had to turn to private leaders for money to do anything big. Public–private partnerships—where local governments ceded businessmen the right to build something like a bridge or develop property and then rent or sell it to make a profit—were the single most important tool municipal leaders had available to them.

The history of urban planning makes clear that "government and markets have always shared responsibility for urban development. From the earliest cities . . . through the first half of the twentieth century, governments designed and built the city's infrastructure." They also helped to design and fund road and sewer construction and the building of transit systems. Much of the land in urban centers also has been set aside for institutional or explicitly public functions such as government facilities, museums, libraries, parks, universities, and places of worship. Local governments often gave "private interests" tax incentives and subsidies to build on this land.

Even more visionary expressions of planning (e.g., Daniel Burnham's work on the 1893 World's Columbian Exposition in Chicago, which inspired the City Beautiful movement) "complemented private investment instead of overriding it." Indeed, after the fair, cities as varied as Chicago, Cleveland, St. Louis, Los Angeles, San Francisco, and Washington, D.C., built new train stations, courthouses, city halls, and other buildings in the image of Greek and Roman architecture like the ones built for the Chicago exposition. Their impact was immediate and great. "The majestic parks, stately boulevards, and palatial public museums, libraries, and governmental buildings . . . triggered a massive wave of real estate entrepreneurship and development in every major metropolis across the country" (Salins, 2009, pp. 46–47).

Parks are another good example of how a broader public good has been married successfully to private acquisitiveness for a long time. The creation of parks was driven by two complementary ideas. First, parks would bring touches of nature to the big city. Nature had restorative qualities that crowded city dwellers could benefit from. Second, there was a democratic impulse to the creation of parks in the sense that these would be places where "the privileges of the garden were enjoyed about equally by all classes." A combination of these ideas led proponents such as Jane Addams to claim that parks would "cure disease" and provide recreation especially for youth that "would divert the city dweller from a life of crime" (Garvin, 2002, pp. 32–33, 35).

It also was thought that parks would serve as a "strategic public investment." Public spending on parks could be justified on the basis that "the money will stimulate private investment." In Europe, the early money supporting parks in the 17th century came from aristocrats. Later it came from government. "It was spent for the specific purpose of attracting a market (i.e., the growing populations of these cities) and generating further real estate development" and the additional taxes it would bring to the city. The same impulse was behind the creation of Regent Street in London in the early-19th century so that it would connect St. James and Regent's Parks.

The public investment was made in Europe and America with different goals in mind. "In Europe, parks were thought of as an integral component of the urban environment; in America they were meant to stand in contrast to the city and provide a refuge from its noise, dirt, and confusion. In Europe, open space was specifically designed to meet the demands of surrounding building occupants; in America, parks were intended for widespread and active public use" (Garvin, 2002, pp. 43, 45, 47).

Ownership or control of open lands in Europe was retained by the surrounding building owners. No such proprietary relationship existed in U.S. cities. Perhaps the sole exception was the way in which Boston's Public Garden had been set aside in 1733 as a "critical mass of open space" necessary to influence the city's subsequent development. What U.S. cities had was plenty of open and as yet undeveloped space that could be set aside and built around as the city grew toward it. Central Park is a notable example of how this worked out in practice, as the city's population, still largely confined to the part of Manhattan south of the park, gradually moved north and filled the rest of Manhattan.

The connection between private enrichment and a broader public good is every bit as real in other kinds of development and redevelopment schemes. It's often harder to see, however, and almost always tougher to sell. To understand this connection at all one must appreciate that American settlements during the colonial period may have been small but were expected to become bigger. That is, they were expected to grow into cities.

People who underwrote the expense of starting these places did so with the idea in mind that these places would become centers of commerce. The value of their property holdings would increase as more commerce was conducted on and around their property or more people came to live and work there. The town that would become a city was first and foremost an investment.

Development *outside* of the most settled parts of the town started at the end of the 18th century, not too long after the successful completion of the American Revolution. The first suburbs were typically incorporated into the city as the city grew outward and engulfed them. Later, in the more urbanized northeast and midwest regions of the country, suburbs resisted being incorporated into the city. Prior to that, suburban developers would sometimes buy property with the idea that the city would grow in their direction. On other occasions, suburban developers provided these infrastructural improvements or provided special amenities to prospective buyers, costs that were passed on to purchasers, and waited for the city to come out to them.

Comparable residential areas inside cities were upscale "private places" that were gated and sometime surrounded by a brick wall. These early gated communities were positioned along major city boulevards such as the ones in St. Louis. Scaled-down versions of the gated and walled private places in the city were extended on either side of these residential blocks, farther east into the city and west into the suburb of University City. In other cities, as in Boston where tidal marsh land was taken and filled so it could be developed for residences in the South End and Back Bay, local governments took aggressive steps to add residential blocks in order to accommodate more well-to-do home buyers. The impulse in all cases was the same. People wanted to escape unpleasant city conditions and trade up to a community with a more congenial environment.

After World War II, innovations in building techniques that made home construction cheaper coupled with the financial benefits available to GIs made large-scale suburban development possible. Levittown developments on Long Island and in Pennsylvania and New Jersey were expressions of this kind of development. Built on farm lands, these new suburban tracts made modest houses available to first-time buyers. It was a model for developing new suburbs that was replicated in many states in the years after World War II.

Compact town-like developments in Columbia, Maryland, and Reston, Virginia, were later built in reaction to the Levittown model. In some ways they drew on Ebenezer Howard's Garden City idea, but only in the sense that they were built some distance from central cities in what started out to be a bucolic setting. At the same time, they weren't anything like the "anti-city" Howard would have had built in the middle cow pastures, forests, and farms. Nor would they have a dedicated manufacturing section built some distance from residential areas. Places like Reston and Columbia had serious urban pretensions. They contained apartment buildings as well as resident-owned houses, economically and racially-mixed residential populations, and brought employers into the center of the town. As such, they more clearly anticipated New Urbanism towns in their layout and the way they put residents close to where they could shop and manicured public spaces where they could socialize.

More ambitious plans to build entirely new towns farther out in the country and away from central cities had first gained currency with the Garden City movement in England during the late-19th century. In the United States, they sometimes sprang up around suburban railroad stations. This was the case for both Lake Forest, Illinois, and Riverside, Illinois. These places, unlike Howard's Garden City, weren't supposed to become self-contained communities surrounded by large open spaces dedicated to agricultural pursuits and manufacturing. They became upper-middle-class suburbs of Chicago (Garvin, 2002, pp. 375–381). Still other new towns (e.g., Chestnut Hill outside Philadelphia and Beverly Hills outside Los Angeles) were developed in the early-20th century as a "vaca-tion refuge" but eventually bumped up against their respective neighboring cities.

Seaside, Florida, and Celebration, Florida, added an experimental twist to the legacy of new towns by embracing "New Urbanism" principles in their layout and buildings. "Its adherents favor[ed] mixed land use patterns that they hope[d] will force residents to live, work, shop, and play in close proximity" just as one might in a small town or suburb. But they also were built to discourage the use of automobiles except to leave the community. They weren't supposed to be scaled-town urban centers like Columbia and Reston (Garvin, 2002, pp. 335–337). In some ways they were more like gated communities with a small but active retail and commercial center (Frantz & Collins, 1999).

Gated communities both in the United States and elsewhere, mostly in Latin America and South Africa, grew in popularity in the late-20th century. Catering to a decidedly upscale clientele, these developments provided residents with a greater sense of personal security, a relatively secure investment, and an opportunity to limit their exposure to people who are not like them. They were exclusive residential compounds consisting of detached single-family houses and as such would never be mistaken for a full-service "community" like new-town-in-town settlements *inside* cities. They were more like the suburban equivalent of the "private places" built inside cities like St. Louis. In the last 15 years, however, gated communities have become more common even for developments with more modest homes or even trailer parks, particularly in rapidly growing regions like the South and Southwest.

Building and rebuilding *inside* cities also was inspired by the idea that overcrowded, dirty, run-down, and impoverished areas needed to be fixed. Vacating and clearing slums was the first step in this process. Rebuilding on vacated and cleared land was the second, and in many ways the more difficult, step in this process. Here, too, public–private partnerships came into play, but usually only after the vacating and clearance of a slum had been accomplished at the government's initiation and with public funds.

The presumed connection between a physically deteriorated area and the unhealthy physical and social state of the area's inhabitants was just as strong as the presumed tie between suburban developments and the superior condition of their residents' personal and social well-being. The earliest campaign to rebuild large sections of central cities was created around *urban renewal* projects that had two goals: eradicating slums and getting developers to do projects on cleared land that would bring in more prosperous businesses and residents. The process of replacing minority and less well-off persons with people who were better educated, had better jobs and incomes, and White has often been referred to as "gentrification."

Slum clearance required the acquisition of property at greatly reduced or no cost to local governments and potential developers so they would build on land that had little or no market value at the time. The idea was to attract outside investors and have them build something that would serve some other higher public use. Sometimes it worked. But a lot of the time it was years before private investment dollars were sunk into urban renewal sites.

The legal appropriation of private property happened in the United States for the first time in New York in 1887 when the state legislature approved the taking of land so that a park might be built on the site. It wasn't until 1954 that the Supreme Court ruled that a piece of property could be taken from a negligent owner and sold to another person. The 1946 D.C. Redevelopment Act had anticipated this by allowing "substandard and blighted areas" that were "injurious to the public health" to be taken and turned over for a *public use* (Garvin, 2002, pp. 449–450).

The physical model for America's urban renewal program parodied parts of Le Corbusier's vision in his 1924 *City of Tomorrow, and Its Planning*. Commercial and residential buildings were tall and combined on superblocks that were separated by larger roads and green spaces. A manufacturing and warehouse district was put off to the side. Whole districts would be condemned

and rebuilt in this way, Le Corbusier reasoned, until the whole city was redeveloped.

Large, publicly subsidized redevelopment projects were seen as the way to create a "slum-free environment" in cities. Title 1 of the federal Housing Act of 1949 provided that the federal government would subsidize two thirds of the difference between a project's cost and the resale price needed to make the new construction financially attractive to developers. Local government picked up the remaining portion of that difference. The Housing Act of 1954 went further by insuring bank mortgages in federally assisted urban renewal areas for up to 95% of the "replacement cost" of new housing (Garvin, 2002, pp. 250, 254). As in all so-called "urban renewal" plans of the 1950s and 1960s, a redevelopment agency assembled land, demolished buildings, prepared sites, and solicited developers to develop plans for the area. Although urban renewal did work in some cities, it often took years before a developer would step forward to build in these areas.

Critics decried the displacement of low-income and minority residents and closing of many local businesses. Many of these areas may have looked run down, said renewal opponents, but they were viable neighborhoods nonetheless (Gans, 1982). Initially, municipalities provided no assistance to help displaced residents and businesses relocate elsewhere. An amendment in 1959 to the original legislation required that there be a relocation plan and some payout to displaced persons. The relocation benefits grew over time and became so great that by the time Congress enacted the Uniform Relocation Assistance and Real Property Acquisition Policies Act of 1970 it made large renewal projects financially untenable. This was just three years before President Nixon terminated funding for any more large-scale urban renewal projects.

The second major thrust to rebuild the rundown parts of central cities involved the creation of *new-towns-in-town*. The primary differences between central city and more distant exurban new-towns-in-town were that the city ones would have looked a lot like Le Corbusier's "superblocks." Park La

Brea and Century City in Los Angeles, Pentagon City in Washington, D.C., and Co-op City in the Bronx are good examples of new-towns-in-towns. These new city districts were supposed to benefit the surrounding city by generating additional employment and taxes. They also were supposed to inspire further development around their peripheries and provide services like retail stores, recreation facilities, and cultural establishments that wouldn't otherwise be available to people living in adjacent neighborhoods. By these measures, Co-op City, Cedar-Riverside, and Roosevelt Island are "flops." On the other hand, both Battery Park in Lower Manhattan and RiverPlace in Portland, Oregon, turned out well on at least several of these criteria (Garvin, 2002, pp. 347–368).

The last urban reclamation initiative had *neighborhood revitalization* rather than neighborhood replacement as its main goal. Some inner-city neighborhoods come back on their own by being "gentrified" by new residents who rehabilitate older, frequently architecturally significant houses. Other neighborhoods, ones that have a strong ethnic history, have been reclaimed by younger members of the families that first settled them.

Neighborhoods that qualify for revitalization on those grounds—and a number that wouldn't—still had their deterioration reversed and abandonment prevented and for far less money than was spent trying to subsidize renewal areas back to life or building brand-new "towns" inside an older city or adjacent to it. Cities as different as Atlanta, New Haven, New York, and St. Louis have sponsored this kind of rehabilitation program in league with area banks and institutions. As Garvin (2002) observed, "These programs involved mortgage insurance, local lending offices, below-market-rate-interest loans, and capital improvement programs." The key to their success was having local institutions make a commitment to neighborhood reinvestment and enter into partnerships with organizations in the affected communities. As they did in earlier urban renewal projects, local governments often made "visible, public improvements" by investing in "new streets, sidewalks, street trees, lighting,

schools, and other community facilities that would make an area more attractive" and increase the market value of housing in the neighborhood (Garvin, 2002, pp. 280–303).

Governments in the Netherlands and England have made the same kinds of investments in the docklands or former industrial areas of several of their own cities. These projects also have important institutional or corporate sponsors, a fact which increases the chance that whatever rebuilding is done will succeed in bringing an area back. The plans for these areas are nothing if not ambitious.

> Attention was paid to using the regeneration schemes to improve the image and character of the whole area, to provide better housing and a better quality of life, and to improve social conditions and promote inclusion, as well as to create attractive sites and conditions for new businesses. (Cadell, Falk, & King, 2008, p. 96)

In short, the people who conceived of these collaborative redevelopment campaigns had much more in mind than revitalizing the area's economy. They were aiming to upgrade and enhance the whole city.

Concern in this country and overseas still exists about these redeveloped areas becoming "gentrified" by more well-to-do people. To the extent that what happened in five areas in St. Louis that were revitalized this way holds true, however, those concerns are misplaced or at least overblown. The redeveloped areas in question kept more of their population than contiguous areas that were not rehabilitated this way and were more racially and economically mixed as well some three decades after their redevelopment had commenced (Monti & Burghoff, 2012).

As we noted in Chapter 3, some inner-city neighborhoods experienced a newer kind of urban renewal during this period of "redevelopment." It focused on the demolition of larger public housing complexes that had been built in the aftermath of World War II for the period of "old style" urban renewal (Hyra, 2012). What was different about this newer phase of urban renewal, according to its critics, was that the people who were displaced this time were almost exclusively low income. Middle-income Blacks were able to take advantage of the "gentrification" going on around them. Their neighborhoods became tourist and cultural centers.

The success of more modest reclamation projects speaks to the promise of so-called *smart growth* development schemes. In general, smart growth projects would encourage the redevelopment of existing communities and more densely built and populated neighborhoods. They also would promote mixed land use by placing neighborhoods within walking distance of community facilities and shopping. "Smart growth" development in its idealized state provides for a variety of housing and transportation options and encourages the kinds of community buy-in that take place in central-city revitalization projects. One of the presumed by-products of successful "smart growth" development projects, of course, would be the preservation of more open space outside of the central city (Knapp & Moore, 2009).

PUBLIC–PRIVATE PARTNERSHIPS IN SOCIAL REFORM

We have seen many privately initiated reform initiatives in the 19th century become publicly supported and government-managed social programs in the 20th century. With the exception of a few elementary schools in city neighborhoods, however, there have been comparatively few public services or agencies taken over by businesses and private voluntary organizations. Government services that have moved into private hands (e.g., turning to religious groups to implement government-funded social programs and businesses running public schools or privatizing public service delivery systems) make for an interesting experiment but can engender a lot of heated public debate.

In general, public–private partnerships have not been utilized nearly as often or in as sustained a way in matters related to social reform. We have not figured out how to make a profit by

reforming people that have been viewed historically as unsalvageable or unworthy. Setting aside efforts to rebuild urban neighborhoods, we haven't learned how to apply the same kinds of strategies and yardsticks for success used in the business world to improve the lives of troubled urban residents. And apart from arguments over job training, affirmative action, drug selling, and gun control, we barely pay attention to information that speaks of the costs of continuing to let so many urban people fail. *What we have accomplished gradually and quite successfully in our ongoing arguments over these issues, however, is the expansion in the number and variety of persons (e.g., people getting welfare or who get AFDC assistance) deemed worthy enough for us to worry about and care for.*

PROGRESSIVISM AND THE 21ST CENTURY CITY

By the end of the 19th century, cities had become a compelling presence on the American scene. Their size, growing number, industrial might, ethnic mix, and political muscle, all the labor disorder, grit, grime, and crime made cities the ultimate venue for staging the great American morality play. If we were to remain a united people in the 20th century, American cities had to be tamed and their people had to be civilized. Everything reformers had thrown at them so far hadn't worked. It was time for reformers to take their game to a higher level.

That next level was called the Progressive Era. During this period, which lasted until the 1920s, reformers availed themselves of every governmental power to restructure the urban environment. These early "environmentalists" moved in two different but complementary directions with their updated reform campaigns. *Some of them "pursued a coercive and moralistic approach" and worked tirelessly to close brothels and saloons,* two institutions that epitomized "urban moral and social breakdown" for Progressive reformers. Another set of more "positive environmentalists" weren't any less committed to fixing cities by reforming their most problematic residents. But they would go about it differently. Instead of destroying vice "through denunciatory rhetoric or legal repression," historian Paul Boyer (1978) noted, *positive environmentalists would create "in the city the kind of physical environment that would gently but irresistibly mold a population of cultivated, moral, and socially responsible city dwellers."*

Their aim, Boyer (1978) observed, was to make a city "where objectionable . . . behavior, finding no nurture, would gradually wither away." Planning and science, including social science, wouldn't just study social groups but control them "through the benevolent manipulation of their physical and social environment." Better housing, more parks, and playgrounds would win the day over gin joints, gambling parlors, opium dens, and whore houses. A beautiful city would dispatch "ugliness, dirt, and disorder" and "surely attract more customers and investors" (Boyer, 1978, pp. 221, 224, 264).

Notwithstanding these differences, the two approaches "shared certain fundamental moral-control purposes: inculcation of a 'higher' standard of individual behavior, the placing of social duty above private desire, the re-creation of the urban masses in the reformers' own image." This meant that reformers would take the great mass of urbanites and provide them with occasions when they could discover they were connected to the whole city and that they should develop sympathy for it. It was supposed that over time people would also acquire a sense of obligation to uphold the city's well-being and that of everyone in it. They would be more mindful and respectful of each other no matter what their social standing and background were. As a practical matter, of course, this meant remaking the masses so they were instilled with a lot more humility and deference for their betters than they were exhibiting at the time (Boyer 1978, pp. 290, 254).

The record of Progressive Era reforms and politicians sympathetic to its message was decidedly mixed. Historian Paul Boyer (1978, pp. 284–291) points out that popular opinion about city life became more favorable and scientists concluded that the threat posed by having so many different kinds of people living in cities had been greatly oversold. Diversity had not become so acceptable that the federal government would turn away legislation severely limiting immigration from foreign countries. But people definitely were beginning to accustom themselves to the idea that having cities didn't mean that civilization was going to crash and burn.

Politics and politicians of the sort that wanted to close bars and the nation's borders to bad outside influences had at least as much to do with the passing of Progressivism as did the softening of popular and scientific thinking about cities and city dwellers. The morally denunciatory part of the Progressive plan to make over the world, the part that held up working-class and immigrant lifestyles to public ridicule and scorn, failed. Candidates backing saloon closings did all right for a time and even managed for a while to have the federal government outlaw liquor. But other quintessential urban sins like gambling and prostitution weren't stopped and even flourished as a result of efforts to outlaw them. Prohibition turned out to be a political mistake of gargantuan proportions for the Progressives. Working-class people didn't like being scolded and having their personal pleasures curtailed by a bunch of self-righteous nags. Immigrant voters didn't forget who had pushed to keep more of their fellow Italians, Jews, and Irishmen from entering the country, restricted immigrants' access to jobs, labeled them mentally deficient, and treated them like second-class citizens.

The more positive parts of Progressive Era "environmentalist" rhetoric and reform initiatives, the parts that wanted to nudge and encourage these same working-class and immigrant people to act better by providing more relief and fewer wagging fingers, actually succeeded better than was expected. The City Beautiful movement, which put muscle to the positive environmentalist message, helped to refashion the downtown core of many American cities before the Depression and inspired even more ambitious rebuilding campaigns in the second half of the 20th century. Tenuous as the connection between making big parts of central cities prettier may have been to improving the social and moral lives of everyday people, cities were updated and cleaned up.

More importantly, perhaps, the very urban masses that reformers hoped to bring over to believe they had a stake in the larger city did, in fact, acquire a sense of having a proprietary stake in the city and a broader view of their role in seeing after its well-being. The cross-class connections that "evangelical volunteers" began to fashion in the early-19th century came to fruition a century later in all manner of neighborhood and citywide redevelopment campaigns in the late-20th century. It also was apparent in the less hostile way late-20th century immigrants were greeted upon their arrival compared to the way their late-19th century counterparts had been treated when they showed up.

The question before us at the top of the 21st century is straightforward and compelling. How might we build on these successes and make a new batch of "Progressives" who can continue rebuilding our cities and incorporating even more immigrants into campaigns to make over the urban world?

If we are true to our Progressive Era roots, then we will continue to turn to business people for leadership and rely on the power and integrative capacity of the market place to make urban magic happen. For instance, latter-day Progressives would openly embrace several business-like ways that governments have tried to reorganize themselves or carry out their work. Foremost among these would be schemes to create metropolitan-wide governments (Phares, 2009). The idea of promoting regional governance has been widely debated since at least the 1930s and applied not just in the United States but in countries such as Mexico and Canada as well. It is considered a rational response to the multiplicity of municipal, county, state, and federal officers and agencies whose overlapping jurisdictions and substantive responsibilities often frustrate coordinated responses to common problems.

Of course, the prospect of giving up or even sharing part of their power is something officials never like to contemplate, which is why so many of the ways in which this idea has been implemented have not been terribly ambitious. Among the easiest to implement have been intergovernmental agreements that enable governments to share services or purchase needed materials from a single source (Krause, 2011). Regional bodies to oversee particular matters like water treatment, cultural affairs, or economic development may be limited in their scope but have the advantage of involving the whole metropolitan area (Hawkins & Andrew, 2011). The most difficult and least likely changes that are made entail the consolidation of different municipal governments or the creation of a "super agency" that effectively takes on the authority to deal with problems that cut across different levels of government.

Two additional paths to fashioning more effective public–private partnerships outside of government can be seen in the recent rise of social entrepreneurship and even more recent arrival of so-called "double-bottom-line" businesses. Social entrepreneurs take nonprofit organizations and find ways to sell part of what they do so that they can continue and even expand their mission to do more good in the world. It's not just the Red Cross that has found a way to market its services and grow the "business side" of its operation. Many small and local nonprofits do this today. Double-bottom-line profit-making organizations have done more social good as an explicit part of their business plan. Ben & Jerry's may be the biggest and best known of our double-bottom-line companies. But it's being shadowed by a growing number of small and medium-sized businesses today, many of them inside our central cities (Brush, Monti, Ryan, & Gannon, 2007; Monti, Ryan, Brush, & Gannon, 2007). The common point of reference for these enterprises is that people have figured out how to build into smaller ventures the very kinds of "giving back" and tithing that were once the exclusive domain of Bible tract societies, Sunday schools, and large corporations.

Furthermore, their work is becoming ever more apparent to larger numbers of city residents and people from each of the city's social classes, races, and ethnic groups.

The work of public–private partnerships in rebuilding inner-city neighborhoods that started shortly after the end of World War II has continued in the 21st century. As we noted earlier, five corporately sponsored and publicly backed redevelopment campaigns that were launched in the central east-west corridor of St. Louis in the 1970s stabilized the neighborhoods most directly affected. They are more attractive and safer than they were four decades ago. More importantly, they have residential populations that don't look anything like those that critics of gentrification imagined would come with inner-city rehabilitation projects. Though not racially or economically balanced in the sense that all races and classes are equally represented, the areas have mixed-race and mixed-income profiles that they didn't have before they were redeveloped. Furthermore, some of the neighborhoods contiguous to these redevelopment sites have seen some positive spillover in their own residential populations.

No redevelopment scheme, no matter how successful it may be in terms of making nicer buildings and more public space for people to share, can guarantee that everyone who ends up living in the rebuilt area will behave wonderfully all the time and get along. As an approach to rebuilding inner cities, however, the comparatively modest size and modestly scaled social expectations for the people living and working in these places holds more promise than the massive urban clearance projects ever delivered.

Early reformers did get this much right. You can fix places and provide opportunities for different kinds of people to learn how to get along and fit in. It takes time and a lot of money, but you can do it.

Questions for Study and Discussion

1. What, if any, connection is there between fixing the physical face of the city and fixing the people who live and work there?

2. Identify an urban problem and outline how public–private partnerships have been used to address it.

3. Describe some of the unanticipated effects of a particular solution that was employed to address a particular urban problem.

4. Describe the ways that government intervention in dealing with a particular urban problem combines strategies and goals that would appeal to both "liberal" and "conservative" reformers.

Website Materials

http://encyclopedia.thefreedictionary.com/Inner+city+decline
http://www. lincolninst.edu/subcenters/making-sense-of-place/cleveland/
http://www.allacademic.com/meta/p_mla_apa_research_citation/2/0/2/1/5/p202150_index.html
http://www.citymayors.com/index.html
http://www.citymayors.com/sections/society_content.html
http://usmayors.org/usmayornewspaper/documents/07_26_99/atlanta_reserved.htm
http://www.good.is/series/urban-renaissance
http://ipsnews.net/news.asp?idnews=44645
http://ipsnews.net/news.asp?idnews=45083
http://ipsnews.net/news.asp?idnews=46217
http://www.nytimes.com/2008/12/03/business/03columbus.html?emc=eta1

10

EMBRACING THE CULTURES OF URBAN PEOPLE AND PLACES

Social analysts and philosophers look at the social world in two very different but surprisingly complementary ways. One might choose other words to describe their respective positions, but the ones Charles, Louise, and Richard Tilly (1975, pp. 1–11) came up with almost 40 years ago worked pretty well then and still make sense today. They grouped these worldviews into two categories: "breakdown" theories and "solidarity" theories.

The scholars who think the world is breaking down see the institutions, customs, codes, habits, values, and beliefs that people have made as badly divided or fractured, perhaps irreparably so. Under such conditions people would be expected to fight with each other a great deal and/or stay out of each other's way for fear that they would end up fighting. Either outcome would put the places they live into something akin to a cultural nosedive or a state of almost continual churning and disunity.

Marxists pay a great deal of attention to the built-in stresses and social class divisions they say all societies have and, importantly, they think people organize around and fight over. At the same time, they also think something new and presumably better will come out of all the battling and disunity. Postmodernists probably are better examples of "breakdown" theorists because they believe that the very idea of a coherent culture and effective social order is a fiction or at least greatly overstated.

The "solidarity" theorists are more hopeful. They see the social world as an unfinished but fundamentally sound work in progress. We may be no more certain than some of our 19th century forebears were that all the work people do will somehow lead to something better than what they had before. However, these theorists don't think the world is so misshapen and broken that people have to tear everything down and start over from scratch. The everyday people that create and keep the world running need not get along or see things the same way all the time, though there have been theorists who insisted that they really should. Most people, however, are seen as capable of getting along and building on what their ancestors left for them most of the time.

Among urban researchers and theorists, the members of the Chicago school of sociology and human ecologists best exemplify the "solidarity" approach to urban society. They have long been identified with reform-oriented projects, whether as researchers describing the growth of metropolitan areas or as analysts of particular neighborhoods or "subculture" groups. Human ecologists who are accustomed to looking at the adaptive accomplishments of whole populations are particularly good at looking at the longer-term capacities of the communities they study. The language of progress that they appropriate is couched in terms of economic expansion and the "fit" between a population and its surrounding environment. "More" isn't necessarily "better." (This is what the concern about developing countries being "over-urbanized" is all about: too many people in cities with too little infrastructure and too few jobs.) But as a first-order approximation of what would pass as "progress," it suggests what one would look for as signs that a people and their cities are working out pretty well.

Social accomplishments and "cultural" progress are entirely different matters. The social agenda of 19th and 20th century reformers had the twin goals of making newcomers and strangers fit in better *and* improve the look and feel of cities to the point that the physical changes would inspire people to act better. Pushing people to "act better" was to be accomplished by the creation of brand-new customs, organizations, and events through which newcomers and strangers might come to identify more with the city as a whole than with their own little subgroups and subcultural worlds. It also was to be accomplished by encouraging them to defer to the leadership of higher-placed and more accomplished people already in the city and becoming compliant clients of all the new institutions (e.g., schools, libraries, companies) that city leaders had created.

The concerns of better-established city people were not misplaced. When Charles, Louise, and Richard Tilly came up with their distinction between "breakdown" and "solidarity" theories they were trying to understand the very rebellious century that Germany, Italy, and France had experienced between 1830 and 1930. Their primary objective was to figure out how nonroutine forms of collective action that had become commonplace—riots, brawls, strikes, and the like—fit into the routine ways that people conducted their affairs before and after they finished rioting, brawling, and striking. But the way they framed the work of 19th and 20th century social

theorists applied equally well to the way researchers, reformers, and social philosophers tried to make sense of urban settlements and people back then and still do today. The reason is simple. The Tillys were studying a period of history and countries that experienced the same unsettling changes that inspired and shaped the research and writing done by the urban sociologists featured in this book.

The present authors played off or repackaged the Tillys' idea with our view that people are either optimistic about the state of urban places and people or pessimistic about them. Our take on these arguments is reproduced below so that you can see the strong parallel between what the Tillys said and what we are saying in this book.

The Optimistic View: Cities are centers of growth, cultural invention, individual freedom, and collective accomplishment. They attract and hold a variety of people who are inclined to mind their own business. At the same time, they are good at coming up with novel solutions to problems when more traditional ways of thinking and behaving don't work or are considered unnecessarily punitive or annoying.

The Pessimistic View: Cities are physically fragmented, overcrowded, and deteriorating. People who live and work there are dragged down by such conditions. As a result, life in the city can only be described as "socially disorganized." People are supposed to look out for each other and follow the rules. The fact that anyone can live there makes it all but impossible for people to create a culture or way of life that everyone can follow much less embrace.

The more *optimistic view* of urban places and people corresponds to the "solidarity theories" that the Tillys favored. They thought that the kinds of collective actions analysts like to dismiss as riotous and disorderly came from the same places—from the same kinds of customs, norms, and groups or organizations—that produced more conventional and rule-abiding kinds of behavior. Their position was that novel, puzzling, and even discordant actions can be understood in terms that we use to describe more customary and even traditional ways of behaving and thinking.

The *pessimistic view* is entirely consistent with the "breakdown theories" that so many observers of civil unrest and social upheaval in the 19th and 20th centuries favored. In this scheme, city people act out—and poorly—either because they are screwed up or the conditions under which they live and work are so bad that most anyone would be driven to act poorly or in self-destructive ways. Unconventional ways of acting and thinking have nothing in common with the way that normal people typically think and act. You need an entirely different vocabulary and set of "theories" to describe and understand them.

Urban analysts and reformers, planners, and policy experts draw on both intellectual traditions in their work. They invoke pessimistic language and images when making the case that urban places and people have serious problems needing immediate remedial attention. They turn to more hopeful ways of talking—and keep both their fingers *and* toes crossed—when they describe how much good their proposed remedies will do for the people and places they aim to help. Some people are tough-to-discourage optimists, to be sure. If you go back and review all the theories and research presented in this book, however, it would be hard to argue that social scientists and philosophers, reformers, planners, and policy makers are more optimistic about the prospects of urban places and people than they are pessimistic.

We understand why. As we have noted throughout this book, our theories and research go back to 19th-century cities in both North America and Europe that were experiencing unprecedented and seemingly out-of-control changes. People had reason to be confused and concerned. The only world they knew was being turned upside down and inside out. Whatever optimism they could muster had to be tempered by the reality of what they saw going on around them, and much of what was going on around them was upsetting and would have made anyone anxious.

The physical and social changes that urban settlements have gone through since the end of World War II created some of the same kinds of

concern and produced the same kind of dispiriting commentary from social scientists. The future of urban places and people did not look good. Depending on where you look, it still doesn't. The dramatic increase in the size and number of cities in the South and West, the rapid growth of suburbs, the deindustrialization and depopulating of older cities, and the marked expansion and repopulating of central business districts have been difficult to absorb, much less make sense of. Equally dramatic changes in 18th-and 19th-century cities had been every bit as difficult to keep up with, manage, and understand. Our pessimism is built on hard facts.

The big difference between our *urbanization* story today and the one that 19th-century thinkers wrote is that we are still going through our period of struggle. We know that 19th-century cities came through theirs in better shape than they were expected to. They didn't crash and crumble or come apart at the seams. There actually was a great deal of growth and progress. The optimists certainly had a great deal they could point to with satisfaction. But the cautionary tale presented by pessimists had more than enough facts to back it up to convince a great many people, including most social scientists, that some of the biggest problems identified in 19th-century cities had not been addressed satisfactorily.

Foremost among the problems that no one seems to know how to deal with today are the massive economic disinvestment and the population losses that many older cities in the Northeast and Midwest experienced during the second half of the 20th century. The incorporation of so many foreign people into our older and still-growing cities remains every bit the challenge it was in the 19th and early-20th centuries. And no one has been able to adequately describe, much less figure out what to do with all the people in this country's cities, suburbs, and towns who aren't employed making things because there are so many people overseas today who are making them cheaper.

The *urbanism* part of the story we have to tell today has kept many if not all of the desultory elements first penned by 19th-century analysts, reformers, and philosophers. More importantly, we have come up with few, if any, positive narrative lines to counter all the bad tales we still tell about life in urban places. The best we have been able to do is say the bad news isn't as bad as people made it out to be. Using this frame of reference, urban dwellers wouldn't be as alienated, unfeeling, unsociable, uncooperative, and irresponsible as scientists and theorists had expected.

Again, the picture wasn't positive. It was less negative than people had feared. After all, it's hard to come up with a more congenial or happy-ending story line when there are too many (or increasingly too few) people in some of our cities; there aren't enough people of the sort we need or would like to fill our businesses and neighborhoods; the ones we'd rather not have to deal with do not seem inclined to leave; and "native" Americans are increasingly outnumbered and outgunned by foreigners who don't look or sound anything like our ancestors, are reluctant to learn English, embrace our customs, or adopt our values.

The different brands of social scientists described in this book are pretty much in agreement on what the current state of urban places is and how well put together the urban society is that the people living and working there have made. Neither is in great shape. These same researchers and commentators differ only on how the urban world came to be this way and what can be done now given all the problems it has.

If the story we tell about America's urban places and society were reimagined as Humpty Dumpty's woeful tale, sociologists from the Chicago school would observe that Humpty used to be pretty solid but had developed some nasty cracks before he fell off the wall. They'd done their best to warn everyone that the egg was going to take a nasty spill, but no one seemed to know what to do to reinforce him so he wouldn't fall. Now that he had fallen, however, reformers and their scientist/analyst/technically expert allies were sure that they could figure out a way to put him back together. Furthermore, the old egg would be sounder and look better than ever thanks to their good work.

Scholars advocating a softer or harder version of Marxism would say that the King cracked Humpty Dumpty and made his fall all but inevitable. On the one hand, they couldn't imagine why anyone would want to reassemble the corrupted and broken egg and wouldn't be surprised that all the King's men had failed when they tried. On the other hand, all the King's subjects would certainly be able to fashion a much finer egg than the one that the King had pushed over the edge.

Postmodern thinkers would argue there never had been an egg or that whatever had been teetering at the top of the wall was only a poor simulation of an egg, which probably is why it wobbled and fell. Inasmuch as Humpty Dumpty had never been whole, the idea of trying to put him back together was pointless. He was destined to be scrambled.

The idea that society would fall and come to a bad end, a brand-new beginning, or had to be substantially rebuilt is our updated version of a 19th-century parable. Depending on who tells it today, the moral of the story is that you are going to have a bad fall but can be fixed, somebody is going to push you from a very high place and you won't recognize yourself after the doctors are through with you, or you're going to end up an icky mess. There is nothing in the story that makes the fall unlikely and unnecessary or makes you think that the people who created the wobbly "society" are anything but incompetent.

Taking a rather different view of the egg and his fate, the authors of this text would argue that Humpty was a lot better put together and more resilient than many people think. Whatever cracks he had were the result of having been hardboiled. So, if he were to slip off the wall, the chances are good that the fall wouldn't have left him disabled or disfigured, much less killed him. He'd figure out what patches and repairs he needed to make and probably would be able to do most of them on his own, thank you very much. He was, after all, a self-made egg.

A "cultural" approach to urban phenomena can no more discount the problems apparent in a given society or settlement than it can the building skills and restorative abilities of the people who made it in the first place. There is a great deal that is "handed down" from one generation to the next and by old-timers to newcomers. The "structures" to which sociologists refer—all the institutions and groups, patterns of commerce and social intercourse and governance—did not appear overnight and they don't come finished. Some of the ones we were left with still worked relatively well. Others may not work nearly as well as they used to. The same is true of the "ideas"—the values, beliefs, perceptions, norms, folkways, and symbolic representations—about society and our place in it that we use to guide and account for our actions or hold in contempt.

Our cities, suburbs, and towns are very much works in progress. So, too, is the way of life that we make and fill those places with. In a cultural sense, we are condemned to talk to ourselves. We revisit and remind ourselves who we are every day, sometimes out loud and thoughtfully and most of the time without thinking much about it. We rework and amend what our ancestors left us, recommit ourselves to finish what they started, and sometimes feel compelled to acknowledge that what worked for them just won't cut it anymore. The result, in every case, is that there is an equally big part of our urban places and way of life that is made and remade every day "from the ground up" and "on the spot."

Somewhere in the middle or wherever it is that the handed-down and made-up-on-the-spot parts of the world we live and work in meet is the intellectual space that a "cultural" approach to making sense of urban places and people occupies and tries to fill. If this approach has a bias, the ideas that inform it probably lead us to see continuity and comity where other observers look for dramatic changes and discord. The glasses we look through aren't rose-colored, but they aren't darkly tinted or cracked, either. The glasses we drink out of are way more than half full.

It isn't hard to come up with a list of the essential elements of a top-down and bottom-up approach to culture that could be used in studies of urban places and people (Borer, 2006). They include the myths, narratives, and images that people have created for their city and about the way of life practiced there and their sense of how these ideas are understood and embraced by people in different parts of the community. There also would be studies of how people from specific subgroups and classes construct an identity and how much these identities overlap. (They would be viewed as being a lot more similar than they are different.) Finally, there would be descriptions of how people and the groups to which they belong and the organizations that represent their interests behave.

While there are sociologists working on all these parts of the cultural landscape, it is difficult to imagine how all the elements of a cultural approach could ever be assembled in one piece of research or tackled by a single scholar. We haven't even tried to do this in the present textbook.

What we have tried to do is introduce students to the range of cultural practices that go into making a way of life that can work for the people who live in cities, suburbs, and towns. We also have suggested that these cultural practices "hang together" and produce a way of life that people living in these places can pick up and contribute to over the course of their own life.

You learned earlier in the book that the late political scientist Norton Long (1958) contended that each social group in the city had its own game and played by its own rules but that the different games were not played in isolation. They were played in tandem and often played together. It was in this way that the "communities of limited liability" of which Gerald Suttles (1972) wrote might intersect and collaborate.

Small businesses like coffee shops or pubs (Oldenburg, 1989; Milligan, 1998; Borer & Monti, 2006) provide settings not just for making a profit but for passing along community gossip and making it possible for people of different social classes or groups to be in each other's presence. Big businesses such as baseball teams play in parks where even larger numbers of people who don't know each other can come together and share each other's company. The stadium becomes a bigger version of the neighborhood pub and coffee shop. People from many different parts of the city, social classes, and races can come together in such places and spaces. They don't have to own any part of these places or spaces to share them.

Cities, suburbs, and towns provide many opportunities for different kinds of people to observe and learn from each other (Monti, 1999; Macgregor, 2010). The trick is to figure out how the "games" played by people you don't know and the rules they prefer to play by can become part of your game and the rules people like you play by. It turns out that the cultural learning curve for this particular trick takes a long time, compels people to accept or at least work with seemingly irreconcilable principles, can be very rough at times, but eventually works out pretty well (Monti, 1999; Monti, 2013).

In an article responding to the influence of anti-urbanism that continues to influence the ways that scholars see, or more likely ignore, the cultural work of urbanites, one of us put it this way:

> The type of civic culture that has been built and continues to be built in American cities is neither liberal nor conservative, but a hybrid culture made up of a hybrid collection of individuals and groups.

And even though communities are collective accomplishments, not everyone plays an equal role in making those decisions or practices them exactly the same way all the time. As such, urban culture is continually changing . . . and [u]rban dwellers can change their ways of thinking and acting (too), but only tend do so within tolerable limits. (Borer 2006, p.186)

The communities Americans build have many paradoxical features that people have learned to live with and even embrace. The study of urban places and people does too.

QUESTIONS FOR STUDY AND DISCUSSION

1. What similarities are there between a "culturalist" approach to understanding urban phenomena and an "ecological" or "Marxist" approach?

2. What are the similarities between a "postmodern" approach and a "cultural" approach?

3. In light of all the evidence provided in this book, are you inclined to agree more with an optimistic or pessimistic view of cities and urban life? Why?

4. How much overlap is there between what we know about urbanization and what we know about urbanism?

GLOSSARY

Alienation   A condition of being estranged or disassociated from other people, the products of one's work, and one's "self."

Anomie   A condition characterized by the absence or confusion of social norms or rules in a society, community, or group.

Assimilation   A process whereby members of ethnic or other minority groups change their practices to conform to the dominant culture.

Authority   Power that has been institutionalized and is recognized, though not necessarily accepted, by the people over whom it is exercised.

Biographical Strangers   Individuals who do not know each other on a personal basis or who have never met.

Bourgeoisie   The owners of the means of production and distribution in capitalist societies.

Built Environment   The human constructed physical and material objects that make up the city, such as buildings, streets, and sidewalks.

Bureaucracy   A formal organization with rules and hierarchical rankings used to achieve and maximize efficiency.

Capitalism   An economic system in which the greater proportion of economic life, particularly ownership of and investment in the production of goods, is carried out by private entities through the process of competition, minimizing costs, and maximizing profit.

Central Business District (CBD)   The commercial, office, transportation, and cultural center of a city; land values are usually among the highest in the city.

Chicago School, The   A collection of scholars from University of Chicago in the early decades of the 20th century whose qualitative and quantitative empirical studies of Chicago and related theoretical contributions helped define urban sociology as a significant subdiscipline.

Citizenship   Full membership in a community in which one lives, works, or was born.

City   A relatively large, dense, and heterogeneously populated place or settlement.

Civic Association   A voluntary organization consisting of individuals with common social and cultural interests and concerns

Civic Engagement   The ways people in a democratic society exercise their rights and fulfill their responsibilities.

Civil Society   The realm of voluntary activity that lies between the state and the market, including the family, community, and other non-governmental associations and extra-economic institutions.

189

Class A large category of people within a system of social stratification who have similar levels of wealth, income, prestige, and life chances.

Comparative Urbanization An approach that replaces limiting notions of cities as being "developed" or "underdeveloped" with one that seeks to identify the commonalities among and across cities of the world.

Community Refers to a (positive, though not necessarily so) form of sustained social cohesion, interaction, and organization that exists between the larger society and individuals who have similar characteristics or attributes (e.g., ethnicity, geography, beliefs)

Creative Class A population of individuals with high amounts of "cultural capital" who tend to work in arts and technology fields.

Crime Acts that violate sanctioned laws and rules for which formal penalties are applied by a recognized authority.

Cultural Strangers Individuals who are from different symbolic worlds or cultures.

Demography The study of the size, composition, growth, and distribution of human populations.

Deviance Acts that violate the relative standards of conduct, expectations, or beliefs of a group, community, or society.

Disorganization The inability to regulate behaviors and activities that are inconsistent with neighborhood or citywide values; ecological factors and structural conditions can lead to variations in crime rates between neighborhoods and cities.

Division of Labor The delegation and assignment of specialized tasks, jobs, or work to be completed by specified individuals, groups, categories, and classes of people.

Enclave Bound to a particular place, like a neighborhood, characterized by the proliferation of commercial establishments and other institutions particularly suited to serving the needs of the resident group.

Entrepreneurship The carrying out of new ideas or practices or the combining older ideas and practices with newer ones.

Ethnicity A shared way of life reflected in language, religion, and material culture such as clothing and food, and cultural products such as music and art; often a key source of both social cohesion and social conflict

Ethnography The study of social groups in their natural environment; it relies on participant observation and field research.

Family A set of people related by blood, marriage, or adoption who share the primary responsibility for reproduction and caring for members of a community or society.

Feudalism The social system that characterized medieval Europe and other preindustrial societies, based upon mutual obligation between nobility and serfs

Gang A group of individuals that engage in common activities, many of which may violate codified laws and regulations.

Gemeinschaft A German term that denotes a sense of close-knit community relations based on shared traditions and values.

Gentrification A process of community and neighborhood change where housing in older neighborhoods is restored, often resulting in higher rents and the displacement of previous tenants who can no longer afford to live there.

Gesellschaft A German term that denotes relationships typified by an impersonal bureaucracy and contractual arrangements rather than informal ones based on kinship and family ties.

Globalization The often uneven development of extensive worldwide patterns of economic, political, and cultural relationships between nations.

Human Ecology The study of the interrelationships between people and their spatial setting and physical environment.

Immigrants People who settle in a country in which they were not born.

Industrialization A process that leads to an significantly increased proportion of a population engaged in specialized factory work and nonagricultural occupations; it increases the number of people living near factories and relying on mechanically produced goods and services.

Inequality The difference in access to and accumulation of wealth, educational opportunities, and cultural activities.

Kinship The network of social relationships that link individuals through common ancestry, marriage, or adoption.

Mechanical Solidarity Social cohesion generated by a minimal division of labor where there is little differentiation in the kinds of labor that individuals engage in.

Megalopolis A continuous stretch of urban settlement that results from cities, suburbs, and towns merging together.

Migrants People who move from one country or region to another, often due to the availability of work.

Neighborhood Collections of people who live close to one another with relatively sustained social contact and interaction.

New Urbanism An approach to designing cities, towns, and neighborhoods aimed at reducing traffic and sprawl and increasing social interactions.

Norms of Reciprocity and Mutual Trust Members of a community share the expectation that when an individual does a favor for someone else, the good they do will be returned at some point in the future.

Organic Solidarity Social cohesion generated by increased specialization where people necessarily rely on the contributions of others to survive and succeed.

Overpopulation An ecological condition in which a society is unable to support all its members with available technology and natural resources.

Physical Determinism A belief that people's lives will improve if they are given a better place to live and work in.

Place A unique location that takes material form and is endowed with meaning and value.

Postmodernism An approach to studying social life that rejects modernist beliefs in scientific knowledge, progress, and "grand theories"; relies on notions of fragmentation and disorganization.

Public Policy Governmental engagement and intervention in response to a perceived social problem.

Public–Private Partnerships Initiatives by city leaders to connect with private investors to undertake projects serve a larger public good.

Proletariat Workers who sell their labor to those who own the means of production.

Race Designation of population based on skin color or other physical features; it is often a key source of both social cohesion and social conflict.

Redevelopment The rebuilding of parts of a city; sometimes large areas are completely demolished before being rebuilt, sometimes older buildings are preserved or updated.

Segregation The practice of physically separating the occupants of some social statuses from the occupants of others.

Slums A heavily populated urban area characterized by substandard housing and squalor.

Social Capital The value of social networks and organizations to get things done together that comes from peoples' relationships with one another.

Social Conflict The struggle over values and meanings or property, income, and power, or both.

Social Order The conformity of individuals to explicit and implicit social rules of behavior.

Social Reform Attempts to change the working and living conditions of citizens and residents.

Space A nonphysical or material area that exists between places.

Status A social characteristic that locates individuals in relation to other people.

Suburbs Settlements located outside the physical and political boundaries of a city that are adjacent to the city or to its other suburbs.

Theory A set of interrelated propositions or ideas intended to explain a phenomenon.

Third Places Locations that serve a social need beyond work and home life (e.g., a local coffee shop).

Underclass The long-term poor who lack the necessary training and skills to become upwardly mobile.

Urban Culturalist Perspective An approach to studying cities by uncovering the meanings and values people endow them with in order to understand the ways that people make sense of the city, themselves, and others.

Urban Political Economy An approach to studying cities by investigating the ways that power relations influence the distribution of scarce resources.

Urban Sprawl The unplanned and unregulated growth of urban areas into surrounding areas.

Urbanism The ways of life or cultures of people in cities; the myths, symbols, and rituals of urbanites.

Urbanization The movement of populations from rural to urban areas; the growth and development, and redevelopment, of cities.

Zoning Legal regulations and restrictions that stipulate land use and architectural design of residential, commercial, and industrial developments.

REFERENCES

A

Abrahamson, M. (2006). *Urban enclaves: Identity and place in the world*. New York, NY: Worth Publishers.

Adleman, R. M. Neighborhood opportunities, race, and class: The Black middle class and residential segregation. *City & Community, 3*(1), 43–63.

Anderson, B. (1983). *Imagined Communities*. New York, NY: Verso.

Anderson, E. (1990). *StreetWise: Race, class, and change in an urban community*. Chicago, IL: University of Chicago Press.

Anderson, E. (1999). *Code of the street: Decency, violence, and the moral life of the inner city*. New York, NY: W. W. Norton.

Anderson, E. (2002). The ideologically driven critique. *American Journal of Sociology, 107(6)*, 1533–1550.

Anderson, E. (2011). *The cosmopolitan canopy: Race and civility in everyday life*. New York, NY: W. W. Norton.

Andrews, R. (2009). Civic engagement, ethnic heterogeneity, and social capital in urban areas. *Urban Affairs Review, 44*(3), 428–440.

Angotti, T. (2013). *The new century of the metropolis: Urban enclaves and orientalism*. New York, NY: Routledge.

Anjaria, J. S. (2009). Guardians of the bourgeois city: Citizenship, public space, and middle-class activism in Mumbai. *City & Community, 8*(4), 391–406.

Aman, W. L. (2013, March). *Mainstreaming the Asian mall*. Paper presented at the meeting of the Urban Affairs Association, San Francisco, CA.

Auyero, J. (2011). Researching the urban margins: What can the United States learn from Latin America and vice versa. *City & Community, 10*(4), 431–436.

B

Bartlett, A., Alix-Garcia, J., & Saah, D. (2012). City growth under conflict conditions: The view from Nyala, Darfur. *City & Community, 11,* 151–170.

Baudrillard, J. (1983). *Simulations*. New York, NY: Semiotext(e).

Baumgartner, M. K (1988). *The moral order of a suburb*. New York, NY: Oxford University Press.

Beauregard, R. (2003). *Voices of decline: The postwar fate of U.S. cities*. New York, NY: Routledge.

Beauregard, R. (2011). *The city revisited: Urban theory from Chicago, Los Angeles, New York*. Minneapolis: University of Minnesota Press.

Beisel, N. (1997). *Imperiled innocents: Anthony Comstock and family reproduction in Victorian America*. Princeton, NJ: Princeton University Press.

Bender, T. (1993). *Community and social change in America*. Baltimore, MD: Johns Hopkins University Press.

Berube, A., Katz, B., & Lang, R. (2005). *Redefining urban & suburban America*. Washington, DC: Brookings Institution Press.

Birch, E. (2009). From townsite to metropolis. In G. Hack, E. Birch, P, Sedway, P. Silver, & M. Silver (Eds.), *Local planning: Contemporary principles and practice*, pp. 3–22. Washington, DC: International City/County Management Association.

Bird, E. (2002). It makes sense to us: Cultural identity in local legends of place. *Journal of Contemporary Ethnography, 31(5),* 519–547.

Bjorkman, L. (2013). A review of *Cities with "slums": From informal settlement eradication to a right to the city in Africa* by Marie Huchzermeyer. *Journal of Urban Affairs, 35*(1), 124–125.

Bobo, L. D. (2000). Reclaiming a Du Boisian perspective on racial attitudes. *The Annals of the American Academy of Political and Social Science, 56*(8), 186–202.

Boorstin, D. J. (1974). *The Americans: The democratic experience.* New York, NY: Vintage Books.

Borer, M. I. (2006). The location of culture: The urban culturalist perspective." *City & Community, 5*(1), 73–98.

Borer, M. I. (2008). *Faithful to Fenway: Believing in Boston, baseball, and America's most beloved ballpark.* New York, NY: New York University Press.

Borer, M. I. (2010). From collective memory to collective imagination: Time, place, and urban redevelopment. *Symbolic Interaction, 33*(1), 96–114.

Borer, M. I., & Monti, D. (2006). Community, commerce, and consumption: businesses as civic associations. In M. Borer (Ed.), *Varieties of urban experience,* pp. 39–62. Lanham, MD: University Press of America.

Bourdieu, P. (1986). Forms of capital. In J. C. Richardson (Ed.), *Handbook of theory and research for the sociology of education,* pp. 241–258. New York, NY: Greenwood Press.

Boyd, M. (2000). Reconstructing Bronzeville: Racial nostalgia and neighborhood development. *Journal of Urban Affairs, 22(2),* 107–122.

Boyd, M. (2008). Defensive development: The role of racial conflict in gentrification. *Urban Affairs Review, 43(6),* 751–776.

Boyer, P. (1978). *Urban masses and moral order in America, 1820–1920.* Cambridge, MA: Harvard University Press.

Boyer, P. (2012). Civility, religion, and American democracy. In C. Clayton & R. Elgar (Eds.), *Civility and democracy in America,* pp. 48–58. Pullman: Washington State Press.

Bridenbaugh, C. (1966). *Cities in the wilderness: The first century of urban life in America, 1625–1742.* London, England: Oxford University Press.

Bridenbaugh, C. (1971). *Cities in revolt: Urban life in America, 1743–1776.* London, England: Oxford University Press.

Bridger, J. (1996). Community imagery and the built environment. *Sociological Quarterly, 37*(3), 353–374.

Brisson, D., & Usher, C. (2007). The effects of informal neighborhood bonding social capital and neighborhood context on homeownership for families living in poverty. *Journal of Urban Affairs, 29*(1), 65–75.

Britton, M. (2011). Close together but worlds apart? Residential integration and interethnic friendship in Houston" *City & Community, 10*(2), 182–204.

Brown-Saracino, J. (2009). *A neighborhood that never changes: Gentrification, social preservation, and the search for authenticity.* Chicago, IL: University of Chicago Press.

Brush, C., Monti, D., Ryan, A., & Gannon, A. (2007). Building ventures through civic capitalism. *Annals of the American Academy of Political and Social Science, 613,* 155–177.

Burgess, E. W. (1925/1967). The growth of the city. In R. Park, E. W. Burgess, & R. McKenzie (Eds.), *The city.* Chicago, IL: University of Chicago Press.

C

Cadell, C., Falk, N., & King, F. *Regeneration in European cities.* York, England: The Joseph Rowntree Foundation.

Carroll, G., & Torfason, M. T. (2011). Restaurant organizational forms and community in the U.S. in 2005. *City & Community, 10*(1), 1–24.

Castells, M. (1977). *The urban question: A Marxist approach.* Cambridge, MA: MIT Press.

Castells, M. (1983). *The city and the grassroots movement.* Berkeley: University of California Press.

Chandrashekar, M. N., Krishne, G., Sridhara, M. V., & Kumar, M. N. (2013, March). Building new mega cities: India's chance to look beyond renewal. Paper presented at the annual meeting of the Urban Affairs Association, San Francisco, CA.

Chaskin, R., & Joseph, M. (2010). Building "Community" in mixed-income developments. *Urban Affairs Review, 45*(3), 299–335.

Chayko, M. (2008). *Portable communities: The social dynamics of online and mobile connectedness.* Albany, NY: SUNY Press.

Chiswick, B., & Miller, P. (2005). Do enclaves matter in immigrant adjustment? *City & Community, 4*(1), 5–36.

Chudacoff, H., and Smith, J. (1988). *The evolution of American urban society*. Englewood Cliffs, NJ: Prentice Hall.

Chudacoff, H., & Smith, J. (2005). *The evolution of American urban society*. Saddle River, NJ: Pearson Prentice Hall.

Coleman, J. (1988). Social capital in the creation of human capital. *American Journal of Sociology, 94,* 95–119.

Corden, C. (1977). *Planned cities: New towns in Britain and America*. Beverly Hills, CA: Sage.

Crankshaw, O. Deindustrialization, professionalization and racial inequality in Cape Town. *Urban Affairs Review, 48*(6), 836–862.

Cressey, D. (1969). *Theft of the nation: The structure and operations of organized crime in America*. New York, NY: Harper and Row.

Cross, G. (1997). Consumer history and the dilemmas of working-class history. *Labor History Review, 62*(3), 261–274.

Cummings, S. (1980). *Self-help in urban America: Patterns of minority economic development*. Port Washington, NY: Kennikat Press.

Cummings, S. (1998). *Left behind in Rosedale: Race relations and the collapse of community institutions*. Boulder, CO: Westview Press.

Cummings, S. (2011, March). *Race, ethnicity, and home-ownership,* Paper presented at the 2011 meeting of the Urban Affairs Association, New Orleans, LA.

Curley, A. (2010). Relocating the poor: Social capital and neighborhood resources. *Journal of Urban Affairs, 32*(1), 79–103.

D

Davis, M. (1998). *Ecology of fear: Los Angeles and the imagination of disaster*. Irvine: University of California Press.

Davis, M. (2002). *The grit beneath the glitter: Tales from the real Las Vegas*. Irvine: University of California Press.

Davis, S. (1986). *Parades and power: Street theatre in nineteenth-century Philadelphia*. Berkeley: University of California Press.

Dawkins, C. (2005). Evidence on the intergenerational persistence of residential segregation by race. *Urban Studies, 42,* 545–555.

Dear, M. (2002). Los Angeles and the Chicago school: Invitation to a debate. *City & Community, 1*(1), 5–32.

Dear, M., & Flusty, S. (1998). Postmodern urbanism. *Annals of the Association of American Geographers, 88* (1), 50–72.

Dekker, K., Volker, B., Lelieveldt, H., & Torenvlied, R. (2010). Civic engagement in urban neighborhoods: Does the network of civic organizations influence participation in neighborhood projects? *Journal of Urban Affairs, 32*(5), 609–632.

Demerath, L., & Levinger, D. (2003). The social qualities of being on foot: A theoretical analysis of pedestrian activity, community, and culture. *City & Community, 2*(3), 217–237.

Domit, M., & Barrionuevo, A. (2010, November 29). Brazilian forces claim victory in gang haven. *The New York Times*, p. A4.

Du Bois, W. E. B. (1996). *The Philadelphia Negro: A social study*. Philadelphia: University of Pennsylvania Press.

Du Bois, W. E. B. (2007). *The souls of Black folk*. New York, NY: Oxford University Press.

Duneier, M. (1999). *Sidewalk*. New York, NY: Farrar, Straus and Giroux.

Duneier, M. (2004). Scrutinizing the heat: On ethnic myths and the importance of shoe leather. *Contemporary Sociology, 33,* 139–150.

Durkheim, E. (1965). *The elementary forms of the religious life*. New York, NY: Free Press.

Durkheim, E. (1947). *The division of labor in society*. Glencoe, IL: Free Press.

E

Eliasoph, N. (1998). *Avoiding politics: How Americans produce apathy in everyday life*. Cambridge, UK: Cambridge University Press.

Engels, F. (1999). *The condition of the working class in England*. Oxford, UK: Oxford University Press.

F

Fasenfest, D., Booza, J., & Metzger, K. (2006). Living together: A new look at racial and ethnic integration in metropolitan neighborhoods, 1990–2000. In A. Berube, B. Katz, & R. Lang (Eds.), *Redefining urban & suburban America*, pp. 93–118. Washington, DC: Brookings Institution Press.

Firey, W. (1945). Sentiment and symbolism as ecological variables. *American Sociological Review, 10,* 140–148.

Fischer, C. (1975). Toward a subcultural theory of urbanism. *American Journal of Sociology, 76,* 847–856.

Fischer, C. (1976). *The urban experience.* New York, NY: Harcourt Brace Jovanovich.

Fisher, C. (1982). *To dwell among friends: Personal networks in town and city.* Chicago, IL: University of Chicago Press.

Fisher, C. (1994). *America calling: A social history of the telephone to 1940.* Berkeley: University of California Press, 1994.

Flint, C. A. (2009). *Wrestling with Moses.* New York, NY: Random House.

Flora, C. B., & Flora, J. L. (2008). *Rural communities: Legacy and change.* Boulder, CO: Westview Press.

Florida, R. (2002). *The rise of the creative class.* New York, NY: Basic Books.

Florida, R. (2005). *Cities and the creative class.* New York, NY: Routledge.

Frantz, D., & Collins, C. (1999). *Celebration, U. S. A.* New York, NY: Owl Books.

Fraser, N. (1992). Rethinking the public sphere: A contribution to the critique of actually existing democracy. In C. Calhoun (Ed.), *Habermas and the public sphere,* pp. 109–142. Cambridge, MA: MIT Press.

Freeman, L. (2008). Is class becoming a more important determinant of neighborhood attainment for African-Americans? *Urban Affairs Review, 44*(1), 3–26

Frey, W. (2011) November 17. Americans still stuck at home. Washington, DC: Brookings Institution.

G

Gans, H. J. (1962). *The urban villagers: Group and class in the life of Italian-Americans.* New York, NY: The Free Press.

Garreau, J. (1991) *Edge city: Life on the new frontier.* New York, NY: Doubleday.

Garvin, A. (2002). *The American city: What works, what doesn't.* New York, NY: McGraw-Hill.

Gau, H. (2010, October 4). Migrant "villages" within a city ignite debate. *The New York Times,* p. A8.

Gieryn, T. (2000). A space for place in sociology. *Annual Review of Sociology, 26,* 463–496.

Glaab, C., & Brown, T. A. (1976). *A history of urban America.* New York, NY: Macmillan.

Glaeser, E., & Vigdor, J. (2012). *The end of the segregated century: Racial separation in America's neighborhoods, 1890–2010.* New York, NY: The Manhattan Institute.

Goldfield, D., & Brownell, B. (1990). *Urban America: A history. boston*: Houghton Mifflin.

Goode, J. (2007). How urban ethnography counters myths about the poor. In G. Gmelch & M. Hutter (Eds.) *Urban life: Readings in the anthropology of the city* (pp. 185–201). Boston, MA: Pearson.

Goodman, M., & Monti, D. (1999). Corporately sponsored redevelopment campaigns and the social stability of urban neighborhoods: St. Louis revisited. *Journal of Urban Affairs, 21,* 101–129.

Gopnik, A. (2010, October 10). Market man: What did Adam Smith really believe? *The New Yorker.*

Gotham, K. F. (2001). Urban sociology and the postmodern challenge, *Humboldt Journal of Social Relations, 26*(1 & 2), 57–79.

Gottdiener, M., & Hutchison, R. (2006). *The new urban sociology.* Boulder, CO: Westview Press.

Gould, S. J. (1981). *The mismeasure of man.* New York, NY: W.W. Norton.

Gould, S. J. (1996). *The mismeasure of man* (revised and expanded ed.). New York, NY: W.W. Norton.

Grazian, D. (2003). *Blue Chicago: The search for authenticity in urban blues clubs.* Chicago, IL: University of Chicago Press.

Granovetter, M. S. (1973). The strength of weak ties. *American Journal of Sociology, 78,* 1360–1380.

Greif, M. (2009). Neighborhood Attachment in the Multiethnic Metropolis." *City & Community, 8(1),* 27–45.

Guest, A., Cover, J., Matsueda, R., & Kubrin, C. (2006). Neighborhood context and neighboring ties. *City & Community, 5*(4), 363–385.

H

Hall, P. *Cities in civilization.* New York, NY: Pantheon.

Halle, D. (Ed.). (2003). *New York and Los Angeles: Politics, society, and culture: A comparative view.* Chicago, IL: University Press of Chicago.

Halle, D., & Beveridge, A. (2001). *New York and Los Angeles: Politics, society and culture: A comparative view.* Chicago, IL: University of Chicago Press.

Halle, D., & Beveridge, A, (2011). The rise and decline of the L.A. and New York schools. In Dennis R. Judd & Dick W. Simpson (Eds.), *The city revisited: Urban theory from Chicago, Los Angeles, and New York.* Minneapolis: University of Minnesota Press.

Hannerz, U. (1980). *Exploring the city: Inquiries towards an urban anthropology.* New York, NY: Columbia University.

Hannigan, J. (1998). *Fantasy city: Pleasure and profit in the postmodern metropolis.* New York, NY: Routledge.

Hampton, K., & Wellman, B. (2003). Neighboring in Netville: How the Internet supports community and social capital in a wired suburb. *City & Community, 2,* 277–311.

Handlon, B. (2010). *Once upon the American Dream: Inner ring suburbs of the metropolitan United States.* Philadelphia, PA: Temple University Press.

Harris, C., & Ullman, E. (1945). *The nature of cities.* Thousand Oaks, CA: Sage.

Harvey, D. (1973). *Social justice and the city.* Athens: University of Georgia Press.

Hawkins, C., & Andrew, S. (2011). Understanding horizontal and vertical relations in the context of economic development joint venture agreements. *Urban Affairs Review, 47*(3), 385–412.

Hawley, A. (1971). *Urban society: An ecological approach.* New York, NY: The Ronald Press.

Hays, R. A., & Kogl, A. (2007). Neighborhood attachment, social capital building, and political participation: A case study of low- and moderate-income residents of Waterloo, Iowa. *Journal of Urban Affairs, 29*(2), 181–205.

Hipp, J., & Perrin, A. (2009). The simultaneous effect of social distance and physical distance on the formation of neighborhood ties. *City & Community, 8*(1), 5–26.

Hohenberg, P., & Lees, L. H. (1995). *The making of modern Europe, 1000–1994.* Cambridge, MA: Harvard University Press.

Holli, M. (1969). *Reform in Detroit.* New York, NY: Oxford University Press.

Holt, M. (1992). *The orphan trains: Placing out in America.* Lincoln: University of Nebraska Press.

Hoyt, H. (1939). *The structure and growth of residential neighborhoods in American cities.* Atlanta, GA: Federal Highway Administration.

Humphreys, L. (1975). *Tearoom trade: Impersonal sex in public places.* Chicago, IL: Aldine.

Hyra, D. (2012). Conceptualizing the New Urban Renewal: Comparing the past to the present. *Urban Affairs Review, 48,* 498–527.

Hyra, D. (2006). Racial uplift? Intra-racial class conflict and the economic revitalization of Harlem and Bronzeville. *City & Community, 5*(1), 71–92.

I

Irwin, J. (1977). *Scenes.* Beverly Hills, CA: Sage.

J

Jackson, K. T. (1986). *Crabgrass frontier: The suburbanization of the United States.* New York, NY: Oxford University Press.

Jackson, P. (1999). Postmodern urbanism and the ethnographic void. *Urban Geography, 20,* 400–402.

Jacobs, J. (1961). *The death and life of great American cities.* New York, NY: Random House.

Jankowiak, W. (2010). Neighbors and kin in Chinese cities. In G. Gmelch, R. Kemper, & W. Zenner (Eds.), *Urban Life: Readings in the anthropology of the city* (pp. 256–268). Long Grove, IL: Waveland Press.

Jonassen, C. T. (1949). Cultural variables in the ecology of an ethnic group. *American Sociological Review, 14*(1), 32–41.

Johnston, R., Poulsen, R., & Forrest, J. (2007). Ethnic and racial segregation in U.S. metropolitan areas, 1980–2000. *Urban Affairs Review, 42,* 479–504.

K

Kahn, J. (2011, July/August). India invents a city: Lavasa is an orderly, high-tech community with everything. Except people. *The Atlantic.* Retrieved from http://www.theatlantic.com/magazine/archive/2011/07/india-invents-a-city/308549/

Karp, D. A. (1973). Hiding in pornographic bookstores: A reconsideration of the nature of urban anonymity. *Urban Life and Culture, 4,* 427–451.

Karp, D. A, Stone, G. P., & Yoels, W. C. (1991). *Being urban: A social psychological view of city life.* New York, NY: Praeger.

Katz, J. (2009). Time for new urban ethnographies. *Ethnography, 11*(1), 25–44.

Kelly, E., & Becker, B. (2000). *Community planning: An introduction to the comprehensive plan.* Washington, DC: Island Press.

Kemper, R. (2010). The extended community: Migration and transformation in Tzintzuntzan, Mexico. In G. Gmelch, R. Kemper, & W. Zenner (Eds.), *Urban life: Readings in the anthropology of the city* (pp. 285–299). Long Grove, IL: Waveland Press.

Kennedy, L. (1992). *Planning the city upon a hill: Boston since 1630.* Amherst: University of Massachusetts Press.

Kimmelman, M. (2013, April 28). Who rules the street in Cairo? The residents who build it. *The New York Times,* p. A1.

Klinenberg, E. (2003). *Heat wave: A social autopsy of disaster in Chicago.* Chicago, IL: University of Chicago Press, 2003.

Kleniewski, N. (1997). *Cities, change and conflict: A political economy of urban life.* St Ann Arbor, MI: Wadsworth.

Knapp, G.-J., & Moore, T. (2009). Smart-growth in brief. In G. Hack, E. Birch, P. Sedway, & M. Silver, (Eds.), *Local planning: Contemporary principles and practice,* pp. 117–121. Washington, DC: International City/County Management Association.

Kornblum, W. (1974). *Blue collar community.* Chicago, IL: University of Chicago Press.

Krause, R. (2011). Policy innovation, intergovernmental relations, and the adoption of climate protection initiatives by U.S. cities. *Journal of Urban Affairs, 33*(1), 45–60.

L

Lang, R. E., & Simmons, P. A. (2001, June). *Boomburbs: The emergence of large, fast-growing cities in the United States.* Washington, DC: Fannie Mae Foundation. Census Note 01–05.

Langer, P. (1984). Sociology—four images of organized diversity, In L. Rodwin & R. Hollister (Eds.), *Cities of the mind: Images and themes of the city in the social sciences.* New York, NY: Plenum Press.

Lees, A. (1985) *Cities perceived: Urban society in European and American Thought, 1820–1940.* New York, NY: Columbia University Press.

Lees, L. H. (1994). Urban public space and imagined communities in the 1980s and 1990s. *Journal of Urban History, 20*(4), 443–465.

LeGates, R., & Hudulah, D. (2013, March). Peri-urban planning for developing East Asia. Paper presented at the annual meeting of the Urban Affairs Association, San Francisco, CA.

Lehrer, J. (2010, December 19). A physicist solves the city. *The New York Times Magazine,* MM46.

Li, M. (1999). *"We Need Two Worlds": Chinese immigrant associations in a Western society.* Amsterdam, Netherlands: Amsterdam University Press.

Lichterman, P. (1996). *The search for political community: American activists reinventing commitment.* Cambridge, UK: Cambridge University Press.

Lichterman, P. (2006). Social capital or group style? Rescuing Tocqueville's insights on civic engagement. *Theory & Society, 35,* 529–63.

Liebow, E. (1967). *Tally's corner: A study of Negro streetcorner men.* Boston, MA: Little, Brown.

Light, I. (1983). *Cities in world perspective.* New York, NY: Macmillan.

Linebaugh, K. (2011, March 23). Detroit's population crashes. *Wall Street Journal.* Retrieved from http://online.wsj.com/article/SB1000142405274 8704461304576216850733151470.html? KEYWORDS=detroit

Lofland, L. H. (1973). *A world of strangers: Order and action in urban space.* Prospect Heights, IL: Waveland Press.

Lofland, L. (1998). *The Public REALM: Exploring the city's quintessential social territory.* New York, NY: Aldine de Gruyter.

Lofland, L. (2002). *The commodification of public space.* College Park: University of Maryland School of Architecture, Urban Studies and Planning Program, University of Maryland, Le Frak Lecture Monograph Series.

Logan, J., & Molotch, H. (1987). *Urban Fortunes: The political economy of place.* Berkeley: University of California Press.

Long, N. (1958). The local community as an ecology of games. *American Journal of Sociology, 64,* 251–261.

M

Macgregor, L. (2010). *Habits of the heartland: Small-town life in modern America.* Ithaca, NY: Cornell University Press.

Macionis, J., & Parrillo, V. (2010). *Cities and urban life.* Boston, MA: Prentice Hall. Mackenzie, P. (2002). Strangers in the city: The *Hukou* and urban citizenship in China. *Journal of International Affairs, 56*(1), 305–319.

Madden, D. (2010). Revisiting the end of public space: Assembling the public in an urban park. *City & Community, 9*(2), 187–207.

Maines, D., & Bridger, J. (1992). Narratives, community, and land use decisions. *Social Science Journal* 29(4), 363–380.

Mann, C. (2011, June). Birth of religion. *National Geographic,* pp.34–59.

Manturuk, K., Lindblad, M., & Quercia, R. (2012). Homeownership and civic engagement in low-income urban neighborhoods: A longitudinal analysis. *Urban Affairs Review, 48*(5), 731–760.

Marx, K., & Engels, F. (1978). The manifesto of the Communist Party. In R. Tucker (Ed.), *The Marx-Engels reader.* New York. NY: W.W. Norton.

Massey, D., & Denton, N. (1993). *American apartheid: Segregation and the making of the underclass.* Cambridge, MA: Harvard University Press.

Massey, D., Rothwell, J., & Domina, T. (2009). The changing bases of segregation in the United States. *The Annals of the American Academy of Political and Social Science, 626,* 74–90.

Mayhew, H. (1968). *London labour and the London poor.* New York, NY: Dover.

McDonnell, K. (1978). *Medieval London suburbs.* London, England: Phillmore & Co.

McKinney, J. C. (1966). *Constructive typology and social theory.* New York, NY: Meredith Publishing.

McLean, S. L., Schultz, D. A., & Steger, M. B. (Eds.). (2002). *Social capital: Critical perspectives on community and "bowling alone."* New York: New York University Press.

McMurry, S. (1995). *Transforming rural life: Dairying families and agricultural change, 1820–1885.* Baltimore, MD: Johns Hopkins University Press.

Mead, G. H. (1932). *The philosophy of the present.* Chicago, IL: University of Chicago Press.

Medina, J. (2013, April 29). New suburban dream born of Asia and Southern California. *The New York Times.*

Mellor, J. R. (1977). *Urban sociology in an urbanized society.* London, England: Routledge.

Merrifield, A. (2002). *Metromarxism: A Marxist tale of the city.* New York, NY: Routledge.

Mesch, G., & Levanon, Y. (2003). Community networking and locally-based social ties in two suburban localities. *City & Community, 2*(4), 335–352.

Meyer, K. (2012, April 12). Who gets to be French? *The New York Times,* p. A27.

Miller, J. (2001). *One of the guys: girls, gangs, and gender.* New York, NY: Oxford University Press.

Miller, Z. (1968). *Boss Cox's Cincinnati: Urban politics in the Progressive Era.* New York, NY: Oxford University Press.

Milligan, M. (1998). Interactional past and present: The social construction of place attachment. *Symbolic Interaction, 21,* 1–33.

Milligan, M. (2003). Displacement and identity discontinuity: The role of nostalgia in establishing new identity categories. *Symbolic Interaction 26*(3), 381–403.

Monkkonen, E. (1990). *America becomes urban: The development of U.S. cities & towns, 1780–1980.* Berkeley: University of California Press.

Monti, D. (1985). *A semblance of justice: St. Louis school desegregation and order in urban America.* Columbia: University of Missouri Press.

Monti, D. (1990). *Race, redevelopment, and the new company town.* Albany: State University of New York Press.

Monti, D. (1994). *Wannabe: Gangs in suburbs and schools.* Oxford, UK: Blackwell.

Monti, D. (1997). Ethnic economies, affirmative action, and mining cultural capital. *The American Sociologist,* 101–112.

Monti, D. (1999). *The American city: A social and cultural history.* Malden, MA: Blackwell.

Monti, D. (2007). Old whines in new bottles: Robert Putnam, Richard Florida, and the "community" problem in contemporary America." In James Jennings (Ed.), *Race, neighborhoods, and the misuse of social capital,* pp. 21–40. New York, NY: Palgrave Macmillan.

Monti, D. (2013). *Engaging strangers: Civil rites, civic capitalism, and public order in an American city.* Lanham, MD: Fairleigh Dickinson University Press.

Monti, D., Ryan, A., Brush, C., & Gannon, A. (2007). Civic capitalism: entrepreneurs, their ventures, and communities. *Journal of Developmental Entrepreneurship, 12*(3), 353–375.

Monti, D., & Burghoff, D. (2012). Corporately-sponsored redevelopment campaigns and the demographic stability of urban neighborhoods: Saint Louis re-revisited. *Journal of Urban Affairs, 34*(5), 513–532.

Monti, D., Butler, C., Curley, A., Tilney, K., & Weiner, M. F. (2003). Private lives and public worlds: Changes in Americans' social ties and civic attachments in the late 20th century. *City & Community, 2*(2), 143–163.

Moore, J. (1978). *Homeboys: gangs, drugs, and prison in the barrios of Los Angeles.* Philadelphia: Temple University Press.

Moore, J. (1978). *Homeboys: gangs, drugs, and prison in the barrios of Los Angeles.* Philadelphia, PA: Temple University Press.

Moore, K. (2005). What's class got to do with it? Community development and racial identity. *Journal of Urban Affairs, 27*(4), 437–451.

Mumford, L. (1961). *The city in history.* New York, NY: Harcourt, Brace & World.

Murray, C. (2012). *Coming apart: The state of White America, 1960–2010.* New York, NY: Random House.

N

Narayan, D. (1999). *Bonds and bridges: Social capital and poverty.* Policy Research Working Paper 2167, Poverty Division, Poverty Reduction and Economic Management Network, The World Bank.

Nelson, A., & Lang, R. (2011). *Megapolitan America: A new vision for understanding America's metropolitan geography.* Washington, DC: American Planning Association.

Neuman, W. (2012, April 21). With Venezuelan food shortages, some blame price controls. *The New York Times,* p. A1.

Newman, K., (1999). *No shame in my game: The working poor in the inner city.* New York, NY: Russell Sage Foundation and Knopf.

Nicolaides, B. (In press). Race, class and suburban engagement in Pasadena, California, 1950–2000. In J. Archer, P. Sandul, & K. Solomonson (Eds.), *Suburban histories: Life, culture, and community.* Minneapolis: University of Minnesota Press.

Nijman, J. (2000). The paradigmatic city. *Annals of the Association of American Geographers, 90*(1), 135–145.

Nissenbaum, S. (1996). *The battle for Christmas.* New York, NY: Alfred A. Knopf.

Nordin, D. S. (2007). *Rich harvest: A history of the Grange 1867–1900.* Jackson: University Press of Mississippi.

O

Oldenburg, R. (1999). *The great good place: Coffee shops, bookstores, bars, hair salons and other hangouts at the heart of a community.* New York, NY: Da Capo Press.

Onishi, N. (2010, November 29). For city dwellers, a taste of the orderly life. *The New York Times,* p. A6.

Open Societies Institute. (2010). *Muslims in Europe: A report on 11 EU cities.* London: Open Societies Institute.

Orum, A. (1995). *City-building in America.* Boulder, CO: Westview Press.

Orum, A., Bata, S., Shumei, L., Jewei, T., Yang, S., & Trung, N. T. (2009). Public Man and Public Space in Shanghai Today. *City & Community, 8*(4), 369–390.

Otterman, S., & Riviera, R. (2012, May 10). Ultra-Orthodox shun their own for reporting child sexual abuse. *The New York Times.*

P

Padilla, F. (1992). *The gang as an American enterprise.* New Brunswick, NJ: Rutgers University Press.

Pahl, R. (1970). *Whose city? And other essays on sociology and planning.* St. Ann Arbor, MI: Longman's Press.

Palen, J. (2008). *The urban world.* Boulder, CO: Paradigm Publishers.

Papachristos, A., Smith, C., Scherer, M., & Fugiero, M (2011). More coffee, less crime? The relationship between gentrification and neighborhood crime rates in Chicago, 1991–2005. *City & Community, 10*(3), 215–240.

Pares, M., Bonet-Marti, J., & Marti-Costa, M. (2012). Does participation really matter in urban regeneration policies? Exploring governance networks in Catalonia (Spain). *Urban Affairs Review, 48*(2), 238–271.

Park, R. E. (1925/1967). The: Suggestions for the investigation of human behavior in the urban environment. In R. Park, E. W. Burgess, & R. D. McKenzie (Eds.), *The city.* Chicago, IL: University of Chicago Press.

Patillo-McCoy, M. (1998). Church culture as a strategy of action in the Black community. *American Sociological Review, 63,* 313–41.

Pfeiffer, D. (2012). Has exurban growth enabled greater racial equity in neighborhood quality? Evidence from the Los Angeles region. *Journal of Urban Affairs, 34*(4), 347–372.

Phares, D. (2009). *Governing metropolitan regions in the 21st Century.* Armonk, NY: M. E. Sharpe.

Pisarki, A. (1987). *Commuting in America: A national report on patterns and trends.* Westport, CT: Eno Foundation.

Polgreen, L. (2010, December 1). India's cities buckle under the strain of new arrivals. *The New York Times.*

Porter, R. (1994). *London: A social history.* London, England: Hamish Hamilton.

Porterfield, A. (2012). Religion's role in contestations over American civility. In C. Clayton & R. Elgar (Eds.), *Civility and democracy in America,* pp. 38–47. Pullman: Washington State Press, 2012.

Portes, A., Haller, W., & Guarnizo, L. E. (2002). Transnational entrepreneurs: An alternative form of immigrant economic adaptation. *American Sociological Review, 67,* 278–298.

Putnam, R. D. (1993a). *Making democracy work: Civic traditions in modern Italy.* Princeton, NJ: Princeton University Press.

Putnam, R. D. (1993b). The prosperous community: Social capital and public life. *The American Prospect, 13,* 35–42.

Putnam, R. (2000). *Bowling alone: The collapse and revival of American community.* New York, NY: Simon and Schuster.

R

Raphael, S., & Stoll, M. (2006). Modest progress: The narrowing spatial mismatch between Blacks and jobs in the 1990s. In A. Berube, B. Katz, & R. Lang (Eds.), *Redefining Urban and Suburban America,* pp. 119–142. Washington, DC: Brookings Institution Press.

Rath, J. (2011). *Promoting ethnic entrepreneurship in European cities.* Publications Office of the European Union, Luxembourg

Richards, L. (1971). *Gentlemen of property and standing: Anti-abolition mobs in Jacksonian America.* London, England: Oxford University Press.

Roberts, B. (2011). The consolidation of the Latin American city and the undermining of social cohesion. *City & Community, 10*(4), 414–423.

Romero, S. (2012, March 5). Slum dwellers are defying Brazil's grand design for Olympics. *The New York Times,* p. A1.

Roof, W. C. (2012). Religious pluralism and civility. In C. Clayton & R. Elgar (Eds.), *Civility and democracy in America,* pp. 59–68. Pullman: Washington State Press.

Ross, B., Levine, M., & Stedman, M. (1991). *Urban politics: Power in metropolitan America.* Itasca, IL: F. E. Peacock.

Rothman, D. J. (1971). *The discovery of the asylum: Social order and disorder in the new republic.* Boston, MA: Little Brown.

Ryan, M. (1997). *Civic wars: Democracy and public life in the American city during the nineteenth century.* Berkeley: University of California Press.

S

Saito, L. (2012). How low-income residents can benefit from urban development: The LA Live community benefits agreement. *City & Community, 11*(2), 129–150.

Salins, P. (2009). Suburban planning in a market economy. In G. Hack, E. Birch, P. Sedway, & M. Silver (Eds.), *Local planning: Contemporary principles and practice,* pp. 46–51. Washington, DC: International City/County Management Association.

Sampson, R. (2012). *Great American city: Chicago and the enduring neighborhood effect.* Chicago, IL: University of Chicago Press.

Sassen, S. (2010). *Cities in a world economy.* Thousand Oaks, CA: Pine Forge.

Sassen, S. (2001). *The global city: New York, London, Tokyo.* Princeton, NJ: Princeton University Press.

Sassen, S. (2002). *Global networks: Linked cities.* New York, NY: Routledge.

Sayare, S. (2012, April 28). After killings in France, Muslims fear a culture of diversity is at risk. *The New York Times,* p. A6.

Schlessinger, A. M. (1999). *The rise of the city: 1878–1898.* Columbus: University of Ohio Press.

Sharkey, P. (2013). *Stuck in place: Urban neighborhoods and the end of progress toward racial equality.* Chicago, IL: University of Chicago Press.

Shen, J., & Wu, F. (2012). Restless urban landscapes in China: A case study of three projects in Shanghai. *Journal of Urban Affairs, 34*(3), 255–278.

Short, J. R. (2004). *Global metropolitan: Globalizing cities in a capitalist world.* New York, NY: Routledge.

Simmel, G. (1971a). The metropolis and the mental life. In D. Levine, *On individuality and social forms.* Chicago, IL: University of Chicago Press.

Simmel, G. 1971b. The stranger. In D. Levine, *On Individuality and Social Forms.* Chicago, IL: University of Chicago Press.

Silverman, R. (1999). Black business, group resources, and the economic detour. *Journal of Black Studies, 30*(2), 232–258.

Sinclair, U. (1960). *The jungle.* New York, NY: Signet.

Singleton, G. (1975). Protestant voluntary organizations and the shaping of Victorian America. *American Quarterly, 27*(5), 549–560.

Sirianni, C., & Friedland, L. (2001). *Civic innovation in America: Community empowerment, public policy and the movement for civic renewal.* Berkeley: University of California Press.

Skocpol, T. (2004). *Diminished democracy: From membership to management in American civic life.* Norman: University of Oklahoma Press.

Small, M. L. (2004). *Villa Victoria: The transformation of social capital in a Boston barrio.* Chicago, IL: University of Chicago Press.

Smith, A. D. *The ethnic origins of nations.* Oxford, UK: Blackwell Publishers, 1985.

Smith, D. A., & Timberlake, M. (1995). *World cities in a world system.* New York, NY: Cambridge University Press.

Soja, E. (1989). *Postmodern geographies: The reassertion of space in Critical Social Theory.* New York, NY: Verso.

Spillman, Lyn. (2002). Introduction: culture and cultural sociology, in L. Spillman (Ed.), *Cultural sociology.* Malden, MA: Blackwell.

Stack, J. (1979). *International conflict in an American city: Boston's Irish, Italians, and Jews, 1935–1944.* Westport, CN: Greenwood Press.

Steffens, L. (1969). *The shame of the cities.* New York, NY: Hill and Wang.

Stein, M. (1994). *The eclipse of community: An interpretation of American studies.* Charlottesville, VA: Harper Publishing.

Stoker, R., Stone, C., & Worgs, D. (2013, March). *The new neighborhood politics in Baltimore.* Paper presented at the meeting of the Urban Affairs Association, San Francisco, CA.

Stone, G. (1954). City shoppers and urban identification: Observations on the social psychology of city life. *American Journal of Sociology, 60*(1), 36–45.

Susser, I. (1982). *Norman Street: Politics and poverty in an urban neighborhood.* New York, NY: Oxford University Press.

Suttles, G. (1984). The cumulative texture of local urban culture. *American Journal of Sociology, 90*(2), 283–302.

Suttles, G. (1968). *The social order of the slum.* Chicago, IL: University of Chicago Press.

Swanstrom, T., Dreier, P., Casey, C., & Flack, R. (2005). In A. Berube, B. Katz, & R. Lang (Eds.), *Redefining urban & suburban America*, pp. 143–166. Washington, DC: Brookings Institution Press.

T

Talen, E. The problem with community planning. *Journal of Planning Literature, 15*(2), 171–183.

Teaford, J. (1984). *The unheralded triumph: City government in America, 1870–1900.* Baltimore, MD: The Johns Hopkins University Press.

Teaford, J. (1993). *The twentieth-century American city.* Baltimore, MD: The Johns Hopkins University Press.

Tierney, J. (2011, February 7). Social scientist sees bias within. *The New York Times*, p. D1.

Tilly, C. (1990). *Coercion, capital and European states, AD 990–1990.* Cambridge, MA: Basil Blackwell.

Tilly, C., Tilly, L., & Tilly, R. (1975). *The rebellious century: 1830–1930.* Cambridge, MA: Harvard University Press.

Tissot, S. (2011). Of dogs and men: The making of spatial boundaries in a gentrifying neighborhood. *City & Community, 10*(3), 265–284.

Tocqueville, A. de. (1863). *Democracy in America, Volume 2* (H. Reeve, Trans., F. Bowen, Ed.). Cambridge, MA: Sever and Francis. [Original work published 1840]

Tocqueville, A. de. (1982). *On democracy, revolution, and society: Selected writings.* Edited by J. Stone & S. Mennell. Chicago, IL: University of Chicago Press.

Tyack, D., & Hansot, E. (1990). *Learning together: A history of coeducation in American public schools.* New Haven, CN: Yale University Press.

U

Usher, C. L. (2007). Trust and well-being in the African American neighborhood. *City & Community, 6*(4), 367–387.

United Nations Human Settlements Programme. (2008). The state of African cities, 2008. New York, NY: United Nations.

United Nations Human Settlements Programme. (2010). The state of Asian cities, 2010/11. New York, NY: United Nations.

V

Van Houwelingen, P. (2012). Neighborhood associations and social capital in Japan. *Urban Affairs Review, 48,* 467–497.

Vallejo, J. (2009). Latina spaces: Middle-class ethnic capital and professional associations in the Latino community. *City & Community, 8*(2), 129–154.

Van Hightower, N. R., & Goton, J. (2002). A Case Study of Community-Based Responses to Rural Woman Battering. *Violence Against Women, 8*(7), 845–72.

Von Schirach, P. (June 15, 2011). Riots in China Indicative of Deeper Troubles? Some begin to question validity of economic model. *Wall Street Journal.*

W

Wacquant, L. (2002). Scrutinizing the street: Poverty, morality, and the pitfalls of urban ethnography. *American Journal of Sociology, 107*(6), 1468–1532.

Wade, R. (1976). *The urban frontier.* Chicago, IL: University of Chicago Press.

Wallerstein, I. (1979). *The capitalist world economy.* Cambridge, UK: Cambridge University Press.

Walton, J. (2001). *Storied land: Community and memory in Monterey*. Berkeley: University of California Press.

Walton, J. (1993). Urban sociology: The contribution and limits of political economy. *Annual Review of Sociology, 19*, 301–320.

Wang, Q., Gleave, S., & Lysenko, T. (2013, March). *A help or hindrance: Racial concentration and African-American entrepreneurship in three U.S. metropolitan areas*. Paper presented at the meeting of the Urban Affairs Association, San Francisco, CA.

Warner, S. B., Jr. (1968). *The private city: Philadelphia in three periods of its growth*. Philadelphia: University of Pennsylvania Press.

Warner, W. L. (1959). *The living and the dead: A study of the symbolic life of Americans*. New Haven, CT: Yale University Press.

Weber, M. (1947). *The theory of social and economic organization*. New York, NY: Free Press.

Weber, M. (1958). *The city*. Glencoe, IL: Free Press.

Weck, S., Hanhorster, H., & Beiswenger, S. (2013, March). *Boundary making and bridging: permeability of neighbourhoods*. Paper presented at the meeting of the Urban Affairs Association, San Francisco, CA.

Wellman, B. (1996). Computer networks as social networks: Collaborative work, telework, and virtual community. *Annual Review of Sociology, 22*, 213–38.

Whyte, W. F. (1966). *Street corner society: The social structure of an Italian slum*. Chicago, IL: University of Chicago Press.

Whyte, W. H. (1956). *Organization man*. New York, NY: Simon & Schuster.

Whyte, W. H. (1974). The best street life in the world. *New York Magazine, 15*, 26–33.

Wilson, W. J. (1980). *The declining significance of race*. Chicago, IL: University of Chicago Press.

Wilson, W. J. (1987). *The truly disadvantaged*. Chicago, IL: University of Chicago Press.

Wirth, L. (1938). Urbanism as a way of life. *American Journal of Sociology, 44*(1), 1–24

Wohl, R. R., & Strauss, A. (1958). Symbolic representation and the urban milieu. *American Journal of Sociology, 63*, 523–532.

Wolff, M. (1973). Notes on the behavior of pedestrians. In A. Birenbaum & E. Sagarin, pp. 100–120. New York, NY: Praeger.

Woods, R. (1970). *The city wilderness*. New York, NY: Arno Press.

Woods, R., & Kennedy, A. (1962). *The zone of emergence: Observations of the lower middle and upper working class communities of Boston, 1905–1914*. Cambridge, MA: MIT Press.

Wu, F. (2012). Neighborhood attachment, social participation, and willingness to stay in China's low-income communities. *Urban Affairs Review, 48*, 547–570.

Wu, Z., Hou, F., & Schimmele. C. (2011). Racial diversity and sense of belonging in urban neighborhoods. *City & Community, 10*(4), 373–392.

Wuthnow, R. (1996). *Sharing the journey: Support groups and America's new quest for community*. New York, NY: Free Press.

Wuthnow, R. (2002). *Loose connections joining together in America's fragmented communities*. Cambridge, MA: Harvard University Press.

Wuthnow, R. (2005). Civil society: Changing from tight to loose connections. In J. Heymann & C. Beem (Eds.), *Unfinished work: Building equality and democracy in an era of working families*, pp. 63–85. New York, NY: New Press.

Wynn, J. (2010a). City tour guides: Urban alchemists at work. *City & Community, 9*, 145–164.

Wynn, J. (2010b). *The tour guide: Walking and talking New York*. Chicago, IL: University of Chicago Press.

Y

Yardley, J. (2013a, April 29). Illegal districts dot New Delhi as city swells. *The New York Times*, p. A6.

Yardley, J. (2013b, June 9). In India, dynamism wrestles with dysfunction. *The New York Times*, p. A1.

Yip, N M., & Yihong, J. (2013, March). *Building the 21st century city: Inclusion, Innovation, and Globalization*. Paper presented at the annual meeting of the Urban Affairs Association, San Francisco, CA.

Z

Zhang, L. (2010). *In search of paradise: Middle class living in a Chinese metropolis*. Ithaca, NY: Cornell University Press.

Zukin, S. (1991). *Landscapes of power: From Detroit to Disney World*. Berkeley: University of California Press.

Zukin, S. (1998). From Coney Island to Las Vegas in the urban imaginary: Discursive practices of growth and decline, *Urban Affairs Review, 33*(5), 627–654.

Zukin, S. (2009). New retail capital and neighborhood change: Boutiques and gentrification in New York City. *City & Community, 8*(1), 47–64.

INTERNET MATERIALS

UN Habitat, 2010. *State of the World's Cities 2010/2011* http://www.unhabitat.org/content.asp?cid=8051&catid=7&typeid=46

http://www.thedialogue.org/PublicationFiles/central%20american%20htas%20report.pdf

http://press.princeton.edu/chapters/i7295.html

http://www.historycooperative.org/cgi-bin/justtop.cgi?act=justtop&url=http://www.historycooperative.org/journals/ahr/109.1/br_104.html

http://www.democracy-asia.org/countryteam/krishna/Civil%20Society%20and%20Polotical%20Participation.pdf

http://www.asiapacificphilanthropy.org/f/backgrounder_india.pdf

http://www.springerlink.com/content/1228x11m4551585r/

http://perl.psc.isr.umich.edu/papers/voluntary.pdf

http://www.asianbarometer.org/newenglish/publications/workingpapers/no.38.pdf

http://ipsnews.net/news.asp?idnews=46452

http://www.dfid.gov.uk/R4D//PDF/Outputs/CentreOnCitizenship/ResSumOct08.pdf

http://siteresources.worldbank.org/INTCPR/Resources/WP36_web.pdf

http://academicjournals.org/AJPSIR/PDF/Pdf2009/Feb/Hassan.pdf

http://www.postcolonialweb.org/africa/ronning2.html

http://muse.jhu.edu/login?uri=/journals/journal_of_democracy/v019/19.1khrouz.pdf

http://www.nai.uu.se/research/areas/collective_organisation_a/

WEBSITE MATERIALS

http://encyclopedia.thefreedictionary.com/Inner+city+decline

http://www.lincolninst.edu/subcenters/making-sense-of-place/cleveland/

http://www.allacademic.com/meta/p_mla_apa_research_citation/2/0/2/1/5/p202150_index.html

http://www.citymayors.com/index.html

http://www.citymayors.com/sections/society_content.html

http://usmayors.org/usmayornewspaper/documents/07_26_99/atlanta_reserved.htm

http://www.good.is/series/urban-renaissance

http://ipsnews.net/news.asp?idnews=44645

http://ipsnews.net/news.asp?idnews=45083

http://ipsnews.net/news.asp?idnews=46217

http://www.nytimes.com/2008/12/03/business/03columbus.html?emc=eta1

INDEX

⑤SAGE research**methods**

The essential online tool for researchers from the world's leading methods publisher

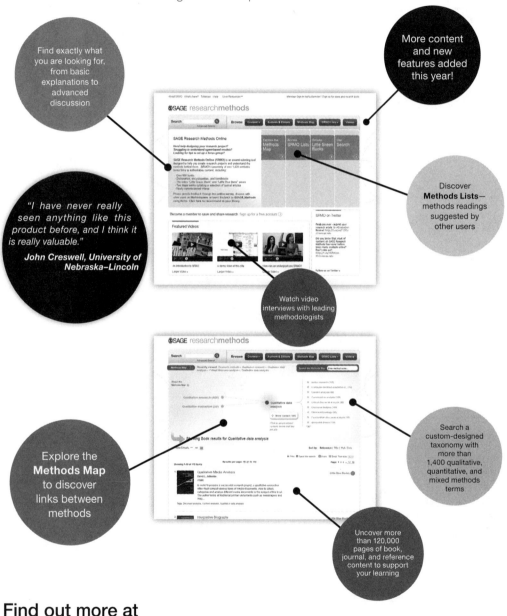

Find exactly what you are looking for, from basic explanations to advanced discussion

More content and new features added this year!

"I have never really seen anything like this product before, and I think it is really valuable."

John Creswell, University of Nebraska–Lincoln

Discover **Methods Lists**— methods readings suggested by other users

Watch video interviews with leading methodologists

Explore the **Methods Map** to discover links between methods

Search a custom-designed taxonomy with more than 1,400 qualitative, quantitative, and mixed methods terms

Uncover more than 120,000 pages of book, journal, and reference content to support your learning

Find out more at
www.sageresearchmethods.com